SEEKING CHANGES

THE POLITICAL DEVELOPMENT IN CONTEMPORARY CHINA

□ Lü Zengkui   Wang Xinying

· Brantly Womack　· Heike Holbig
· Maria Heimer　· John P. Burns
· Akio Takahara and Robert Benewick
· Young Nam Cho　· Barry Naughton
· Ross Garnaut　· Arif Dirlik
· Peter Rutland　· Ashwani Saith
· Khuong M. VU　· Mark Beeson

全国百佳出版社
中央编译出版社
CCTP　Central Compilation & Translation Press

CONTENTS

Democracy and the Governing Party:
A Theoretical Perspective

Brantly Womack [*]

In the past few years the leadership of the Communist Party of China has been developing a political guiding ideology that would sustain and justify the Party as a governing party (*zhizheng dang* 执政党, also translated as "ruling party") on the basis of its capacity to serve the current needs and interests of China as a modernizing and prosperous country. In September 2004, the Central Committee adopted a major guideline for political reform, the "Resolution on Developing the Party's Governing Capacity" (Zhong Gong ZhongYang GuanYu JiaQiang Dang De ZhiZheng NengLi JianShe 中共中央关于加强党的执政能力建设的决定). [1] The Resolution stresses that the fate of Chinese socialism, the fate of the Chinese people and the fate of the Communist Party of China hangs upon the successful adaptation of Party to the leadership challenges of being a governing party for a relatively prosperous country.

Restructuring the Party as a governing party is not considered an easy task. As the Resolution puts it, "It was not easy for a proletarian political party to achieve power, but to handle power over the long term—and especially to handle it well—is even more difficult. "[2] The task as described by the Resolution is not to continue the revolution, but to adapt the party-

---

[*] Brantly Womack is professor of Foreign Affairs at the University of Virginia. He has published extensively on China and East and Southeast Asia. He is author and co-author of numerous books, such as *Foundations of Mao Zedong's Political Thought and Politics in China*, *Politics in China*, and *Contemporary Chinese Politics in Historical Perspective*. His most recent book, *China and Vietnam: The Politics of Asymmetry*, has been published by Cambridge University Press in 2005. His current research interests include asymmetry in international relations and political reform in China. An earlier version of this paper was presented at 政治文明与中国政治现代化 [Political Civilization and Modernization in China], 中国人民大学 [Renmin University of China], Beijing, June 2004. My thanks to Lowell Dittmer, Zhang Wenxian, Xiao Yanzhong and other participants for their comments.

© *Journal of Chinese Political Science*, Vol. 10, No. 1, April 2005.

1 Xinhua News Net (新华网), Sept 26, 2004.

2 Ibid.

state structure created by revolution to a complex environment in which the only expected transformations are economic. Adaptation involves some features common in other forms of modern government, such as rule of law, encouragement of economic development and equity, and citizen institutions. However, the purpose of the Resolution is not to provide guidance for a transition to a modern government similar to other modern governments, but rather to preserve China's unique form of party governance under modern conditions.

The formulation of the problem of the governing party began with Jiang Zemin in the second half of the 1990s and is best known by the label of his "Three Represents" (*san ge daibiao* "三个代表"). The Three Represents attempt to provide an ongoing legitimation and policy guidance for Party rule without relying on the historical justification of the 1949 revolution or even on Deng Xiaoping's "second revolution", and without relying on the future promise of the achievement of a communist transformation of society. The Three Represents promise stability on the basis of the Party's inclusive and effective promotion of popular interests within a framework of a rule of law administered by the state and guaranteeing the appropriate autonomy of individuals and groups. In effect, the Three Represents attempt to preserve the existing political structure by binding its governance to popular interests. The goal is thus party-state democracy, the achievement of the effective power of the people within the framework of a single political party that cannot be challenged by other political parties.

The historical reasons for the Party's shift toward the idea of a governing party are clear. First, the party-state has remained the central institution of the reform era, and any change to a different political system might be profoundly disruptive. The example of the former Soviet Union is quite convincing in demonstrating that transformations of political systems can be harmful. The problem is not unique to communist regimes. As the philosopher David Hume pointed out in 1752:

> It is not with forms of government, as with other artificial contrivances; where an old engine may be rejected, if we can discover another more accurate and commodious, or where trials may safely be made, even though the success be doubtful. An established government has an infinite advantage, by that very circumstance of its being established; the bulk of mankind being governed by authority, not reason, and never attributing authority to any thing that has not

the recommendation of antiquity. To tamper, therefore, in this affair, or try experiments merely upon the credit of supposed argument and philosophy, can never be the part of a wise magistrate, who will bear a reverence to what carries the marks of age; and though he may attempt some improvements for the public good, yet will he adjust his innovations, as much as possible, to the ancient fabric, and preserve entire the chief pillars and supports of the constitution. [3]

Secondly, the Party's success in managing reform since 1980 compares quite favorably with other political systems. Clearly the Party has acquired "performance legitimacy" that the European communist parties lacked in the 1980s. Thirdly, however, the political assets of the Party have shifted during the reform era. Although successful efforts have been made to recruit younger and better-educated leaders, the movement of economic activity away from state-owned enterprises and collective farming toward privately organized businesses has eroded the Party's presence in new and important areas of Chinese society. Finally, just as the 1956 uprisings in Poland and Hungary led to a realization that "contradictions among the people" were possible even under socialism, the disturbances of 1989 have led the Party to reconsider its mechanisms for maintaining its leadership of the people. Continuing problems of corruption and of popular alienation indicate institutional weaknesses toward abuse of power and insensitivity to popular concerns that might endanger the party-state if they are not corrected.

Although the rational for the governing party is clear, party-state democracy is quite different from legislative democracy, and there is no existing model for its success in the long term. Therefore the chief theoretical question posed by the goal of establishing a governing party is quite simple: Is party-state democracy possible? But this question is neither as important nor as simple as it seems.

Regardless of whether party-state democracy is an achievable or sustainable goal, it could be argued that the governing party is the best feasible policy direction for the Party. Even if legislative democracy is the only stable form of democracy, the continued liberalization of the party-state might minimize the trauma of transition, and if no transition occurred

---

3　David Hume, "Idea of a Perfect Commonwealth", in Charles Hendel (ed.), *David Hume's Political Essays*, New York: Liberal Arts Press, 1953, pp. 145 – 158.

then a soft authoritarian state could still be preferable to a less soft one.

Lastly, it has been argued that China's most basic political need is the rule of law rather than democratic rule. The Three Represents contribute directly to the rule of law by stressing the importance of controlling corruption. More generally, the emphasis on a governing party rather than a revolutionary party puts greater emphasis on laws and their administration (yi fa zhizheng 以法执政). Thus it is possible to justify the measures suggested by the Fourth Plenum as a step forward without answering the question of a step towards what goal.

The question of the theoretical possibility of party-state democracy is less simple than it might appear because essentially it is an abstract question of the compatibility of the minimum conditions of a democratic system and of the minimum conditions of the party-state. If party-state democracy is impossible in theory, then of course it should be impossible in practice. On the other hand, even if party-state democracy is possible in theory, there may be circumstances in which it cannot be realized in practice. Just as a legislative democracy may be too weak to provide effective governance, a party-state democracy might be too strong to permit the power of the people to have any real effect on the decisions or behavior of the leadership. Another possibility is that the population can be too alienated from the party-state to utilize the new mechanisms of party-state democracy.

Despite these cautions concerning the practical consequences of theoretical discussions of party-state democracy, the topic remains significant and in need of serious consideration. There are fundamental differences between a party-state and a legislative democracy, and all existing modern democracies are legislative democracies. The "governing party" that Hu Jintao has in mind is not simply a Chinese version of the Japanese LDP or the Singapore PAP, because these parties operate within the framework of contested elections. The fate of the LDP demonstrated that Japan did not have a governing party, but rather a legislative democracy under the long term control of a single political party.

The argument for a governing party cannot be that party-state democracy is a new form of legislative democracy. It must be argued that modern democracy is a broader category than legislative democracy. As we will see, such an assertion contradicts the assumptions of a half-century of Western democratic theory, and there is at present no broader democratic theory that can encompass both legislative democracy and party-state democracy. In order to argue for the possibility of party-state democracy, one must also assert that legislative democracy is not the essence of democracy, but rather one path of democracy, and that there exists the possibility of other paths.

Since the identification of democracy with legislative democracy is so entrenched in contemporary political thought around the world, the first task of this essay is to explore the limitations of legislative democracy as a comprehensive democratic theory. We will then consider the relationship of people and public authority in China. Finally we will consider whether party-state democracy implicit in the Fourth Plenum's idea of the governing party could possibly fit within a more general notion of modern democracy, and what its prerequisites would be.

▪ The Limits of Legislative Democracy

By "legislative democracy" I am referring to what is often called "parliamentary democracy" or "liberal democracy". Most often in the contemporary West, however, it is simply called "democracy". It refers to a system of government in which the formulation of laws for society is the highest political act, and the legitimacy of the legislative process is secured by the free formation, articulation and aggregation of citizen interests, and electoral control of representatives by the citizenry. In order for the citizenry to exercise its rights, it requires freedom of expression and information, freedom of political organization, and decisionmaking processes based on majority rule but limited by the vital interests of minorities and by the limits placed on the state by society. The most basic law is the constitution, which defines the functions and limits of the state within the larger interests of society.

Legislative democracies differ in their selection of chief executives (hence the distinction between "presidential" and "parliamentary" democracies), but regardless of the amount of attention lavished on the chief executive, the core political function is the authoritative formulation of the will of the people by the legislature. The executive operates not only in accordance with the laws, but also primarily in order to make the laws effective. The judiciary provides authoritative judgments of disputes arising under the laws, including conflicts between ordinary legislation and the constitution.

Of course, when the term "democracy" was coined in Athens, it did not have this meaning. It referred to the direct power of the people to decide public matters, and it was distinguished from "aristocracy" (rule by the nobles) as well as from "monarchy" (rule by the king). The claim that legislative democracy merits the name "democracy" was made by John Locke, who argued that a legislative process based on majority rule was necessary to control and displace the abuses of privilege by the monarch and nobility. [4] The power of the people and the protection of society from state excesses required a powerful elected legislature. Essentially the justification for the procedures of legislative democracy was founded on the substantive claim that this would secure the real power of the people. The classic claim for legislative democracy was put most famously by Abraham Lincoln in 1863 as "government of the people, by the people, and for the people", and by John Stuart Mill as "the government of the whole people by the whole people, equally represented". [5]

Even before the twentieth century contradictions were evident between the substantive claim that legislative democracy guaranteed the power of the people and the procedural outcomes of legislative democracy. Thomas Jefferson, the author of the immortal line that "all men are created equal", was himself a slave owner. Abraham Lincoln preserved the unity of the United States of America despite the votes of the southern states to secede. John Stuart Mill worried about the "tyranny of the majority", that is, the power of the legislative state to interfere with the private behavior of citizens. [6] Moreover, according to Mill, democracy required a high level of civilization, and savage peoples had to be enlightened by their colonial masters before legislative democracy could be effective. [7] In general, the nineteenth century democrats saw democratization as a work in progress, and the imperfections of democracy as signs that the job was not yet finished. Before the extension of the right to vote to the entire populations

---

4　John Locke, *Two Treatises of Government*, Peter Laslett (ed.), New York: Mentor Books, 1965; original 1698.

5　John Stuart Mill, *Considerations on Representative Government*, Chicago: Henry Regnery, 1966; original 1861.

6　John Stuart Mill, "On Liberty", 1869.

7　John Stuart Mill, *Considerations on Representative Government*.

of Western countries and the completion of the education of the savages elsewhere, the shortcomings of legislative democracy could be attributed to its incompleteness rather than to inherent structural problems.

Although the classic notions of democracy inspired the transition to legislative regimes in Europe and the extension of the franchise to the whole citizenry, by the end of the nineteenth century serious doubts had been raised concerning the capacity of legislative democracy to serve as the mouthpiece for the voice of the people. Besides the radical critiques of capitalist democracy offered by Marxists and anarchists, the failure of the growing strength of the social democratic parties in Europe to make much difference in European politics led to a disillusionment regarding political parties and elections. Gaetano Mosca argued in *The Ruling Class* that in any large state there would always be a minority political class who actually ran things. [8] Robert Michels strengthened the argument for an inevitable elitism in electoral politics by carefully analyzing the incorporation of the rising leaders of the social democratic parties into the existing political arrangements. In his *Political Parties* he suggested that there was an "iron law of oligarchy" by which the leadership of all groups would have more in common with their fellow members of the elite than with their followers. [9] Meanwhile Walter Lippmann in his classic *Public Opinion* emphasized the shaping of public opinion by elites and the stereotyping of public choice by the very limited set of alternatives that can be presented for a vote. [10] Given the inevitable elitism in democracies and the shaping of the public mind by the government, it is not surprising that fascism would dismiss legislative institutions and attempt to build a direct, one-way relationship between the leader and the nation, or that communism would dismiss bourgeois democracy as a political facade for class rule.

Victory in the Second World War gave a new confidence to Western democracy, but it did not answer the questions raised about its efficacy as a means of rule by the people. Joseph Schumpeter in his work *Capitalism, Socialism and Democracy* began a new line of defining democracy by shifting attention away from the general question of the "power of the people" and

---

8 Gaetano Mosca, *The Ruling Class*, H. Kahn(tr.), New York: McGraw Hill, 1939; original 1895.

9 Robert Michels, *Political Parties*, C. Paul(tr.), New York: Free Press, 1962; original 1911.

10 Walter Lippmann, *Public Opinion*, New York: Free Press, 1922.

toward the most prominent institutional features of modern Western democracy. [11] Schumpeter explicitly rejected "the classical notion of democracy" with its normative emphasis on the role of the people and redefined democracy in terms of the empirical political processes of legislative states. Schumpeter's redefinition of democracy as electoral competition for power was developed into a calculus of party competition for votes by Anthony Downs in *An Economic Theory of Democracy*. [12] Downs argued that the logic of two-party electoral competition drives both candidates to the center of the political spectrum and leaves voters with little choice, but he presented this as a basic logic of democracy, not as a questioning of the democratic character of competitive elections. In various writings in the 1960s and 1970s Robert Dahl developed a comparative theory of democracy based on a generalization of the characteristics and prerequisites of legislative majority rule, and by the time of Samuel Huntington's *The Third Wave: Democratization in the Late Twentieth Century,* it was out of the question that a form of government that did not conform to the legislative democratic model could still be considered democratic. [13] Moreover, despite the institutional definition of democracy, the assumption was that any government that did not meet the standards of legislative democracy would necessarily be authoritarian or worse. To be sure, democratic theorists were often critical of democratic politics, and Robert Dahl hesitated to rank any existing democracies above "polyarchy"[14]. However, with few exceptions (C. P. MacPherson being the most impressive) [15] the critics did not expand the notion of democracy beyond legislative democracy.

Regardless of the questions that can be raised about the relationship of citizen power and public authority in legislative democracy, the popularity of this form of government is profoundly impressive. While it can be agued that the people don't really get what they want in legislative democracy, it

---

11 Joseph Schumpeter, *Capitalism, Socialism and Democracy,* New York: Harper and Row, 1950.

12 Anthony Downs, *An Economic Theory of Democracy,* New York: Harper and Row, 1957.

13 Samuel Huntington, *The Third Wave: Democratization in the Late Twentieth Century,* Norman: University of Oklahoma Press, 1991.

14 Robert Dahl, *Polyarchy: Participation and Opposition,* New Haven: Yale University Press, 1971.

15 C. P. MacPherson, *The Real World of Democracy,* New York: Oxford University Press, 1975.

is clear that they want what they get. The legitimacy of legislative democracy is certainly enhanced by habituation, and in countries like the United States it is further enhanced by a sense of prosperity, power and superiority that is attributed to its political structure, but it is also robust when it is challenged, as in India by Indira Gandhi, or overturned, as in the Philippines by Ferdinand Marcos, and it is attractive to people living under other political systems. The American presidential election of 2000, in which more people voted for Al Gore than for George W. Bush and election irregularities occurred in Florida, did not lead to a general alienation from the political system. Many would agree with Winston Churchill's joke that democracy is a terrible form of government except when compared to the alternatives. Thus, to doubt whether legislative democracy is in fact democratic is itself an undemocratic act—it clearly goes against the will of the people.

Why is legislative democracy so popular? It would be difficult to argue that it selects the most competent candidates for office. To take an American example, anyone who would argue that George W. Bush is the best possible president is unlikely to have thought that Bill Clinton was the best possible president, and yet they were both elected by the same system. More generally, despite the popularity of the democratic system, politicians are usually held in low regard, and electoral participation is often quite low.

Ultimately, legislative democracy is popular not because it expresses the will of the people or because it produces the best political leadership, but because it is a participatory system in which the current leadership appears to be at risk to popular opinion, and it is also a system that does not threaten the complex society of developed nations. Because legislative democracy is inclusive and participatory, and citizens are free to make up their own minds and to participate as much as they want, there is a sense that the system is fair even if the results are unsatisfactory. If a citizen does not approve of an elected representative, the citizen should have tried harder to elect someone else. In any case, because the elected officials remain at risk to the electorate in the next election, it is unlikely that they will threaten overtly the interests of a significant part of the electorate. Thus democratic politics tends to be cautious. The middle of the political spectrum predominates, and while people like to hear grand proposals during election campaigns the politicians rarely risk the political costs of transformative new programs.

Before concluding the discussion of legislative democracy, it should be noted that the process of transition to legislative democracy has been considerably more volatile than the settled politics of developed democracies. The political shifts in European communism that began with the election of Solidarity in Poland on June 4, 1989 were anything but cautious, and subsequent democratic politics in former communist states has moved around the political spectrum, including back to reconstructed democratic rebirths of former ruling communist parties. The key problem in post-communist states has not been the conservative caution characteristic of developed democracies, but rather the weakening of state capacity in a situation of economic and political disorder. Hence, even if legislative democracy is accepted as the most desirable form of government and the only form of modern democracy, the transition to democracy might reasonably be viewed as a perilous passage with no guarantee of success.

The importance of this brief critical look at legislative democracy for our consideration of party-state democracy is two-fold. First, the common assumption that legislative democracy is synonymous with democracy, or at least with modern democracy, must be questioned. Although legislative democracy can be a popular and effective form of government, it is not simply "the power of the people". Thus the characteristics of legislative democracy should not be used as an unquestioned standard for judging the relationship of popular interests and power to public authority in another form of government. Secondly, if legislative democracy—with all of its problems—is still considered a democracy, then the standard of what is a modern democracy should be reconsidered. Either the standard can be set for a pure democracy that is unattainable in a large modern state—full, direct participation of the citizenry in public affairs—or the standard should take into account the satisfaction of the people with their system of government and their confidence that their interests are served.

Even though legislative democracy is a very interesting and impressive system of government, and many of its features might provide useful lessons for other forms of government, I think that it is important to bring the people back in to the definition of democracy. The question of the relationship of the people to government is too important and too complex to be reduced to a shopping list of legislative characteristics. Moreover, questions about democracy as "the power of the people" are most properly endogenous questions. They are about the power of this particular people in this particular state. All politics is local, and therefore democracy without Chinese characteristics is not Chinese democracy.

▪ A Chinese Path?

Legislative democracy has never played a major role in Chinese politics. Ch'ien Tuan-sheng (Qian Duansheng 钱端升) provided the classic narration and critique of China's constitutional history during the Republican period[16], and Mao Zedong in 1949 clearly affirmed a Marxist critique of bourgeois democracy and a party-state model of governance in "On the People's Democratic Dictatorship", issued on the 28th anniversary of the founding of the CPC. [17] Although laws, constitutions, and the system of People's Congresses have played a role in the politics of the PRC since 1949 and especially in the reform era, they do not play the central role that they enjoy in legislative democracy, and they do not operate in the institutional configuration of competitive political parties. Moreover, even with the political reforms of the past twenty years, a transition to legislative democracy would involve a political transformation more profound than anything China has experienced since 1949, and such a transformation is not envisioned in the idea of a governing party.

While legislative democracy may have been peripheral to China's politics over the past century, the power of the people was central to the success of the protracted rural revolution. As Mao argued in "Be Concerned with the Well-Being of the Masses", the only strength that the CPC could rely on against militarily superior enemies was the support of the people. [18] Through trial and error Mao and the CPC developed the mass line and mass-regarding habits of leadership. The key mistake to be avoided was alienation

---

16 Ch'ien Tuan-sheng, *The Government and Politics of China 1912—1949*, Stanford: Stanford University Press, 1950.

17 Mao Tse-tung, "On the People's Democratic Dictatorship", *Selected Works of Mao Tse-tung*, Beijing: Foreign Languages Press, 1967, *Vol. 4*, pp. 411 – 424.

18 Mao, "Be Concerned with the Well-Being of the Masses", *Selected Works of Mao Tse-tung*, Beijing: Foreign Languages Press, 1967, *Vol. 1*, pp. 147 – 252.

from the masses (*tuoli qunzhong* 脱离群众) . [19] Because the rural revolution transformed the village structure and mobilized the masses, it created a political and military power that eventually overwhelmed the Guomindang and its allies. In effect, the rural revolution was a quasi-democratic system[20] because the CPC pursued mass-regarding policies without democratic institutions in the context of a life-and-death struggle with the Guomindang.

After victory in 1949, the situation became more complex. On the one hand, Mao Zedong and the CPC remained committed to the people's welfare, and mass mobilization remained the major technique for accomplishing economic and political goals. On the other hand, the goals of socialist transformation were not as immediate or obvious to the masses as the earlier goals of land reform and fighting the Japanese, and the CPC now controlled the state. Revolutionary transformation remained the goal of the party-state, but, in contrast to the base area period, the top-down authority structure was not conditioned by a powerful domestic opponent. The people's democratic dictatorship was indeed a dictatorship, however, democratic its intentions.

It is unquestionably true that Mao Zedong bore personal responsibility for the catastrophes of the Great Leap Forward and the Cultural Revolution. Without his initiative, the Great Leap Forward would not have been launched, and if launched it would have terminated at the Lushan Plenum. The Cultural Revolution was even more dependent on Mao's personal intervention and authority. Even if another Party leader or group had wanted to launch such a movement, no one but Mao had the personal authority to "bombard the headquarters". Nevertheless, the excesses of these movements depended on systemic weaknesses as well. Just as the rest of the Party leadership could not question Mao's directives, there were no institutions within the Party or state that permitted alternative viewpoints or provided for the defense of basic interests. Although Mao provided a theoretical justification for acknowledging contradictions among the people[21] and argued for democratic centralism and self-criticism by leading

19 Brantly Womack, *Foundations of Mao Zedong's Political Thought, 1917—1935*, Honolulu: The University Press of Hawaii, 1982.

20 Brantly Womack, "The Party and the People: Revolutionary and Post-Revolutionary Politics in China and Vietnam", *World Politics*, Vol. 39, No. 4, July 1987, pp. 479 – 507.

21 Mao, "On the Correct Handling of Contradictions Among the People", *Selected Works of Mao Tse-tung, Vol. 5*, Beijing: Foreign Languages Press, 1977, pp. 384 – 421.

cadres[22], he did not provide mechanisms that would protect individuals from possible abuse of power. Democratic centralism was a matter of the work style and moral responsibility of leading cadres.

Even if Mao had died before 1957 the Chinese party-state would still have faced major challenges of political structural reform. The problems of bureaucratism, of official corruption, and of unrealistic political demands would have been severe even without the catastrophes of the Great Leap Forward and Cultural Revolution. Indeed, it is possible that without Mao's leftism the party-state would have been less open to structural reform. The Cultural Revolution laid bare the structural problems of party-state dictatorship and united the people and the leadership behind the "second revolution" of the reform era.

In the 1980s Deng Xiaoping boldly addressed the substantive mistakes of the leftist period. The importance of material welfare, individual incentives, and markets were acknowledged, and the dogmatic inhibitions that had stifled the emergence of a modern economy were removed. The need for changes in the political system was also articulated and progress was made, but essentially the new direction of the second revolution was guaranteed by the Party's new general line and its improved work style rather than by major systemic changes. Individual freedoms expanded and the realm of public discussion improved, but only because the Party now permitted it. The Party did not adopt suggestions for political structural reform made in 1986—1988 because it felt that they were unnecessary. The political structure of the second revolution remained similar to that of the first revolution, even if the content of the two revolutions was quite different.

The events of the spring of 1989 were profoundly traumatic for Chinese politics. Besides the vivid trauma of June 4, there was the more general question of how the party-state would relate to the new economy and society that arose in response to the reform era. Neither permissiveness nor control addressed the basic challenge of the integration of new societal forces into the political structure. After the death of Deng Xiaoping, Jiang Zemin articulated the political challenge facing the party-state as the "Three Represents".

---

22 Mao, "Speech at the 7000 Cadre Conference", *Peking Review,* July 1, 1977; original 1962.

The purpose of the Three Represents is to shape the CPC into a governing party that can maintain the current party-state system indefinitely by providing inclusive, effective and responsive political leadership. As Jiang Zemin put it,

> ... all Party members should strengthen and improve the Party-building work according to the requirements of the "Three Represents" so that our Party can remain forever in an impregnable position with great support from the people of all ethnic groups and lead them to go forward steadily. [23]

Jiang also emphasized the central importance of popular support:

> ... our Party, as a party in power, must pay close attention to the relationship between the Party and the masses, and the feelings of the people. Whether the people are for or against it is the basic factor deciding the rise and fall of a political party or a political power. [24]

Jiang goes on to give the example of the Qin dynasty, which defeated itself through its unpopular policies.

The Three Represents is not a complete program of political reform, but it does address some fundamental problems facing the CPC today. The first of the Three Represents, that the Party should represent the advanced productive forces, addresses an important problem of inclusiveness. The second, that the Party should represent advanced culture, is possibly a commitment to cultural diversity, though it is most often interpreted to mean that the Party should inculcate socialist morality and Marxist ideology. [25] The third, that the Party should represent the fundamental interests of the overwhelming majority of the population, reiterates the most basic commitment of the CPC, but in the context of current politics it is used to emphasize anti-corruption measures and Party openness to mass concerns.

The Three Represents remain the theoretical banner of reform, but the measures suggested by the Fourth Plenum include greater attention to the rule of law and to inner-Party democracy. Perhaps the best authoritative

---

23 Jiang Zemin, "Strengthen the Training of Cadres", 2000, in Jiang Zemin, On the "Three Represents", Beijing: Foreign Languages Press, 2002, pp. 38 – 58.

24 Jiang, "Promote the Building of a Clean Government", 2000, in ibid. , pp. 119 – 147.

25 Jiang, "Speech at the Publicity Directors' Conference", 2001, in ibid. , pp. 148 – 165.

statement of this trend is the following paragraph from President Hu Jintao's address on the 110th anniversary of Mao Zedong's birth:

We must continue to actively and steadily promote reform of the political structure and vigorously build socialist political civilization. To build a well-off society in an all-around manner and open up new vistas for the cause of socialism with Chinese characteristics, we must develop socialist democracy; fully arouse the enthusiasm, initiative, and creativity of the broad masses of the people; enhance the vitality of the party and state; and consolidate and develop the political situation marked by ethnic unity, liveliness, dynamism, stability, and harmony. We must integrate adherence to the party's leadership, the people's status as the masters of their own affairs, and governance of the country according to law into the practice of reforming the political structure, building socialist democracy, and achieving socialist modernization; develop inner-party democracy to promote the development of democracy among the people; and systematize, standardize, and prescribe procedures for practicing socialist democracy. We must proceed from China's conditions; further improve the democratic system; focus on improving the system of people's congresses, the system of CPC-led multiparty cooperation and political consultation, the system of autonomy for ethnic minority regions, and the system of grassroots democracy; expand citizens' political participation in an orderly manner; promote scientific and democratic decision-making; and ensure that the people exercise their rights according to law in democratic elections, democratic decision-making, democratic management, and democratic supervision. We must bring into play the characteristics and strengths of our country's socialist party system and increase cooperation and collaboration with democratic parties. We must comprehensively implement the party's policy of religious freedom, manage religious affairs according to law, uphold the principle of independent administration, and actively guide religion in adapting to the socialist society. We must further strengthen the socialist legal system, strengthen and improve legislative work, tighten supervision over law enforcement, do a better job in implementing the strategy of governing the country according to law, and build a law-governed socialist country. We must further reform and improve the party's style of leadership and governance, uphold the principle of putting the party in charge of the overall situation and having the party coordinate all areas of work, exercise the reins of government according to law, and improve the party's leadership over the country and society. We must further deepen reform of the administrative management system and reform of the judicial system, improve administrative efficiency, promote fairness and justice in all sectors of society, and do a better job in serving the people. [26]

If Hu Jintao's expectations regarding political reform are fulfilled, then the Chinese political path in the future will parallel modern legislative democracy in many respects. Representative institutions and the rule of law will be strengthened, popular participation will be encouraged, especially at the grassroots, and religious freedom will be respected. Just as important are the increasing similarities in political perspective, values and tasks between China and the non-communist world. The leadership's actions during the SARS epidemic in 2003 showed a pattern of response as well as a concern for public opinion and the media familiar in democratic states. Although China is much more goal-oriented in its policies than developed countries, policy content reflects common values. For instance, the "five balances" outlined by Premier Wen Jiabao in his Government Work Report to the Second Session of the Tenth National People's Congress[27], balancing urban and rural development, balancing development among regions, balancing economic and social development, balancing development of man and nature, and balancing domestic development and opening wider to the outside world, would resonate with the concerns of the leadership of any developing country. Wen's general goal of "all-round, sustainable, and balanced socio-economic development" is one that no one could reasonably dispute, even if the concrete trade-offs involved in specific plans were open to question.

Likewise, although China's political path has been unique, it has not been a rut. No country's political path over the past 55 years has seen more fluctuation and changes in direction. Even though China's basic political structure has not changed since 1949, its politics has been determined more by the dynamic flux of policies than by institutional continuities. One of the ideological postulates of the idea of the governing party is that Marxism must adjust to changed circumstances, and that the world of a prosperous China requires theoretical reorientation.

---

26 Hu Jintao, "Speech at a Forum in Commemoration of Comrade Mao Zedong's 110th Birth Anniversary", 2003, translated in *Foreign Broadcast Information Service*, December 26, 2003 (FBIS-CHI-2003-1226).

27 Wen Jiabao, "Government Work Report", *People's Daily Online*, 5 March, 2004.

Perhaps the most basic reorientation has been from a vanguard role of leading China from socialism to communism to a more complex leadership role. On the eve of victory in 1949, Mao Zedong was confident that a people's democratic dictatorship was necessary, that the Soviet Union provided a model for the transition to socialism, and that eventually the state would wither away as the goal of communism came closer. For Jiang Zemin, the fundamental challenge that gave rise to the Three Represents was how to preserve the Party's leadership position "forever" by including new societal forces and directions while remaining faithful to mass interests. Leadership is determined by present interests rather than by a future transformation. The path is now infinitely long, and the goal has faded away.

Despite the critique of leftism and the Cultural Revolution and profound differences from Mao's politics, China's present political horizons are still shaped by its past, and by a past different from that of the West. Three basic types of path dependency can be differentiated, one relating to the momentum of success, one relating to the correction of mistakes, and finally one relating to the context of leadership. The most obvious form of path dependency concerns previous successes. The CPC is justly proud of the success of the rural revolution, of China standing on its own feet, and of the amazing economic growth during the reform era. These accomplishments shape its identity and its internal sense of legitimacy. In so far as future policies and leaders can be plausibly related to these past successes they will be preferred. There will of course be constant discussions of what policies were actually responsible for success and how the present situation has changed, but such discussions are themselves a blend of past and present, and thus are the essence of continuity.

Even the admission of past mistakes and their correction involves a kind of path dependency. Certainly a failure, if serious enough, can lead individuals to the complete rejection of their previous thinking and a sudden acceptance of a radical—and even a foreign—alternative. The best example might be the rejection of Confucianism after the fall of the Qing Dynasty and rise of radical ideologies among the "new youth". Even in such cases, however, a society cannot simply jump off of its own track and onto another. First, the failure usually creates a practical situation of chaos that must be dealt with. History is not a video tape. A society cannot simply back up, erase, and try again, it must cope with the ruins of its failures. Second, the attempted transfer of political institutions and ideas is at best a difficult process. Democracy in the West, for instance, grew slowly, and it emerged as an indigenous reaction to indigenous challenges. Transplanting democracy involves reducing its reality to a formula and then institutionalizing it in a traumatized society that is unfamiliar with it.

The last aspect of path dependency is leadership context. Leadership continuity is by no means absolute—new leaders feel constrained to distinguish themselves from their predecessors—however, especially in a political system in which the new leadership is designated by the old, the prerequisites for becoming a successor preclude a dramatic shift. In contrast to Genghis Khan, who conquered China from the saddle, a new leader must now be adept at running along beside the stirrup of the current leader. And in contrast to Genghis Khan, who had to learn to get out of the saddle in order to rule China, a new leader faces the difficult task of getting into the saddle. To put the problem less metaphorically, the formal transfer of power is encumbered by continuing informal relationships.

None of these path dependencies prevent change, especially over time, and sometimes they can have the unexpected effect of encouraging radical initiatives. For example, the Guangxu Emperor's hundred days of reform in 1898 and Mikhail Gorbachev's perestroika and glasnost were radical precisely because the initiators were hemmed in by their governing structures. However, the outcome of both of these innovations suggests that the limitations imposed by the existing context of leadership are real.

■ Party-state Democracy

I use the term "party-state democracy" rather than "socialist democracy" with some hesitation, since "socialist democracy" is the official term and the one used by President Hu in the above quotation. However, from a broader perspective of world politics "socialist democracy" is an ambiguous term. Social democratic parties compete in many legislative democracies, and "socialist" is often used to refer to the public ownership of the means of production rather than to a state in which a revolutionary party has a leadership role. We could call party-state democracy "communist democracy", since all of the states so described are led by communist parties, but we must respect Marx's description of communist society as one that no longer needs politics and the state. The term "party-state democracy" highlights the chief characteristic of the political system, namely, that the communist party holds the prerogative of political leadership and the state is the administrative organ of public affairs. Political leadership and state administration can be distinguished but not separated, and therefore the hyphenated term "party-state" is appropriate. It would appear to fit all remaining communist countries, although only Vietnam is sufficiently similar to China in its current political situation for this discussion to be relevant.

Just as we have been cautious about the term "party-state", we need also to be cautious about the term "democracy". On the one hand, we have already argued that party-state democracy is fundamentally different from legislative democracy. On the other, it would be difficult to deny that the measures outlined by President Hu and detailed in the Resolution of the Fourth Plenum would make China more democratic rather than less democratic. If a party-state can move in a more democratic direction, then the criteria for more and less democracy must be broader than whether or not a system is or isn't a legislative democracy. If the influence of the people becomes stronger and more effective in a party-state, one can say that it has become more democratic. If the influence of the people becomes less, then it has become less democratic.

We have not addressed the question of whether party-state democracy can be a stable democratic system, but before we do so, it is worth pausing to reflect on the significance of the trend of party-state democratization. Even if party-state democratization is only transitional to a legislative democracy, it could be considered an essential path to a feasible democracy. Moreover, even if rule of law rather than legislative democracy is considered more important for China[28], party-state democratization may be a prerequisite for rule of law. [29] So regardless of whether Hu Jintao's goal of a permanent governing party can be attained, party-state democratization can be considered valuable in its own right.

---

28 Pan Wei, "Toward a Consultative Rule of Law Regime in China", *Journal of Contemporary China*, Vol. 12, No. 34, February 2003, pp. 3 – 44.

29 Randy Peerenbohm, "A Government of Laws", *Journal of Contemporary China*, Vol. 12, No. 34, February 2003, pp. 45 – 68.

Now the key theoretical question of the prerequisites for a stable party-state democracy can be addressed. Stability requires that party-state democracy be a democratic system rather than a temporary condition, and the requirements for a system are that it be complete, indifferent to its concrete content, and not self-destructive. By "complete" I mean that it is not a subsystem whose relevance is determined by external, higher considerations. If a democratic system is a tool for some other purpose, and it is suspended when it conflicts with the higher purpose, then its proper functioning would not determine its real functioning: It would be an incomplete system. Another important illustration of incompleteness would be a system that did not cover all citizens. It would be incomplete in the obvious sense of not including everyone, but it also would presuppose a higher authority with the power to exclude some and thereby limit the system.

Secondly, if a system is not indifferent to its concrete content, it is not functioning as an abstract procedure. If a system stipulates a specific requirement or right for a category, for instance "all employees", "all citizens", "all representatives", then everyone fitting that category should be treated equally. If not, there are either implicit subfunctions affecting the application of the democratic system, for instance "all employees (on good terms with their employers)", "all citizens (of acceptable class background)", "all representatives (of some groups but not others)", or the system is simply weak and ignored in practice. The requirements of completeness and indifference are complementary in that they require that the system have independent significance above and below, above towards restrictions by higher authorities and below towards inequalities and exceptions in application.

The third system criterion, non-self-destructiveness, is different from the first two in that it is oriented toward an internal problem rather than external ones. Basically, this criterion requires the definition of the system to be compatible with its abstractness. For instance, a system that stipulated "all those who get here first shall rule the world" is not really a system, because it self-destructs after the first person arrives. Similarly, if democracy permitted the redefinition of citizens by authorities the system would lose its abstract identity over time. To be a system, democracy must be indifferent as to point in time.

It is also necessary to define "democracy" in terms more basic than the characteristics of legislative democracy. I propose that the most basic characteristic of democracy is consensus, that is, the unforced general acceptance of the legitimacy of the system. Consensus has three prerequisites, the expectation of benefit, the decisive influence of the majority, and the protection of the minority. If people do not expect to benefit from being in a system they will be indifferent to it regardless of its structure. Majority rule in some form is necessary, because any other system presumes a basic inequality. In any large state the number of people actually in power is small, but democratic legitimacy requires that the ultimate foundation of political power be majority rule. The leadership and its policies must be at risk to the interests and opinions of the majority. Protection of the basic interests of the minority is also necessary because any member of a current majority might at some time be a member of the minority, and in any case mistreatment of a minority is self-destructive for the system.

Can China's party-state be a democratic system? Let us consider the democratic prerequisites first. The first, expectation of benefit, is obvious. The party-state has provided impressive benefits, from the basic ones of social order to rapid and broad-based economic growth. In general, party-states are executive political structures that are powerful in pursuing policy objectives. As long as the other prerequisites are met, the expectation of benefit is a strong point for party-state democracy.

Majority rule is more problematic. If democratic centralism in the party-state is understood as the unquestioned command of higher authorities, and the democratic moment of democratic centralism is only a matter of the work style of the leader, then there is no majority rule, but rather only a concern for majority interest on the part of the leadership. Of course, such concern is good, and it might be called a democratic sentiment, but it is not a democratic system. On the other hand, it would be naive to think that decisions can always be questioned in a democracy. In any state binding decisions must be made, and leaders must be obeyed. The key question is whether the routines of the system allow the popularity or unpopularity of leaders and their policies to determine their fate.

But, outside of a legislative democracy, what would a majority be? Could the masses be a form of the majority? Certainly it would be a mistake to identify a majority with "fifty percent plus one"; that would be a sufficient but not necessary condition, a minimum definition of a majority. If the masses are the overwhelming majority of the population, they are certainly a majority. The problem is not with there being too many people, but rather with how their interests and opinions are known and articulated, and the mechanism for mass rule.

To what extent could inner-Party democracy serve as a link in majority rule? Certainly it would be meaningless to talk of party-state democracy without inner-Party democracy. The idea of the Party as the vanguard of the working class suggests that it might represent the majority, but majority rule implies control from below. If greater inner-Party democracy meant more transparency of leadership, more collegial decisionmaking, and a greater deliberative role for Party congresses, then inner-Party democracy could play a major role in party-state democracy. However, the Party itself would remain a minority of the population, and so its own comprehensiveness of membership and political openness would be essential to a broader democratic function. Moreover, the citizen institutions of the state, especially the people's congress system and the rule of law, would have priority.

The most difficult aspect of party-state democracy is the protection of the interests of the minority. At a minimum this requires recognition and protection of basic rights. The party-state's non-interference with the proper autonomy of individuals and groups cannot simply be a matter of current policy. Autonomy must exist in a law-based zone of immunity from improper interference, not in a fluctuating zone of indifference subject to policy changes and administrative style. Beyond the minimum, a culture of respect for diversity and for personal autonomy needs to be cultivated.

In order for party-state democracy to be a democratic system, the prerequisites of a system must also be addressed. The first system requirement is completeness, and here the first of the Three Represents is particularly important. The Party must be inclusive of all productive elements in society. If groups are excluded from the Party, then whatever rule is used to exclude them is higher than democracy, and so democracy cannot operate as a system. The second system requirement is indifference to content. In part the second of the Three Represents corresponds to this, since it implies an openness of policy content. More importantly, indifference implies rule of law. Rule of law is the operating system of any democratic system, because otherwise the discretion of the powerful is not controlled by public regulation. Corruption is one symptom of inadequate rule of law.

The final system requirement, non-self-destruction, implies that the party-state cannot redefine itself in a way that excludes part of the public. An example of such exclusion would be class struggle.

The above discussion of party-state democracy as a democratic system is only a brief sketch of its theoretical possibility. There are many fundamental issues that are not addressed, such as the ethos and functioning of a non-competitive democracy, the role of state consultative institutions such as the people's congress system, the relationship of legal institutions to the Party, and so forth. The point here, however, is not to present a complete theory of party-state democracy, but to open up the question of its theoretical possibility in the context of contemporary Chinese politics.

▪ The Feasibility of Party-state Democracy

Even if the theoretical possibility of party-state democracy is accepted, the question of its feasibility remains to be addressed. Here the question of feasibility will be discussed only from a theoretical standpoint. The questions of what specific policies must be adopted, or whether or not the current political reforms associated with the Three Represents are adequate, are beyond the scope of this paper. The fundamental conditions of feasibility relate to the nature of democracy, that is, to the power of the people. Feasibility is not primarily a matter of the correct policies, in an abstract sense, but rather popular political consensus.

The first criterion of feasibility is that the process of party-state democratization has broad credibility. The people must consider the process as their own, rather than as top-down policy. This is particularly difficult for a party-state because the public's involvement in decision-making is consultative rather than deliberative. In legislative democracies many people disagree with the government's policies but accept the political system as their own. In party-states it is not uncommon for people to agree with policies and to have a high regard for the abilities of current leaders and yet to be alienated from the political system. A feeling of significant participation must be developed in the democratization process; otherwise, regardless of the policies, the people will not regard the system as their own. The processes of broad consultation in the writing of the 1954 and 1982 constitutions are good examples of public processes that help to establish a broader sense of policy ownership. By contrast, the process of developing the Resolution of the Fourth Plenum was extensive within leadership circles, but it was not public. [30] It is crucial, however, that popular involvement with democratization policies be more than window-dressing for Party decisions.

The second criterion is committed leadership by the Party. This might seem to be in some tension with the first criterion, but in fact they are complementary. If party-state democracy is to be achieved, then certainly the Party must act as the vanguard of the people in the democratization process. If it appears to act only as the rearguard of its own interests as an elite in power, then party-state democratization might serve as a transition to legislative democracy, but it would not be credible as a permanent system. If the Party responds only to crises and does not move toward democracy on its own, then the question can be raised of why it should have a special role in a democratic system. If the Party talks about democratization but makes slow and half-hearted practical moves in that direction, it would frustrate the public and alienate it from the eventual political outcomes. If the Party is to have a special role in a democratic system, it must earn that role not by defending its power but by leading China to democracy. It must be clear to all that public interest is more important than leadership convenience.

A final criterion is the emergence of what might be called domestic multipolarity. As the autonomy of individuals and groups receives more recognition and encouragement, the diversity of Chinese society and culture will increase and will express itself. Just as in foreign affairs multipolarity requires respect for the autonomy of all states and criticizes unilateral action by the most powerful, democratization requires an increasing

---

30　See "'Zhong gong zhongyang guanyu jiaqiang dang de zhizheng nengli jianshe de jueding' de yansheng ji"中共中央关于加强党的执政能力建设的决定 [A Record of the Emergence of the Resolution on Developing the Party's Governing Capacity], Renmin wang 人民网 [People's Daily Online], September 28, 2004.

broad public sphere in which all feel at ease in expressing themselves. Democratization is not a narrow path, but an increasingly broad road, and, given the role of the Party in a party-state democracy, broadening must occur within the Party as well as in its tolerance of other views. Similarly, relations between the center and localities must respect the autonomy and situation of the localities. The creation of the Hong Kong SAR and the "one country, two systems" policies towards Taiwan are impressive steps in this direction.

Beyond the problems of the theoretical feasibility of party-state democracy are problems of practical and political feasibility that are beyond the scope of this paper. There is a long way to go between the present initiatives in political reform and the goal of party-state democracy. However, the CPC began as a small group of young urban revolutionaries, and it has traveled a long way in its time. One characteristic of the early CPC that is needed for democratization is the collective courage to take risks. Before 1949, participation in revolution was a risky business, and reliance on the masses was necessary for survival. At the present time, the need for political forms suitable to a modern and prosperous China presents the party with a new challenge, that of institutionalizing a close and interactive relationship with the people. As Mao Zedong said to his revolutionary comrades in 1927, the task is to march at their head and lead them.

Remaking the CCP's Ideology:
Determinants, Progress, and Limits under Hu Jintao

Heike Holbig *

▪ Ideology Is Dead, Long Live Ideology

> The Chinese Communist Party can't do
> without its forefather, but simply
> reeling off the forefather's words all the
> time won't do either (Huang, 2002, p. 16).

In the eyes of most contemporary witnesses, the fall of the Berlin Wall and the collapse of the Soviet Union signalled the end of ideology in general, and of socialism and Marxism in particular. [1] Almost two decades later, those communist one-party regimes that managed to survive at that time still exist. Particularly in China, increasingly perceived in the West as a strategic competitor due to its economic success and its rise as a new "authoritarian great power" (Gat, 2007), we can observe a renaissance of socialism and Marxism, accompanied by a renewed debate on the role of ideology. While Hu Jintao's leadership since he took over as general secretary of the Chinese Communist Party (CCP) in November 2002 has been labelled "populist"—a term normally used to describe politicians' tactical behaviour in election campaigns—it may be more adequately characterized as demonstrating a re-emphasis on ideology.

Hu Jintao's early pilgrimages to Xibaipo and other historical sites of the Communist Revolution, his handshakes with members of the working masses,

---

* Dr. Heike Holbig is a senior research fellow at the GIGA Institute of Asian Studies and editor of the Journal of Current Chinese Affairs. As a specialist in PRC domestic politics and a member of GIGA's "Legitimacy and Efficiency of Political Systems" research programme, her research topics include the Communist Party's quest for political legitimacy in the course of reform and the role of ideology.

1 An earlier version of this paper was presented at the Asia Centre's annual seminar on *Chinese Contemporary Politics* on June 27, 2008, in Paris. The author wants to thank the participants of the Paris seminar and three anonymous referees for their valuable comments.

and his televised reproduction of memorized Marxist and Maoist tenets were designed to evoke core elements of party ideology. A watershed resolution entitled *Strengthening the Construction of the Party's Governing Capacity,* approved by the Central Committee of the CCP in September 2004, demanded that Marxism take on the "guiding status" (*zhudao diwei)* in the ideological sphere (*Renmin Ribao,* 2004d) . In late 2005, the CCP launched a new Academy of Marxism under the auspices of the prestigious Chinese Academy of Social Science and bestowed it with the mission of modernizing Marxist theory. Hundreds of millions of CNY have been earmarked by the Politburo to fund research projects in the field of theoretical innovation of Marxist theory as well the compilation of new Marxist textbooks. With a "modern Marxist theory", the party hopes to achieve a new ideological framework which can be used to integrate an increasingly complex society at home and even to play an pioneering international role in adapting Marxism to modern market economies (Holbig, 2006a) . Another example of the re-emphasis on ideology under Hu Jintao is the campaign to "preserve the party's progressive nature" (*baochi dang de xianjinxing)* launched by the CCP in early 2005, which is in fact the broadest and most systematic inner-party education campaign since the start of economic reforms. In the course of 18 months, all 70 million party members were supposed to prove their loyal commitment to the party's cause by informing themselves on the most recent developments of Sinicized Marxism and socialist party theory (*Renmin Ribao,* 2005a, 2005b) .

How can we explain this re-emphasis on party ideology, more than two decades after the predicted "end of ideology" and despite a track record of economic success and the satisfaction of material needs, both of which were supposed to render ideology fully obsolete? To answer this question, we will look into the reasons for and the factors shaping the remaking of party ideology under Hu Jintao, and we will assess the progress and limits of this process. After a theoretical discussion of the role of ideology, we will analyse in detail the (re) formulation of the "mainstream ideology" since 2002. In addition to looking at party documents, top leaders' speeches, promulgations and other evidence found at the "surface" of official discourse, it is important to take into account relevant debates which have been held among intellectual and party elites over recent years in order to better understand the motives, reflections and sometimes conflicts behind the remaking of the CCP ideology. Based on the analysis of elite debates[2], it will be argued here that the re-emphasis on ideology has been the consequence of perceived challenges to the legitimacy of CCP rule. While the doomsday narrative of some Chinese scholars, who warn of an outright "legitimacy crisis" (*hefaxing weiji)* of the party regime, may not represent the perceptions of the broader public, it does hint at some uneasiness on the part of political and intellectual elites about the regime's stability (Gilley and Holbig, 2009). Contrary to many Western commentators, who see China's successful economic performance as the most important if not the only source of regime legitimacy, Chinese party theorists and scholars have come to regard Deng Xiaoping's formula of performance-based legitimacy as increasingly fragile and precarious. As will be demonstrated below, in order to tackle the perceived "performance dilemma" of party rule, a majority has commended the adaptation and innovation of party ideology as the main resource for relegitimizing CCP rule.

▪ Ideology and Regime Legitimacy

In recent years, a considerable number of social science publications on contemporary China have been devoted to "bringing the Party back in" (cf. , for example, the collection from Brødsgaard and Zheng, 2004). This has been a highly commendable and productive undertaking, balancing the earlier scholarly neglect of state-centred approaches and top-down mechanisms in the wake of Chinese reform policies, the pluralization of social life, and the alleged "pragmatism" of party leaders since Deng Xiaoping. Most of these studies readdressing the party's role, however, have focused on organizational issues: how the party is organized; how its various departments at the central and local levels function and interact with state organs; how cadres are selected, promoted and trained; etc. Ideology, on the other hand, has mostly remained a blind spot in the field. This is a problem, not only in light of Schurmann's classic *Ideology and Organization in China,* which aptly demonstrated the crucial role of ideology in China's political system (Schurmann, 1968). As Sun Yan, in

---

2 Part of the evidence from Chinese elite debate used in this article was identified in an ongoing collaborative research project with Bruce Gilley, where we analysed approximately 200 Chinese articles published between 2000 and 2007 dealing with the issue of the CCP's political legitimacy; cf. Gilley and Holbig(2009).

her study *The Chinese Reassessment of Socialism, 1976—1992,* has shown more recently, ideology should not be dismissed lightly as a factor in explaining Chinese politics. On the empirical side, she finds that the power struggles and factional infighting among political elites in the post-Mao era still very often originate from ideological cleavages rather than the other way around. Whether this centrality of ideology stems, as she notes, from a cultural preoccupation with the primacy of ideas in framing political action and the "Confucian exaltation of doctrine" is debatable. In a less culturalist, yet not less convincing, way she argues with the hindsight from Soviet experience that "the change of ideology is the decisive criterion for determining the degree of empirical change" (Sun, 1995, p. 16).

These findings support this article's proposition that it is too early to ring in the end of ideology in China, a proposition which is made here not only with respect to the specific history and nature of authoritarian party rule but also, more generally, with a view to the ongoing process of social and institutional change at large. In other words, ideology is treated here not as a rigid and static repertoire of constant world-views, but rather as a dynamic system for interpreting social reality (Salamun, 1988). More particularly, ideology is understood here as a "unified system of meanings for which political actors claim exclusive authority" (Herrmann-Pillath, 2005; cf. also Freeden, 2006). Similarly, it has been defined as a "cognitive structure with legitimizing functions" (Strath, 2006).

Particularly in countries which experience rapid economic and social transition—as China has over the past three decades—ideology plays a most crucial role in mediating the highly volatile social perceptions of transition. On the one hand, official ideology has to be flexible enough to adapt to changing social norms, interests and expectations in order to support the perception of a "smooth" transition. If properly designed, ideological reform that is able to mediate the subjective assessments of the costs and benefits of transition can enhance social tolerance of the pains of transition and contribute to the continuous reproduction of regime legitimacy. At the same time, however, such transition poses a difficult test to regime legitimacy, as social expectations of future change are faced with fundamental uncertainty. In this situation, ideological continuity can help to stabilize social expectations and reduce anxieties and resistance, particularly among those who find themselves among the less privileged in the transition process. In this sense, ideological reform has to strike a dynamic balance between ideological adaptability on the one hand and ideological continuity on the other. In other words, it is a path-dependent process which directly affects regime legitimacy (Holbig, 2009; cf. North, 1990).

It is important to note that in order for ideology to fulfil its legitimating functions, it is not necessary that it be internalized by the whole populace in the sense of deep-rooted ideological beliefs and convictions. Rather, ideology can be expected to be "effective" in the sense that it serves as a symbolic resource for the formation of public opinion and as a framework for the social construction of reality (Wohlgemuth, 2002). Particularly in socialist states, the ideological hegemony claimed by Communist parties in the public sphere almost systematically tends to produce a cynical discourse.[3] Over the longest periods of socialist rule the widespread cynicism has actually served to vent popular grudges and thus to stabilize party hegemony in the public sphere. In a way, cynical interpretations of official discourse can therefore be seen to confirm rather than subvert the role of ideology in shaping public opinion and framing social perceptions of reality (Herrmann-Pillath, 2005). Efforts to mobilize "true" ideological commitment and demonstrations of "honest belief" are typically focused on political elites, particularly on Communist Party cadres who form the rank and file of the administrative staff at all levels of the party, state and military hierarchies. The ideological commitment of this elite, aroused during repeated education campaigns, can be used as a test of political loyalty vis-à-vis the regime. Also, based on doctrines of the Communist Party as "vanguard" of the masses, this purported elite commitment can be publicized as representing the consent of the whole populace, at least symbolically.

---

3 James Scott has described the emergence of "hidden transcripts" behind the "public transcript" of official discourse, stating, "Whether he believes in the rules or not, only a fool would fail to appreciate the possible benefits of deploying such readily available ideological resources". Typically, the "hidden transcripts" take the form of "rumours, gossip, folktales, jokes, songs, rituals, codes, euphemisms [...]", genres which share as a common characteristic the fact that they can be articulated in the public sphere and disguise their authors at the same time (Scott, 1990, p. 95).

Thus, from a theoretical point of view, it does not seem implausible that the vast resources spent on the (re) formulation and propagation of ideology may in some way "pay off". Particularly in a system that is undergoing rapid transition and thus leaves people with fundamental uncertainties concerning future institutional change, ideological reform may help to legitimize political power by stabilizing social expectations, smoothing the transition process and shaping the perception of legitimate rule. On the other hand, it is precisely the dependence on official ideology to maintain regime legitimacy which reveals the heightened vulnerability of socialist systems. According to Lance Gore, who has analysed the collapse of socialist systems in the Soviet Bloc in 1989, the dominant ideology played a critical role in both the existence and the demise of Communism. In his account, the seemingly bottom-up revolution of 1989 was not caused in the first instance by the moral indignation, widespread disappointment, and frustration of the people. Rather, it was initiated by segments of the ruling elite who, in order to cope with perennial problems such as economic stagnation, social division, corruption and abuse of power, had adopted reforms which reformulated or even renounced the sacred tenets of the ruling ideology and led to the wholesale abandonment of the communist ideal (Gorbachev's *Glasnost* being the most illustrative example). It can therefore be argued that compared to other, mostly "weaker" authoritarian systems, socialist systems are much more easily thrown out of balance once reforms extend beyond the Communist grand tradition and the ruling ideology is unravelled (Gore, 2003).

■ International and Domestic Challenges to Socialist Ideology and Party Legitimacy

Chinese party theorists and scholars generally agree that various international and domestic factors have put the CCP's ideology under heavy pressure. Internationally, the collapse of the Soviet Union and its hallmark socialist ideology stands out as the most striking example and has served as a reference point of the internal debate within the CCP since then. It was not until the Taiwanese Guomindang's loss of power in 2000, however, that the CCP came forward with an explicit counterstrategy intended to adapt its dominant ideology to a changing environment. In fact, the concept of Three Represents, since its very launch in early 2000, has been advertised as the core element of the ideological reconstruction of the CCP's legitimacy as ruling party. [4] Legitimacy is no longer claimed with reference to the CCP's long revolutionary history and traditional ideological dogmas, but instead with an emphasis on the innovativeness of party theory and the vitality of the CCP, which result from its ability to adapt its dominant ideology to an ever-changing environment and to reform itself from within (ibid. ; Schubert, 2008). Chinese commentators have claimed explicitly that by formulating the Three Represents, the party leadership has, wisely and with foresight, reacted to challenges which other formerly ruling parties worldwide—among them East European Communist parties and Taiwan's Guomindang—did not manage to tackle, thus resulting in them losing their ruling position (for example, cf. Yin, 2002; confirmed in personal communications with researchers from the CCP's Central Party School in February 2008).

Economic globalization, the impact of Western culture and technology, and the Internet revolution are also seen as challenging the CCP's socialist ideology. New mentalities imported to China from abroad, such as individualism, religious mysticism, pragmatism or nihilism, have led to an unknown degree of ideological pluralization. They are competing, if not clashing with, the "mainstream ideology" and the party's exclusive claim to truth that goes along with it (Lu, 2005, 2006). On the domestic front, the decay of party ideology has been found to be due to the exhaustion of people's direct experience with the Communist Revolution; the discrediting experiences of Maoist campaigns, which culminated during the years of the Cultural Revolution; and, most importantly, widespread perceptions in the populace of social inequality and injustice. As various scholars have illustrated quite vividly in recent years, economic reforms have indeed produced a disturbing degree of social inequality, reflected in an alarmingly high and still increasing Gini coefficient (Zhang, 2005; Long and Wang,

---

4   The precise definition of the "Three Represents" (Sange daibiao) formula is "the importance of the Communist Party in modernizing the nation—representing the demands for the development of advanced social productive forces, the direction of advanced culture, and the fundamental interests of the greatest majority of the people". It was first formulated by the former CCP general secretary Jiang Zemin in early 2000 (Lu, 2002; for a detailed analysis of the concept cf. Holbig, 2009).

2005). With growing income disparities between regions, between industries, between social strata, and between cities and rural areas, social contradictions are on the rise. Interest conflicts run most deeply between the urban and rural workers on the one hand and the newly rich— entrepreneurs, the urban white-collar elite, and also party and government cadres who have learned to maximize their personal profits in the socialist market economy—on the other. The prioritization of economic growth has resulted in political incentive structures for cadres which have bred corruption and abuse of power, local "palace economies", and a common disregard for social matters.

Some scholars have stressed the fact that it is particularly workers and farmers—the traditional proletarian class base of the CCP—who have found themselves the "losers" in the economic reforms, as the victims of "relative deprivation" (xiangdui bei boduo). They are feeling betrayed by their vanguard, and are thus loosing their faith in the socialist ideology and in the party's ability to lead them into a better future (for example, cf. Sun and Sun, 2003; Lu, 2005). In 2002, two authors from the Ningxia Party School published an alarming portrait of urban citizens losing their faith in the party-state. According to a survey among city dwellers in Ningxia, approximately 25% did not believe in the cause of socialist construction any more, 50% doubted the CCP's role as vanguard of the working class, 65% felt that they were no longer the "masters in their own house" (guojia de zhuren), and 79% had lost their close emotional ties to the party. It was high time for the party to develop an awareness of the looming peril (youhuan yishi) (Bu and Liu, 2002).

Based on Samuel Huntington's concept of the "King's dilemma"[5], which has been translated into Chinese as "performance dilemma" (zhengji kunju), social scientists have in recent years denounced the mistaken belief that economic growth and rising living standards alone suffice to safeguard the CCP's legitimacy. Criticizing Deng Xiaoping's pragmatic approach to economic reform explicitly, or at least implicitly, they warn that political legitimacy derived from performance and material well-being is highly fragile

---

5   According to Samuel Huntington, autocratic rulers may undermine their basis of power by adopting reforms, improving economic performance and thus breeding demands for political participation and democratic freedom, but may risk the same result if they do not do so (Huntington, 1970, p. 177).

because it depends on continuously high economic growth rates which cannot be guaranteed by the CCP forever. To make things worse, in the age of economic globalization and world market interdependencies, economic performance is gradually growing beyond the control of the Communist party-state. Already in 2005—three years before the international financial crisis would strike China—Chinese scholars warned that should China's economic success falter one day, the party's performance-based legitimacy would crumble within a short time (Long and Wang, 2005) .

The perceived dilemma is grounded in the fear that even with sustained economic growth, the satisfaction of material needs will be followed by the emergence of immaterial needs, such as demands for political participation and for pluralized lifestyles, mentalities and beliefs. Autonomous usage of the Internet and other commercialized media and the formation of a "third realm" of associations and non-profit organizations have put increasing pressure on CCP rule and foreshadow a crisis of confidence if not an outright crisis of party legitimacy. The widespread attitude of distrust is described in one article as "taking up the bowl and fishing for the fat meat, putting down the chopsticks and cursing their mother" (ibid.). After more than two decades, two scholars from Shenzhen University have stated, economic reforms have thus arrived at a crossroads. If the social ills are not remedied in due time, they argue, Chinese society might even fall back to the level of development of the pre-reform period (Xu and Yang, 2005) .

Given the alarm generated by this analysis, the modernization of socialist ideology is praised by a surprisingly large number of Chinese scholars and party theorists as a panacea for tackling the attested fragility of the CCP's performance-based legitimacy. Ideology is seen to lay at the very heart of party legitimacy, to be its "essence", "key criterion" or the "key factor for public identification" with the party (Lu, 2005; Sun and Sun, 2003; Zhang, 2003). To conceptualize the role of ideology, authors sometimes refer to the classics of Western social science—for example, to David Easton's concept of "ideological legitimacy", to Douglass North's theory of institutional and ideological change, or to a classical trinity of "ideology", "performance" and "rules and norms"—as sources of political legitimacy ascribed to Western scholarship (Ma, 2003) .

According to a scholarly article by Li Haiqing from the Central Party School published in the party's authoritative theory organ *Qiushi* (Seeking Truth) in 2005, ideology fulfils various functions crucial to political, social and economic life (the author refers to, among others, Douglass North's theory of institutional change). Ideology interprets political and social order and thus lays the foundation for citizens' identification with and support of this order; it serves to mobilize people's enthusiasm and confidence, particularly by making long-term, collective goals more attractive and generating incentives to sacrifice short-term, individual interests; and it works as political "cement", unifying cognitive, normative and behavioural standards throughout society. Besides these direct functions, ideology is ascribed some indirect functions which help to activate economic and social life—such as discouraging "free rider" mentalities, harmonizing the norms and values of different social groups, and solving the problems of the non-market allocation of economic resources by establishing common standards of what is "good and bad", "right and wrong"—thus reducing social transaction costs and lubricating economic life (Li, 2005).

A more recent *Qiushi* article, written in 2008 by two scholars from the People's University in Beijing, also dwelt on the crucial functions of ideology in legitimating party rule. Referring to Max Weber, Jürgen Habermas, Michael Freeden, and Robert Dahl, among others, the authors argue that no political party can do without a distinct ideology if it wants people to trust and identify with it. Ideology, in other words, serves as the cohesive force and "political soul" of parties worldwide, being the main instrument with which to mobilize support and active commitment to the party's cause. In China, socialist ideology, which was adopted from the Soviet Union and adapted to domestic needs under the leadership of Mao Zedong, has played a crucial role in legitimizing party rule over the decades. As Deng Xiaoping himself made very clear while stressing economic construction and development, the CCP must never abandon the Four Cardinal Principles: the socialist road, the dictatorship of the proletariat, the leadership of the Communist Party, and Marxism-Leninism and Mao Zedong Thought. In particular, Marxism plays a most dominant role in guiding political beliefs and behaviours, even serving as a "guiding principle for speaking and acting in daily life" (Nie and Hu, 2008).

Compared to past periods of "ideological frenzy", the authors reflect, Chinese people today are no longer assessing their political leaders according to the party's programme and principles, but rather according to its capacity and efficiency in solving real social problems. This trend, however, does not at all mean, as some have falsely argued, that the role of ideology has been fading (*danhua*). Rather, ideology has become more realistic (*shixianhua*). Socialist ideology, according to the authors, should not be regarded as signalling simply a remote ideal, but as a practical means to satisfy people's actual needs under the conditions of social transformation. The real challenge posed to socialist ideology is that of increasing social injustice, which could lead to an identity crisis (*rentong weiji)* or even to a legitimacy crisis in China. If the party wants to maintain its ideology-based legitimacy, therefore, it has to take stringent measures to restore social justice (ibid.) .

These are just a few examples of Chinese party theorists and scholars ascribing highly positive political, social, and even economic functions to ideology. In the face of new social mentalities and pluralized ideas, values and interests, their recommendation is not to discard the claim of a dominant ideology altogether, but instead to further develop Marxist and socialist ideology in order to accommodate these new mentalities and pluralized ideas. Thus, these authors are among the large number of proponents of ideological innovation, adaptation, and modernization as one, if not *the,* prerequisite for relegitimating party rule. Given the broad agreement among political and intellectual elites about the important role of ideology in legitimating the party-state, the re-emphasis on Marxism and socialism as well as the stressing of social equality and justice observed under Hu Jintao should not be attributed solely to the growing impact of the New Left upon the CCP leadership in a narrow sense. Also, it should not be interpreted as a departure from the priorities of economic growth and efficiency, reform and opening up. Rather, the party leadership under Hu Jintao seems to have operated during the past five years on the grounds of a broader consensus that while economic performance is a crucial source of regime legitimacy, it is not a sufficient condition, and that to maintain party legitimacy in the longer run, ideological reform and modernization are crucial.

▪ Ideological Reform under Hu Jintao: Progress and Limits

From Three Represents towards Three for the People

When assessing the process of ideological reform undertaken under Hu Jintao since he took over as CCP general secretary in November 2002, it is important to note that he faced a difficult legacy, left to him by his predecessor. The elitist connotations of Jiang Zemin's version of the Three Represents, which officially opened the CCP's doors to the new economic elites, had met with strong resistance from inside the CCP (Lewis and Xue, 2003). In summer 2000, Zhang Dejiang, former party secretary of Zhejiang province and now member of the Politburo since 2002, had accused the party leadership of "muddle-headed thinking" and warned that the recruitment of private entrepreneurs into the CCP would make indistinct the party's nature and its standard as vanguard fighter of the working class [...] The basic masses of workers and peasants [...] would be led to misunderstand the party ideologically and distance themselves from the party emotionally (Zhang, 2000).

Similarly, party theorist Lin Yanzhi warned in June 2001 that if entrepreneurs were officially admitted into the CCP, it would

> create serious conceptual chaos within the party, and destroy the unified foundation of political thought of the party that is now united, and break through the baseline of what the party is able to accommodate in terms of its advanced class nature. [...] Expanding opportunities for private entrepreneurs to join the party carries the important function of "sowing discord", or sowing discord between the party and its relationship with the masses of workers (Lin, 2001).

Based on essentially Marxist arguments, these and other articles warned that the Three Represents as advocated by Jiang Zemin had crossed the boundaries of "proper" ideological discourse and thus had endangered the political legitimacy of CCP rule. While resistance inside the CCP could not hinder the Three Represents from entering the party constitution at the Sixteenth Party Congress in November 2002 as the legacy of retiring CCP general-secretary Jiang Zemin, public controversy flared when the new concept, together with provisions to protect private property rights, was to be introduced into the Chinese constitution. As of late 2002 and through the following year, educated elites used the Internet to rage against what they regarded as state protection of the exploiting classes and their illegally generated incomes. A Beijing high school professor warned publicly in December 2002 of a looming "capitalist fascist dictatorship" (Kuang, 2002). Other netizens followed suit, venting their anger at the "capitalists" and "exploiters" whose admission into the Communist Party foreshadowed the latter's corruptibility and degeneration. By summer 2003, the party leadership decided to ban all discussion of the issue in the media, in party organizations and in academic circles, fearing that the public articulation of collective anger could grow beyond state control (Heilmann, Schulte-Kulkmann, and Shih, 2004).

The new party leadership under Hu Jintao obviously faced an ideological dilemma: while it could not openly work against Jiang Zemin's legacy, it also could not let the delegitimizing potential of such vehement articulation of dissent inside and outside the CCP continue to grow unabatedly. To solve this dilemma, it used a two-pronged strategy. For the sake of formal ideological continuity, the Three Represents remained omnipresent in official discourse as a reliable stereotype in documents emanating from the party centre and in official media coverage, from late 2002 until the present. In particular, state media repeatedly stressed the innovative and "scientific" character of the Three Represents in order to reflect the party's effort to reconstruct the CCP's legitimacy as a ruling party capable of reform and self-modernization.

> The important thinking of the "Three Represents" has for the first time [...] profoundly revealed the scientific connotation of the party's progressiveness from the angle of the combined intrinsic quality and actual role of a Marxist party, and clearly answered the questions of what the party's progressiveness is and how to maintain it under new historical conditions (*Renmin Ribao*, 2005d).

At the same time, however, when looking at the new authoritative exegesis of the canonical text of the Three Represents, one finds a subtle reinterpretation of the formerly elitist notion in more orthodox populist terms. One element is a shift of emphasis from the "first" term, namely, the "representation of the development of the advanced social productive forces", which had been stressed earlier in the name of the CCP's casting its lots with the beneficiaries of its economic reforms (Lewis and Xue, 2003), to the third term, namely, the "representation of the fundamental interests of the greatest majority of the people". A comparison of official booklets used over time for cadre training makes this shift of emphasis from the newly affluent to the broader masses most visible (cf. compare Lu, 2002; Yue, 2003). Another element is the "translation" of the Three Represents into the Three For the People (*Sange wei min*), a new slogan introduced by Hu Jintao in a speech in February 2003: "The party must exercise its power for the people, have passion for the people, and seek benefits of the people" (*quan wei min suo yong, qing wei min suo xi, li wei min suo mou*) (*Renmin Ribao*, 2003a). Similarly, the essence of the Three Represents was now interpreted in official discourse as "establishing a party that is devoted to the public interest and governing for the people" (*li dang wei gong, zhizheng wei min*) (*Renmin Ribao*, 2003b). As these subtle rhetorical changes reveal, by summer 2003 the Three Represents had been boiled down to an ideological formula which generally reflected a new "people-centred" mentality on the part of the fourth generation leaders. The complex theoretical edifice built under Jiang Zemin to allow for the admission of new economic elites into the CCP while upholding its role as "vanguard of the working class" had been rendered more or less obsolete.

The Scientific Outlook on Development

Hu Jintao came forth with a new theoretical concept that claimed to embody the collective wisdom of the fourth leadership generation within only a year of assuming the post of party chief. The so-called Scientific Outlook on Development (*kexue fazhan guan*) was discussed in party circles as of fall 2003, if not earlier, and was introduced to the public as a concept of "comprehensive, coordinated, and sustainable development" in January 2004 (*Renmin Ribao*, 2004a, 2004b). The National People's Congress adopted it as a new guideline for social and economic development in March of the same year and integrated it into the eleventh five-year programme of social and economic development (2006—2010) in 2005. In October 2007, the Seventeenth Party Congress of the CCP decided to include the Scientific Outlook on Development in its revised party constitution. While it had taken his predecessors decades to leave their imprint on party theory—alive or post-mortem—Hu Jintao managed to do so within one congress period of five years.

At first glance, the new concept was one of practical politics, reacting to long-standing criticisms of China's quantity-driven growth formula by emphasizing the social and ecological aspects of development and adapting to the international language of "sustainable" (*kechixu*) development. In the domestic context, however, particular emphasis was given to the "scientific" (*kexue*) nature of the new concept, signifying the CCP's innovative capacities and its objective qualification to formulate and implement a strategy to tackle the widely perceived social ills of growing income disparities and inequalities. The "scientific" nature was reflected specifically in the so-called "five coordinations" (*wu ge tongchou*), which formed an integral part of the new concept. According to the party documents, these included

> overall coordination of urban and rural development, of regional development, of economic and social development, of the harmonious development of man and nature, and of domestic development and opening the country to the outside world (*Renmin Ribao*, 2004c).

As Yu Quan, a veteran member of the National Committee of the Chinese People's Political Consultative Conference and leftist scholar, put it, not without admiration,

> An interpretation of the "Scientific Outlook on Development" is developing the economy in a planned way and in a proportionate and coordinated way. In other words, it is a planned economy (cited from English translation in BBC, 2007).

While it might entail some general nostalgia for the pre-reform period, this surprising comment also reveals the susceptibility of the Scientific Outlook on Development concept to being seen as framing a grand vision devised in a top-down manner by a benevolent party to cure the people's economic and social woes. With this grand vision of "overall balancing", the party attempted to fulfil social expectations that it would not let the trend of growing disparities go unheeded but would actively arrange for re-distribution between the socio-economically privileged and the underprivi-leged, at least in the longer run. The party-state was rendered the only au-thority capable of commanding a "fair" redistribution of resources and of guaranteeing effective institutional mechanisms for compensation. In this way, the Scientific Outlook on Development not only claimed to present an innovative embodiment of the new leaders' "people-centred" outlook but also projected a specific redistributive role of the party-state in pursuing social equality and justice which, in turn, supported the normative justification of its leading position in the country's modernization process. In light of the perceived crisis in the party's performance-based legitimacy illustrated above, the "scientific" concept, at the level of ideology, was clearly designed to tackle this crisis by reinforcing the CCP's historical claim to the monopoly on truth as well as the monopoly on power.

Harmonious Socialist Society

The Harmonious Socialist Society (*shehuizhuyi hexie shehui)* was another formula introduced under Hu Jintao to refine the party's management of the social expectations implicit in the Scientific Outlook on Development. The concept of a Harmonious Society was first mentioned in the resolution of the Sixteenth Party Congress in November 2002 and was defined at the fourth plenary session in September 2004 as a society built on "democracy and rule of law, justice and equality, trust and truthfulness, amity and vitality, order and stability, and a harmonious relation with nature" (*Renmin Ribao*, 2004d). With respect to social relations, the new vision described a society "in which all the people will do their best, each individual has his proper place, and everybody will get along in harmony with each other" (ibid.). In February 2005, Hu Jintao, in a long speech that was only published four months later (obviously in the context of a new climax of social protests), expounded on the concept in person. He made the concept's relevance to the legitimacy of CCP rule very clear when he stated that the creation of a Harmonious Socialist Society was "essential for consolidating the party's social foundation to govern and achieving the party's historical governing mission" (*Renmin Ribao*, 2005c). Together with the Scientific Outlook on Development, though with less rhetorical weight, the goal of building a "harmonious" country was written into the CCP's party constitution in October 2007 (cf. new paragraph 10 of the CCP's Constitution's "General Program", *Xinhua*, 2007).

Besides being another manifestation of the new leaders' "people-centred" outlook, the new concept represents two remarkable innovations with respect to party ideology. Firstly, the notion of a Harmonious Socialist

Society explicitly acknowledges the existence of serious social contradictions and interprets them as a "natural" consequence of social and economic transition. In his February 2005 speech, Hu Jintao named as being among the most pressing social problems "people's growing and increasingly diverse material and cultural needs", "the increasingly complex interests in different social sectors", and "the greater fluidity of personnel flows, social organization and management". He also admitted "the appearance of all sorts of thoughts and cultures", the fact that "people's mental activities have become noticeably more independent, selective, changeable, and different", as well as "people's heightening awareness of democracy and the law and growing enthusiasm for political participation" (Renmin Ribao, 2005c). In contrast to former party rhetoric which prioritized the need to maintain social stability through Leninist means of party-state control, we find here an outright recognition of social complexity, of diverging social interests and of pluralist tendencies translating into demands for political participation. Of course, the discourse of a Harmonious Society should not be misread as a signal that democratic reforms are to be launched. Rather, it appears to be a strategic attempt by the new leadership to rationally tackle the root causes of growing social contradictions, which are increasingly perceived as a risk to social stability and to the political legitimacy of CCP rule.

Secondly, in a highly idealized reading, the concept of a Harmonious Socialist Society can be understood to present a new mode of governance which combines elements of traditional Confucianism and of a "liberal" governance style of individual self-realization and self-responsibility. On the one hand, the term social "harmony" (hexie) evokes traditional values of social self-governance based on the Confucian ethics of individual self-discipline and contribution to social order and stability. The new discourse of "harmonious" social governance clearly resonates with larger efforts to revitalize Confucian values, norms and responsibilities that have been observed since the late 1980s. As Sébastien Billioud has shown, however, the relationship between the party-state and Confucianism has been a very complicated and ambiguous one, with bottom-up demands for Confucianist rituals, morality, spirituality and inspiration for children's education sometimes approved, at other times ignored, and at still other times controlled by official authorities (Billioud, 2007; Billioud and Thoraval,

2007, 2008).

According to Ai Jiawen's detailed analysis of Chinese intellectuals' discourse on Confucianism, three different approaches can be identified: while the socialist approach, drawing on the essence of Chinese culture and tradition, hopes to enrich and renovate Marxism, two other approaches—Confucian (*rujia*) and liberal—contain more or less subversive critiques of Marxism and the CCP, such as Kang Xiaoguang's vision of discarding Marxism, "Confucianizing" the CCP, and establishing a Chinese "Confucian authoritarian regime" (Kang, 2005, 2007). In this complex situation, it is impossible to trace a homogeneous view of Confucianism. Instead, Ai Jiawen recommends speaking of a "refunctioning" of Confucianism undertaken by the official party-state by lifting the tradition out of its previous context, reconceptualizing it, and investing it with new meanings (Ai, 2008). In this sense, official discourse can be seen as avoiding a head-on collision with those interpretations of Confucianism that openly challenge Marxism, and instead as emphasizing those elements of a reimagined tradition which are compatible with Marxism: love of order and stability, strong leadership, and social harmony. The notion of a Harmonious Socialist Society thus manifests as the intersection of Marxism—which has been shown in turn to contain ideas of social harmony (Liu, 2002)—and a "refunctioned" Confucianism compatible with upholding party rule and its dominant ideology. In the same vein, in recent years Chinese urban communities (*shequ*) have been advocated as testing grounds for creating a "harmonious society" where members of the educated and affluent middle class are co-opted by the party as "virtuous citizens" to reinforce its ruling capacity and consolidate its legitimacy (Tomba, 2007).

At the same time, by projecting the ideal of a society "in which all the people will do their best and each individual has his proper place", the new concept gives rise to social expectations that it will not only satisfy people's basic material needs but will also create conditions that allow everyone a fair chance to develop his or her individual abilities to the fullest and thus to contribute to the "creative vitality of society as a whole" (*shehui de chuangzao huoli*) (*Renmin Ribao*, 2005c). In a sense, one is reminded here of "liberal" governance styles in modern industrial states which guarantee their citizens equal opportunities while assigning to them the responsibility of taking the risks of individual choice. It differs from this "Western" liberal reading, however, in that Chinese citizens—or at least the urban elites addressed here—are "reponsibilized" to develop their individual potential to the fullest in order to contribute collectively to the nation's material well-being and development. In this idealized version of a Harmonious Socialist Society, the legitimacy of party rule is validated in terms of social expectations of a more symmetric distribution of rights and responsibilities between the individual and the state, of equal and just participation in national welfare, and of an individual commitment to the nation's cause. In this newly devised mode of social governance, recourse to the Confucianist tradition is woven into the fabric of a discourse of nation building—making the past serve the present, as a Chinese proverb goes.

Again, the concept of a Harmonious Socialist Society assigns to the party a central role in the dynamic process of social engineering and nation building—signified, last but not least, by the unavoidable attribute "socialist". As has been illustrated, the CCP seeks to justify its historical governing mission and ruling position by reference to a unique blend of traditional Confucianist values and seemingly liberal, yet collectively bound, norms of social governance. This example demonstrates most vividly how ideological innovation, while trying to adapt to the pressures arising from social transition, remains anchored to an orthodox set of socialist legitimacy doctrines underpinned by strategically vague links to the great tradition of Confucianism and visions of an even greater future for the Chinese nation.

Theoretical System of Socialism with Chinese Characteristics

Party rhetoric under Hu Jintao reveals an obsession with the attribute "socialist" (*shehuizhuyi*), which has been attached to almost all new political and ideological concepts. Due to space limitations, it is not possible to analyse in detail here all the variations on the "socialist" theme formulated during recent years; "socialist political civilization" (*shehuizhuyi zhengzhi wenming*), "socialist democratic politics" (*shehuizhuyi minzhu zhengzhi*, 2002) (Holbig, 2002), the "socialist new countryside" (*shehuizhuyi xin nongcun*, 2005/2006) (Holbig, 2006b), or the "socialist concept of honour and disgrace" (*shehuizhuyi rong ru guan*, 2006) (*Renmin Ribao*, 2006a, 2006b; cf. Holbig, 2006b). Suffice it to repeat here that these concepts are designed, in a more or less subtle manner, to contribute to the ideological legitimation of the CCP's leadership claim.

The legitimizing function of party rhetoric is revealed most clearly in Hu Jintao's report to the CCP's Seventeenth Party Congress in October 2007. While the preceding report to the Sixteenth Party Congress in November 2002 had given much prominence to the concept of "socialism with Chinese characteristics" (*Zhongguo tese de shehuizhuyi*), the 2007 report now climbed one step up on the ladder of abstraction, outlining the concept of a "theoretical system of socialism with Chinese characteristics" (*Zhongguo tese shehuizhuyi lilun tixi*). A separate chapter of the report, titled "The Great Historical Process of Reform and Opening Up", which deviated from the standard pattern of former party congress reports, insisted on continuing the course of reform and opening up while at the same time holding up the Four Cardinal Principles (see above). Drawing a linear path from Mao Zedong Thought via Deng Xiaoping Theory and Jiang Zemin's Three Represents to the Scientific Outlook on Development and the Harmonious Socialist Society formulated under Hu Jintao, the latter two concepts were praised as the most recent innovations of the "theoretical system of socialism with Chinese characteristics" and as essential contributions to the ongoing "Sinicization of Marxism". In accordance with this argumentation, the CCP's party constitution was amended to include the following new passage:

> The fundamental reason behind all of China's achievements and progress since the reform and opening up policy was introduced is, in the final analysis, that the Party has blazed a path of socialism with Chinese characteristics and established a system of theories of socialism with Chinese characteristics. All Party members must cherish the path and the system that the Party explored and created after going through all the hardships, keep to the path and uphold the system for a long time to come and constantly develop them (*Xinhua*, 2007).

As this passage shows, the success of reform and opening up "proves" the CCP's correct decision to uphold Marxist and socialist tenets which have to be constantly adapted to the country's reality and further developed theoretically. Conversely, the ongoing Sinicization of Marxism and the theoretical development of socialism are presented as the ultimate reasons behind the past achievements of economic reforms and as the guarantors of future success. Based on this teleological argumentation, the CCP's leading position is validated in terms of the party leadership's theoretical innovativeness not only in retrospect but also with a view to the future.

Conclusion: From a Performance-based to an Ideology-based Legitimacy for CCP Rule

The re-emphasis on party ideology under Hu Jintao, which has been highlighted in this paper, should not be underestimated as a simple face-lifting measure for CCP rhetoric resulting from conservative pressure by some leftist party veterans and intellectuals. Rather, it has to be understood as a broader reaction to perceived challenges to the legitimacy of CCP rule which have been debated among party and academic elites since 2001. Among the many domestic and international factors seen as challenging party rule, the so-called "performance dilemma" features most prominently in elite discourse: while in the event of continued economic success and rising living standards the party is anxious about the prospect of growing demands for civil rights and political participation, which could undermine the CCP's power monopoly, there is also a noticeable fear that the party could plunge headlong into a serious "legitimacy crisis" in the event of worsening economic performance. In an increasingly globalized and inter-dependent economy, the risks of a growth slump or even a depression are growing, and with them the risk of growing social disparities at home. Seen against this background, the recourse to and remaking of CCP ideology appears as a logical answer to the perceived fragility of performance-based legitimacy. Based on a broad consensus among Chinese party and intellectual elites, the adaptation of Marxist and socialist ideology to the needs of modern Chinese society is recommended as a panacea for tackling domestic and international challenges and for relegitimizing party rule.

As described above, the populist reinterpretation of Jiang Zemin's elitist concept of Three Represents as well as the formulation of the Scientific Outlook on Development and the Harmonious Socialist Society have been core elements of the ideological innovation and "modernization" over the recent years under Hu Jintao. At the practical level, these concepts imply a new emphasis on social equality and justice: socialist core values reflecting the traditional common interest orientation and concern for the "masses" of the party's leadership. At the theoretical level, the new concepts have been woven together to form a new "system of theories of socialism with Chinese characteristics" designed to legitimize the CCP's monopoly on power and truth. The party's claim to theoretical innovativeness is itself an important ingredient of this ideological strategy to relegitimize CCP rule.

In this process of remaking Marxist and socialist ideology, the party is walking a tightrope between ideological flexibility and continuity. Faced with the need to adapt to the ongoing evolution of social structures, interests, values and expectations on the one hand, and the obligation to uphold the "forefather's" values on the other, the CCP is following an increasingly narrow path of ideological reform. As this paper has shown, the specific process of remaking party ideology under Hu Jintao reveals a consistent attempt to reconcile both needs by blending modernized versions of Marxist and socialist tenets (with a particular emphasis on social equality and justice propagated as socialist core values), and of "Confucian" traits and other elements of Chinese tradition and culture—including appeals to national resurrection. While the space to frame and negotiate liberal prescriptions for political reform seems to have been shrinking over the past five years, the idea that party rule can be relegitimized with a refurbished CCP ideology with nationalist underpinnings has clearly gained currency under Hu Jintao. In the eyes of party leaders, the alleged "pragmatism" of the CCP's course of reform and opening up does not signal a departure from socialist ideology, but rather its most innovative application.

■ References

Ai, Jiawen, "The Refunctioning of Confucianism: The Mainland Chinese Intellectual Response to Confucianism since the 1980s", in *Issues & Studies,* Vol. 44, No. 2, June 2008, pp. 29 – 78.

BBC, see *BBC Monitoring Global Newsline Asia Pacific Economic File.*

BBC Monitoring Global Newsline Asia Pacific Economic File (2007), "Chinese 'Leftist Scholar' Urges Hu Jintao to Preserve Public Ownership", 13 January, 2007 (original article: *Ming Pao,* 11 October, 2007).

Sébastien Billioud, "Confucianism, 'Cultural Tradition', and Official Discourse in China at the Start of the New Century", in *China Perspectives,* No. 3, 2007, pp. 50 – 65.

Sébastien Billioud, and Joel Thoraval, "The Development of Contemporary Confucianism (part 2). An shen li ming or the religious dimension of Confucianism", in *China Perspectives*, No. 3, 2008, pp. 88 – 106.

Sébastien Billioud, and Joel Thoraval, "The Development of Contemporary Confucianism (part 1). Jiaohua: The Confucian Revival Today as an Educative Project", in *China Perspectives*, No. 4, 2007, pp. 4 – 20.

Kjeld Erik Brødsgaard, and Yongnian Zheng, *Bringing the Party Back in: How China is Governed*, Singapore: Eastern Universities Press, 2004.

Bu, Qinghu and Dong Liu, "Zhongguo Gongchandang zhizheng de hefaxing ji chengshi qunzhong de panduan" (The CCP's Ruling Legitimacy and Urban Masses' Assessments), in *Ningxia Dangxiao Xuebao* (Journal of Ningxia Communist Party School), Vol. 4, No. 3, 2002, pp. 20 – 22.

Michael Freeden, "Ideology and Political Theory", in *Journal of Political Ideologies*, Vol. 11, No. 1, 2006, pp. 3 – 22.

Azar Gat, "The Return of Authoritarian Great Powers", in *Foreign Affairs*, July/ August, online: http://www. foreignaffairs. org/2007 0701 faessay86405/azar-gat/ the-return-of-authoritarian-great-powers. html, September 11, 2007.

Bruce Gilley, and Heike Holbig, "The Debate on Party Legitimacy in China: A Mixed Quantitative/ Qualitative Analysis", in *Journal of Contemporary China*, Vol. 18, No. 59, 2009, pp. 339 – 358.

Lance L. P. Gore, "Rethinking the Collapse of Communism: The Role of Ideology Then and Now", in Gungwu Wang and Yongnian Zheng (eds.), *Damage Control: The Chinese Communist Party in the Jiang Zemin Era*, Singapore: Eastern Universities Press, 2003, pp. 27 – 63.

Sebastian Heilmann, Nicole Schulte-Kulkmann, and Lea Shih, "'Die Farbe der Macht hat sich geändert': Kontroversen um die Verfassungsreform in der VR China", in *China aktuell*, No. 1, January 2004, pp. 33 – 39.

Carsten Herrmann-Pillath, "Culture, Economic Style and the Nature of the Chinese Economic System", in *China aktuell*, No. 2, January/ February 2005, pp. 32 – 51.

Heike Holbig, "Ideological Reform and Political Legitimacy in China: Challenges in the Post-Jiang Era", in Thomas Heberer and Gunter Schubert (eds.), *Regime Legitimacy in Contemporary China: Institutional Change and Stability*, London: Routledge, 2009, pp. 13 – 34.

Heike Holbig, "Kampagne zur theoretischen Erneuerung des Marxismus", in *China aktuell—Journal of Current Chinese Affairs*, No. 1, 2006a, pp. 107 – 108.

Heike Holbig, " Ideologische Gratwanderung—Die Jahrestagung des Nationalen Volkskongresses", in *China aktuell—Journal of Current Chinese Affairs,* No. 2, 2006b, pp. 51 – 59.

Heike Holbig, "Der XVI. Parteitag der KPCh. Teil II: Politische Weichenstellungen", in *China aktuell,* No. 12, 2002, pp. 1402 – 1412.

Jifu Huang, "Lun Zhongguo Gongchandang Zhizheng Hefaxing de Tedian" (On the Characteristics of the Legitimacy of CCP Rule), in *Tanqiu* (Exploring Truth), No. 72, 2002, pp. 16 – 17.

Samuel Huntington, *Political Order in Changing Societies,* New Haven: Yale University Press, 1970.

Xiaoguang Kang, "Ruan liliang jianshe yu Rujia wenhua fuxing" (The Construction of Soft Power and the Revival of Confucian Culture), in *Tianya* (Frontiers), No. 1, 2007, pp. 32 – 38.

Xiaoguang Kang, *Ren zheng* (Rule by morality), Singapore: Singapore University Press, 2005.

Xinnian Kuang, "Weishenme women xuyao yige hufa yundong?" (Why Do We Need a Campaign to Protect the Constitution?), online: www. tianyaclub. com/new/Publicforum, December 12, 2002.

John W. Lewis, and Litai Xue, "Social Change and Political Reform in China: Meeting the Challenge of Success", in *China Quarterly,* No. 176, December 2003, pp. 926 – 942.

Haiqing Li, "Zhengzhi hefaxing de yishixingtai weidu" (The Ideological Dimension of Political Legitimacy), in *Qiushi* (Seeking Truth), No. 9, 2005, pp. 66 – 69.

Yanzhi Lin, "How the Communist Party should ' Lead' the Capitalist Class", in *Shehui Kexue zhanxian* (Social Sciences Battlefront), No. 3, June 2001; English translation cited from BBC Monitoring Global Newsline Asia Pacific Political File, July 16, 2001.

Guanjun Liu, "Makesizhuyi zhexue shiye zhong de hexie fazhan tujing jiqi shixian lujing" (The Blueprint of Harmonious Development and Its Path to Actualize in Marxist Philosophy), in *Ziran Bianzhengfa Yanjiu* (Studies in Dielactics of Nature), No. 6, 2002, pp. 4 – 6.

Taijiang Long, and Bangzuo Wang, "Jingji zengzhang yu hefaxing de ' zhengji kunju' " (Economic Growth and the "Political Performance Trap" of Legitimacy, and the Legitimacy Foundation in Chinese Politics), in *Fudan Xuebao—Shehui Kexue Ban*

(Fudan Journal—Social Sciences), No. 3, 2005. pp. 169 – 176.

Ailin Lu, "Xin shiqi weihu yu peiyu dang de hefaxing ziyuan de lujing xuanze" (The Strategic Choice to Maintain and Cultivate the Legitimacy Resources of the CCP in the New Era), in *Qiushi* (Seeking Truth), No. 1, 2006, pp. 18 – 21.

Ailin Lu, "Shehui zhuanxing qi Zhongguo Gongchandang zhizheng hefaxing ziyuan de weihu yu chonggao" (The Maintenance and Reconstruction of the Resources of CCP's Ruling Legitimacy During Social Transformation), in *Lilun yu Gaige* (Theory and Reform), No. 6, 2005, pp. 56 – 60.

Hao Lu, (ed.), "*Yi 'Sange daibiao' wei gangling quanmian jiaqiang dang de jianshe*" (Comprehensively Strengthening Party Building with the 'Three Represents' as Guiding Principle), Beijing: Dangjian duwu chubanshe (Party Construction Literature Publishing House), 2002.

Baocheng Ma, "*Zhengzhi hefaxing*" (Political legitimacy), Beijing: Zhongguo shehui chubanshe (China Social Press), 2003.

Pingping Nie, and Qizhu Hu, "Zhizheng dang hefaxing the yishixingtai shiyu fenxi" (Analysis of the Ruling Party's Legitimacy from the Perspective of Ideology), in *Qiushi* (Seeking Truth), No. 2, 2008, pp. 19 – 22.

Douglass C. North, *Institutions, Institutional Change, and Economic Performance,* Cambridge et al.: Cambridge University Press, 1990.

Renmin Ribao (a), "Yixiang zhongda er jinpo de zhanlüe renwu. Yi lun shuli shehuizhuyi rong ru guan" (An Important and Urgent Strategic Task: On the Socialist Concept of Honour and Disgrace, Part One), 18 March, 2006.

Renmin Ribao (b), "Yige gulao er zhanxin de shidai huati. Er lun shehuizhuyi rong ru guan" (An Ancient as well as Brand-new Topic of Epochal Relevance: On the Socialist Concept of Honour and Disgrace, Part Two), 21 March, 2006.

Renmin Ribao (a), "Zhonggong zhongyang guanyu zai quandang kaizhan yi shijian 'sange daibiao' zhongyao sixiang wei zhuyao neirong de baochi gongchandangyuan xianjinxing jiaoyu huodong de yijian" (Views of the CCP Central Committee on Launching a Party-wide Education Campaign to Preserve the Progressiveness of CCP Members, with the Three Represents as Its Main Content), 10 January, 2005.

Renmin Ribao (b), "Dali jiaqiang dang de xianjinxing jianshe, Jiji tuidong quanmian jianshe xiaokang shehui jincheng" (Making our Greatest Efforts to Strengthen the Construction of the Party's Progressiveness, Doing our Best to Promote the All-around Construction of a Comparatively Well-off Society), 15 January, 2005.

Renmin Ribao (c), "Zai shengbuji zhuyao lingdao ganbu tigao goujian shehuizhuyi hexie shehui nengli zhuanti yantaoban shang de jianghua" (Speech Delivered at a Study Session for Important Leading Cadres at the Provincial and Ministerial Level on How to Improve the Capacity to Build a Harmonious Socialist Society), 27 June, 2005.

Renmin Ribao (d), "'Dang de xianjinxing jianshe' shi Makesizhuyi dangjian lilun de zhongda chuangxin" ('Building the Party's Progressiveness' is an Important Innovation of the Marxist Theory of Party Construction), 4 July, 2005.

Renmin Ribao (a), "Quanmian jianshe xiaokang shehui shijian de shenghua" (Raising the All-around Construction of a Comparatively Well-off Society to a Higher Level), 12 January, 2004.

Renmin Ribao (b), "Tigao renshi, tongyi sixiang, laogu shuli he renzhen luoshi kexue fazhanguan" (Raising Knowledge, Unifying Thoughts, Solidly Establishing and Diligently Implementing the Scientific Outlook on Development), 22 February, 2004.

Renmin Ribao (c), "Chongfen renshi kexue fazhanguan de zhidao yiyi" (Fully Acknowledging the Guiding Role of the Scientific Outlook on Development), 22 March, 2004.

Renmin Ribao (d), "Zhongyong zhongyang guanyu jiaqiang dang de zhizheng nengli jianshe de jueding" (Resolution of the CCP Central Committee on Strengthening the Construction of the Party's Governing Capacity), 27 September, 2004.

Renmin Ribao (a), "Xuexi guanche 'sange daibiao' zhongyao sixiang he shiliu da jingshen yao chi zhi yi heng" (Implementing the Important Thought of the "Three Represents" and the Spirit of the Sixteenth Party Congress Has to be Studied Assiduously and Perseveringly), 19 February, 2004.

Renmin Ribao (b), "Zai 'sange daibiao' zhongyao sixiang lilun yanjiuhui shang de jianghua" (Speech Delivered at the Theory Symposium on the Important Thought of the "Three Represents"), 2 July, 2003.

Kurt Salamun, *Ideologie und Aufkläung: Weltanschauungstheorie und Politik,* Wien et al.: Böhlau, 1988.

Gunter Schubert, "One-Party Rule and the Question of Legitimacy in Contemporary China", in *Journal of Contemporary China,* Vol. 17, No. 54, 2008, pp. 191–204.

Franz Schurmann, *Ideology and Organization in Communist China,* Berkeley and Los Angeles: University of California Press, 1968.

James Scott, *Domination and the Arts of Resistance: Hidden Transcripts,* New Haven: Yale University Press, 1990.

Bo Strath, "Ideology and History", in *Journal of Political Ideologies,* Vol. 11, No. 1, 2006, pp. 23 - 42.

Xiaowei Sun, and Yan Sun, "Yishixingtai: Zhongguo gongchandang zhezhi quanwei hefaxing Rentong de sixiang jichu" (Ideology: The Ideological Fundament of Identification with the Legitimacy of the CCP's Political Authority), in *Daizong Xuekan* (Journal of Daizong), Vol. 7, No. 3, 2003, pp. 5 - 6.

Yan Sun, *The Chinese Reassessment of Socialism, 1976—1992,* Princeton, New Jersey: Princeton University Press, 1995.

Luigi Tomba, "Baolei Zhongguo: Yezhu xiaoqu de kongjian yu zhili" (Fortress China: Space and Governance in China's Proprietary Communities), in Zengke He, Thomas Heberer, and Gunter Schubert (eds.), *Chengxiang gongmin canyu he zhengzhi hefaxing* (Citizen Participation in Rural and Urban Areas and Political Legitimacy), Beijing: Zhongyang bianyi chubanshe (Central Compilation and Translation Press), 2007, pp. 285 - 302.

Michael Wohlgemuth, "Evolutionary Approaches to Politics", in *Kyklos,* Vol. 55, No. 2, 2002, pp. 2232 - 2246.

Xinhua see *Xinhua News Agency English language service,* English translation adopted from "Full Text of Constitution of Communist Party of China" (amended and adopted at the Seventeenth National Congress of the Communist Party of China on October 21, 2007), 25 October, 2007.

Haibo Xu, and Xianping Yang, "'Goujian Hexie Shehui' yu Zhongguo Gongchandang de zhizheng hefaxing" (The Building of a 'Harmonious Society' and the CCP's Ruling Legitimacy), in *Shenzhen Daxue Xuebao* (The Journal of Shenzhen University— Humanity & Social Sciences), Vol. 22, No. 6, November 2005, pp. 41 - 45.

Desi Yin, "Lüelun 'Sange Daibiao' yu zhizheng dang de hefaxing" (A Brief Comment on the 'Three Represents' and the Legitimacy of Ruling Parties), in *Tanqiu* (Exploring Truth), No. 2, 2002, pp. 4 - 9.

Qiwei Yue, *Ru dang xu zhi* (What you have to know to join the Party), Shanghai: Shanghai renmin chubanshe (Shanghai People's Publishing House), 2003.

Dejiang Zhang, Several Issues to be Studied and Resolved in Strengthening the Work of Party Building in Non-Public Enterprises, originally published in: *Dangjian Yanjiu* (Research on Party Building), No. 4 (Summer), 2000; reprinted in *Zhenli de zhuiqiu* (Pursuing Truth), May 2001.

Feng Zhang, "Lun zhengqiang dang zhizheng de hefaxing" (On Increasing the CCP's Ruling Legitimacy), in *Zhongyang Shehuizhuyi Xuebao* (Journal of the Central Institute of Socialism), Vol. 134, No. 2, April 2005, pp. 5 – 10.

Lianguo Zhang, "'Sange Daibiao': Shichang jingji tiaojian xia qianghua Zhonggong zhizheng hefaxing de xitong gongcheng" ("Three Represents": System Engineering to Strengthen the Legitimacy of CCP Rule Under Market Economy Conditions), in *Jiangsu Shehuikexue* (Jiangsu Social Sciences), No. 4, 2003, pp. 192 – 197.

The Cadre Responsibility System and the Changing Needs of the Party

Maria Heimer *

A contended issue currently debated is whether the Chinese Communist Party (CCP) can adapt to the new era. There are two diverging views on this highly ideologically charged issue. One commonly held view is that the party cannot adapt mainly because Leninist institutions are not able, almost by definition, to survive large-scale changes and marketisation. [1] The other view maintains that the party-state *is* already adapting. The government's overall role in the economy has been reduced, and government agencies and personnel are being downsized as a result. The Chinese authorities have delegated many government functions to service organisation that perform administrative duties for them. [2] China is remaking its public management [3] and is also gradually transforming the internal functioning of the party-state. [4] It is the latter view that has come to predominate, in particular among

---

* Maria Heimer is a researcher in the Department of Government of Uppsala University in Sweden. She is the author of *Doing Fieldwork in China* (co-editor), and her articles have appeared in the *Den Ny Verden, Forum for Development Studies, The Journal of Peasant Studies, China: An International Journal, The China Quarterly,* and *Hong Kong Journal of Social Sciences,* etc.

1 See for example, Merle Goldman and Roderick MacFarquhar, "Dynamic Economy, Declining Party-State", in Merle Goldman and Roderick MacFarquhar (eds.), *The Paradox of China's Post-Mao Reforms*, Cambridge, MA: Harvard University Press, 1999; and David Shambaugh, "The Chinese State in the Post-Mao Era", in David Shambaugh (ed.), *The Modern Chinese State*, Cambridge: Cambridge University Press, 2000.

2 See for example, Zheng Yongnian, *Globalization and State Transformation in China,* Cambridge: Cambridge University Press, 2004; Yang Dali, "Rationalizing the Chinese State: The Political Economy of Government Reform", in Chao Chien-min and Bruce J. Dickson (eds.), *Remaking the Chinese State: Strategies, Society, and Security,* London: Routledge, 2001; and Kenneth W. Forster, "Administrative Restructuring and the Emergence of Sectoral Associations in China" (paper presented at the Association for Asian Studies Annual Meeting, Washington, D. C. , 7 April, 2002).

3 Peter Nan-Shong Lee and Carlos Wing-Hung Lo (eds.), *Remaking China's Public Management,* Westport, C. T. : Quorum Books, 2001.

4 Maria Heimer, "Remaking the Communist Party-State: The Cadre Responsibility System at the Local Level in China", *China: An International Journal,* Vol. 1, No. 1, 2003.

scholars who carry out empirical research. The former view that the CCP cannot adapt has, to some extent, been overtaken by development in China. Moving on from this particular issue of debate, the questions we pose should instead be: where is the party going and can the Chinese party-state solve the many urgent social problems it is presently facing?

The latter question takes on a special salience as the Chinese government will have to deal with a great many social problems. The gap between coastal areas and the inland, as well as between different income groups, has been growing. According to a recent study by the Chinese Academy of Social Sciences, the Gini coefficient was 0. 46 in 2000, far higher than that of India and fast approaching Latin American figures. [5] Poverty and unemployment are on the rise, not only in rural areas but also in urban areas. The new Chinese leaders, Hu Jintao and Wen Jiabao, have gone to great lengths to portray themselves as men of the people, and they have adopted a people-oriented approach to government (*yiren weiben*). To appreciate the shift of policy, their people-oriented approach must be interpreted in the light of their predecessors' growth-oriented policies of the 1990s. Jiang Zemin and his administration put economic growth first and had a reputation for representing the rich and powerful. [6] To "put people first" (*qinmin*) might have replaced the old slogan to "serve the people" (*wei renmin fuwu*) as a legitimising device, but the new approach has also translated into concrete policies. At the first National People's Congress meeting headed by Wen Jiabao in March 2004, China said goodbye to blind pursuit of GDP growth and promoted the scientific concept of development which also takes into account social development and environmental protection. China's GDP growth rate was slowed down to 7% in 2004 in order to strike a better balance between economic growth and social development. [7] At the same time, the total GDP volume is to be doubled in around 20 years, making it uncertain how much weight will be placed on social development. [8] One of the concrete measures taken to raise

---

5 "How Wide is the Gap of China's Individual Income?", see http://fpeng. people daily. com. cn//200108/31/eng20010831_78962. html.

6 Cheng Li, "The 'New Deal': Politics and Policies of the Hu Administration", *Journal of Asian and African Studies,* Vol. 38, Nos. 4-5, 2003.

7 "China Says Good-bye to Blind Pursuit of GDP Growth", see http://english. peopledaily. com. cn/200403/05.

8 "China to Rank the Third of the World in National Strength as a Whole in 2020", see http:// english. peopledaily. com. cn/200403/05.

rural income is to reduce the agricultural tax by more than 1% per year, with agricultural taxes to be eliminated in five years. [9]

This chapter will explore to what extent political institutions can be adapted to the changing needs of the CCP by taking the cadre responsibility system as a case. The main focus is whether the cadre responsibility system can be adapted to solve urgent social problems such as rising poverty and inequality between regions. An organisational approach is favoured to analyse the renewal of the CCP. The cadre responsibility system is the instrument used by the central government to steer local leaders and by which it holds them accountable. The priorities of the centre are channelled downwards through the responsibility system. In this way, a focus on the cadre responsibility system enables us to see what priorities are communicated to lower levels as well as to study the implementation of central policy. To what extent has the people-oriented approach of the new central leaders had an impact at the local organisational level, and has the emphasis on poverty and inequality trickled down to lower levels? Two of the top priorities of the new leadership coming into power are to reduce poverty and inequality. Poverty reduction was elevated to a key task in China's national development and became manifest in the Ninth Five-Year-Plan (1996—2000). In 2000, a "Develop the Western regions" (Xibu dakaifa) programme was launched and secured more funds, particularly for infrastructure, to the Western provinces. As a consequence of the large social problems, demonstrations, small and large, occur frequently. These social problems are, of course, also political problems that may ultimately endanger social stability and party rule.

To study party changes, it is argued here that to do it from the local level is the best method. One important reason why a local approach is valuable is that macro-level changes are very likely to be first observed at the local level. Changes are likely to be spotted first at the local level for two reasons: first, initiatives to new policies are often taken locally, and only later adopted by the centre for national implementation, as were the household responsibility system, the emergence of township enterprises, and entrepreneurs joining the Communist Party. Second, when the initiative

---

9 See the government work report delivered by Premier Wen Jiabao to the National People's Congress, 5 March, 2004.

is taken by the central government, the centre has adopted a system of first trying out proposed policies in local experimental sites in order to study the process of implementation and its consequences. Recent examples are elections above the village level, and the tax for fee reform for which Anhui province volunteered to be the experiment site. Sometimes the reforms tried out are either postponed or abandoned. The two approaches may be merged, for example, when localities succeed in getting the centre's support to continue to carry on with their experiment model or when the centre becomes inspired by local examples to carry out their own experiments. With regard to the cadre responsibility system, it is only in use below the central level which illustrates that its primary function lies in managing lower levels.

▪ The Basic Features of the Cadre Responsibility System

The cadre responsibility system is based on the nomenklatura and, likewise, constitutes the source of political control of the CCP, but it is also a method of governance. The nomenklatura is a list of leading positions over whose appointments the party exercises full control. Party committees exercise authority over the appointment of senior personnel, as well as promotion, dismissal and transfer one step down the administrative hierarchy. [10] The cadre responsibility system (*gangwei zerenzhi*) , on the other hand, is foremost about the employment of this appointment power. One component of the cadre responsibility system is the evaluation of leading cadres' work performance, which is one factor underlying the promotion, dismissal and transfer decisions made by the party organisation department. The second component is how the centre makes use of promotion, dismissal and transfers to enforce their authority and steer local leaders, which includes the patterns of promotion and rotation. Local leaders are promoted to higher levels or hold positions at two levels simultaneously, and leading cadres are rotated between two administrative

---

10　John P. Burns, "China's Nomenklatura System", *Problems of Communism*, Vol. XXXVI, No. 5, 1987; *The Chinese Communist Party's Nomenklatura System: A Documentary Study of Party Control of Leadership Selection, 1979—1984*, Armonk, NY: M. E. Sharpe, 1989; and "Strengthening Central CCP Control of Leadership Selection: The 1990 Nomenklatura", *The China Quarterly*, No. 138, 1994.

levels or between geographical areas at the same level. The nomenklatura is usually described to reach one level down, but in my view this choice of terminology is misleading as it gives the impression that the county controls the township, etc. which is only partly correct. The county party committee manages the county bureau leaders as well as the township leaders, and the two level leaders hold the same rank so it may be more correct to say that the nomenklatura reaches one rank down. This clarification turns out to be relevant when discussing the rotation between administrative levels.

Cadre responsibility is thus one mode of overall cadre management. It is important to be explicit about what type of cadres it manages: both the nomenklatura and the cadre responsibility system only deal with leading cadres (*lingdao ganbu*), to be distinguished from *bianzhi* which covers all employees in a given unit, and concerns overall cadre management. [11] One difference, however, between the nomenklatura and the cadre responsibility system is that the former encompasses leading cadres of all units while the latter mainly involves leading cadres of all levels, namely the party secretary and government head of local governments (*diyi bashou*).

I have described the cadre responsibility system in detail elsewhere and will only briefly mention its basic features here so we are able to address its potential for adjustment. [12] I focus on township leading cadres—the party secretary and township government head—but the system is reproduced from the province level down to the township. The first component is the evaluation of local leaders. Party secretaries and township heads literally sign performance contracts (*gangwei mubiao zerenshu*) with the county level. In these contracts, township leaders pledge to attain certain targets laid down by higher levels and are held personally responsible for achieving them. The content of performance contracts varies between areas and over time, reflecting the priorities of not only the central, but also of local, authorities. It is a sophisticated system as performance targets are internally

---

11   The term *bianzhi* refers to the authorised number of personnel (the number of established posts) in a party or government administrative organ, service organisation, or working unit, see Kjeld Erik Brodsgaard, "Institutional Reform and the Bianzhi System in China", *The China Quarterly*, No. 170, 2002.

12   Maria Heimer, "State Capacity and Local Agent Control in China: CCP Cadre Management from a Township Perspective", *The China Quarterly*, No. 173, 2003. The description of the cadre responsibility system in this chapter is largely drawn from this article.

ranked in importance: soft targets (*yiban zhibiao*), hard targets (*ying zhibiao*) and priority targets with veto power (*yipiao foujue*) sometimes also called bottom line targets. Veto power implies that if township leaders fail to attain these priority targets, it would cancel out all other work performance, however successful, in the comprehensive evaluation at the end of the year. The different targets are important in order to understand which policies are emphasized by the central government. At the end of the year, leaders are evaluated by higher levels upon the various targets in the performance contract. As part of the annual evaluation by higher levels, lower levels also pass their judgements on their leaders through questionnaires and opinion polls. Colleagues from the leader's own work unit and representatives from the subordinate unit take part in an appraisal meeting. Ordinary citizens can only go through the channel of petitioning to provide input in the evaluation process. O'Brien and Li have shown how the number of complaint letters is a criterion in the evaluation of local leaders. [13] Petitioning and staging demonstrations do also indirectly affect the evaluation of leaders' work performance through the priority target of upholding social order.

The second component of the cadre responsibility system is the CCP's governance methods to incorporate leading cadres of lower levels into higher levels, including promotion to holding two posts simultaneously, and rotation between geographical areas and administrative levels. An example of promotion to holding a concurrent post at a higher level is when a successful township party secretary is simultaneously being posted as the county vice-party secretary. Huang Yasheng identifies this cross-posting and has found for the provincial level that about 17% of all provincial party secretaries were members of the Politburo in the Fourteenth Central Committee. [14] Rotation between geographical areas implies that the top leaders are recruited from outside the township or the county where they work, and horizontal rotation has increasingly been applied since the 1990s. Rotation between different administrative levels is less often discussed than rotation between geographical areas but is more important

---

13　Kevin J. O'Brien and Li Lianjiang, "The Politics of Lodging Complaints in Rural China", *The China Quarterly*, No. 138, 1995.

14　Yasheng Huang, "Managing Chinese Bureaucrats: An Institutional Economic Perspective", *Political Studies*, Vol. 50, 2002, p. 70.

when studying party control. Frank Pieke has highlighted how township leading cadres and cadres who head bureaus under the county government are both under the purview of the organisation department of the county party committee, and consequently rotate between the county and the township level. [15] Rotation between vertical levels deserves more attention. In his sample above, Huang Yasheng only examines whether provincial party secretaries had served as party secretaries or governors in other provinces immediately prior to assuming their current posts, and whether ministerial officials had moved to another ministry. He did not examine the rotation between ministry and provincial top posts. At least below the province level, vertical rotation may be as frequent, and would demonstrate vertical integration.

Cadre management has undergone large changes in recent decades, but there are also important continuities from the pre-reform era. Does the cadre responsibility system have the ability to adjust to the changing needs of the party?

■ The Adjustment Potential of the Cadre Responsibility System

Scholars familiar with cadre management in the pre-reform era may question how much has really changed since then. While new features, such as economic incentives, have certainly been introduced, old features remain and have been adjusted to changing circumstances.

To the outside observer, the most obvious change is that the overall goal of the Communist Party has radically shifted from achieving socialism or communism to promoting economic growth. To many, it seems counterintuitive that an old Leninist system can put economic development as its top priority. One scholar of communist systems has described the Soviet type of command structure as goal-rational. [16] The final goal is communism from which intermediate goals are allegedly derived. The cadre

---

15 Frank Pieke, "Contours of an Anthropology of the Chinese State: Political Structure, Agency and Economic Development in Rural China", *Journal of Royal Anthropological Institute*, Vol. 10, 2004.

16 T. H. Rigby, "Introduction: Political Legitimacy, Weber and Communist Mono-organisational Systems", pp. 1 – 26, in T. H. Rigby and Ferenc Fehér, *Political Legitimation in Communist States*, London: MacMillan, 1982, pp. 10 – 12.

administration, most commonly found in communist systems, is analysed as a distinct form of administration defined by its emphasis ongoals. [17] Another analyst of cadre administrations writes that this type of public administration is highly sensitive to the changing preferences on the part of their leaders who can turn the mighty organisation to work for new goals. [18] In this way, it is even built into the system that the cadre organisation should easily adapt to changing circumstances and the reformulation of goals. It is the goal-rationality and the flexibility of the system, rather than a specific goal, which are the cadre administration's main characteristics. Using this analytical framework to understand communist organisation, it is less surprising that the CCP can first work towards the goal of communism and then shift to make economic development its overriding goal using the same cadre organisation. The CCP has introduced market reform not only into its economic system, but also into its cadre management system.

A market governed model named New Public Management provides a suitable framework to understand the changes the cadre administration in China is undergoing. The model is based on the view that the experience of the private sector is superior and it should therefore be applied to the state administration, that is to say, that government should function in accordance with the same principles as private enterprises. The primary objective of this school is to downsize government administration. A second, and subordinate, objective is to apply important market principles into the operation of government administration. [19] The market reforms that China has applied are similar to those reforms that have swept public administrations in both the developed and developing world. The basic features of the cadre responsibility system described above—decentralisation of authority, employment of contracts, setting of quantitative goals, introducing competition among state bureaucrats, use of economic incentives to encourage goal fulfilment, and taking the help of clients to measure

---

17 Göran Therborn, *Vad Gör Den Härskande Klassen När Den Härskar?: Statsapparater och Statsmakt under Feodalism, Kapitalism och Socialism?*, Stockholm: Zenit, 1980, pp. 52 – 54.

18 Bo Rothstein, *Just Institutions Matter: The Moral and Political Logic of the Universal Welfare State*, Cambridge: Cambridge University Press, 1998, p. 91.

19 For a good introduction to the New Public Management model, see Peter Self, *Government by the Market? The Politics of Public Choice*, Boulder, CO: Westview Press, 1993; and Patrick Dunleavy and Christopher Hood, "From Old Public Administration to New Public Management", *Public Money and Management*, July-September 1994.

government performance—are all elements of the New Public Management. At the same time, there are important continuities with the past. [20] How can seemingly opposite models, the communist cadre organisation and New Public Management, be merged in the cadre responsibility system? The reason is that there are important similarities between Leninist systems and the market model of public administration first employed in Margaret Thatcher's Britain. Both models emphasize goals, rather than rules and the process itself, thereby building flexibility into the system. Both cadre administrations and New Public Management are the types of public administration that most closely resemble private companies in their organisation. [21]

The adjustment potential of the cadre responsibility system should, therefore, be great. The flexibility is built into the system, and the organisation should be responsive to the changing goals of central leaders. What have been the concrete changes in cadre management of local leaders since the beginning of reform? We cannot discuss changes and continuities of exact features with any degree of certainty since our knowledge of the actual practice of local political institutions in the pre-reform era is limited, and neither do we have sufficient knowledge about today's organisation. The most noticeable continuity with the past is that the performance targets of today do not differ greatly from the quotas of the old planning system. The difference is that performance targets are fewer and internally ranked, clearly signalling the priorities of the centre. Hard targets tend to be economic in nature, invariably operationalised in quantitative figures and relatively easy to measure, such as the increase of GDP, tax revenues handed up to higher levels, etc. Priority targets with veto power, in contrast, are used for the fundaments of the system, or for policies that take on a special urgency. At least with regard to the priority target to uphold social order (shehui zhi 'an) , it is measured by its effects rather than a target to be achieved. Hard targets may be important goals under ordinary circumstances, but priority targets with veto power will simply have to be carried out, under ordinary or extraordinary circumstances. In certain

---

20 It is important to underline that change and development is not a linear process. While we see decentralisation of some areas, we see recentralisation of others.

21 Rothstein, *Just Institutions Matter,* p. 91.

ways, cadre management has become more institutionalised. The performance contracts that leading cadres sign are an innovation in the reform era, and are most likely modelled on the household responsibility contracts. As a result, the responsibility is more clearly spelled out as it is the highest local leaders—the party secretary and the government head—who shoulder the final responsibility.

Competition between local leaders from different townships and counties was always a feature of cadre management, but now also economic incentives are used to spur them on. The opinions of the masses provided input into evaluation in the pre-reform era too, but are supposed to play a larger role today and their role has become more institutionalised in recent years. In the new regulations on leading cadres, an article has been added to the temporary regulations that stipulates that a cadre should normally be removed from his or her position if more than one-third of the pollers grade the cadre to be unqualified, and he or she has been verified by the authority as being not up to standard. [22] New regulations for intra-party supervision also stipulate a larger role for the public when cadre promotion is decided. [23] Scholars writing about local organisation in the pre-reform era identified cross-posting and rotation between geographical areas and administrative levels as methods of cadre management then, so these seem to be continuous features of CCP cadre management. [24] With the reservation that we know too little of both the pre-reform and post-reform systems, there are however indications that the logic of cross-posting and rotation has changed. Oksenberg's study from 1969 indicates that grade 1 and model unit areas were less likely to have outside cadres assigned to them[25] but today higher levels have increased their political control over strategically important areas; very often the areas important for economic

---

22 "Regulations on the Work of Selecting and Appointing Leading Party and Government Cadres", Article 55, Central Committee of the Communist Party of China, 9 July, 2002, http://www. china. org. cn/english/features/45399. htm (accessed 12 November, 2002).

23 Joseph Fewsmith, "The Third Plenary Session of the 16th Central Committee", *China Leadership Monitor*, No. 9, 2003.

24 See for example, Frederick C. Teiwes, *Provincial Party Personnel in Mainland China 1956—1966*, New York: Columbia University, 1967; and Michel Oksenberg, "Local Leaders in Rural China, 1962—1965: Individual Attributes, Bureaucratic Positions, and Political Recruitment", in Doak Barnett (ed.), *Chinese Communist Politics in Action*, Seattle, WA: University of Washington Press, 1969.

25 Oksenberg, "Local Leaders in Rural China, 1962—1965", pp. 199 – 200.

development and tax revenues. [26] If this observation is correct, it would mean that the CCP has let go of, or at least pays less attention to, problem areas, which holds large implications for tackling the problems of poverty and inequality.

To what extent is the cadre responsibility system uniformly applied in the whole of China? There are clearly many variations between areas. First of all, I argue against the view that variation between areas per se is a measure of loss of central control. It is an empirical question whether the variation of the system is a sign of central control or loss of it. More importantly, we should use the variations to learn more about CCP rule and the way the CCP governs. When Huang Yasheng examines the centre's political and administrative control over provincial government leaders, he uses similarity across regions as a measure of central control. [27] With regard to the setting of performance targets, variation across regions reflecting the priorities of central and local authorities does not necessarily mean loss of central control but could even imply an increase of central control in some instances. The centre does not have the same policies towards all areas. There are two national *yipiao foujue,* priority targets with veto power: family planning and social order. In Sichuan province, environmental protection (*baohu huanjing)* was a *yipiao foujue.* [28] One interpretation of this local priority target would be that provincial leaders in Sichuan are especially concerned about the protection of environment, but it is much more likely that the centre is targeting the province because environmental problems there will lead to floods and damage in other parts of the country and affect its financial centre, Shanghai. In this example, variation is evidence of central enforcement. Variation could, on the other hand, be evidence of weakening central control if central priority targets are downgraded in importance in some areas. The Chinese government attaches great importance to social stability as expressed in the priority target of upholding social order. If less emphasis were placed on social order in areas where

---

26 Heimer, "State Capacity and Local Agent Control in China".

27 Huang Yasheng, *Inflation and Investment Controls in China: The Political Economy of Central-Local Relations during the Reform Era,* Cambridge: Cambridge University Press, 1996.

28 Interview with a division chief of the office for West China Development in Sichuan province (Autumn 2003). At the county level and below, though, I found no evidence that environmental protection was a *yipiao foujue.*

social unrest is a grave problem, this would indicate the weakening of central control (or at least that the centre cares more about other targets in that area) .

The cadre responsibility system, and the nomenklatura, are sometimes mistaken to be more than they actually are. I argue that the cadre responsibility system must be analysed as a governance tool or method of cadre management of the CCP, it is nothing more and nothing less. If the efficiency of the system is to be evaluated, it has to be measured against the goals of the principals that use this system as a tool. John Burns examines how well the nomenklatura has served the CCP and finds that the nomenklatura system has been partially impaired during long periods of time since it was selecting corrupt officials for public office and could not check widespread corruption in the party. [29] However, this reasoning presumes that the CCP places relatively large weight on fighting corruption, which can be questioned on a number of grounds. [30] We cannot estimate the impact of the cadre responsibility system by looking at goals on which the system does not place emphasis. Its critics point out that cadres still do all they can to please their superiors by apparently reaching the targets laid out in their contracts and evaluation forms, even if they have to distort data, and even when their acts are detrimental to the peasants' interests. [31] Again, we cannot automatically assume that the critics' concern is the same as the party's concern. This is not to say that criticism should not be voiced, but the point is that criticism should be directed against the party itself rather than claiming its management tools are inefficient. I fully concur with Burns who writes that: "The nomenklatura system, then, is as relevant as the CCP itself. "[32] Therefore, the cadre responsibility system is, in my opinion,

---

29 See his contribution to this book or John P. Burns, "The Relevance of the Nomenklatura System to the Chinese Communist Party in a New Era", a paper presented to the international conference on The Chinese Communist Party in a New Era: Renewal and Reform held in Singapore, 9-10 December, 2003.

30 For further reasoning on the relationship between corruption and development and the role of fighting corruption in checking cadres' behaviour, see Maria Heimer, "The Local State and Developmental Projects in China", in Richard Boyd and Tak-Wing Ngo (eds.), Asian States: Beyond the Developmental Perspective, London: Routledge, 2004.

31 See Stig Thogersen, "Parasites or Civilisers: The Legitimacy of the Chinese Communist Party in Rural Areas", China: An International Journal, Vol. 1, No. 2, 2003, p. 203.

32 Burns, "The Relevance of the Nomenklatura System", p. 7.

foremost *an analytical tool* that helps us to see which are the goals that the central government wants to promote, how well they manage to do so, and a tool to understand why cadres behave as they do. In turn, it helps us to analyse Chinese policy implementation and politics. This is by no means a straightforward process and should certainly not be portrayed as such. The system provided political incentives for local leaders to promote growth, but in an indirect and an unexpected way.[33]

Given that flexibility is built into the system, and the previous reformulations of the party's goals and methods discussed above, it should be possible for the Chinese government to upgrade the importance of social problems in the cadre responsibility system. Have they done so?

If the central authorities would upgrade the importance of solving the social problems of poverty and regional inequality in the cadre responsibility system in order to facilitate their implementation, we would expect them to write these targets into the performance contract of the government head, rather than treating them as a task for a subordinate leader such as the director of poverty reduction bureau or a vice-government head/ vice-party secretary. Some policies emphasized by the centre, such as fighting SARS in the spring of 2003, for example, are not always written into the performance contracts, but the more continuous priority policies are. Reducing poverty and inequality would have to be made important hard targets in the comprehensive evaluation of work performance, and the government head be made accountable for these targets rather than targets related to economic development. It seems as if the centre is only able to push a few priority policies at the same time through the cadre responsibility system: In that sense cadre management has not changed significantly since the pre-reform era. When two priority targets conflict, at least one of them is going to be difficult to implement. Unlike the target of economic growth, the targets of poverty reduction and inequality do not conflict to the same extent with the priority target to uphold social order. Reducing poverty and inequality should presumably ease social tension and contribute to social stability.

---

33 Maria Heimer, "Local State Corporatism and Private Business", *The Journal of Peasant Studies*, Vol. 30, No. 3/4, 2003.

■ Solving the Problem of Poverty and Regional Inequality

To attack the problems of poverty and regional inequality, central leaders need to rely on the local political institutions to carry out their programmes. The focus here is not on the two policies but on their organisation in order to discuss whether the cadre responsibility system can be adapted to the changing needs of the party as well as to evaluate how the implementation of the poverty reduction and the Western development programme is going. [34]

The government programmes to alleviate poverty and to develop the Western regions of China have different stated objectives, but are overlapping. Whereas the main objective of the government's programme to alleviate poverty is to assist the poor, the main purpose of the Western development programme is to promote the development of China's interior and reduce the gap between the coastal and the inland regions. Poverty reduction and the Western development programme are related in that, first, poverty reduction in China itself is very development oriented. The Chinese term for poverty alleviation is *Fupin Kaifa*, literally establishing that poverty should be reduced through development. Since its initiation, poverty reduction policies have focused on creating the proper conditions for regional economic development rather than directly assisting the poor. Second, even though it is not its main objective, the Western development programme is assumed to reduce rural poverty: "The implementation of the large-scale development strategy for the western region is also helpful for poverty alleviation and will have a far-reaching influence on the reduction of the impoverishment rate. "[35] The implementation of the Western development programme is to link up with poverty reduction to promote economic development in poor areas.

The two programmes both focus on geographical areas. Since the "8-7" poverty reduction plan in 1994, the Chinese authorities have targeted 592

---

34 The discussion is based on on-going fieldwork carried out for my current project. Fieldwork has been conducted in three poor counties: one county which is not a nationally designated poor county in Yunnan province in 2003, and one nationally designated key poor county in each of Sichuan and Shanxi provinces in 2004.

35 Government White Paper: The Development-Oriented Poverty Reduction Program for Rural China.

key poor counties (first called *pingkun xian,* today they are called *zhongdian xian*) to which they concentrate their resources. [36] In the new national poverty reduction strategy from 2001, all the 592 national key counties are situated in the central and Western part of China. Poverty reduction work is the central task of party and government leaders in these 592 key counties who should place poverty reduction as their overarching goal. [37] The Western development programme covers the following areas: Chongqing municipality, Sichuan, Guizhou, Yunnan, Shanxi, Gansu and Qinghai Provinces, and Tibet, Ningxia Hui, Xinjiang Uygur, Inner Mongolia and Guangxi Zhuang Autonomous Regions. Within these areas, the central and local governments have a number of large key projects. [38]

The poverty reduction policy was formulated for the first time in 1986 and has a permanent organisation, whereas the Western development programme was launched in 2000 and does not have a permanent organisational system. With regard to poverty reduction, central authorities exercise the cadre responsibility system as spelled out in the 2001 Outline of the reformulated national poverty alleviation plan. The division of responsibility between different administrative levels is not entirely clear. The Outline states that the main responsibility lies at the province level but the key work is performed at the county level. It is the highest leaders of the party and government (*diyi bashou*) at the local level who should shoulder the responsibility for poverty reduction. The effectiveness of poverty reduction work shall be an important target in the evaluation of the top leaders' work performance, according to the Outline. [39] The central government has not, as far as I can tell, issued a similar directive for the Western development programme which is supported by findings from the local level.

Together with the national office for poverty alleviation, a leading group for poverty reduction at the national level was established in 1986. The

---

36 Under the 8-7 plan, all resources had to be concentrated in the selected counties, but under the new poverty reduction plan some money is also spent on poor residing outside the key counties, taking the village as the unit.

37 "Zhongguo Nongcun Fupin Kaifa Gangyao (2001—2010nian)" [Outline for Poverty Alleviation and Development of China's Rural Areas (2001—2010)], article 29.

38 David S. G. Goodman, "The Politics of the West: Equality, Nation-building and Civilisation", *Provincial China,* No. 2, 2002.

39 "Zhongguo Nongcun Fupin Kaifa Gangyao (2001—2010 nian)", article 29.

leading group is directly under the State Council, holds ministerial status and is usually led by the vice-premier in charge of agriculture.[40] The leading group and its executive office are reproduced at the different administrative levels. A State Council leading group for Western development was formed in 2000, and the executive office of the leading group was set up within the State Development Planning Commission which illustrates the influence of that organ over the Western development programme at large. Today, the head of the leading group is Vice-Premier Zeng Peiyan.[41] Looking at organisation at the national level, poverty reduction and the Western development programme seem equally important as both leading groups are headed by a vice-premier, although the latter, due to the responsibilities allocated to him, may carry more weight than the vice-premier in charge of agriculture.

From the central level, we turn our attention to the local level which is crucial in political organisation. In the three provinces where I conducted fieldwork, Yunnan, Sichuan and Shanxi province, the picture is quite consistent when looking at the leading groups and the organisational setup. The leading group for poverty reduction is either led by the county mayor or the party secretary, whereas leading groups for Western development only exist on paper. One governor claimed that all the government affairs belong to the Western development programme so there is no need to establish a special leading group.[42] While the poverty alleviation bureau is a separate unit with its own director, the office for Western development is inside the development planning commission whose director is also the director of the Western development office. There is no need to establish a separate office because the work of the planning commission is the same work or content as that of the Western development programme.[43] The majority of the projects of the planning commission are "in the spirit of the

---

40 Today, its leader is Vice-Premier Hui Liangyu.

41 Its leaders were then reported to be the former Premier Zhu Rongji and deputy leader the former Vice-Premier Wen Jiabao. Zeng Peiyan was previously the Head of the State Development Planning Commission.

42 Interview with a division chief of the office for West China Development in Sichuan province (Autumn 2003).

43 Interview with the director of a development planning commission cum Western development office in a Sichuan municipality (Spring 2004).

xibu dakaifa"[44]. It means that in actuality there is no specific organisation for the Western development programme; the organisation carrying its name is really an empty one, but the policy is managed by the development planning commission and the local government as a whole. We will discuss the implications below, now it is sufficient to say that the Western development programme may be held more important than poverty reduction but it is incorporated into the overall work of government.

Performance targets give an indication of how higher levels govern lower levels. In the Yunnan county, the district level had given the county poverty reduction targets which were then divided among the 23 townships and included in the mayors' performance contracts. [45] Township mayors signed a performance contract with, and were accountable to, the county. Altogether there were 12 targets relating to poverty reduction in the performance contract which township leaders were evaluated upon. [46] According to the director of the poverty alleviation bureau, the most important target was to solve the problem of food and clothing for a certain number of people (*jiejue wenbao renkou*): for 2003 the number was 30, 000 people. [47] This is mirrored at the township level where the most important target to complete was to make 1, 500 people escape poverty (*jiejue wenbao renkou*) in 2002. Next in priority was the target to prevent 3, 800 people from returning to poverty (*gonggu wenbao renkou*) in 2002, and to complete the plan of the three key projects. [48] Poverty reduction targets were hard targets in the evaluation in the sense that completion of the targets rendered bonus and non-completion caused fines. It is difficult, however, to judge the relative status of poverty reduction targets to the other 17 hard targets in the evaluation, especially the economic development targets. [49] In the two

---

44 Interview YA4 with the vice-director of the Western development office under the development planning bureau in a Yunnan county (Spring 2003).

45 See document "X shi 2001 nian fupin kaifa mubiao guanli zerenzhuang".

46 See document "X shi 2002 nian fupin kaifa mubiao guanli zerenzhuang". It is a county-level municipality.

47 Interview YA2 with the director of the poverty alleviation office in a Yunnan county (Spring 2003).

48 Interview YAa1 with the head of the poverty alleviation office in a Yunnan township (Spring 2003); and see document "X shi 2002 nian fupin kaifa mubiao guanli zerenzhuang".

49 Interview YA6 with the director of the poverty alleviation office in a Yunnan county (Spring 2003); and see also documents "Guanyu duixian 2002 niandu mubiao guanli zerenzhi de tongzhi" and "X shi 2002 niandu xiangzhen mubiao guanli zerenzhi jiang".

nationally designated key poor counties in Sichuan and Shanxi that I visited, to raise the average income of farmers (*nongmin shouru*) is an important target but difficult to separate from more comprehensive economic targets such as the target to increase GDP: the reasoning was that when GDP increases, the average income of farmers will also increase or vice versa. [50]

In contrast to poverty reduction, the Western development programme has no targets of its own in the annual evaluation of local leaders. Central authorities do not exercise the cadre responsibility system for the Western development programme so the township leaders do not sign performance contracts with regard to the initiative to develop the Western region. According to a section chief of the development planning commission, it would be difficult to set up a performance contract for the Western development programme since there is no specific meaning attached to the policy. However, there are targets and performance contracts for particular projects that fall under the Western development programme and which were managed by different bureaus. One such project was to relocate farmers (*yidi ban qian*) but although it is managed by the development planning bureau it has a poverty reduction dimension. [51] In the comprehensive evaluation, the Western development programme is likely to be measured by economic development indicators. Through an analysis of the organisation of the Western development programme, it is possible to deduce the nature of the policy. The Western development programme is, in my opinion, a significant increase in budgetary resources to various sectors in the Western provinces, but not a policy with a specific content. There are close parallels with the Coastal development strategy initiated in the 1980s, although the Western development strategy is much less focused in comparison. Like the Coastal development strategy, key projects are written into the performance contracts and the success of the Western development programme is measured in the targets of GDP, the level of investment, in particular foreign investment, etc.

---

50 Interview SiA2 with the director of the poverty reduction bureau in a Sichuan county (Spring 2004); and Interview ShCa1 with the party secretary of a Shanxi village (Spring 2004).

51 Interview YA3 with a section chief of the development planning commission in a Yunnan county (Spring 2003); see also document "X shi 2001—2002 nian guojia yidi fupin banqian shidian gongcheng xiangmu". It is a county-level municipality.

The Western development programme and poverty reduction seem both to be either measured by economic development indicators or overshadowed by them—even in the key poor counties in Western provinces in which poverty reduction was supposed to be the central task of local leaders. Poverty reduction targets are hard targets in the evaluation of the leading cadres, but there are strong indications that reducing poverty is taken to be the same as economic development and the specific poverty reduction targets are of lesser importance. According to one director coordinating the evaluation, when poverty reduction gets a low score but development indicators are good, the unit under evaluation can still gain a high score. When the work to reduce poverty is done well but the GDP is poor, on the other hand, the unit under evaluation may not get a high score. [52] The assumption seems to be that an increase of GDP automatically leads to an increase of farmers' income, although there is no inspection to check whether an increase of the GDP benefits the poor households living below the national poverty line of 625 yuan or even below an annual income of 1,000 yuan. Judging from the way poverty reduction policies are carried out, however, probability is low that growth will actually benefit the households whose income is below average in poor places. I conclude that under the current design of the cadre responsibility system, the work to reduce poverty and regional inequality is assessed by economic development indicators. In this way, the problems of regional inequality and poverty can only become more important in the evaluation than economic growth through the *yipiao foujue* target of upholding social order. It is therefore the *effect* of the problems of poverty and regional inequality that is measured in the cadre responsibility system, rather than the implementation of poverty alleviation or the Western development programme as such. If social problems such as poverty and inequality cause social discontent and widespread unrest, social development may then, but only then, be given higher priority than economic growth.

▪ Concluding Discussion

The people-oriented approach and the new leaders' emphasis on balanced

---

52 Interview SiA5 with the director of the evaluation office under the party committee in a Sichuan county (Spring 2004).

development have not yet taken hold at the local organisational level. An analysis of the cadre responsibility system at the local level shows that there is still a single-handed focus on GDP growth. So far, policies have not changed much from the previous leadership. In the current design, social problems such as poverty will only kick in through the *yipiao foujue* targets measured by their effect on social stability. Given the mixed messages given from the centre—more weight should be given to social development but at the same time the total GDP volume is to be doubled in 20 years—it is not really surprising. A policy to put economic growth first has been implemented for two decades, and if the policy is going to change there needs to be a strong message from the central government. This is not to say that Chinese leaders ignore social issues but they seem to view economic growth as the best means to solve social problems. However, the new leadership has become conscious that additional policies are needed, and one of the concrete measures taken to raise rural income is to reduce the agricultural tax by more than 1% per year, with agricultural taxes to be eliminated in five years. The separate policy to reduce agricultural tax has been given high priority and was effectively implemented in my field sites in Sichuan and Shanxi in April 2004 even though it was only announced in March the same year. In fact, the work to reduce agricultural tax began before the National People's Congress meeting in March 2004, together with overall tax reform, which is one reason why the policy is going to be implemented well ahead of the set time frame. To reduce the burden on peasants (*jianqing nongmin fudan*) counted as a priority target with veto power, but as part of the larger target to maintain social order. [53]

The findings here affirm that the cadre responsibility system is flexible enough to adjust to the changing needs of the CCP and to solve urgent social problems, but the CCP has not yet given sufficient priority to the social problems of poverty and regional inequality. From the beginning of reform up until today, the party has been better at promoting development than at attacking social problems. I argue that it is not the political system itself that is at fault, but the party's objectives. I agree with Hu Angang and Wang Shaoguang that the capacity of the state to solve social problems has

---

53 Interview SiAa1 with the township head, the chairman of the local People' s Congress and the vice-party secretary of a Sichuan township (Spring 2004).

been reduced, but I differ from them in that I see it as a consequence of a deliberate strategy to roll back the state on social issues. [54] Again, the Chinese government falls into line with New Public Management and the trend of the rest of the world. The Chinese government has in the reform era chosen to withdraw and delegate the responsibility for social issues to local governments without providing budgetary funds for it. In poor areas, local funds are not sufficient and township officials have no budgetary resources to carry out central-level policies for which they are held responsible. Neither do they today have legal local taxation rights to raise resources for that purpose. When social problems cause widespread unrest, the Chinese government's capacity to deal with this will be contingent on not having rolled back the state too far. Hopefully, the new leadership will have changed course before problems reach that level.

If the new leadership want to "put people first" and pay more attention to social issues, they have to push it through the cadre responsibility system. Up until today, they have not done so. New initiatives require time, however, and within the next one or two years we might be able to spot a change at the local level if the new leaders are serious about it.

---

54 Wang Shaoguang and Hu Angang, *The Chinese Economy in Crisis: State Capacity and Tax Reform*, Armonk, NY: M. E. Sharpe, 2001; and *The Political Economy of Uneven Development: The Case of China*, Armonk, NY: M. E. Sharpe, 1999.

The Chinese Communist Party's Nomenklatura System as a Leadership Selection Mechanism: An Evaluation

John P. Burns [*]

■ Introduction

Like all communist parties in power, the Chinese Communist Party (CCP) has developed a system to manage the selection of leaders of public organizations. The system is based on Leninist principles of party organization and state-society relations, the most important of which is that the party holds a monopoly of power. [1] The system, developed in the context of a centrally planned economy and disabled or non-existent civil society, is arguably the defining characteristic of the party. The principal function of the system is to maintain the CCP in power. Because the party continues to exercise monopoly power in China, arguably the nomenklatura system has performed very well. For the past 50 years or more the CCP has been able to select China's top leaders more or less unchallenged.

* John P. Burns is a Chair Professor of Politics and Public Administration of The University of Hong Kong. He obtained undergraduate degrees from St. Olaf College and Oxford University, and a Ph. D. in political science from Columbia University. His research interests focus on public sector human resource management, civil service reform, party-state relations, and public sector reform. He is the author or editor of eight books, and his articles have appeared in the *China Quarterly, Journal of Contemporary China, Pacific Affairs, and Public Administration and Development*. He is a member of the Editorial Committee of the *China Quarterly* and served on the HKSAR Government's Civil Service Training and Development Advisory Committee from 1997 to 2003.

The author grateful for comments on a first draft of this paper to the participants of the Conference on "the Chinese Communist Party in a New Era: Renewal and Reform, " sponsored by the East Asian Institute, National University of Singapore, Singapore, December 9-10, 2003 and especially to Zheng Yongnian and Kjeld Erik Brodsgaard, and to Kenneth Lieberthal and Ken Qingxin Wang. All remaining errors are my own. The author grateful to the Hong Kong Research Grants Council for supporting this research.

1 Janos Kornai, *The Socialist System: the Political Economy of Communism*, Princeton, NJ: Princeton University Press, 1992, pp. 33 – 48.

In addition to its primary function of maintaining the CCP in power, however, the nomenklatura system also serves as a mechanism for selecting specific kinds of leaders, namely, those who are competent and loyal, to facilitate China's development needs. Given the party's monopoly position this function is of growing importance for the development of the country. In so far as performance is relevant to the CCP maintaining its position in power, and arguably it is, the two functions are linked. It is from the latter perspective that I evaluate the performance of the nomenklatura system. I argue that from this perspective the nomenklatura system has served neither the CCP nor China very well.

CCP management of leadership selection in China has had a checkered past. During some periods, such as the Cultural Revolution, the system completely collapsed, while, during other periods (for example, 1952—1953), the system was disabled by elite infighting and corruption. Even during the Jiang Zemin era the system has been moderately impaired by corruption. Arguably the system performed at its best in 1954—1955 during a period of organizational rationalization when elite conflict was low and party discipline relatively high. That is, the performance of the nomenklatura system as a leadership selection mechanism has varied even when the position of the CCP as an institution was apparently more secure and the party less decayed than it is now. I conclude that elite unity and party discipline best explain variation in the performance of the nomenklatura system. When these have broken down, the ability of the nomenklatura system to select competent and loyal leaders has been undermined.

▪ Background

The nomenklatura system is, in essence, a leadership selection system that gives territorial party committees at each administrative level monopoly power to select officials for posts within their jurisdiction. Jurisdictions are determined at the center by the Politburo. Each party committee from the Central Committee on down has a list of positions over which it has final selection authority. Generally, the lists are divided into two parts: A list of positions over which the party committee must first give its approval before an appointment may be made and a list of positions the filling of which must be reported to the Organization Department (OD). The OD may veto appointments on the second list. [2] The system also includes lists of

reserve candidates for each position that are also managed by territorial party
committees and sets of principles and procedures for matching candidates to
positions.

Vertical Dimensions

In 1998 the Central Committee's nomenklatura included about 2, 500
officials at the rank of minister/provincial governor and a further 39, 000
officials at bureau level whose appointment must be reported to the Central
Committee (see Figure 1). The number of ministerial/provincial-level
positions has remained remarkably stable over time, while the number of
bureau-level posts has increased by more than 48% since 1984. The
numbers of bureau-level posts fell briefly in 1989—1990 and again in
1993—1994, the latter dip undoubtedly the result of a government
downsizing campaign. [3] The decline in 1989—1990 may have been the
result of retrenchment and political fallout from the June 4, 1989 episode.

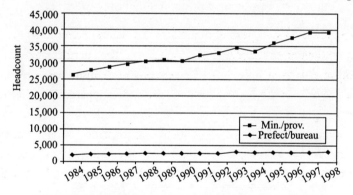

Figure 1 Central Committee nomenklatura, 1984—1998
Source: Organization Department, Central Party History
Research Office, Central Archives, Zhongguo gongchandang
zuzhishi ziliao, Vol. 2, Appendix 1, Beijing: Zhonggong dangshi
chubanshe, 2000, p. 1357.

Authority to make leadership selection decisions, although relatively
centralized, has sometimes been decentralized to supra-provincial regional
party bureaus (1952—1954) and to provincial and prefectural party committees

---

2 John P. Burns, *The Chinese Communist Party's Nomenklatura System*, Armonk, NY: M. E.
Sharpe, 1989.
3 John P. Burns "Downsizing the Chinese State: Government Retrenchment in the 1990s", *The
China Quarterly*, No. 175, September 2003, pp. 775 - 802.

(since 1984). From 1952 to 1954, for example, the Politburo set up six regional administrations covering groups of provinces and gave the regional party bureaus their own leadership selection authority. Authority was re-centralized in 1954, however, when the bureaus were abolished. [4] Since 1984, nomenklatura authority has extended one level down the administrative hierarchy. Prior to 1984 officials were required to seek the prior permission of the Central Committee before prefectural-level appointments could be made. [5] In 1983, officials made some 5, 845 appointments at prefectural/bureau level all of which would have obtained prior approval from the Central Committee. [6] With the decentralization of nomenklatura authority in 1984 prior approval was necessary for only ministerial/provincial-level appointments (less than 100 new appointments were made in 1984). In some cases, the number of posts requiring central approval fell drastically (e. g. , in the People's Bank of China, by 87%). [7] Still the central OD, since 1984, has had to process several thousand cases a year, either to give prior or post-appointment approval (see Figure 2).

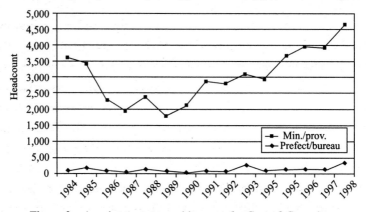

Figure 2 *Appointments to positions on the Central Committee nomenklatura, 1984—1998*

Source: Organization Department, Central Party History Research Office, Central Archives, *Zhongguo gongchandang zuzhishi ziliao,* Vol. 2, Appendix 1, Beijing: Zhonggong dangshi chubanshe, 2000, p. 1427.

4　Burns, *The Chinese Communist Party's Nomenklatura System,* p. x.

5　Ibid. , p. xviii.

6　Organization Department, Central Party History Research Office, Central Archives, *Zhongguo gongchandang zuzhi shi ziliao: Zhonghua renmin gongheguo zhengzhuan zuzhi 1949—1997* (Chinese Communist Party Organization History Materials: People's Republic of China Organization of Organs of Political Power, 1949—1997), Vol. 2, Appendix 1, Beijing: Zhonggong dangshi chubanshi, 2000, p. 1427.

7　Burns, *The Chinese Communist Party's Nomenklatura System,* p. xviii[0].

Horizontal Dimensions

The horizontal dimensions of the nomenklatura system include: (1)
changes to the locus of authority to select leaders (periodic de-
concentration of authority at the center) ; and (2) the changes to the scope
of party control.

Although the OD, on behalf of the Politburo, has retained operational
control over the nomenklatura system since 1949, from time to time it has
delegated authority to other high-level party bodies to make leadership
selection decisions. Thus, in 1953, for example, when the Central
Committee consisted of many agencies that shadowed government
ministries and commissions, these party agencies made leadership selection
decisions. These party agencies included the Planning and Industry
Department, the Finance and Trade Department, the Communications and
Transportation Department, the Rural Work Department and the Political
Work Department. The Propaganda and United Front Work Departments
also had their own leadership selection authority. Still this authority was
exercised under the supervision of the OD. [8] In the 1990s, the OD also
delegated leadership selection authority to two central party organizations
with responsibilities for financial institutions and key state-owned
enterprises. The CCP's Central Financial Work Committee (*zhongyang
jinrong gongzuo weiyuanhui*) , headed from 1998 to 2003 by Wen Jiabao,
and the Central Enterprise Work Committee (*zhongyang qiye gongzuo
weiyuanhui*) , headed by Wu Bangguo from 2000 to 2003, both
subordinate to the Central Leading Group for Finance and Economics,
selected leaders for key financial institutions and state-owned enterprises. [9]

Which positions to include in the published nomenklatura and the degree
of secrecy surrounding its publication are political questions. Unlike the
pre-1984 lists, the party made the 1984 and 1990 nomenklatura lists relatively

---

8　Ibid. , p. xvi.
9　Central Committee, "Zhonggong zhongyang guanyu wanshan jinrong xitong dangde lingdao tizhi,
　jiaqiang he gaijin jinrong xitong dangde gongzuo youguan wen-tide tongzhi" (Notice on Several
　Questions on Perfecting the Financial System and the Party's Leadership System, Strengthening
　and Improving the Financial System and the Party's Work), May 19, 1998 in Central Financial
　Work Committee Organization Department (ed.), *Dangde zuzhi gongzuo shiyong shouce*
　(Handbook of the Party's Organization Work), Beijing: Central Party School Press, 1999, p. 190.

accessible to outsiders (they were published in collections of organization and personnel documents sold in official book stores or otherwise available) [10], while the party has not published the 1998 lists as openly. The apparent increasing secrecy surrounding the party's behind-the-scenes role comes as China has entered the World Trade Organization which requires increasingly transparent decision-making. Leaders may be attempting to conceal from outsiders the role of the party in, especially, economic policy making.

The scope of the Central Committee's published nomenklatura (and presumably the nomenklatura of local party committees) has changed from time to time reflecting (1) the increasing institutionalization of the Chinese political system[11] and (2) the Politburo's perception of its political needs. In 1990, for example, the party added positions to the published nomenklatura that clearly had been controlled by the Central Committee previously, but not reported. These included the Politburo, the Central Committee, the Central Military Commission, and the President and Vice President of the PRC (see Table 1). The 1990 version, then, was a more complete and honest account of the party's role. The 1990 version omitted the nation's top universities in line with party thinking at the time that controlling them no longer required Central Committee attention. [12] They were included once again, however, in the 1998 list, indicating, perhaps, the party's changed perception of the importance of universities to stability and the party's continued survival. Most state-owned enterprises were dropped from the Central Committee nomenklatura in the 1990 list. [13] They have been moved to the list of positions to be reported to the Organization Department.

10　The 1984 lists were published in People's Bank of China Personnel Bureau (ed.), *Renshi gongzuo wenjian xuanbian*, Beijing: China Finance Press, 1985; while the 1990 lists were published in Ministry of Personnel (ed.), *Renshi gongzuo wenjian xuanbian*, Vol. 13, Beijing: China Personnel Press, 1990. The 1984 lists were discussed in a document in the Ministry of Labor and Personnel Policy Research Office (ed.), *Renshi gongzuo wenjian xuanbian*, Vol. 7, Beijing: Ministry of Personnel Policy and Regulation Bureau, 1986, pp. 39 – 42.

11　Lyman H. Miller, "Institutions in Chinese Politics: Trends and Prospects", in Library of Congress *China's Future: Implications for US Interests: Conference Report*, Washington, D. C. : Library of Congress, 1999.

12　John P. Burns, "Strengthening Central CCP Control of Leadership Selection: The 1990 Nomenklatura", *The China Quarterly*, No. 138, June 1994, pp. 474 – 480.

13　These comments refer to the list of positions that must receive prior Organization Department approval before an appointment may be made.

Table 1 Structure of the Central Committee nomenklatura, 1984—1998 *

	1984	1990	1998
Party Central		X	X
Central Party Bureaucracy	X	X	X
President, Vice President; Chairman, Vice Chairman of Central Military Commission (CMC)		X@	X
National People's Congress	X#	X#	X
Chinese People's Political Consultative Conference	X#	X#	X
State Council, Banks, Corporations, Diplomats	X^	X^	X
Judiciary, Procuratorate	X#	X#	X
Mass Organizations	X	X	X
Provincial-level Organizations	X	X	X
Universities	X		X
State-owned Enterprises, Service Units	X		

Notes: * Refers only to the list of positions over which the party committee must give prior approval before an appointment may be made; @ Chairman and Vice Chairman of the CMC were classified as Party Central; # Included as a single category; ^ Included People's Armed Police.

Sources: John P. Burns, *The Chinese Communist Party's Nomenklatura System*, Armonk, NY: M. E. Sharpe, 1989, pp. 122 – 130; John P. Burns, "Strengthening Central CCP Control of Leadership Selection: The 1990 Nomenklatura", *The China Quarterly*, No. 138, June 1994, pp. 474 – 480; Hon S. Chan, "Continuity and Change in Cadre Personnel Management in China: From the 1990 to the 1998 Nomenklatura System, 1990—1998", *The China Quarterly*, No. 179, September 2004, pp. 703 – 734.

Functions

The nomenklatura system has served several functions the significance of which has varied over time. From a system perspective the nomenklatura's most enduring and principal function is to enable the party to realize effective control of the state and, more broadly, the commanding heights of the economy. Arguably the party has adhered to this goal unwaveringly since 1949. In this regard the nomenklatura system functions as a patronage system that allows the party to reward its supporters and punish its enemies. Patronage allows the party to build support for its rule. The patronage system also permits the party to use public organizations as an employer of last resort, an important policy instrument to preserve stability under conditions of high unemployment. Also, from a system perspective, the nomenklatura seeks to place competent and loyal leaders in positions of power, which enables the system to develop efficiently. I am concerned with this function in this chapter.

From the perspective of organizations, the nomenklatura system serves the function of political communication, laying out for insiders and outsiders the system of official statuses. This allows participants to understand their place in the political system. Moreover, the system acts as a political road map because higher status organizations (those on the Central Committee's nomenklatura, for example) may legitimately make demands on senior party leaders for assistance and support.

From the perspective of individuals, the nomenklatura system provides the structure for systems of reciprocal relations (networks) that can assist the life chances of members and their extended kin/friends. [14] In this sense the nomenklatura system has provided a structure for party factionalism that has system-wide implications. Because of information asymmetry and the incompleteness of the legal system, the access the nomenklatura system provides for members and their networks may advantage them in everything from job applications to tendering and licensing requests. This function of the nomenklatura may have grown with the development of the market economy. Even under conditions of the unbridled pursuit of Weberian-type efficiency, norms that value advancing family interests and information asymmetry may continue to permit nomenklatura networks to play a valuable role in the distribution of rewards.

The development of a market economy, and a rapidly growing private sector, have severely challenged Leninist institutions such as the nomenklatura system. The reforms have thrown open new opportunities for individuals to accumulate resources outside of party control, which poses a danger to party rule. The party has met this development with both repression and co-optation. The CCP has repressed attempts to establish

---

14 Andrew G. Walder, "Sociological Dimensions of China's Economic Transition: Organization, Stratification, and Social Mobility", paper prepared for the Conference "China's Economic Transition", University of Toronto, November 15-17, 2002.

political parties and trade unions outside of party control and continues to manage the media. The party uses and manages the increasing number of non-government organizations that have come to characterize civil society in China "with Chinese characteristics". CCP policy also calls for co-opting the new business elite and professionals into the party. Jiang Zemin's theory of the "three represents" provides the ideological foundation for the policy. [15] Whether these measures will succeed or not remains to be seen.

■ Evaluation of the CCP's Nomenklatura System

Considerable evidence indicates that China's officials, in general, are increasingly selected based on performance. [16] Civil service reforms have abolished life tenure, raised educational levels, and brought in formal rules that require competitive selection and promotion based on ability. Career paths of public officials in the reform era have advantaged those with a formal university degree. [17] Rapidly increasing formal educational levels are a relatively recent phenomenon. Education levels fell in the early and mid-1950s and stayed relatively flat during the Cultural Revolution (1966—1976). [18] Aggregate data is consistent with the interpretation that advancement is linked to educational levels for China's leaders as well, especially since the early 1980s (see Figure 3).

15 Zemin Jiang Speech delivered on the 80th Anniversary of the CCP, *China Daily,* July 2, 2001, pp. 4 - 6 and Guoguang Wu, "From the July 1 Speech to the Sixteenth Party Congress: Ideology, Party Construction and Leadership Transition", in David M. Finkelstein and Maryanne Kivlehan (eds.), *China's Leadership in the 21st Century,* Armonk, NY: M. E. Sharpe, 2003, pp. 167 - 185.

16 Walder, "Sociological Dimensions of China's Economic Transition: Organization", pp. 9-12; and Maria Heimer, *Market Forces and Communist Power: Local Political Institutions and Economic Development in China,* Uppsala: Uppsala University, 2000.

17 Andrew G. Walder, Bobai Li and Donald J. Treiman, "Politics and Life Chances in a State Socialist Regime: Dual Career Paths into the Urban Chinese Elite, 1949—1996", *American Sociological Review,* Vol. 65, No. 2, 2000, pp. 191 - 209.

18 Organization Department, Central Party History Research Office, Central Archives, *Zhongguo gongchandang zuzhi shi ziliao: guodu shiqi he shehui zhuyi jianshe shiqi* 1949—1966 (Chinese Communist Party Organization History Materials: the Transition Period and the Period of Socialist Construction 1949—1966), Vol. 5, Beijing: Zhonggong dangshi chubanshe, 2000, pp. 1350 - 1352.

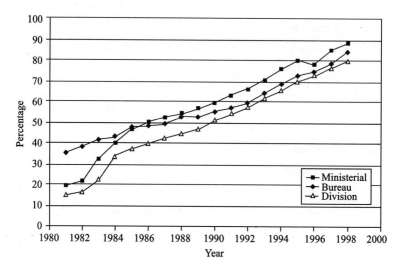

Figure 3 *Leading Cadres in China with University Education, 1981—1998*
Note: University education here includes both university and college (associate) degrees.

Source: Organization Department, *Dangzheng lingdao ganbu tongji ziliao huibian* (Collected Statistical Materials on Party and Government Leading Cadres), Beijing: Dangjian duwu chubanshe, 1999, p. 5, 8, 10.

An evaluation of China's leadership selection system, however, reveals that while the CCP has stressed performance and ability as important selection criteria, selection decisions in practice have also valued nepotism and favoritism, on the one hand, and rewarded corruption, on the other. A high performing leadership selection system has both process and outcomes dimensions (see Table 2). The system should be able to: (1) produce leaders effectively (process); and (2) produce leaders who perform well and who can meet the expectations of the competent political authority and the community (outcomes). The first dimension refers to the process of selecting leaders and requires, among other things, clearly articulated and agreed upon rules, selection criteria, and participants, as well as

Table 2 *Evaluation of Leadership Selection Cases*

		Outcomes	
		Effective	Ineffective or impaired
Process	Effective	1954—1955	1990s
	Ineffective or impaired	?	Cultural Revolution, 1952—1953 and mid-1980s

timeliness. In particular, leaders should be selected according to the official
and agreed criteria, whatever they may be. In the context of China, for
example, the criteria have varied over time but have included both merit or
ability, on the one hand, and political loyalty, on the other ("red" and
"expert"). [19] Leaders chosen by nepotism, favoritism, or through
corruption, are evidence of an impaired leadership selection system. I argue
that for substantial periods of time China's nomenklatura system has been
procedurally impaired.

The second dimension refers to the result or outcome of the selection
process and requires that the selected leaders perform well. They should
meet the expectations of both the competent political authority and the
community. Where leaders, for example, engage in corruption they
clearly have not performed well. I argue that widespread corruption in
China is evidence that relatively large numbers of leaders selected through
the nomenklatura system have failed to perform well.

Arguably the most important variables for explaining the performance of
the nomenklatura system are elite-level conflict and party discipline (see
Table 3). I hypothesize that a high level of elite-level conflict (unbounded)

Table 3 *Nomenklatura System Contexts*

		Party discipline	
		High	Low
Elite conflict	High	1958—1960	Cultural Revolution, 1952—1953?
	Low	1954—1955	mid-1980s and 1990s

impairs the nomenklatura system either because leaders cannot agree on
personnel appointments, thus causing delay or inaction, or because strong
individual leaders attempt to hijack the system and impose leaders who are
not supported by the organization. I hypothesize that the lack of party
discipline impairs the system because high levels of corruption and/or
factionalism result in the selection of the incompetent or those who pervert
public (CCP) policy for their own ends. Although elite-level conflict and
party discipline are closely related (elite-level conflict usually produces party
indiscipline [factionalism]) they are conceptually different variables and
may vary independently. Thus, low levels of elite conflict may co-exist

---

19 Franz Schurmann, *Ideology and Organization in Communist China*, Berkeley, CA: University
of California Press, 1966.

with party indiscipline (for example, corruption) if the elite tolerate indiscipline as they apparently did during the 1990s. Relatively high levels of elite conflict may co-exist with relative party discipline as apparently occurred in 1958—1960 (see below) .

I argue that when elite-level conflict has been high and party discipline low as during the Cultural Revolution and perhaps during other periods such as 1952—1953, the system has been wholly ineffective or greatly impaired. During these times the nomenklatura system broke down procedurally and served neither national nor collective party goals. Alternatively, when elite-level conflict has been low (bounded) and party discipline high as during the period 1954—1955, the nomenklatura system has been a relatively effective leadership selection device. I argue that for substantial periods during China's post-1949 history, the nomenklatura system has been an unreliable leadership selection instrument, serving neither the party as a collective entity nor the nation very well.

System Effective: 1954—1955

Arguably the period from mid-1954 to late 1955 represents the nomenklatura system at its most effective. In February 1954, the party dismissed Gao Gang and Rao Shushi, thus ending a debilitating elite-level confrontation between the two leaders and Mao Zedong. The handling of Gao and Rao must have indicated to other leaders that challenging Mao and the party center was unwise, even dangerous. The period 1954—1955 was, then, one of relatively low elite-level conflict. It was also a period of relatively high party discipline. By mid-1954 the CCP had led three campaigns to root out corruption. Two of these campaigns (the *sanfan* campaign in 1951—1952 and the new *sanfan* campaign in 1953) were aimed at the party and state bureaucracy and were designed, in part, to improve party discipline. As a result of the first campaign some 173,000 leading cadres were punished for "corruption, waste and bureaucratism"[20]. The new *sanfan* campaign focused more on the "bureaucratism, subjectivism and decentralism" of middle—and upper-level leaders. [21] It is likely that the

---

20 Harry Harding, *Organizing China: The Problem of Bureaucracy, 1949—1976*, Stanford, CA: Stanford University Press, 1981, p. 54.
21 Ibid. , p. 62.

net effect of the two campaigns and an earlier party rectification campaign was to heighten party discipline.

The period from mid-1954 through 1955 was a period of organizational rationalization. [22] In June 1954, the CCP abolished the regional administrative committees and party bureaus that had provided Gao and Rao with their platforms to challenge the center, and centralized power in Beijing. The period 1954—1955 was also one of "tidying up" the system of assignments and promotions. In tandem with the development of a planned economy, party organization departments played the leading role in personnel appointments. "Throughout the period" central personnel organs made or approved all appointments of county magistrates and party first secretaries, all provincial appointments above the level of bureau director, and all central government and party appointments above the level of deputy bureau director. During the same time the party also specified more clearly criteria for appointment and promotion (administrative ability and political reliability). Although officials sometimes resisted the reassignments made during the period, especially being sent down to lower-level units, the system successfully transferred over 90,000 cadres by July 1954, indicating its robustness. There were also sometimes job mismatches. Still, a survey in 1955 indicated that only 11.7% of engineering graduates and 17.7% of technical middle school graduates had yet to be given appropriate assignments.

As it began, the process of organizational rationalization "generated remarkably little controversy" and "little disagreement among top Chinese leaders"[23]. Even Mao openly supported the increasing formalization and centralization of the Chinese state and supported the further development of the technical skills of the bureaucracy. The period, then, was arguably the heyday of China's nomenklatura system which was both procedurally effective and apparently produced leaders who were valued by the political authority.

System Ineffective: Cultural Revolution

To be effective the nomenklatura system requires a single political center

---

22　Ibid., pp. 65 – 86.
23　Ibid., p. 85.

and relatively high levels of party discipline, neither of which condition prevailed during the Cultural Revolution.

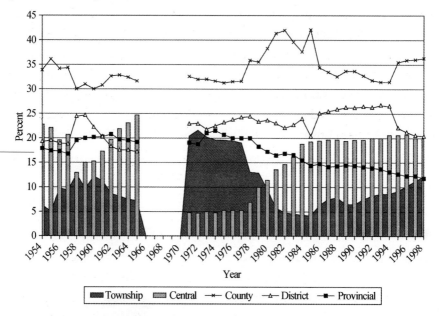

Figure 4 *Distribution of Cadres by Administrative Level, 1954—1998*

Source: Organization Department, Central Party History Research Office, Central Archives, *Zhongguo gongchandang zuzhishi ziliao,* Vol. 2, Appendix 1, Beijing: Zhonggong dangshi chubanshe, 2000, pp. 1333 – 1334.

Beginning in 1966 Mao Zedong mobilized radical leaders within the CCP to attack and remove from office what became large numbers of officials at all administrative levels throughout the country. [24] The campaign against the bureaucracy reportedly resulted in at least 80% of officials (most of whom were leaders) being removed from office by 1968. [25] Aggregate

---

24 See Byung-joon Ahn, *Chinese Politics and the Cultural Revolution,* Seattle, WA: University of Washington Press, 1976; Melvin Gurtov, "The Foreign Ministry and Foreign Affairs in the Chinese Cultural Revolution", in Thomas W. Robinson (ed.), *The Cultural Revolution in China,* Berkeley, CA: University of California Press, 1971, pp. 113 – 164; Harry Harding, "Maoist Theories of Policy-Making and Organization", in ibid., pp. 113 – 164; Harding, *Organizing China,* pp. 235 – 328; Hong Yung Lee, *From Revolutionary Cadres to Party Technocrats in Socialist China,* Berkeley, CA: University of California Press, 1991, pp. 77 – 162.

25 Zhou Enlai apparently told Edgar Snow that the number of officials working in central agencies was cut from 60, 000 to 10, 000. Descriptions of the new revolutionary committees set up at provincial level indicated similar reductions. Throughout 1968 reports indicated that the number of employees of county governments had been cut by between 75% and 90% (Harry Harding, *Organizing China,* p. 288).

data from the period indicate that huge reductions were made in the number of central-level cadres during the Cultural Revolution, numbers that did not begin to pick up again until the early 1980s (see Figure 4). During the same time, the number of township officials expanded rapidly, however, indicating that many central-level cadres were "sent down" to township level. (Indeed, for the entire period 1954 to 1998 the percentage of central-level cadres was inversely correlated [−0.81647] with the percentage of township-level cadres, indicating also the impact of the Great Leap Forward on the relative distribution of officials.) From 1978 to 1982 when higher-level cadres were being re-called during the post-Cultural Revolution era, the percentage of township-level officials fell dramatically. It has crept up since that time. The percentage of provincial-level officials, stable before and after the Cultural Revolution, has declined steadily relative to other categories of officials since the Cultural Revolution. The relative strength of county-and district-level officials also changed little before and after the Cultural Revolution, although there have been substantial changes especially at county level since. Because of the collapse of the organization-personnel system from 1966 to 1970 published statistics for the period are unavailable.

As we have seen, prior to the Cultural Revolution organization departments had responsibility for managing the system throughout the country.

Although they appear to have been effective managers of the nomenklatura system until 1966, beginning then, official accounts indicate that they became "paralyzed" (*tanhuan*) until at least 1973 (and probably until 1976). [26]

The fate of the central OD was symptomatic of the disarray that characterized leadership selection in general during the period. Like other central party and government agencies, the OD was badly affected by the Cultural Revolution. A few days after the Cultural Revolution Temporary Preparatory Committee was set up within the OD on August 15, 1966 under the leadership of Zeng Di (a Deputy Head of the OD), the Committee

---

26　Modern China's Personnel Management Editorial Group, *Dangdai Zhongguo renshi guanli* (Modern China's Personnel Management), Beijing: Dangdai Zhongguo chubanshe, 1994, p. 57.

convened a meeting of all OD employees during which the then Head of the Department (An Ziwen) and five of seven deputy heads were severely criticized. As a result, the head, all deputy heads (except presumably Zeng Di), and many division chief-level officials of the department stopped work and were investigated. (From 1967 to 1971, together with over 500 other leading cadres, An Ziwen was incarcerated in Qincheng maximum security prison.[27] He died on June 25, 1980.) Under these circumstances the OD's management of the central nomenklatura effectively ceased. The Preparatory Committee under Zeng Di's leadership continued in power until January 18, 1967 when "several mass organizations seized its authority by force"[28]. The attack on the OD's deputy leaders was then stepped up. In May, Kang Sheng, by then a Politburo Standing Committee member[29] and Advisor to the Cultural Revolution Small Group set up in May 1966, appointed first Zhu Guang from the PLA and then in October Guo Yufeng, a PLA major general to take over the OD. Under Kang and Guo's leadership further attacks were launched on the leadership of the department.[30] In March 1968 Guo submitted a report to the "party center" demanding that the department be thoroughly re-organized. Still, during 1968 Kang Sheng was able to use the OD to launch attacks on other central leaders. Thus, on August 23 he instructed the OD to brand 37 of the 60-member 8th Central Supervisory Committee (*zhongyang jiancha weiyuanhui*)[31] as "renegades, spies and counterrevolutionary revisionists". Kang and Guo contemplated a thorough clean out of the Organization

---

27   Michael Schoenhals, "The Central Case Examination Group, 1966—1979", *The China Quarterly*, No. 145, March 1996, p. 105.

28   Organization Department, Central Party History Research Office, Central Archives, "*Zhongguo gongchandang zuzhi shi ziliao: 'wenhua dageming' shiqi*" (Chinese Communist Party Organization History Materials: "Cultural Revolution" Period), Vol. 6, Beijing: Zhonggong danshi chubanshe, 2000, p. 70.

29   In May 1966, Kang was only an alternate Politburo member, but he was promoted in August 1966 to the Politburo Standing Committee by the 11th Plenum of the 8th Central Committee (see Organization Department, Central Party History Research Office, Central Archives, 2000, p. 24). From August 1966 he seems to have had responsibility for organization and personnel work.

30   Organization Department, "*Zhongguo gongchandang zuzhi shi ziliao: 'wenhua dageming' shiqi*", p. 70.

31   The Committee, set up in 1955 to carry out party discipline and investigation work, was chaired by Dong Biwu until 1966. See Organization Department, "*Zhongguo gongchandang zuzhi shi ziliao: 'wenhua dageming' shiqi*", pp. 48 – 51.

Department and on February 21, 1969 the "party center" approved Guo's plan to send to the countryside virtually all employees of the department for re-education through labor. A nucleus of 55, only 35 of whom were cadres, remained in the office in Beijing.

From 1970 the OD was placed under the direction of the Central Organization and Propaganda Group (zhongyang zuzhi xuanchuan zu) set up "under the leadership of the Politburo"[32]. Chaired by Kang Sheng, members included Jiang Qing, Zhang Chunqiao, Yao Wenyuan, Ji Dengkui and Li Desheng. When Kang became too ill to continue as leader and Li was transferred to Shenyang, Jiang Qing and her associates effectively took over the group. Rebuilding the OD commenced in 1971 when the number of employees was increased first to 85 and then, by August 1971, to 113. New appointments to leadership positions in the OD in 1969 and 1971 brought in PLA officers and the Head of the First Office of the Central Case Examination Group. [33]

This brief account indicates that there was considerable resistance to the radicals' takeover of the OD, which was finally completed only with the clean-out in 1969. Clearly the OD was in no position to manage the central nomenklatura from 1966 to 1969. Similar takeovers occurred locally that "paralyzed" local government organization departments from 1967 to 1971. [34]

The Cultural Revolution had devastating consequences for cadre management. First, about 60% of top leaders lost their positions. [35] Of these the "purge" rate was about 70% at the center and 54% of local leaderships. [36] The extent of the purges was indicated by radical Zhang Chunqiao's view that:

32 Tianxun Fan and Bo Zhao (eds.), *Zhongguo gongchandang zuzhi gongzuo dashiji* (Chronology of Chinese Communist Party Organization Work), Beijing: Zhongguo guoji guangbo chubanshe, 1991, p. 233.

33 Schoenhals, "The Central Case Examination Group, 1966—1979".

34 Modern China's Personnel Management Editorial Group, *Dangdai Zhongguo renshi guanli* (Modern China's Personnel Management), Beijing: Dangdai Zhongguo chubanshe, 1994, p. 54.

35 Hong Yung Lee, *From Revolutionary Cadres to Party Technocrats in Socialist China*, Berkeley, C. A. : University of California Press, 1991, p. 80.

36 Ibid. , p. 81.

> every official has made mistakes and every mistake will be opposed. As a result, there is now no single county party committee member who can be trusted, no single prefectural party committee member who can be trusted; among the provincial party committee members and those of the center, no one can be trusted except Chairman Mao. [37]

The criteria of those to be purged was ambiguous and constantly changing. [38] As a result dismissals from office made during the Cultural Revolution in the name of the nomenklatura system were suspect.

Second, conflict over recruitment and promotion criteria was intense at the early stages of the Cultural Revolution and after Deng Xiaoping was reinstated in office in March 1973. [39] The radicals declared that the differential power relationships and reward structures of the pre-CR bureaucracy had served as the basis for the emergence of a new ruling class that had to be overthrown. The radicals argued that class background and age were the appropriate selection criteria. Thus, having one-third of every leadership group consist of young people became an official policy. Conservatives accused the radicals of "two surprises". "One recruited unqualified persons to the party, and the second promoted them to high office by skipping several grades—a practice that Deng Xiaoping satirically labelled helicopter promotion. " By 1973 a backlash set in against the newly appointed young cadres ("young men are unstable, [and] men without moustaches are immature"). [40] Until the arrest of the Gang of Four in 1976, however, many party committees continued the radicals' policy in spite of the conservatives' criticism by creating new leadership positions for the young cadres.

Third, the appointment and dismissal of leading cadres occurred through highly irregular procedures. [41] The radicals used all sorts of "illegal" methods to promote their followers to positions of power, including arbitrary promotions of the unqualified, promotions based solely on factional affiliation, waiving party recruitment procedures to take in "those who had

---

37   Ibid. , p. 143.

38   Ibid. , p. 91.

39   Ibid. , pp. 121 − 129.

40   Ibid. , p. 137.

41   Modern China's Personnel Management Editorial Group, *Dangdai Zhongguo renshi guanli* (Modern China's Personnel Management), Beijing: Dangdai Zhongguo chubanshe, 1994, p. 54.

rebelled", and setting up new temporary party branches to recruit their followers. [42] As a result, some individuals who were not even party members became party secretaries.

Fourth, effective operation of the nomenklatura system depended on extensive and accurate files on each cadre. During the Cultural Revolution the radicals who temporarily took over organization and personnel departments filled personnel files with inaccurate and wild accusations about the supposed crimes of many leaders. The official evaluation of this period criticized the Gang of Four for "violating party rules and regulations, randomly destroying the party's cadre management principle, and disregarding materials in the dossier, frequently changing the conclusions that had been reached organizationally and adding forged materials"[43].

During the CR Mao Zedong and the radicals destroyed the formal authority of the Chinese party/state and with it the party's leadership selection system.

System Partially Impaired: 1952—1953, Mid-1980s, and 1990s

I have identified three intermediate cases where the nomenklatura system has been partially impaired by relatively high levels of elite conflict and/or relatively low levels of party discipline. In the first two cases (1952—1953 and mid-1980s) the process and outcomes of the leadership selection system were both somewhat impaired. In the last case (1990s) although the leadership selection system was relatively effective procedurally, outcomes were tainted by corruption, especially by the sale and purchase of official posts.

The CCP's leadership selection system was severely tested in 1952— 1953, during the early years of the People's Republic. During this time Mao's conflict with Gao Gang and Rao Shushi had a debilitating effect on the work of organization departments, especially the central OD in Beijing, and high levels of corruption were evidence that the system was not producing appropriate leaders.

Gao and Rao were accused of establishing tight personal control over

---

42 Lee, *From Revolutionary Cadres to Party Technocrats in Socialist China,* p. 125.
43 Ibid. , p. 126.

their regional governments and party bureaus (Gao in the Northeast and Rao in Huadong) and of then using their local power to demand changes in the central party and state leadership. [44] In 1952 and early 1953, as part of attempts to centralize power, the CCP moved the heads of the regional bureaus to Beijing. Gao, also a Politburo member, arrived in late 1952 to become Chairman of the State Planning Commission and Rao in early 1953 to take over the OD. [45] At the National Conference on Financial and Economic Work in June-August 1953, Gao, supported by Rao, attacked Liu Shaoqi and Zhou Enlai over their support for a new tax system. They stepped up their attack at the National Organization Work Conference in September-October, 1953. A core issue was a list of new Politburo members prepared by An Ziwen, then Deputy Head of the OD with close ties to Liu Shaoqi, who was the Politburo and Secretariat member in charge of organization and personnel work at the time. The list had not been approved by Rao, who took over the OD in February 1953. [46] The origins of the new Politburo list are obscure, but go to the very heart of the leadership selection process. According to one account:

> Mao raised the matter of arrangements for leaders of the regions with Gao and asked him to consider the matter. Gao went to An in the spring of 1953 and, using Mao's name, instructed him to prepare a Politburo list including the existing members and the key figures of the regions. It was not An's job to do this and he hesitated, correctly understanding that this was something within Mao's responsibilities. But in the face of Gao's representation he finally produced the list. People aware of the list were befuddled as to how someone of An's rank could produce it, and thus they were susceptible to Gao's claim that Liu was behind it. In producing the list, An reportedly accepted Gao's guidelines and dutifully added those region leaders not already on the Politburo— Bo Yibo, Deng Xiaoping, Rao Shushi and Lin Biao. Gao Gang, however, assertively spread the rumor that Lin was not on the list. [47]

In July, Rao, seeking to take effective control of the OD, attacked An at a meeting of OD bureau chiefs and at other meetings, attacks that were

44 Harding, *Organizing China*, p. 68.
45 Frederick C. Teiwes, *Politics at Mao's Court: Gao Gang and Party Factionalism in the Early 1950s*, Armonk, NY: M. E. Sharpe, 1990, p. 20.
46 Ibid. , p. 80.
47 Ibid. , pp. 96 - 97.

not approved by the Politburo.[48] Still, An Ziwen apparently acted beyond his authority and subsequently received a formal disciplinary warning and criticism as a result. Mao later referred to "a slate of candidates for the Politburo illicitly put together by An Ziwen"[49].

Gao Gang used the list to play one group of senior officials off against another. In communications with senior army officers he pointed out how the list favored cadres from the "white areas", especially Liu Shaoqi over those from "red areas", especially the army and Lin Biao. He also criticized the proposed rapid promotion of Bo Yibo, a Liu lieutenant, to the Politburo.[50] Gao contacted leaders, seeking a reorganization of the party and government. He offered various posts to prospective allies and made use of An's list to gain the support of disgruntled army leaders.[51] In the end both Gao and Rao were purged in February 1954 for attempting to split the party.

Although the Politburo list was not acted on, the episode demonstrates, first, that leaders were being selected primarily for factional ends, that is, to further the careers of senior figures such as Politburo member Gao Gang. Second, the case demonstrates how senior leaders could override established processes to influence outcomes. Although not as serious as the Cultural Revolution cases discussed above, the Gao-Rao Affair indicates that leadership selection at the time was weakly institutionalized and outcomes were unsure.

During the early 1950s party discipline also was relatively weak. As it shifted from its role as an opposition force pursuing military conquest to a governing party, the CCP faced a severe shortage of cadres which it sought to rectify by recruiting thousands of new officials.[52] From October 1949 to September 1952, the party recruited nearly 3 million new cadres increasing their number from 720,000 to 3,310,000.[53] Given high levels of unemployment, the new positions were undoubtedly attractive.[54] To fill

---

48   Ibid. , p. 81.
49   Ibid. , p. 97.
50   Ibid. , pp. 98 – 99.
51   Ibid. , p. 6.
52   Ying-mao Kau, "Patterns of Recruitment and Mobility of Urban Cadres", in John W. Lewis (ed.), *The City in Communist China*, Stanford, CA: Stanford University Press, 1971, pp. 98 – 99; and Harding, *Organizing China*, pp. 34 – 37.
53   Kau, "Patterns of Recruitment and Mobility of Urban Cadres", p. 103.
54   Ezra Vogel, *Canton under Communism: Programs and Politics in a Provincial Capital, 1949— 1968*, New York: Harper, 1969, p. 66.

the gaps the CCP made rapid promotions of cadres who were often not qualified for the positions. In Wuhan, for example, "a number of early top appointees were only semiliterate, with so little administrative ability and professional competence that the party eventually found it necessary to dismiss them"[55]. According to Kau "the quality of cadres who were hastily recruited early on was sometimes appalling" and illiteracy among newly recruited government officials was widespread.[56] Lax admissions standards had allowed many unqualified individuals into the party—they sought to join the winning side rather than to join out of ideological conviction.[57] This sort of environment encouraged corruption and, indeed, many officials became corrupt. As we have seen, during the 1951—1952 anti-corruption (*sanfan* and new *sanfan*) campaigns, authorities removed 4.5% (over 100,000 punished[58], see above) of state cadres from office for corruption.[59] I conclude that in the early days of the People's Republic the nomenklatura system was partially impaired because it selected for promotion many incompetent officials and relatively large numbers of officials who either were, or later became, corrupt.

Our discussion of the period 1952—1953 has highlighted both elite-level conflict and party indiscipline as undermining the leadership selection system. The leadership learned from the Gao and Rao affair of the importance of isolating dissident leaders so that they could not organize opposition. The period 1958—1960 reveals that when the party is able to contain elite-level conflict it may not be a sufficient condition to impair the leadership selection system. For example, the nomenklatura system appears to have been reasonably effective even during the period surrounding the Great Leap Forward (GLF), especially 1958 to 1960. The anti-rightist campaign that preceded the GLF removed from office critics of the party's collectivization and other policies which paved the way for implementation of urban and rural communes and the Great Leap.[60] Although Mao was

---

55 Kau, "Patterns of Recruitment and Mobility of Urban Cadres", p. 101; and Ezra Vogel, *Canton under Communism,* p. 59.

56 Kau, "Patterns of Recruitment and Mobility of Urban Cadres", p. 102.

57 Harding, *Organizing China,* p. 47.

58 Harding reports 173,000 punished.

59 Kau, "Patterns of Recruitment and Mobility of Urban Cadres", pp. 113 – 114.

60 Roderick MacFarquhar, *The Origins of the Cultural Revolution, Vol. 2: The Great Leap Forward 1958—1960,* Oxford: Oxford University Press, 1983.

challenged by Peng Dehuai at the Lushan Plenum in August 1959 and
Peng, Zhang Wentian (Deputy Foreign Minister), Huang Kecheng
(Chief of Staff), and Zhou Xiaozhou (Hunan Party Secretary) were
dismissed from their posts[61] they were relatively isolated from other senior
party leaders[62] and appear to have had little influence on the leadership
selection system. Unlike Gao Gang and Rao Shushi, who used the
organization and personnel system to further their own ambitions, Peng
Dehuai appears to have opposed Mao on a policy issue. The period 1958—
1960 was also characterized by relatively high levels of party discipline.[63] I
conclude, then, that bounded elite-level conflict has not been a sufficient
condition to impair the nomenklatura system.

The nomenklatura system was also partially impaired during the mid-
1980s. Although elite-level conflict was relatively low, both procedural
irregularities (nepotism and favoritism) and corruption affected leadership
selection decisions during the period. According to a survey of the
children of more than 1,700 central and provincial leaders conducted in
the early 1990s, about 3,100 held official positions above the government
bureau or military division level. Another 900 were the principal leaders
of large and medium-sized state-owned enterprises (SOEs).[64] According
to one source children in leading positions who gained their early foothold
in party or government through family connections include Deng Pufang,
Deng Nan, Chen Yuan, Xi Jinping, Bo Xilai, Yao Mingwei, Hu
Deping, Fu Rui, Wan Jifei, Li Xiaolin, Liao Hui, Chen Haosu, Li
Tielin, Lin Yongsan, He Guangwei, and Zhou Xiaochuan.[65] In
addition, many cadre children found leading positions in the military and
corporate worlds.

During the mid-1980s, to induce their elders to retire a large number of
sons and daughters of high-level cadres were given middle-level official
positions as compensation.

61　Ibid. , p. 234.
62　Ibid. , pp. 228 – 233.
63　Vogel, *Canton under Communism,* p. 247.
64　Cheng Li, *China's Leaders: The New Generation,* Lanham, MD: Rowman and Littlefield,
　　2001, pp. 128 – 129.
65　Ibid. , p. 132.

> It became a common practice for veteran leaders to retire with the "compensation" of having their children appointed to leadership posts... elderly leaders could continue their privileged lifestyles if their children succeeded them in official positions. In fact, official status has become particularly important over the past decade because political power can often lead to tremendous economic wealth as official corruption becomes rampant. [66]

Thus, paradoxically, "nepotism and favoritism in elite recruitment have become prevalent at a time when educational criteria and technical expertise are more important than class background and revolutionary experience" for cadres as a whole. [67]

It could be argued that because the primary function of the nomenklatura system was to maintain the CCP's position in power, using its nomenklatura authority to compensate the elders demonstrated that the system was effective. While this may be so, the appointment of so many officials based on nepotism and favoritism also demonstrates that leadership selection decisions were made on criteria other than competence or party loyalty, criteria that I am using (and the CCP also uses) to evaluate the system.

The emergence of corruption as a serious problem dates from the early 1980s. As early as 1982, Chinese leaders publicly acknowledged that corruption had reached "crisis levels"[68]. As Manion points out, the volume of corrupt activities exploded in the early 1980s, continued to grow in the 1980s and 1990s, and "increasingly involved large sums and probably a greater number of senior officials"[69]. Since the 1980s corruption has ranked at or near the top of every public opinion poll as the most urgent problem confronting the country, with ordinary citizens describing it as serious and its growth unabated or more rapid than ever. [70] If anti-corruption campaigns are excluded (when many more cases were reported than during other times), a trend line for the data in Figure 5 shows the number of cases increased from less than 5, 000 per year in 1980 to over 50, 000 per year in

---

66 Ibid. , p. 129.

67 Ibid. , p. 128.

68 Melanie Manion, *Corruption by Design: Building Clean Government in Mainland China and Hong Kong*, Cambridge, MA: Harvard University Press, 2004, p. 88.

69 Ibid. , p. 122.

70 Ibid. , p. 124.

1996. [71] Given the low probability of being prosecuted (from 1993—1998
fewer than half of the corruption cases being investigated led to criminal
charges being filed and only 6. 6% of these led to corrupt officials being
sentenced) [72], engaging in corrupt practices appears to have been a relatively
low risk activity. I conclude, then, that during the mid-1980s not only
was the nomenklatura system selecting leaders based on criteria such as
nepotism and favoritism in relatively large numbers, but that it was also
selecting corrupt officials for public office. That is, the nomenklatura
system was at least partially impaired.

In the 1990s although the system was procedurally relatively effective,
outcomes have been partially impaired by corruption. As we have seen,
corrupt activity increased rapidly during the 1990s (see Figure 5) . [73] The

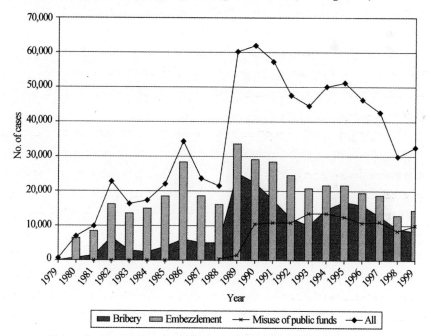

Figure 5 Corruption Cases Filed and Investigated by Procuratory

Source: Melanie Manion, *Corruption by Design: Building Clean Government in
Mainland China and Hong Kong,* Cambridge, MA: Harvard University Press, 2004,
Table 3. 1.

---

71   Ibid. , Figure 3. 1.

71   Ibid. , Figure 3. 1.

72   Angang Hu, *Zhongguo: tiaozhan fubai* (China: Fighting Against Corruption), Hangzhou: Zhejiang
renmin chubanshe, 2001; and Angang Hu in *South China Morning Post,* March 24, 2001.

73   Cheng Li, *China's Leaders,* p. 148, 149.

CCP's leadership selection system was then producing officials who later became corrupt, and promoting officials who were already corrupt. A new twist to the corruption saga, however, was the emergence in the 1990s of the practice of buying and selling official posts, including leading positions. In so far as this practice was widespread, it seriously undermined the system.

During the mid-1990s the press published numerous cases of officials selling government positions. By 1996, *People's Daily* pointed out that "some extremely power-hungry people go all out to bribe organizational and personnel departments. Some subordinates directly bribe their superiors, who are in charge of transfers, deployments, and promotions, with bribes worth hundreds of thousands of dollars. "[74] Corrupt personnel practices have been reported primarily in local government. In 1997 and 1998, for example, the press reported that officials sold scores of government jobs in Wenzhou City (Zhejiang) , Pizhou County (Jiangsu) , Beihai City (Guangxi) , Huaibei City (Anhui) , Tieling City (Liaoning) , Guanfeng County (Jiangxi) , and in Heilongjiang Province. [75] When former NPC Vice Chairman Cheng Kejie was Governor of Guangxi province from 1994 to 1998 he accepted bribes totalling RMB 280, 000 *yuan* and US $ 3, 000 to arrange for the promotion of three local government officials to senior positions in the Beihai City government. [76] From 1999 to 2000, officials bribed their way into powerful positions including leading positions in county-level organization departments. [77] I have no way of knowing how extensive these corrupt practices were but they do indicate that the CCP's leadership selection system was at least

---

74 *People's Daily (Renmin ribao)*, January 17, 1996 (in FBIS-CHI-96-034 January 17, 1996).

75 *People's Daily (Renmin ribao)*, March 24, 1998 (in FBIS-CHI-98-097 April 7, 1998); *China Daily* in *South China Morning Post*, September 22, 1998; *New China News Agency (Xinhua)*, October 29, 1998 (in FBIS-CHI-98-310 November 6, 1998); *Sing Tao Daily (Sing Tao Jih Pao)* (Hong Kong), May 13, 1998 (in FBIS-CHI-98-133 May 13, 1998); *Ming Pao* (Hong Kong), October 28, 1998 (in FBIS-CHI-98-301 October 28, 1998); and *Outlook (Liaowang)*, March 10, 1997 (in FBIS-CHI-97-071 March 10, 1997).

76 *Wenhui bao* (Hong Kong), August 1, 2000.

77 Xiao Zhong (ed.), *Zhonggongde shenceng fubai* (Deep Layered Corruption of the CCP), Hong Kong: Xiafeier chuban youxian gongzi, 2003, pp. 406 − 413. On May 7, 1998, the Central Organization Department set up a 24-hour hotline to receive information on corrupt personnel practices. From then until November 1998, nearly 1, 000 informants called the hotline. See *New China News Agency (Xinhua)*, October 29, 1998 (in FBIS-CHI-98-310 November 6, 1998).

moderately impaired during the 1990s, a trend that appears to have continued.

We must admit that, at least formally, the CCP has taken many steps to prevent or minimize corruption. Although there is no evidence that the CCP has sought out and promoted corrupt officials to leading positions, the structure of incentives has done little to prevent such an outcome. Rules that require leading officials to declare their assets and to undergo audits before being transferred or promoted are not being effectively enforced. [78] The two parties to a corrupt transaction have every incentive to keep it hidden. The nomenklatura system does not screen out the corrupt in part because the CCP is unable to subordinate itself to an independent anticorruption agency. To do otherwise would result in the party losing its monopoly position. Accordingly, corruption is likely to impair the leadership selection system for the foreseeable future.

Although the nomenklatura system has continued to be an effective mechanism to keep the CCP in power, as a mechanism for selecting competent officials and those loyal to the party as an institution, for much of the past 50 years the system has served neither the CCP nor the country particularly well. I have argued that the system operated most effectively in the mid-1950s during a period of organizational rationalization. During the Cultural Revolution the system collapsed under the weight of elite infighting and weakened party discipline. Elite conflict and corruption also undermined the system in 1952—1953. More recently, the system performed badly in the mid-1980s when it selected many leaders through nepotism and promoted the corrupt. In the 1990s, although the system was procedurally stronger, corruption also undermined leader selection outcomes. Given this patchy performance what can we expect in the future?

▪ Conclusion: The CCP in a New Era

As many have observed, two decades of economic reform, the move toward a market economy, increasing integration with the world economy, rapidly rising living standards, higher educational levels, and

---

78 *Xinhua,* March 24, 1997 (in FBIS-CHI-97-083, March 24, 1997).

greater access to information have had a marked impact on the environment in which the CCP operates. [79] In spite of these contextual changes, there are striking continuities in the organization of the party. First, the internal structure of the party remains Leninist and formal institutions have changed little during the past 50 years. In practice, power continues to be centralized in the Politburo, its Standing Committee, the Secretary General and the head of the Central Military Commission. [80] Second, the CCP, like other communist parties, continues to be an elite party, recruiting less than five percent of the total population, a practice that should enable the party to remain relatively disciplined. Third, the incentives for joining the party have remained broadly unchanged as well. Although most people join out of rational calculation (to influence policy or for personal gain) we must acknowledge that some join out of a sense of duty or love of country (that is, for norm-based or affective reasons). [81] Fourth, the party continues to exercise monopoly power in society and vigorously suppresses challenges to its authority, such as those posed by the China Democratic Party and the Falungong in the 1990s. [82] Fifth, the party continues to rely heavily on traditional Leninist institutions of control, such as the nomenklatura system and the military. We have already seen, however, that in some respects the nomenklatura system has been at least partially impaired for decades.

Socio-economic change in the 1980s and 1990s has undermined support for the party, especially from farmers and workers in state-owned enterprises. Although China is not a democracy the CCP has felt it necessary to scramble for new bases of support. Accordingly the party has

---

79 Carol Lee Hamrin, "Social Dynamics and New Generation Politics", in Finkelstein and Kivlehan (eds.), *China's Leadership in the 21st Century*, pp. 204 – 222; David Shambaugh, "Remaining Relevant: The Challenges for the Party in Late-Leninist China", in ibid., pp. 271 – 286; and Bruce Dickson, *Red Capitalists in China: The Party, Private Entrepreneurs, and Prospects for Political Change*, Cambridge: Cambridge University Press, 2003.

80 To be sure the transition from a charismatic leader to a technocratic leadership has had an impact on the relationships among these institutions and between them and the Central Committee. See Susan Shirk, *The Political Logic of Reform in China*, Berkeley, CA: University of California Press, 1993.

81 James L. Perry and Lois R. Wise, "The Motivational Bases of Public Service", in David H. Rosenbloom, Deborah D. Goldman, and Patricia W. Ingraham, *Contemporary Public Administration*, New York: McGraw Hill, 1994, pp. 251 – 261.

82 Bruce Dickson, *Red Capitalists in China*.

shed its class-based ideology[83] and begun recruiting from among the urban middle class and private entrepreneurs. [84] The strategy seeks to co-opt these groups and re-penetrate the commanding heights of society and the economy, including the private sector. How successful this strategy will be only time will tell.

Although the literature on the evolution of one-party states suggests a variety of possible trajectories for China[85], the Chinese political system fits comfortably with the notion of an "established one-party state"[86]. According to Huntington, one-party states face challenges both internal (succession problems and the management of elite-level conflict during a transition phase) and external (challenges from a technical-managerial class, interest groups, critical intellectuals, and "local and popular groups" demanding to participate during an adaptation phase). [87] Established one-party states may adapt to these challenges but do not necessarily or even mostly become "democratic"[88].

According to Huntington, the principal difference between revolutionary and established one-party systems is the scope of politics. The increasing complexity of society means that to function effectively, established one-party systems must relax political controls. Economics, technology, and various social units "require greater degrees of autonomy to accomplish effectively the ends of the system" and de-politicization becomes the order of the day. Accordingly, the extent to which the party continues to monopolize politics in an established one-party system depends on the extent

---

83　Zemin Jiang Speech delivered on the 80th Anniversary of the CCP, pp. 4 – 6. Guoguang Wu, "From the July 1 Speech to the Sixteenth Party Congress: Ideology, Party Construction and Leadership Transition", in Finkelstein and Kivlehan (eds.), *China's Leadership in the 21st Century*, pp. 167 – 185.

84　Bruce Dickson, "Economics as the Central Task: Do Entrepreneurs Matter?", in ibid., pp. 186 – 203; and Bruce Dickson, *Red Capitalists in China*.

85　Shambaugh, "Remaining Relevant"; Shiping Zheng, *Party vs. State in Post-1949 China: the Institutional Dilemma*, Cambridge: Cambridge University Press, 1997; Gordon Chang, *The Coming Collapse of China*, New York: Random House, 2001; Minxin Pei, *From Reform to Revolution: The Demise of Communism in China and the Soviet Union*, Cambridge, MA: Harvard University Press, 1994; and Bruce Dickson, *Red Capitalists in China*.

86　Samuel P. Huntington, "Social and Institutional Dynamics of One-Party Systems", in Samuel P. Huntington and Clement H. Moore (eds.), *Authoritarian Politics in Modern Society: The Dynamics of Established Party Systems*, New York: Basic Books, 1970, pp. 3 – 47.

87　Ibid., p. 33.

88　Dickson, *Red Capitalists in China*, pp. 157 – 167.

to which decisions continue to be made on political rather than technical or functional grounds.[89] In so far as decisions are made on political grounds, the extent of the party's influence is much broader. Leadership selection decisions based on nepotism, favoritism, and corruption are political grounds. We have seen that the incentives to continue to make leadership decisions on these grounds are strong but they entail a loss of legitimacy. In this sense they undermine the nomenklatura system as a tool enabling the CCP to maintain its position in power.

I have identified the levels of elite conflict and party discipline as key variables for explaining the performance of the CCP's leadership selection system. Unbounded elite conflicts in China, such as the Cultural Revolution, have been associated with the "consolidation" phase of the country's development where the resolution of succession crises was important.[90] Rule by a charismatic leader and relatively low levels of institutionalization characterized this stage. China's leaders no longer rule through charisma and considerable institutionalization has taken place.[91] The 1980s, for example, saw a proliferation of party and state institutions, regularization of institutional process, and emphasis on institutional discipline that has continued into the 1990s.[92] Institutional restraints on China's leaders "have been stronger than ever during the past few years"[93]. The CCP's management of the leadership succession in 2002—2003 is evidence of a new higher level of institutionalization especially at the top. Where elite conflict has emerged, such as during the June 4, 1989 incident, the party has moved quickly to isolate the dissenting leaders and prevent them from organizing to oppose the center. (The party's monopoly position requires it to deal harshly with elite dissent, which arguably is not a characteristic of a highly institutionalized political system. Thus, the CCP must continue to arrest, detain, and isolate dissenting leaders to enable the party to maintain its monopoly position.)

Maintaining party discipline is probably the greatest challenge in the new era. Although there are many challenges to party discipline including

---

89 Huntington, "Social and Institutional Dynamics of One-Party Systems", p. 41.
90 Ibid. , pp. 26 – 32.
91 Miller, "Institutions in Chinese Politics: Trends and Prospects".
92 Ibid. , pp. 24 – 28.
93 Cheng Li, *China's Leader*, p. 129.

ideological change and a new membership base, managing corruption is, perhaps, the most serious challenge. As we have seen, corruption emerged as a serious problem in the 1980s and 1990s, causing a serious rift between the interests of officials and society. Corruption continues at crisis levels. In March 2003, the President of the Supreme People's Court revealed that 85,000 officials had been found guilty of corruption since 1997. Since then, authorities have dismissed the Minister of Land and Resources for corruption and fired two provincial party secretaries accused of corruption.[94] In 2003, 13 ministry/province-level officials were convicted of corruption, the largest number of high-ranking officials to be dealt with in a single year.[95]

Some have argued that corruption has become less of a problem in recent years. For example, China's corruption " score " on Transparency International's Corruption Perception Index has improved in recent years (from 2.16 out of 10 in 1995 to 3.5 out of 10 in 2002).[96] Official party surveys reveal that people now perceive corruption to be a less serious problem than they did in the 1990s.[97] Still, the evidence of a sea change in this arena is very thin and officials continue to describe corruption in China as "rampant"[98]. Corruption at epidemic proportions seriously undermines the performance of the nomenklatura system and is an indication of considerable organizational decay.

The continued stability of established one-party systems such as China depends on " the maintenance by the party of its monopoly of the legitimation of the system". This, in turn, depends on the identity of interest between party and society.[99] Corruption is a serious challenge to the shared interests of the party and society. In so far as it undermines the performance of the nomenklatura system, it also undermines the usefulness of the system as a tool for maintaining the party in power.

---

94 Ching, Frank, "Still Corrupt—But Not as Much", *South China Morning Post*, December 3, 2003.

95 *China Daily*, December 26, 2003.

96 Ching, "Still Corrupt—But Not as Much", and Jon S. T. Quah, *Curing Corruption in Asia: a Comparative Study of Six Countries*, Singapore: Eastern Universities Press, 2003.

97 Ching, "Still Corrupt—But Not as Much".

98 *China Daily*, December 26, 2003. See also *China Daily*, December 5, 11, and 23, 2003.

99 Huntington, "Social and Institutional Dynamics of One-Party Systems", p. 42.

Party Work in the Urban Communities

Akio Takahara and Robert Benewick [*]

■ Introduction

Following the reforms of basic-level governance in the countryside, the Chinese Communist Party (CCP) is now implementing community construction in the urban areas. The rural reforms centred on the introduction of free elections for the village committees and on enhancing the transparency of the village finances, with a view to increasing the accountability of the village authorities to the villagers. On the other hand, the aims of urban community construction involve improvements in various areas, including: providing services such as welfare, sanitation, environment, and public security; implementing democracy and autonomy at the grassroots level; and maintaining and strengthening the control over the urban populace.

The need for urban community construction stemmed largely from the progress in marketisation, particularly the reforms in state-owned enterprises and in the government. [1] In the past, under the *danwei* (unit) system that developed in China in the days of the planned economy, much of the

[*] Akio Takahara is Professor of Contemporary Chinese Politics at the Graduate School of Law and Politics, University of Tokyo. He served as Visiting Scholar at the Consulate-General of Japan in Hong Kong (1989—1991) and the Japanese Embassy in Beijing (1996—1998). He also served as a Member of the Governing Body of the Institute of Development Studies, UK (1999—2003). His publications include *The Politics of Wage Policy in Post-Revolutionary China, New Developments in East Asian Security* (co-editor, in Japanese), and *Beyond the Borders: Contemporary Asian Studies Volume One* (co-editor, in Japanese).

Robert Benewick is Emeritus Professor of Politics, University of Sussex, and Research Associate at the Centre for the Study of Democracy, University of Westminster.

We are grateful to Sarah Cook, Ford Foundation, who was instrumental in arranging the fieldwork, the Leverhulme trust and the British Academy for their generous support and to Xia Jianzhong and our many friends and colleagues in China for their wisdom and support.

[1] For an analysis of the reform of the *danwei,* see David Bray, *Social Space and Governance in Urban China: The Danwei (Workunit) System from Origins to Reform,* Stanford, CA: Stanford University Press, 2005; Xiaobo Lu and Elizabeth J. Perry (eds.), *Danwei: The Changing Chinese Workplace in Historical and Comparative Perspective,* Armonk, NY: M. E. Sharpe, 1997.

above-mentioned services were provided by the *danwei*. *Danwei* was not only a workplace but also a small society in which people were born, went to school, worked, lived, and died. Now facing increasingly severe competition in the market, enterprises are no longer able to afford the services for their staff and workers as they constitute a heavy financial burden. In the industrialised countries, it is mainly the government that provides such services. In the case of China, however, the CCP aimed for "small government, big society", and a major aspect of the government reforms has been to change the functions and reduce the size of the government. It is regarded that the government, as well as the enterprises, is unable to bear the full burden of the provision of services to the urban residents.

Besides the provision of services, another function of the *danwei* was to control the urban residents. *Danwei* kept dossiers on staff and workers and gave them not only political education but also ration coupons and permission to visit other cities. When the Regulation for Organising Urban Street Offices was promulgated at the end of 1954, the major purpose of it was to control those that did not belong to any *danwei*. [2] For this purpose, it was stipulated that the area of jurisdiction of a Street office would be the same as that of a police station. [3] Along with the promotion of reforms, however, there is an increasing number of staff and workers that leave their *danwei,* either because they are fired, or because they seek better opportunities in the labour market. At the same time, a great number of migrant workers from the countryside have entered the cities and now dwell in the urban neighbourhoods. Thus, the CCP has found a need to strengthen their control and power at the urban grassroots. This includes the need for better control over their stray party members, many of whom had been "contaminated" by the "evil teaching" of *Falun Gong*.

It follows that there has been a streamlining of government which has led to a devolution and decentralisation of many of its functions to the lower

---

2   Being dispatched offices of the district government, the Street offices constitute the lowest level of government in urban China. Below the Street offices, there are the residents committees, which are stipulated in the constitution as residents' autonomous organisations.

3   See clause 3 of the Regulation, in Pang Senquan, "A Study Report on Revising the 'Regulation for Organising Urban Street Offices'" (in Chinese), in Policy Research Centre of the Ministry of Civil Affairs (ed.), *Zhongguo Shehui Fuli yu Shehui Jinbu Baogao (2003)*, Shehui kexue wenxian chubanshe, 2003, p. 210.

levels of government. The relationships between the basic level of government, i. e. the Street office and the residents committees are changing both structurally and substantively. The need for younger, better-educated, professional leaders at the urban grassroots has been accepted. How the enhancement of social capital and the creation of community residents committees affect the distribution of power has to be tested. In order to understand the distribution or redistribution of power at the basic level of urban government and below, it may be more rewarding to shift focus from the new community committees to the role of the party, which is stipulated as the core of leadership in community construction. [4] In this view the community residents committee is just one element among those in a complex web of local governance with the party at the centre.

This chapter discusses the question of party work in community construction. It discusses the different ideas about what the party should do in urban communities, and attempts to examine the results of the implementation of different approaches. While nobody could challenge the leading role of the party in community construction, there were a variety of interpretations of the nature and the form of party leadership at the grassroots level. A delicate issue was the relationship between party leadership and the autonomy of the community. The debate around party work in community construction was related to the different ideas about the importance of autonomy, which, in turn, brought about different definitions of the area of a community and the location of power.

In the next part of this chapter, we shall investigate the two major patterns of community construction that took place in the experimental cities, focusing on the treatment of autonomy. On the one hand, there are the experiments in the more affluent, coastal cities such as Shanghai, Beijing, Tianjin, and Qingdao, where the city governments were able to invest generously in the social infrastructure for the building of urban communities. We chose the case of Qingdao, which is well known for its emphasis on the provision of welfare services. On the other hand,

---

4 Stipulated in "Ministry of Civil Affairs" Opinion on Promoting Urban Community Construction Nationwide, which was approved and transmitted in the joint circular issued by the General Offices of the party centre and the State Council on 13 December, 2000. This document is collected in Liang Wanfu (ed.), *Urban Community Construction with Chinese Characteristics, Volume* 2 (in Chinese), Liaoning University Press, 2001, pp. 1 – 10.

Shenyang, which is at the heart of the depressed, heavy industrial area in the north-east, opted for the promotion of autonomy, since they found that autonomy was a more economical way of social management. Perhaps this was an important reason why the Ministry of Civil Affairs in late 2000 chose the Shenyang model to be disseminated to other cities in China.

In the final part of this chapter, we shall assess the work of the party in the implementation of community construction. Actually, the party has proved to be effective in two areas in particular. First, the party at the street level, when strengthened, was instrumental in coordinating the work of various vertical departments. That coordination of vertical departments (*tiaotiao*) at the local level (*kuaikuai*) could only be achieved by the party, which possesses the leverage of personnel evaluation and appointment. How effective this party function of coordination has been at the level of the community is questionable, however. It appears that the party organisations at the level of the community have yet to establish the control over the party cells in the *danwei* that exist in their area or jurisdiction.

Second, it turns out that the mobilisation of the residents for various community activities has been difficult without the effort and contribution of the party members. Unlike the rural villages that possess substantial assets in the form of land and rural enterprises, urban communities hardly own anything and the residents do not feel they have a stake in participating. Besides, many urban residents actually still belong to their *danwei,* and find little incentive to take part in community activities. Thus, the contribution of the party members to community construction has been necessary in many communities. At the same time, however, their contribution has not been sufficient. From the viewpoint of the party, this represents an aspect of loosening discipline and control at the grassroots level, which is supposed to be the foundation of their rule.

Overall, it seems that urban community construction has proved to be another niche in marketisation, in which the party has found an indispensable role to play. Having said that, there are a few further questions to be answered: how well can the party play this role, and how much power and authority can the party maintain as the democratic election of the community residents committee becomes prevalent? Can a democratic synergy be achieved between the party branch and the community residents committee? Is the control function compatible with the rule of law? These are analogous to the questions regarding basic-level governance in the countryside and in enterprises and other *danwei*. How the party solves the problems in community construction is an important indicator for its future role in a fully marketised society.

▪ Patterns of Community Construction[5]

Emphasising Services and Management: The Case of Qingdao[6]

"Community" Construction at the Street-level

Qingdao is one of the earliest cities to experiment with community construction since the mid-1990s. It has defined community broadly, and has focused on improving the welfare services to, and the management of, the city residents by strengthening the party and government at the Street-level.

In 1999, the Qingdao city party committee and its organisation department chose Sifang district to experiment with the reorganisation of the Street party committee into the Street party work committee. While the previous committee had no power over other offices at the Street-level that were dispatched from the district departments, the new work committee was empowered to be the core of leadership of all the offices and activities at the Street-level. [7] The new work committee was to discuss and decide on all the important affairs of community construction and development, and mobilise the resources and coordinate the related works of the various offices and units. In 2000, it was decided to implement this method in all the districts in Qingdao.

Specifically, the Community Management Committee was to be established at the Street-level, involving the dispatched offices of specialised

---

5 This part is taken from Robert Benewick and Akio Takahara, "Eight Grannies with Nine Teeth Between Them: Community Construction in China", *Journal of Chinese Political Science*, Vol. 7, No. 1 and 2, 2002, pp. 1 – 18.

6 Based on interviews with Qingdao city and district officials, Street officials and cadres of Community Residents Committees, September 2000, and "CCP Qingdao City Committee and Qingdao City People's Government, Some Opinions on Further Promoting the Work of Strengthening Urban Basic-level Basis through Community Construction", 3 July, 2000.

7 The district department and the Street party work committee jointly conducted the assessment and appointment of the cadres to these offices.

departments and cadres of residents committees, and functioning as the coordination and implementation organ for community construction and management.

Also at the Street-level, a Community Affairs Reception Centre (*shequ shiwu shouli zhongxin*) was to be established, providing legal advice and administrative services to the residents. The Street office was also required to develop organs for social services such as introducing jobs, medication and health, education and training, and home-help.

In addition, the Community Representative Council was to be established at the Street-level. Organised by the Street party work committee, the Council was to play a consultative role, consisting of the representatives of enterprises and government-affiliated institutions, social organisations and residents, and members of the people's congresses and the Chinese People's Political Consultative Conferences at various levels. The Council was to meet regularly and discuss important affairs and problems of the community, and supervise and check the work of the Street office and other Street-level dispatched offices of the district departments.

As for the finances of the Street offices, it was decided that they were no longer allowed to run their own businesses. The Street office was to be cut off from their enterprises completely, in terms of personnel, finances, and property, and instead receive a transfer from the district finances. For instance, in the case of Shinan district, the district financial department started to transfer 10 million RMB per year to each Street office to cover their expenses. The objective of this change in the financial arrangement was to let the Street offices concentrate on city management and community construction, rather than on businesses and the making of profits. The amount of profits made was no longer included in the list of achievements used in assessing the Street office officials.

"Community" construction at the residents' committee level

At the level of the residents committees, these committees had been amalgamated and were to be reorganised into community residents committees (CRCs). The 786 residents committees of the four inner-city districts had been consolidated to 569. [8] The tasks of the CRCs were to

---

8 These figures exclude the Family Committees, the number of which was reduced from 390 to 178. They are just like residents committees, but their membership consists of the family members of staff and workers who all belong to a certain work unit.

organise the residents and conduct the following: improving the environment and beautifying the residential area; cleaning and sanitation work; services for the convenience of the residents; social welfare services; security; construction of "spiritual civilisation"; ideological education; etc. The CRCs were also expected actively to provide public affairs services, and support the government in urban management, maintaining social stability, family planning, and so on.

The members of the CRCs were to be elected democratically by the Residents Representative Council, which also discussed and decided on the important affairs of the CRCs. The city bureau of civil affairs hoped that there would be direct elections of the CRCs by all the residents in the future. [9] Also, a Community Democratic Consultative Council was to be established in each CRC, consisting of the CRC director, community work assistant, representative of the real estate management firm, representatives of the work units and the police station, Street office officials, residents' representatives, and members of the people's congresses and the Chinese People's Political Consultative Conferences at various levels. This Council was to provide opinions about community work, coordinate and solve problems that have emerged, and assess the work of the members of the CRC.

A characteristic of Qingdao's experience was the introduction of specialised community workers, recruited from among the young and well-educated, laid-off workers. [10] They were employed by the Street office, and after receiving a month's training at the district, were dispatched one each to the residents committees (now the CRCs). Their salaries are paid jointly by the district and the Street office, and are set at the level of the average wage of the total urban work force, which was an annual 8,504 RMB, that is, just over 700 RMB per month, in 1999. [11]

There was another scheme to send down staff of the district government and its affiliated institutions to the CRCs. Every district was to send down

---

9   Experiments with direct elections had started in CRCs in Sifang district.

10   They had to be under 41, have been to senior high-school, and have a local urban registered residence (*chengshi hukou*).

11   So the annual salary of a community worker was 8,504 RMB in 2000. Cf. the supplement paid to the CRC director was increased in 1998 from 135 RMB to 300 RMB. It was planned to be doubled to 600 RMB in 2001.

100 of these staff at deputy division-chief and section-chief levels to the CRCs for one year, making them deputy-secretaries of party branches or assistant-director of the CRCs. They were supposed to reinforce the work of CRCs through their knowledge of policies and high cultural standards.

Qingdao made it clear that the party organisation was to play the core leadership role, and the government was to play the organising role, in community construction. The slogan explaining the new work arrangement for community construction was, "the leadership of the party committee, organisation by the government, participation by all parties, joining forces and promotion by all". One party branch was established along with each CRC[12], and as at the autumn of 2000 the party branch secretary was concurrently director of the CRC in 63% of cases. [13]

Resources for Community Construction

The funds required for the improvement in welfare services came from various sources. First, they came from the income of the city's bureau of civil affairs. Thirty per cent of the sales of welfare lotteries could be retained in the social welfare fund, and distributed to the districts according to their sales. Also, 5% of the profits of disabled people's enterprises, exempted from income tax, were retained by the bureau of civil affairs.

Second, there might be expenditures from the districts' finances. Most of the fiscal expenditures were made on an ad hoc basis for certain projects, except for Sifang district that had earmarked 500,000 RMB for community construction each year. [14]

Third, the resources of the work units in the communities were to be mobilised. This was apparently not easy to actualise. Qingdao's officials regarded that this was particularly difficult to do if the area of a "community" was restricted to a couple of residents committees.

Discussion

Qingdao officials explained that they had focused on improving the

---

12 Before this was not the case. Although figures are unavailable for the situation in Qingdao, at the national level only 69.9% of residents committees had party cells at the end of 1998.

13 Qingdao City Bureau of Civil Affairs, "Pay Effort to Foster and Improve Community Functions and Promote the Deepening Development of Community Construction".

14 Licang district was also going to include "community construction" among the expenditure items on a regular basis.

delivery of welfare services in constructing communities. For this purpose, they said the best method was to empower the Street-level, and the Street party work committee in particular, to take the lead in interest coordination, decision-making and implementation.

Not only the money required, but also some personnel were sent from the city and the district to the Street office and the CRC. The recruitment of community workers was a way to solve the problem of unemployment, to which the development of welfare services was also considered conducive. On the other hand, the secondment of district officials to CRCs was one way to deal with the government organisational reform, which required the number of personnel to be reduced. Thus, community construction was regarded as a good opportunity for the government to alleviate the pains of enterprise and government reforms.

Improving services thus meant strengthening of management by the Street party committees and Street offices. The role of the party was also an important point at the level of the CRCs, as was clear from the fact that 63% of the party branch secretaries were concurrently directors of the CRCs. The functions of the CRCs overlapped those of the Street offices, and their institutional structures looked very similar. The CRCs, although they were the residents' autonomous organisations by name, had been co-opted and turned into the agents of the "administrative community".

Emphasising Participation: The Case of Shenyang[15]

Defining Communities

Shenyang, the capital of Liaoning province and the industrial centre of the north-east, used to be deeply embedded in the planned economy and has been seriously affected by the enterprise reforms. Since the workers could no longer depend on the work units for the delivery of social services, there had to be a new "tray", that is the community, to carry the work. After studying the experiences of other cities such as Qingdao, Nanjing, Shanghai, and Beijing, the leaders of the Shenyang city party committee and the city government decided to implement a different model of community construction. This was because the problems they confronted

---

15　Based on interviews with officials at the city, district and street levels and cadres of the Community Committees, conducted in Shenyang in September 2000.

in the process of reforms were larger than those of other cities.

Shenyang, from the beginning, defined the area of a community to be formed from amalgamated residents committees, thus excluding the Street office from the community. A central idea was to separate the government and the community along with the reform policy to separate the government and the enterprise, and not to let the residents committee become another layer of government. Shenyang officials decided to amalgamate 2-3 residents committees to form a "community", which was defined by geographical concerns, population size, functional facilities available, the sense of identity among the residents, and the distribution of work units. They thought that Streets were inappropriate to be communities, because they were government, and because they were too big to implement direct elections. In 1999, 2, 753 residents committees were consolidated into 1, 277 Community Committees. [16]

Officials of the Bureau of Civil Affairs had proposed to reorganise the constituencies of the deputies to the people's congress. If the newly defined communities became the constituencies, this would be conducive to enhancing the residents' identity with the community. The city party committee and the people's congress had agreed that some deputies in the next election should be chosen from constituencies based on communities. Already, the deputies visited communities to listen to the views of the residents, and every community had chosen one liaison officer who would convey the views of the residents to the standing committee of the people's congress. The communities were to enjoy the following rights and perform the following functions. [17] First, the right of autonomy, which consisted of five elements: the right to decide on their internal affairs; the right to select and recall their staff (recall by the request of 60% of the residents); financial rights; the right to manage ordinary affairs and goods; [18] the right

---

16   At a conference on communities held in Hangzhou in 1999, some criticised that the Shenyang model was illegal, because it had dropped "Residents" from the name despite the Law on Organising Residents Committees, and because they were hiring cadres living outside the community. Although this made Shenyang officials nervous, they maintained the support from MoCA.

17   The Shenyang city government was preparing a draft regulation that clearly defined the rights and powers of the communities.

18   According to an official of the civil affairs department, they used to need the approval of the Street office even to use some sheets of paper.

to reject any irrational request for money and other contributions (*tanpai*) . But their second "right" was to cooperate with the government and manage affairs according to the laws. This was the function the government had passed on to the community, so the necessary expenditure had to be covered by the government. The work included the management of migrants, provision of social welfare, security, and environmental protection. The third right was that of supervising the government, the court, and the prosecutor's office. But at the same time, the officials were also preparing a mechanism for the government to assess the performance of the community cadres.

As for the role of the party, Shenyang officials did see the need to establish more party branches at the community level. This was to facilitate the management of the party members who were no longer managed by the work unit party committees, and to conduct the ideological and political work. However, they also uttered an impressive statement that the people's city should be managed by the people and not by the party. Through the promotion of basic-level democracy, they said they were returning power to the people and making them the true masters of society.

The organisation of the communities consisted of four main bodies. First, there was the Community Party Organisation which had to be the "core of leadership". Second, there was the Community Members' Congress (*shequ chengyuan dahui*), or the Community Members' Representative Congress (*shequ chengyuan daibiao dahui*), depending on whether they have direct elections of the Community Committee or not. This was the highest body for decision-making. The majority of the representatives were the leaders of apartment buildings (*louzhang)* and the leaders of apartment units (consisting of flats using the same building entrance and stairs) (*danyuanzhang)* . Third, there was the Community Committee, which implements the decisions. After amalgamating the residents committees, the number of members was reduced from over 13,000 to 6,400. The average age came down from above 70 years to 45.1. The idea was to professionalise the members, and after openly inviting applications, elections were conducted. The competition ratio was 3.3 applications to 1 post. Of those elected, over 60% used to be in a managerial position in their former work units. [19] In Shenyang, in addition

---

19 However, over 3,000 of the former members of the residents committees were re-elected.

to the elected members, one or more policemen in charge of the area became ex officio members. Fourth, there was the Consultative Committee (*yishi xieshang weiyuanhui*), which consisted of three to 20 members, depending on the size of the community. The membership was similar to that of the equivalent in Qingdao. This Committee exercised the power of the Community Members' Congress or the Community Members' Representative Congress when they were not in session.

Officially, the relationship between the Street office and the Community Committees is one of guidance, and not leadership. However, there is a section (*ke,* that is one rank below the division, *chu*) in charge of community work in both the Street office and the district. They were supposed to solve any problems that the communities were unable to solve.

In the government reforms that were scheduled to start at the end of 2000, Shenyang was considering the reduction of personnel, and organisation of the Street offices in particular. They would rather strengthen the district and weaken the Street offices, which is the opposite to the idea of cities such as Qingdao and Shanghai. This apparently was not unrelated to the deep-rooted problem they were facing: it was difficult for the government, and the Street offices in particular, to get rid of their habit of giving orders and instructions to the community. Shenyang officials took this problem seriously and, in June 2000, the mayor disallowed the establishment at the community level of any organisations directly under the vertical departmental systems. At the same time, communities were prohibited from establishing organisations that bore the same name as any upper-level organisation. [20]

There were organisational arrangements at the city, the district and the Street level for the coordination of various governmental departments. At the city level, there was the Community Construction Leadership Small Group, which is headed by the mayor. The office of this leadership small group was located in the bureau of civil affairs. At the district level, there was the Community Construction Party and Government Liaison Meeting, which decided on the annual plan of community construction. The district

---

20 For example, there is the Communist Youth League at the level of Street office and above, but communities only have the Youth Association (*qingshaonian xiehui*). The latter receives no money nor personnel but only guidance from the former.

Community Construction Guidance Committee, involving various departments, provided the specific guidance on community work. For example, they decided on promoting sports activities in the communities, and guided them on the contents and methodology.

Resources for Community Construction

Funds for community construction came mainly from the district. For a new project, the communities themselves could draw their own plans, which would be assessed and approved by the Street office. The Street office would then send the plans to the district assessment committee for their assessment and approval. The district had started to earmark some budget for this committee.

What was emphasised in Shenyang was resource sharing within the community. Work units with facilities such as hospitals and gymnasiums opened them to other community members. Note here that a distinct characteristic of Shenyang was to acknowledge work units also as members of a community. In addition, donations from individuals were collected for specific purposes, such as the holding of an arts festival.

Discussion

Thus, there were difficulties in implementing autonomy thoroughly, partly because of work habit, but particularly because the communities were still dependent upon the Street offices and the district (and the city) for funds. There was also an acknowledged difficulty in mobilising the interest of the residents in community work.

Nevertheless, there was a clear target to enhance democracy and the autonomy of the community. Unlike other cities such as Qingdao, Shenyang was not allowing anybody dispatched from the district or the Street office in the community Committees (except for the policemen). They were keen to mobilise the resources within the communities, and stressed that work units were also members of the community. The bureau of civil affairs seemed genuinely keen to promote residents' participation in community work, including direct elections of Committee members.

Why was this the special way of community construction, for a city that faced bigger problems than others in the process of reforms? This partly stemmed from the fact that Shenyang was less wealthy and had a stronger need to cultivate and mobilise the resources and initiative at the societal level. When we remember the fact that most of the 26 experimental cases of community construction were located in relatively affluent big cities, we think we understand the reason why the Ministry of Civil Affairs opted not for the Qingdao model or the Shanghai model, but for the Shenyang model to be disseminated to other cities in China, a view that was eventually endorsed by the party centre and the State Council in late 2000.

■ Party Leadership in Community Construction

From the above cases, we can identify two lines of thought regarding party leadership in community construction. On the one hand, there is an idea to emphasise the central role of party leadership in the communities. This view is widely shared by such institutions as the Central Organisation Department and the relatively affluent, coastal cities that experimented with community construction. Regarding the functions of the community, emphasis was placed on control and management and provision of services. Even in medium-and small-sized cities, the leaders of the Central Organisation Department have stressed the need for implementation of ' the most important task of community management and services' through the strengthening of party organisations. [21] According to the director of the organisation department in Jianghan district, Wuhan city, which is well known for its experiment with community construction, the specific tasks of the party organisation in the community as defined by party committees at various levels can be summarised as follows: to propagate and implement thoroughly the line and policy of the party and the laws and regulations of the state, and make decisions on the important affairs of the community; to exercise leadership on the community residents committee and on the work of mass organisations such as the Communist Youth League and the Women's Federation; to organise and coordinate the party organisations and party members that belong to the units within the community to participate in community construction; to strengthen its own organisation and let the party members play a vanguard and model role in the work of the community; to implement well the work on educating and managing

---

21　See the reporting on the National Conference on the Exchange of Work Experiences on Party Construction in Streets and Communities in Medium-and Small-sized Cities, held in January 2002, in *Shequ*, Nos. 2 – 3, 2002, 8 February, 2002, particularly p. 4.

community workers; to implement well ideological and political education and maintain social stability. [22] These, in fact, are much larger roles than are stipulated in the document, "The Opinions of the Ministry of Civil Affairs on Promoting Urban Community Construction Nationwide", which was approved and transmitted by the General Offices of the party centre and the State Council. [23] With such a mandate, there seems to be no doubt that institutionally the party is in a commanding position.

The other line of thought on community construction, however, emphasises the importance of autonomy. When autonomy is regarded vital, whether for the sake of democratisation or because of the need to seek an economical way of social management, the leadership role of the party is acknowledged but considered separate from the construction of the community as such. This is the position taken by the Ministry of Civil Affairs and by the civil affairs department in poorer cities such as Shenyang. Thus, they argue that the nature of the leadership of the party over the autonomy of the community residents should be that of guidance rather than wholesale substitution, or running things all by itself. [24]

From our findings, we can identify the following effects and problems of party work in the implementation of community construction. First, the party at the Street-level can be instrumental in the coordination of different departments, and solve the friction between vertical departments (tiaotiao) and localities (kuaikuai) at the basic level. Previously, the party committee at the Street-level lacked the power to manage the party members that belonged to those offices at the Street-level that were dispatched by the bureaus of the district government. Moreover, there was no relation between

---

22 Hu Ming, "On the Unification of Institutional and Non-institutional Factors for the Leadership Role Played by the Party Organisations in Communities" (in Chinese), *Shanghai Dangshi yu Dangjian*, No. 9, 2003, collected in *Zhongguo Gongchandang*, No. 12, 2003, pp. 113 – 116.

23 This document listed the following as the major tasks of the party organisation in the community: to propagate and implement thoroughly the line and policy of the party and the laws and regulations of the state, and unite and organise the members of the party branch and the residents to fulfil the tasks assigned to the community; to support and guarantee the implementation of autonomy by the community residents committee according to law and its execution of duties; and to strengthen its own organisation, implement well its work on ideological and political work, and let the party members play a vanguard and model role in community construction.

24 This was the remark made by one representative at the National Conference on the Exchange of Work Experiences on Party Construction in Streets and Communities in Medium- and Small-sized Cities, held in January 2002, in *Shequ*, Nos. 2-3, February 2002, p. 8.

the Street-level party committee and the party members of the *danwei* that existed at the Street-level, either. Therefore, it was difficult for the former to deal with the latter, particularly if the designated administrative-level of that *danwei* was higher than Street-level. By providing the Street-level party committee with the power to co-manage these party members, that is by enabling the former to take part in the assessment of the latter, the Street-level party committee have come to possess effective leverage in mobilising the vertical departments and their party members in community construction.

This is all the more important because it has turned out that, compared to village autonomy, it is more difficult to secure the participation of residents in the various activities of the urban community. This is partly because a number of urban residents generally do not feel they have a stake in community construction. Compared to the villages that own a substantial amount of assets, such as land and village enterprises, urban communities are penniless. The work of urban communities is targeted mainly at the weak and unfortunate members of society, and if you are still employed by a *danwei* that is doing relatively well, working in the growing private sector or involved in a property owners' committee, there is not much incentive for you to participate in community activities.

It also turns out that even the party members lack enthusiasm for community work. According to a survey conducted in Hunan province, 66% of the 767 party members who were employed answered that they were unwilling to take part in community activities, and 79% of them said they were unwilling to attend education sessions organised by the party organisation of the community after work. [25] A report from Hangzhou city, Zhejiang province, reveals that there is a widespread phenomenon of "laid-off party members distrusting communities, party members with jobs in *danwei* deriding communities, retired party members ignoring communities, and resident party members not helping communities" [26]. Although the party has been empowered at the Street-level, the party organisation at the

---

25 Li Chi, "Create the Mechanism and Method for the Education and Management of Party Members in Communities" (in Chinese), *Zhongguo Gongchandang*, No. 4, 2003, p. 113.

26 Zhou Gansong, "New Situation, New Requirements, New Problems and New Countermeasures Regarding Current Work on Community Party Construction" (in Chinese), *Zhonggong Hangzhoushiwei Dangxiao Xuebao*, No. 1, 2004, pp. 58 – 63, collected in *Zhongguo Gongchandang*, No. 4, 2004, pp. 118 – 124.

community-level is yet to attain the effective mechanism and leverage to control the members of other party organisations belonging to the *danwei*.

Another issue concerns the relationship between party leadership and community autonomy. There are many cases of friction between the party organisation and the CRC, (aka Community Committee) and between the party secretary and the director of the CRC. [27] There is a parallel here with the relationship between the party secretary and the elected village leader, and between the party secretary and the manager of an enterprise. A survey in Beijing reveals that not much attention to autonomy has been paid by the party organisations, which tend to intervene extensively in the work of the CRCs. [28] This phenomenon, which is apparently widespread, leads to the imbalance between the large amount of their work and the limited amount of their funding. In other cases, since only the CRC is elected by the residents, the party organisation in the community is regarded as secondary and is only playing a subsidiary role in decision-making. [29]

Recent arguments that have arisen from praxis indicate that party leadership and community autonomy are compatible. [30] As elsewhere, the CCP has advocated a virtual merger of the party organisation and the CRC; the secretary can take part in the election and become the CRC director or a deputy director, and/or the CRC director or deputy director can be elected by the party members as the secretary or a deputy secretary. [31] In reality, besides the party secretary, the two organs have

---

27 Xu Yong and Chen Weidong *et al.*, *Zhongguo Chengshi Shequ Zizhi* (Community Autonomy in Chinese Cities), Wuhan Chubanshe, 2002, p. 275.

28 Task Force for Beijing Urban Community Party Construction, "Survey on the Situation of Beijing Urban Community Party Construction" (in Chinese), *Chengshi Wenti*, No. 4, 2003, pp. 66 – 68, collected in *Zhongguo Gongchandang*, No. 10, 2003, p. 124.

29 Hu Ming, "On the Unification of Institutional and Non-institutional Factors for the Leadership Role Played by the Party Organisations in Communities", p. 115.

30 See also Lu Hanlong, "From Party and Government Administration to Community Governance", Institute of Sociology, Shanghai Academy of Social Sciences, Construction of Grassroots Organisations in Urban China: A Research Report on Chinese Neighbourhood Committees, May 2003.

31 Yu Yunyao, *Dang de Jianshe Ruogan Shijian he Lilun Wenti* (Some questions on the practice and theory of party construction), Dangjian Duwu Chubanshe, 2002, p. 589. This is from a remark made by Yu Yunyao at a discussion meeting on party construction work at streets and communities, held in October 1999. Yu was then a deputy director of the Party Central Organisation Department.

virtually merged in many communities. [32] Naturally, there are objections to this arrangement from those who argue that it could neutralise autonomy and also compromise the social position of the party by loading it with cumbersome administrative functions. [33] It can also be argued, however, that if there is a full merger, the party secretary in effect will be elected by the residents, which points to a way of democratisation with Chinese characteristics.

▪ Concluding Remarks

The urban community in China was originally designed as an autonomous entity that would provide the residents with services, which used to be a function of the work unit, also known as the *danwei*. Available evidence suggests, however, that the autonomy of the community has been largely compromised in the actual process of community construction in a number of cities. We have identified the causes from both above and below, as it were. First, urban communities were expected to fulfil another function of maintaining and strengthening the control over the urban populace. Generally, therefore, there is a strong emphasis on the leadership of the party organisation, which tends to neutralise the principle of the exercise of autonomy by the residents. As long as the party attempts to hold on to its dictatorship, there does not seem to be any room left for autonomy at the societal level. However, there is a curious symbiosis between control and autonomy at the basic level of Chinese society. Particularly in the poorer areas where the government cannot invest much in the provision of services, autonomy has been promoted as an economical means for social management. In implementing autonomy in those areas, however, it still has to be the party that constitutes the core entity, around which social forces cluster.

This relates to the second factor of socio-economics. It has proved to be rather difficult to motivate the residents to participate in the work of the community. Unlike the countryside, where the village possesses substantial

---

32 Xu Yong and Chen Weidong, *Zhongguo Chengshi Shequ Zizhi*, p. 275, and pp. 276–277.

33 An argument by Lin Shangli, professor at Fudan University, introduced in Kazuko Kojima and Ryosei Kokubun, "The '*Shequ* Construction' Programme and the Chinese Communist Party", *The Copenhagen Journal of Asian Studies*, No. 16, 2002, pp. 100–101.

assets in the form of land and rural enterprises, land in the cities is owned by the state and controlled by the government, and the community is generally not allowed to run its own businesses for making profit. Where destitute, the community tends to attract little support from the residents, particularly those that can still turn to the *danwei* or to the market for the services that they need. Available evidence suggests that even the party members are generally reluctant to come out for support. Nevertheless, it is still the party members that the community leaders rely on to take the lead in implementing the various activities of the community.

Thus, judging from the actual implementation process, it seems that the leadership role of the party is indispensable for an effective operation of the community. From the standpoint of the party, community construction has thus provided a good opportunity to strengthen its organisation at the basic level and consolidate the basis of its power. The difficulty in playing this role, however, reveals the enormous challenge that the party is facing. The experience of party work in community construction represents another case of its uphill struggle: the party has yet to prove that it can tighten its grip on society in the centrifugal process of marketisation.

The Politics of Lawmaking in Chinese Local People's Congresses

Young Nam Cho [*]

With the advent of a market economy and the implementation of governance according to law policy in China, laws have increasingly grown in importance as both a tool of government to rule the country and a measure for ordinary people to safeguard their rights and interests. As a consequence, legislative politics, which takes place in the National People's Congress (NPC) and local people's congresses, has become a process of serious decision-making. At the same time, China's lawmaking system, as Tanner successfully illustrated, has shifted from a unitary, hierarchical system to "a multi-stage, multiarena" system chiefly composed of the Chinese Communist Party (CCP), the State Council and the NPC. Power in the lawmaking system is distributed among various individuals and organizations too. [1] In fact, as Tanner, Chang and Cao showed, the NPC played a decisive role in two examples of legislation even in the 1980s: the

* Young Nam Cho is an associate professor of the Graduate School of International Studies at Seoul National University. He was a visiting Fellow of the Center for Contemporary Chinese Studies at Peking University (1997—1998), visiting scholar in the Department of Political Science at Nankai University in Tianjin (2001—2002), and visiting scholar of Harvard-Yenching Institute (2006—2007). His research focuses on the Chinese legislative system, rule of law, state-society relations, and elite politics. He has published three books in Korean and has written articles in *China Quarterly, Asian Survey, Issues & Studies, Asian Perspective, Development and Society, and Korean Journal of Defense Analysis.* Dr Cho graduated from the Department of East Asian History at Seoul National University in 1989. He received an M. A. and Ph. D. in political science from Seoul National University in 1996 and 1999, respectively.

This work was supported by Korean Research Foundation Grant (KRF-2004-003).

1 Murray Scot Tanner, *The Politics of Lawmaking in China: Institutions, Processes, and Democratic Prospects*, Oxford: Oxford University Press, 1999, pp. 34, 132, 234 – 235. On other studies on the NPC's lawmaking function and procedures, see Kevin O'Brien, *Reform without footnote continued Liberalization: China's National People's Congress and the Politics of Institutional Change*, New York: Cambridge University Press, 1990, pp. 158 – 164, 130 – 141; Tanner, "Organization and politics in China's post-Mao lawmaking system", in Pitman B. Potter (ed.), *Domestic Law Reforms in Post-Mao China*, Armonk: M. E. Sharpe, 1994, pp. 56 – 93; Ann Seidman, Robert B. Seidman and Janice Payne (eds.), *Legislative Drafting for Market Reform: Some Lessons from China*, London: Macmillan, 1997.

Enterprise Bankruptcy Law in 1986 and the State-owned Industrial Enterprise Law in 1988. [2]

Is there a pattern similar to the development of the NPC in the legislative politics of the provincial people's congresses? Local legislatures across the country have pioneered local laws to satisfy the urgent needs for economic reforms and development in their respective regions, given that the NPC did not enact pertinent laws. [3] And compared to legislative supervision, local legislative bodies can act more firmly and safely in the case of legislation, because they have been gradually recognized as the proper authority of lawmaking in the reform era. [4] Under these circumstances, local people's congresses can attempt to consolidate the lawmaking power given to them by institutionalizing the lawmaking process and broadening their organizational capacities, confronting governments, when necessary, instead of tamely conceding to or co-operating with them.

This article analyses the politics of lawmaking in Chinese provincial people's congresses in order to make visible the changes in the political processes that occurred in the reform era. To this end, it briefly examines the shifting relations between the Party, governments and legislatures, as well as lawmaking institutions themselves since the 1990s. It then investigates the specific roles and activities of major forces, including government agencies, legislative committees and social organizations, by analysing two cases of lawmaking.

When the introduction of a market economy and governance according

---

2 Tanner, *The Politics of Lawmaking*, pp. 135 – 205; Ta-kuang Chang, "The Making of the Chinese Bankruptcy Law: A Study in the Chinese Legislative Process", *Harvard International Law Journal*, Vol. 28, No. 2, 1987, pp. 370 – 371; Cao Siyuan, *Pochan fengyun (A Stormy Situation of Bankruptcy)*, Beijing: Zhongyang bianyi chubanshe, 1996, pp. 1 – 169.

3 Local legislatures have been able to do this chiefly because China has implemented the decentralization policy of legislative powers since the early 1980s. See Sen Lin, "A New Pattern of Decentralization in China: The Increase of Provincial Powers in Economic Legislation", *China Information*, Vol. 7, No. 3, 1992—1993, pp. 27 – 38.

4 Kevin O'Brien, "Chinese People's Congresses and Legislative Embeddedness: Understanding Early Organizational Development", *Comparative Political Studies*, Vol. 27, No. 1, 1994, pp. 80 – 109; An Chen, *Restructuring Political Power in China: Alliance and Opposition, 1978—1998*, Boulder: Lynne Rienner Publishers, 1999, pp. 183 – 227; Young Nam Cho, "From 'Rubber Stamps' to 'Iron Stamps': The Emergence of Chinese People's Congresses as Supervisory Powerhouses", *The China Quarterly*, No. 171, 2002, pp. 724 – 740; Cho, "Symbiotic neighbour or Extra-court Judge? The Supervision over Courts by Chinese Local People's Congresses", *The China Quarterly*, No. 176, 2003, pp. 1068 – 1083.

to law policy compelled the Party to open the political arena of lawmaking, the political process in China, although the country remained a party-state, became more consultative and sophisticated, while political actors became more diversified and competitive. In local legislative politics, the simple time of the Party's leadership and government's domination ended, as government agencies, legislative committees and various social organizations began to take part in open-ended "contestation of persuasion", frequently clashing and co-operating with each other on a case-by-case basis to augment their organizational interests. Provincial people's congresses, after having secured their lawmaking authority since the late 1990s, have played two distinct roles: the co-ordinators of conflicts of interests and the representatives of various social groups' voices. In addition, social organizations have been emerging as new forces in lawmaking, supported by local legislatures in their attempt to improve their stand against government dominance in lawmaking politics.

I selected the Shanghai Municipal People's Congress as a case for this study. Although Shanghai cannot be seen as a representative case of how local people's congresses operate in China, its innovations in strengthening its legislature's lawmaking functions make it a pioneer and possible model for other local legislatures. Shanghai, one of the leading areas of Chinese economic reform and development, has witnessed the strengthening of its legislature's lawmaking function. In particular, its legislature has become a pioneer in the arena of lawmaking by promulgating substantial "creative local laws" in the absence of pertinent laws enacted by the NPC. Some of the local laws in Shanghai became models for legislation later enacted by the NPCs and other local people's congresses. [5]

Relations between the Legislature and the Party: Not a Key Issue in Local Legislative Politics

In principle, Chinese legislatures should report to, and get prior approval

---

5 Xu Zuxiong and Zhu Yanwen (eds.), *Minzhufazhi yu renda zhidu* (*Democratic Legal System and People's Congress Institutions*), Shanghai: Fudan daxue chubanshe, 1999, pp. 236 - 245, 266 - 272; interview with a senior leader of the Shanghai legislature, 13 August, 2003, Shanghai.

from, the Party in all important matters of lawmaking.[6] But in practice, the Party's leadership has radically shifted its course from direct participation in the making of individual laws to an indirect and comprehensive role that oversees the lawmaking processes as a whole.[7] In this sense, legislative— Party relations are no longer a key issue in local lawmaking politics, different from the relations between the NPC and the Party centre.[8] Locally the relations between the legislative and the executive are the crucial issue, as discussed in more detail below.

The Shanghai legislature until around the early 1990s had to report almost all legal bills to the Party in order to get approval before a draft could be deliberated. However, since then the legislature has been able to enact most local laws without the Party's prior review except in a few cases. Instead, the legislature now just compiles and reports annual legislative plans (*jihua* 计划) at the beginning of every year, and five-year plans (*guihua* 规划), on the basis of proposals submitted by government agencies, legislative committees and its members. For example, the legislature reported a five-year legislative plan to the Party for the first time in 1998, and reported the second five-year plan in 2003.[9] A directive from Huang Ju, the Shanghai Party secretary from 1994 to 2002, made this possible.[10]

The Shanghai legislature, of course, still referred some individual cases of lawmaking to the Party for consideration in the 1990s. But they were very few: of 153 local laws enacted from 1990 to 2000 in Shanghai, the author's

---

6　Chen Tiedi, "Chongfen fahui renda dangzude hexin baozhang zuoyong" (To Guarantee the Secured Core Roles of Party Groups in People's Congresses), *Shanghai renda yuekan* (*Monthly People Congresses in Shanghai*), No. 11, 2000, pp. 5 – 7; Huang Ju, "Nuli ba Shanghai de renda gongzuo zuode genghao" (To Make Efforts so that People's Congresses in Shanghai Well Play Their Roles), *Shanghai renda yuekan*, No. 6, June 1998, pp. 3-6.

7　On the changing relationship between the Party and the NPC and, in particular, on the detailed contents and significance of the Central Document No. 8, see Tanner, *The Politics of Lawmaking in China*, pp. 48 – 49, 51 – 71; Peng Chong, *Minzhu fazhi lunji* (*Collections on Democracy and Rule of Law*), Beijing: Zhongguo minzhu fazhi chubanshe, 1993, pp. 173 – 175; Cai Dingjian, *Zhongguo renda zhidu* (*People's Congress System in China*), Beijing: Shehui kexue wenxian cubanshe, 1993, pp. 253 – 254.

8　On the more detailed description of the relations between the Party and legislatures, see Cho, "From 'Rubber Stamps' to 'Iron Stamps'", pp. 726 – 731.

9　Shanghai renda changweihui yanjiushi (ed.), *Shijian yu tansuo* (*Practice and Exploration*), Vol. 4, Shanghai: Fudan daxue chubanshe, 2003, pp. 130 – 131; Xiao Dong, "Zhonggong Shanghai shiwei pizhun benshi wunian lifa guihua (The Shanghai Party Committee Approved the Five-year Legislative Plan of This Period), *Shanghai renda yuekan*, No. 5, 1999, pp. 5-6.

10　Interview with a senior leader of the Shanghai legislature, 13 August, 2003, Shanghai.

documentation and interview data indicate that the legislature reported only five to the Party. And since 2000, a senior legislative leader attested, the legislature has not reported a single draft law to the Party. [11] In addition, the Party interfered in the aforementioned five cases mainly at the legislature's request.

The five cases of lawmaking that the Shanghai legislature reported to the Party can be divided into three categories. The first was important laws, such as the Trade Unions Regulation introduced in 1995. [12] The second was sensitive laws, such as the Religious Affairs Regulation in 1995. This was considered to be very sensitive because the prestigious leaders of Catholic and Protestant churches in the country were concentrated in Shanghai, and Shanghai had more than one million people affiliated with religions. Besides, government agencies and religious organizations, when the law was discussed, had very different notions as to its purpose: the former stressed control and the latter emphasized protection. [13] The Conscription Work Regulation in 1994 and the Civil Defence Regulation in 1999 were considered sensitive cases as they were directly related to the military. The Party was therefore asked to get involved. [14] The third category was difficult laws, that is, those where the legislature failed to resolve severe differences of opinion and asked the Party to make a final decision. The Firework Security Regulation in 1994 belongs to this category. When the legislature enacted the local law which strictly prohibited setting off fireworks in the city during holidays, it encountered substantial objections from citizens. The legislature sent the draft law to the Party and asked that it decide whether the legislature was to be promulgated. [15]

There are two possible causes for the Party being less involved today in the making of new laws. Most important is the Party's limited capability. The number of laws produced by the Shanghai legislature has dramatically increased since the 1990s. As Table 1 notes, the legislature promulgated 153 local laws between 1990 and 2000, compared to only 50 in the decade

---

11 Ibid.
12 "Difang lifa bufa jiakuaide wunian" (Five Years of Speedy Footsteps in Local Lawmaking), *Shanghai renda yuekan*, No. 9, 1997, pp. 6 – 8.
13 Xu and Zhu, *Democratic Legal System*, pp. 266 – 272.
14 Chen, "To Guarantee the Secured Core Roles of Party Groups", p. 6.
15 Interview with a senior leader of the Shanghai legislature, 13 August, 2003, Shanghai.

from 1980 to 1989. As a result, it is actually beyond the Party's capability to review all individual legal bills. In addition, the majority of local laws which are related to economic policies do not need the Party's involvement in terms of political sensitivity. For instance, 59 (43%) of the 136 local laws the Shanghai legislature enacted from 1980 to 1998 belong to this category. A roughly similar relation can be found for provincial people's congresses in other regions: more than 50% of local laws are concerned with economic reforms. [16] Resolving technical problems and co-ordinating different opinions among government agencies and social groups is a key task in enacting such local laws, and this requires a thorough investigation and coordination by lawmaking bodies, not the political decisions of the Party.

Relations between the Legislative and the Executive, and the Institutionalization of the Lawmaking Process against "Departmentalism"

In the Chinese system of lawmaking, "departmentalism" (*bumenzhuyi* 部门主义) is considered to be the most crucial and tricky issue in the whole reform era, and the Tenth NPC period (2003—2007) is no exception. [17] It refers to the phenomenon that governments in general and their agencies in particular make efforts, by way of lawmaking, to expand organizational interests and evade corresponding responsibilities. [18] They can do this because

---

16 About 60% of local laws that Heilongjiang, Hebei and Gansu legislatures promulgated in the past two decades are related with economic reform and development. See Li Linke, "Jiaqiang lifa gongzuo, baozhang jingji fazhan" (To Strengthen Lawmaking Work and Guarantee Economic Development), *Difang renda jianshe (Construction of Local People's Congresses)*, No. 2, February 1999, pp. 7 – 8; Ma Bin, "Difang lifa jige lilun wenti yu Gansu 20nian difang lifa shijian" (Several Theoretical Problems in Local Lawmaking and 20 Year's Practice of Local Lawmaking in Gansu), *Rendayanjiu (Study of People's Congresses)*, No. 6, 1999, available at www. rdyj. com. cn/rdqk-6-t. thml.

17 Wu Bangguo, "Tigao lifa zhiliang shi benjie lifa gongzuode zhongdian" (To Enhance Lawmaking Quality is the Focal Point of Legislation Work in This Period of the NPC), *Zhongguo renda (China's People's Congresses)*, No. 21, 2003, pp. 2-6.

18 Tanner, *The Politics of Lawmaking*, pp. 120 – 21. Chinese articles criticizing the problems of "departmentalism" are too numerous to cite. See Ji Liangru, "Lüelun difang lifa zhongde bumen zhuyi" (A Brief Discussion on Departmentalism in Local Lawmaking), *Renda gongzuo tongxun (Bulletin of People's Congresses)*, No. 14, 1995, pp. 21 – 24; Liu Yunlong, "Difang lifazhong bumen liyi qingxiangde biaoxian, weihai, chengyin ji duice" (Appearances, Harms, Causes and Countermeasures of the Tendency of Departmental Selfishness in Local Lawmaking), *Renda gongzuo tongxun*, No. 10, 1996, pp. 13 – 15, 35.

Table 1 *Number of Local Laws and Administrative Regulations in Shanghai, 1980—2000*

Years	Total number	Local laws		Administrative regulations	
		Number	%	Number	%
1980—1989	451	50	11.08	401	88.92
1990—1996	408	84	20.58	324	79.42
1996—2000	183	69	37.71	114	62.29
Total	1,042	203	19.48	839	80.52

Notes: Local laws are enacted by the Shanghai People's Congress, and administrative regulations by the Shanghai government.

Source: Ying Songnian and Yuan Shuhong (eds.), *Zouxiang yifa zhengfu (Towards Governments Based on Laws)*, Beijing: Falü chubanshe, 2001, p. 506.

governments, as compared to legislatures, dominate the lawmaking processes, especially as far as preparing legislative plans and drafting laws is concerned. This originates in their decisively more advantageous position in terms of capacity (information, organizational and personnel supports) . Therefore, the most challenging task facing Chinese legislatures has been to cope with "departmentalism", and several measures have been proposed and adopted to overcome this problem. [19] These are discussed in some detail below.

The Shanghai government, not the legislature, overwhelmingly led the lawmaking processes in the 1980s. The legislature, in a strict sense, did not enact but just passed local laws which were prepared, considered and proclaimed by the government until the mid-1980s. [20] The government also proposed and drafted most local laws after the 1990s. For instance, the total number of local laws that were compiled in annual lawmaking plans by the Shanghai legislature from 2000 to 2002 was 41: of these, the government

19　Wu Hong, "Kefu difang lifa zhong bumen liyi qingxiangde jidian sikao" (Several Considerations to Overcome Departmental Selfishness in Local Lawmaking), *Minzu fazhi jianshe (Construction of Democracy and Rule by Law)*, No. 2, 2001, pp. 37 – 38; Liu Mianyi, "Cong chengxude jiaodu tan kefu lifa zhongde bumen liyi" (A Discussion to Overcome Departmental Selfishness in Procedure's Perspective), *Zhongguo renda*, No. 16, 2003, pp. 6, 12 – 13.

20　Xu Xianghua (ed.), *Xin shiqi Zhongguo lifa fansi (A Reflection on Chinese Lawmaking in the New Era)*, Shanghai: Xuelin chubanshe, 2004, p. 276. On detailed lawmaking cases in that period, see Cai Bingwen (ed.), *Shanghai renmin daibiao dahui zhi (Annals of Shanghai People's Congress)*, Shanghai: Shanghai shehui kexueyuan chubanshe, 1998, pp. 259 – 269.

proposed 35 (85. 4%). [21] And of 40 local laws enacted in Shanghai from 1998 to 2002, the government drafted 34 (85%). [22] This shows that the legislative-executive relations in Shanghai also fit in with the "90% rule", which applies to most legislative bodies in the world: cabinet proposes at least 90% of legislative agenda, and at least 90% of what it proposes is adopted. [23]

The Shanghai legislature, like legislative bodies in other countries, cannot and will not be able to dominate the lawmaking process in the contemporary administrative state, as the "90% rule" suggests. In particular, legislatures' roles are limited to economic policymaking. [24] So when the roles of legislatures in the lawmaking process are evaluated, the focus should be on the degree to which the legislature, by rejecting or amending drafts proposed by the government, is able to constrain the executive branch and prevent it from making policy unilaterally. [25] The Shanghai People's Congress has certainly moved in this direction since the late 1990s.

Most of all, the legal-political conditions for the Shanghai legislature have improved. That is, local laws have gained more weight relative to administrative regulations (xingzheng guizhang 行政规章) promulgated by government, since governance according to law policy has been more firmly rooted in the 1990s. As Table 1 shows, the percentage of local laws among all regulations has increased from 11. 08% during 1980 to 1989 to 37. 71% during 1996 to 2000. This suggests that administrative lawmaking power has given way to some augmentation of the lawmaking authority of legislatures. This tendency has been intensified with China's entry into the World Trade Organization (WTO) in 2001 and the implementation of the

21　Fazhi gongzuo weiyuanhui, "Shanghaishi renda changweihui niandu shenyi fagui caoan jihua (2000, 2001, 2002)" (Annual legislative Plans of the Shanghai People's Congress Standing Committee in 2000, 2001 and 2002), available at www. spcsc. sh. cn.

22　Gu Ping, "Guanyu gaijin fagui qicao gongzuode sikao" (A Consideration on the Reform of Drafting Work of Local Laws), Shanghai renda yuekan, No. 1, 2003, available at www. spcsc. sh. cn.

23　David M. Olson, Democratic Legislative Institutions: A Comparative View, Armonk: M. E. Sharpe, 1994, p. 84.

24　David M. Olson and Michael L. Mezey, "Parliaments and Public Policy", in Olson and Mezey (eds.), Legislatures in the Policy Process, Cambridge: Cambridge University Press, 1991, pp. 4 - 5.

25　Michael L. Mezey, Comparative Legislatures, Durham: Duke University Press, 1979, pp. 25 - 26.

Administrative Licensing Law in 2004. [26]

In addition, the organizational capability of the Shanghai legislature has been strengthened. For example, of the 65 members of the Standing Committee of Shanghai People's Congress, about half are full-time members (*zhuanzhi weiyuan* 专职委员), an increase of about 10% compared with the previous period (1998—2002). The increase in the ratio of full-time members is significant, because they are most responsible for the investigation and deliberation of drafted laws. [27] For reference, all six members of the Legislative Affairs Work Committee and six out of nine in the Legislative Committee are full-timers. The number of legislative staff has also increased. Now, 160 staffers directly or indirectly perform lawmaking-related work: 30 of them specialize in lawmaking affairs, with most being law graduates. [28]

Finally, the legislatures, in an effort to cope with "departmentalism", have also introduced several new institutions and thus increased their lawmaking authority. These include the changing of lawmaking guidelines from "experience-based legislation" (*jingyan lifa* 经验立法) to "legislation in advance" (*chaoqian lifa* 超前立法), the strengthening of legislature's initiative in lawmaking plans, more diversified drafters, the introduction of "opening-up legislation" (*kaimen lifa* 开门立法), and stricter deliberation of legislative drafts. [29] The NPC, based on its own experience, has made efforts to dissipate nationwide improved lawmaking systems, and local people's congresses have been willing to accept the NPC's suggestions. The Legislation Law in 2000 can be considered the sum of previous experiences, and its enactment became a watershed in the institutionalization of Chinese

26 Dali L. Yang, *Remaking the Chinese Leviathan: Market Transition and the Politics of Governance in China*, Stanford: Stanford University Press, 2004, pp. 161 – 164; Yuan Xudon, "Xingzheng xukefa dui difang lifa yingxiangde jidian sikao"(Several Considerations on the Effect of the Administrative Licensing Law on Local Lawmaking"), *Zhongguo renda*, No. 22, 2003, pp. 11 – 13.

27 Cai Dingjian and Wang Chenguang (eds.), *Renmin daibiao dahui ershinian fazhan yu gaige (20 Years' Development and Reform of People's Congresses)*, Beijing: Zhongguo jiancha chubanshe, 2001, p. 95.

28 Interview with a senior leader of the Shanghai legislature, 17 February, 2004, Shanghai.

29 On the lawmaking processes, see Tanner, *The Politics of Lawmaking*, pp. 209 – 230; Cai Dingjian, *Zhongguo renmin daibiao zhidu (People's Congress System in China)*, revised ed., Beijing: Falü chubanshe, 1998, pp. 301 – 319. On Shanghai's case, see Shanghai renda, *Practice and Exploration*, pp. 128 – 147; Xu, *A Reflection on Chinese Lawmaking*, pp. 245 – 311.

lawmaking systems. Among the few important innovations, the following two are the most important.

Much stricter deliberation of drafted laws. The most effective measure to cope with "departmentalism" is to conduct more thorough deliberation of drafted laws in accordance with regulations specified by legislatures themselves. This is because legislatures exercise their authority during the deliberation stage of lawmaking, while governments have better means for agenda-setting and drafting laws.

Two new systems in this regard are worth mentioning. The first is the introduction of the two-step-deliberation and three-reading (*liangshen sandu* 两审三读) system. [30] Until the early 1990s, most local legislatures passed drafted laws after just a first deliberation. Consequently, laws proposed and drafted by governments were passed without substantive changes, and legislative deliberation tended to be considered a necessary formality. Since the Shanghai legislature introduced the system in 1998, all drafts of laws have to be deliberated at least twice and read three times in plenary sessions or standing committee meetings, except for trivial amendments to a few words and phrases. Because the legislature convenes regular meetings of its standing committee once every two months, it can deliberate drafts for at least four months. [31]

The second is the introduction of a unified investigation and deliberation system. In common with most legislative bodies in liberal democracies, the Shanghai legislature's special committees (*zhuanweihui* 专委会) used to take chief responsibility for deliberating legislative drafts. On the one hand, this system has the merit that relevant committees can exercise their special capabilities in the deliberation processes. On the other, it entails several

---

30 The NPC officially introduced a two-step deliberation system in 1987 and has practised a three-step system since 1998 with the purpose of enhancing the "quality" of legislation. During the same period, several provincial people's congresses also introduced a three-step system, including Tianjin and Anhui. Of course, the stricter deliberation system cannot automatically guarantee Chinese legislatures' lawmaking authority. In fact, the NPC and local people's congresses still complain about the non-co-operative attitude and sometimes obstruction of governments during deliberation of draft laws. See Cai and Wang, *20 Years' Development and Reform of People's Congresses,* pp. 427 - 440.

31 Shanghai renda, *Practice and Exploration,* pp. 128 - 147; Wan Zongyan, "Guanyu difang lifa shenyi zhidude ruogan wenti" (On Several Problems of Deliberation System in Local Lawmaking), *Shanghai renda yuekan,* No. 10, 2002, available at www. spcsc. sh. cn; interview with a senior leader of the Shanghai legislature, 17 February, 2004, Shanghai.

problems. For example, legislatures will hardly be able to address "departmentalism" because of the close relationship between special committees responsible for deliberation and government agencies drafting laws. In addition, special committees tend to pay more attention to the contents of drafted laws than to legal formality, so that local laws deliberated by special committees sometimes conflict with "parent laws" and other local laws.

To redress these problems, the Shanghai People's Congress established the Legislative Affairs Work Committee (*fagongwei* 法工委) in 1998 which conducted a unified deliberation of all drafted laws. According to the provisions of the Legislation Law, the Legislative Committee (*fazhiwei* 法制委) was established in 2001 for the same purpose, and the legislature changed the Work Committee into a staff office of the Legislative Committee. A division of labour between the Legislative Committee and other special committees was then put in effect. Special committees conduct the preliminary deliberation of drafted laws, and present deliberating reports in written form for the first deliberation meeting. Also, special committee members, as non-voting observers, can participate in the unified deliberation of the Legislative Committee. The Legislative Committee then takes over unified deliberation after the first deliberation and reports the deliberating opinions and the proposals for revising the original draft laws in written form to the legislature when the second deliberation resumes.[32] The legislature generally respects the Committee's suggestions. In this way, the Legislative Committee, as a kind of "prestigious committee" in the lawmaking organ, exercises leadership in the process of deliberating legislative drafts, and can help redress parts of problems of "departmentalism. "[33]

"*Opening-up legislation.* " Another innovation employed to cope with "departmentalism" is "opening-up legislation" or "democratic legislation" (*minzhu lifa* 民主立法). This refers to measures that the legislature, in an effort to make up for its weaker capability relative to government, encourages social organizations and the public to actively participate in

---

32 Shanghai renda, *Practice and Exploration*, pp. 50 – 67; Wan, "On Several Problems of Deliberation System"; Interview with a senior leader of the Shanghai legislature, 13 August, 2003, Shanghai.

33 Xu, *A Reflection on Chinese Lawmaking*, pp. 100, 292 – 293, 299.

drafting and deliberating legal bills. [34] Two institutions are important: legislative hearings and soliciting public opinions by publicizing drafts.

China's first legislation hearing was convened in Guangdong in 1999, when the legislature enacted a regulation of construction project bidding. [35] The Legislation Law confirmed this procedure in 2000, and now most provincial legislatures employ legislative hearings when they promulgate important local laws. The NPC also convened legislative hearings when it revised the Marriage Law in 2001. The Shanghai legislature is no exception. It has held four legislative hearings since it introduced them in 2001. [36] By employing legislative hearings, the legislature can redress parts of "departmentalism" in the name of public opinion: that is, legislative hearings provide the legislature with a base to fend off government agencies' requests. [37]

The system of soliciting public opinion has been widely employed across the country since the late 1990s. Recently, Chinese legislatures have often put drafts for laws that would seriously influence ordinary people's lives in local newspapers, and gathered public comments and suggestions. For example, the Shanghai legislature has solicited public suggestions on ten draft laws since 1998. [38] In addition, the legislature sends almost all draft laws to lower-level people's congresses and social organizations, and seeks their comments and suggestions. The legislature, it is argued, has recently paid much attention to public suggestions when deliberating, and in this sense, public opinion has become significant in the lawmaking process since the late 1990s. [39]

---

34 Ibid. , pp. 156 – 157.

35 Ling Su, "Zhe shijishang ye shi benjie renda changweihui gongzuode jiben jingyan" (This is also Substantively Fundamental Experiences of This Period's People's Congress), *Renmin zhi sheng (People's Voice)*, No. 1, 2003, pp. 4 – 9.

36 Shanghai renda, *Practice and Exploration*, p. 62; Gan Guanghua, "Shanghai: xiaoyuan shanghai shigu chuli youfa keyi" (Shanghai: Provided Local Laws to Deal with Injury Accidents at Schools), *Zhongguo renda*, No. 19, 2001, pp. 9 – 11.

37 On the significance of introducing legislative hearings, see Laura Paler, "China's Legislation Law and the making of a more orderly and representative legislative system", *The China Quarterly*, No. 182, 2005, pp. 301 – 318.

38 Wen Qing, "Shanghai: difang lifa 24nian zhuduo chuangxin" (Shanghai: Various Innovations of Local Lawmaking for 24 years), *Renminwang*, 27 August, 2004, available at www. people. com. cn.

39 Interview with a senior leader of the Shanghai legislature, 17 February, 2004, Shanghai.

▪ Two Case Studies of Lawmaking

In the following two cases, social organizations as well as legislature committees and government agencies clashed and co-operated with each other in lawmaking based on their interests. And the Shanghai legislature played crucial roles in co-ordinating conflicting interests and representing various groups' voices. Finally, the Party was not involved in the lawmaking process, and the roles of government agencies were more limited than anticipated.

The legislation of the Labour Contract Regulation. When the Shanghai People's Congress enacted the Labour Contract Regulation in 2001, there were severe conflicts among government agencies, legislative committees and social organizations. This was because the local law was closely related with the interests of social groups: both labour and business could be seriously affected depending upon how the law was enacted. Therefore, trade unions and business organizations, such as the Federation of Industry and Commerce (*gongshanglian* 工商联) and trade associations (*hangye xiehui* 行业协会), made the utmost effort to steer the lawmaking process towards their interests. [40] In addition, both executive agencies [the Labour Bureau and the Economy Committee) and legislative committees (the Financial and Economic Affairs Committee (*caijingwei* 财经委) and the Legislative Committee] were deeply involved in the lawmaking process as promoters of certain social groups' interests and co-ordinators of conflicting interests.

A drafting group was composed of three executive agencies (the Labour Bureau, the Economy Committee and the Legislative Affairs Office), two legislative committees (the Legislative Affairs Work Committee and the Financial and Economic Affairs Committee) and the Shanghai General Trade Union (SGTU). In the actual drafting process, according to a leader of the SGTU, the Labour Bureau and the Union played core roles, and

---

40 Trade unions have been able to participate in legislation since the late 1980s with the permission of the Party. Anita Chan, "Revolution or corporatism? Workers and trade unions in post-Mao China", in David S. G. Goodman and Beverley Hooper (eds.), *China's Quiet Revolution: New Interactions between State and Society*, New York: St. Martin's Press, 1994, pp. 177 - 178; Gordon White, Jude Howell and Shang Xiaoyuan, *In Search of Civil Society: Market Reform and Social Change in Contemporary China*, Oxford: Clarendon Press, 1996, pp. 53 - 55.

other participating members just read and suggested several comments on the draft. In the drafting stage, the SGTU tried to secure labourers' interests, while the Labour Bureau as a representative of government attempted to take care of the opinions of both labour and business. During this process, against conventional wisdom that suggested the Bureau and the SGTU would form an alliance against a coalition composed of business-related executive agencies and social organizations, the Bureau and the Union severely clashed because the former, a Union leader insisted, took sides with business on key issues. As a result, the draft generally met the demands of business.[41]

There were three primary issues in the lawmaking process. The first was the aim of the legislation. The first article of the Labour Law enacted in 1994, a "mother law" of the Labour Contract Regulation, stipulates that: "This law was enacted to safeguard the lawful rights and interests of labourers, co-ordinate labour relations, and establish and maintain a labour contract system appropriate to the socialist market economy." On this basis, the SGTU argued that the regulation also ought to "safeguard the lawful rights and interests of labourers" as its primary goal. In contrast, business organizations and economic-related government agencies argued that the primary goal should be "to safeguard the lawful rights and interests of both parties of labour contract". It is reasonable, they argued, that the regulation was to protect the interests of both business enterprises and labourers, because enterprises were a main contacting party in labour contracts.

The second issue was whether the regulation should or should not maintain the "10 + 3 provision", and this was critical for the business circle. The former Shanghai Labour Provision introduced in 1994 had an article that an enterprise could not cancel labour contracts or lay off workers who were within three years of retirement after having worked for the company for more than ten years. The SGTU insisted on maintaining the provision to protect elderly labourers' rights and interests, while the business coalition criticized it as a legacy of the planned economy, lagging far behind

---

41 Shanghai renda changweihui fagongwei (ed.), "*Shanghaishi laodong hetong tiaoli*" *shiyi (An Interpretation of the Shanghai Labour Contract Regulation)*, Shanghai: Shanghai renmin chubanshe, 2002, pp. 104 – 109; interviews with senior leaders of the SGTU and the Federation of Industry and Commerce, 17 and 18 February, 2004, Shanghai.

the times.

The most important issue was about granting trade unions the right to interfere with labour contracts, which was critical for the trade unions' status and roles in enterprises. Labourers, the Union argued, were such weak parties compared to enterprises in labour contracts that trade unions should have the right to be involved in labour agreements. Therefore, the provision that "an enterprise should listen to the opinions of the trade union when it would unilaterally cancel labour contracts, and the cancellation of contracts would be invalid and void without prior consultation with the trade union" should be inserted into the regulation. Business organizations did not agree with this argument on the ground that trade unions were not a contracting party. [42]

In regard to these three issues, the legislative committees presented different opinion reports when they deliberated the draft. The Financial and Economic Affairs Committee firmly sided with the SGTU: in the report of deliberating opinions, the Committee defended the Union's three arguments. [43] The Legislative Committee had different ideas. First, it did not accept the SGTU's argument in relation to the law's mission. As a result, the first article of the regulation states that: "This regulation was enacted to co-ordinate labour relations, and establish and maintain a labour contract system appropriate to the socialist market economy. " Secondly, the Committee also rejected the "10 + 3 provision". This provision, the Committee argued, was a kind of discrimination unfavourable to Chinese enterprises after China's accession to the WTO; the elderly labourers themselves would be victims, because companies would avoid making contracts with them because of this condition. However, the Committee accepted the demand that trade unions should have the right to interfere with labour contracts.

Why did the two legislative committees suggest different deliberating opinions? The most important factor is that special committees have cosy

---

42　Interviews with senior leaders of the SGTU and the Federation of Industry and Commerce, 17 and 18 February, 2004, Shanghai; Shanghai renda, *An Interpretation of the Shanghai Labour Contract Regulation*, pp. 104 – 109; Zheng Guangjun, "Xinxi renmin tancheng zhiyan: Shirenda changweihui shenyi laodong hetong tiaoli caoan" (Minded People Candidly Spoke without Reservation: The Municipal People's Congress Deliberated the Draft Law of the Labour Contract Regulation"), *Shanghai renda yuekan*, No. 10, 2003, available at www. spcsc. sh. cn.

43　Shanghai renda, *An Interpretation of the Shanghai Labour Contract Regulation*, pp. 111 – 115.

and close relations with certain executive agencies and social organizations outside governments. [44] Certain legislative committees, executive agencies and social organizations, belonging to "a similar *xitong* (系统)", have maintained ongoing working relations, and personnel interchanges between them have occurred quite often. For example, the members of the Financial and Economic Affairs Committee are mostly recruited from among those in leading positions of relevant government agencies and social organizations including trade unions. The situations of other committees are similar. For this reason, legislative committees tend to represent the voices of certain executive agencies and social organizations when they deliberate drafted laws.

By contrast, the Legislative Committee does not keep up such a cosy relationship with executive agencies and social organizations. Significantly, the Committee as an organ responsible for the unified deliberation of drafted laws has few reasons and motives to maintain ongoing working relations with them. Neither are certain constituents overrepresented among the members of the Legislative Committee. This is the main reason that the Committee can deliberate legal bills on the basis of legal rationality, and can co-ordinate conflicts of interest among major forces. In particular, it tends to restrict other special committees when it thinks that they are inordinately favouring a certain government agency or social group. [45]

Meanwhile, some senior leaders of the SGTU thought that the Labour Contract Regulation reflected their opinions relatively faithfully. Concerning the mission of the local law, the regulation did not correspond to the Union's preference, but it did not meet the business alliance's demands either. Originally, the SGTU had thought that the regulation did not need to include the legislation's mission, because the Labour Law had already stated it in its first article. But in the lawmaking process, the business

---

44　Tanner argued that the special committee members' behaviour seemed to be far closer to the professional legislator model than the iron triangles model. Tanner, *The Politics of Lawmaking*, p. 108. In fact, there is not a consistent model which explains every case of lawmaking in Chinese legislatures. However, the author's interview data and literature materials about the provincial people's congresses in Tianjin, Shanghai and Guangdong indicate that iron triangles model rather than professional legislator can apply to the behaviours of the special committees' members.

45　Xu, *A Reflection on Chinese Lawmaking*, pp. 292 – 293; interview with a senior leader of the Shanghai legislature, 13 August, 2003, Shanghai.

coalition made an attempt to change the main aim of the local law and the SGTU took a firm position against this. In order to block further attempts by the business coalition, the Union submitted a new proposal that the regulation should not include either argument, and finally the regulation made no mention of it at all. [46]

The SGTU was not at all dissatisfied with the outcome in the conflict about the "10 +3 provision" either. From the outset, the SGTU had not intended to argue too strongly for this provision, because the leaders already knew that it was unreasonable and inappropriate in a market economy. Free labour contract systems were widespread in Shanghai, and this special article could not play a crucial role in protecting the rights and interests of most labourers. Some workers even thought that it was not bad for them to retire early and to find new jobs if they could get enough compensation. Therefore the SGTU sought to use the "10 +3 provision" as a bargaining chip, so it could agree to its cancellation. Instead, the SGTU strongly insisted on the insertion of an article that gave trade unions the right to interfere with labour contracts, and in the end the Union was successful. [47]

In short, the final version of the regulation was a result of compromises between confronting forces, in which the legislature played a vital roles in co-ordinating conflicts of interests. The SGTU obtained a substantive achievement by making the Regulation allow trade unions to interfere in labour contracts as lawful agents, while business enterprises were able to repeal the "10 +3 provision".

The amendments of the Consumers' Rights Protection Regulation. The revision of the Consumers' Rights Protection Regulation in 2002 brought about as much conflict as the Labour Contract Regulation. The law could have an enormous effect not only on the interests of ordinary citizens and business enterprises but also on those of some executive agencies and social organizations. Preparation for the draft revision started in late 2000. The government's Industrial and Commercial Administration Bureau and the legislature's Legislative Affairs Work Committee took the official role of drafting. But in the actual process, the Shanghai Consumer Association

46 Interview with a senior leader of the SGTU, 18 February, 2004, Shanghai.
47 Ibid.

(SCA) led the drafting, and the Legislative Affairs Work Committee supported it by reviewing the draft. [48]

Three issues were highlighted at the drafting stage, two of which were critical for the SCA to enlarge its organizational interests. The first issue was the limits of the SCA's mediation. The SCA and the Industrial and Commercial Administration Bureau argued that three items about which consumers had raised serious complaints should be included in the remit of its mediation: "profit-making" education (yinglixing peixun 营利性培训), medical services, and "commercial" houses (shangpinfang 商品房). In contrast, the Education Committee and the government's Public Health Bureau, and the social organizations of educational and medical areas insisted that education and medical services were "public goods" rather than general consumer goods, and thus they should not be subject to mediation. In particular, because a specified regulation dealing with medical disputes had already been enacted, it was not necessary for the regulation to duplicate it.

The second issue was about the introduction of the "three systems" to strengthen the SCA's authority. In order to safeguard consumers' rights and interests, the Association and the Bureau argued, its supervisory authority over the production and sale of business enterprises should be strengthened; as such a measure, the revised regulation should introduce the "three systems": the publication of consumer information and consumer complaints, and annual supervisory deliberation. But business organizations and economic agencies opposed the introduction of any measures to intensify the Association's power without provisions to check and punish its potential malfunctions.

The third issue was the introduction of a recall system. Such a system was indispensable, the Association and the Bureau strongly argued, to redress consumer complaints about products such as electric home appliances and cars. Indeed, consumers in some countries were able to get compensation for defective goods under pertinent laws, while Chinese consumers could not because such laws did not exist. Business organizations

---

48 Shanghaishi renda changweihui fagongwei (ed.), "Shanghaishi xiaofeizhe quanyi baohu tiaoli" shiyi (An Interpretation of the Shanghai Consumers' Rights Protection Regulation), Shanghai: Shanghai renmin chubanshe, 2003, pp. 153 – 154, 171 – 175.

and related government agencies disagreed with this argument: even the "mother law" did not mention recall, and other regions throughout the country had not yet introduced it. [49]

When the Shanghai legislature started deliberating the draft revision, the SCA, in a very systematic and active fashion, launched a series of lobbying activities in an attempt to rally public support and to persuade the legislature members. The Association conducted opinion polls by telephone several times and made public the results which supported its position concerning the three issues. It also held various forums in which representatives of consumers and enterprises, professionals such as lawyers and scholars, government officials and members of the legislative committees were invited to discuss the draft. In a forum, the secretary-general of the Hong Kong Consumers' Association, who was invited by the Association, explained its activities in detail, and emphasized the necessity of strengthening the authority and function of the SCA in front of the legislature committee members. [50] This active lobbying by the SCA gave rise to serious concerns among some legislative leaders as to how to deal with the increasing pressure of interest groups in the lawmaking process. [51]

Notwithstanding the intense lobbying by the SCA, the Education Committee, the Public Health Bureau and relevant social organizations strongly opposed its argument once again at the deliberation stage. Facing strong objections, the Industrial and Commercial Administration Bureau and the Association had to withdraw some of their original demands. Most of all, education and medical services were finally excluded from mediation; only "commercial" houses remained in the draft. The main reason why education and medical services were excluded while houses remained was that the lobbying power of the education and "medical-related coalition was far stronger than that of the construction" and sales-related coalition. [52] The introduction of the "three systems" had been deleted too. But the Bureau and the Association maintained their firm stance towards the introduction of a recall system with strong support from the public. [53]

---

49 Ibid. , pp. 155 – 161; interview with senior leaders of the SCA, 18 February, 2004, Shanghai.
50 Interview with a senior leader of the Shanghai legislature, 13 August, 2003, Shanghai; interview with senior leaders of the SCA, 18 February, 2004, Shanghai.
51 Shanghai renda, *Practice and Exploration*, p. 63.
52 Interview with senior leaders of the SCA, 18 February, 2004, Shanghai.
53 Ibid.

The legislative committees also confronted each other when they deliberated the draft revision. The Financial and Economic Affairs Committee responsible for preliminary deliberation supported the arguments of the SCA as anticipated. [54] In contrast, the Education, Science, Culture and Health Committee (*jiaokewenweiwei* 教科文卫委), which has a cosy relationship with education-and medical-related executive agencies and social organizations, opposed it. Meanwhile, the Legislative Committee adopted a position close to the education and medical coalition: it excluded education and medical services from mediation and rejected the "three systems". The Committee, however, agreed to the introduction of a recall system and included "commercial" houses within the mediation items. [55]

In sum, the lawmaking processes of the Labour Contract and the Consumers' Rights Regulations indicated a common characteristic of lawmaking politics in Chinese local legislatures. Executive agencies, legislative committees and social organizations formed alliances and confronted each other at every stage of the lawmaking process, and the legislature played a co-ordinating role. The final versions of the two regulations reflect these conflicts and compromises.

▪ Conclusion

The relations between the legislative and the executive in lawmaking processes, from a comprehensive perspective, are co-operative and harmonious relative to those in legislative supervision, while social organizations' active participation in lawmaking tends to be limited to a few cases which are directly concerned with their critical interests. Significantly, the majority of enacted local laws deal with economic policies which need specified technical knowledge. And these cases do not contain so many sensitive issues that can induce interest conflicts between government agencies and legislative committees. In fact, legislature and government, under the leadership of the territorial Party in a province, have made concerted efforts to promulgate economic-related local laws in order to speed up regional economic development. In this sense, we cannot

---

54 Shanghaishi renda, *An Interpretation of the Shanghai Consumers' Rights Protection Regulation*, pp. 162 – 165.

55 Ibid. , pp. 166 – 175.

overestimate the distinguished roles of legislatures and social organizations in lawmaking politics.

Meanwhile, there is a different aspect of lawmaking politics when local people's congresses enact local laws containing conflicts of interests between lawmaking forces. In these cases, local legislatures, not governments, take the initiative and exercise pivotal roles as co-ordinators of confronting interests and representatives of various forces' voices. At the same time, relevant social organizations and even ordinary people actively participate in lawmaking processes. As a consequence, legislative politics changes into a more consultative and sophisticated decision-making process. The case studies illustrated this point.

Finally, the evaluation of the legislative development in China is in order. Most of all, a balanced view on the strengthening roles of the legislature is needed. Chinese legislatures, like representative bodies in other countries, fulfil four functions: legislation, supervision, representation and regime maintenance. To put it simply, the roles of Chinese legislatures have been unevenly strengthened: their lawmaking power has already been recognized as their own proper authority, and Chinese legislatures can exercise it in a stable fashion; and local legislatures, not yet the NPC, have started to exert a substantive power in overseeing state organs while their roles are still very limited in representation. Therefore, we should not think of the strengthened lawmaking role of Chinese legislatures as the emergence of representative politics. In particular, caution in this regard is necessary given that the main functions of legislatures in liberal democracies have shifted from legislation to supervision and representation since the 1970s. Chinese legislatures, however, can be considered to have successfully strengthened their roles through institutionalization prior to liberalization. [56] Established powers' recognition of the lawmaking authority of legislatures, the intensification of legislatures' initiative in lawmaking processes, and the distinguished co-ordinating and representative roles of legislatures prove this path of Chinese legislative development.

---

56 See O'Brien, *Reform without Liberalization*, pp. 3 – 8; Murray Scot Tanner, "The National People's Congress", in Merle Goldman and Roderick Macfarquhar (eds.), *The Paradox of China's Post-Mao Reforms*, Cambridge, MA: Harvard University Press, 1999, pp. 101 – 104, 125 – 128.

Singularity and Replicability in China's Developmental Experience

Barry Naughton *

What lessons does China's experience offer? It is perilous to try to extract simple lessons from such a complex experience. The Chinese environment is singular: size, factor endowment, policy trajectory, and historical conditions are all unique. Yet because of China's importance and developmental success, people will continuously draw conclusions about the meaning of the Chinese experience. In turn, we can draw lessons both from the insights and from the shortcomings of existing ways that China's experience is interpreted. I start with some simple propositions:

▪ Introduction: Five Paradoxical Propositions

1. China is an important model and many draw lessons from its developmental success.

2. There is no consensus about what these lessons are, and many supposed lessons are inconsistent, incompatible or just plain wrong.

3. Despite China's remarkable institutional creativity, **no** specific institution which one can responsibly recommend should be replicated in other developing economies.

4. Institutional innovation in China involved modifying and strengthening, as well as abandoning, existing hierarchies. Chinese institutional innovation was highly specific to the existing institutional context, and made use of existing organizational capital at each step of the transition process.

5. Since no country has an institutional endowment similar to that of China, no country should adapt China's specific experiences. However,

---

* Barry Naughton is Professor of Chinese Economy and Sokwanlok Chair of Chinese International Affairs at the University of California, San Diego. He is the author of *Growing Out of the Plan: Chinese Economic Reform, 1978—1993*, and *The Chinese Economy: Transitions and Growth*.

the *process* of institutional innovation in China can provide many lessons about the nature of institutions and the interactions between institutions and the development process. Developing countries may be able to strengthen their capacity for institutional innovation by examining China's experience.

The influence of the Chinese model has usually come not in the form of discrete lessons, but rather as a contribution to the updating of world views; that is, in revising the economic ideologies and viewpoints used to steer through complex economic phenomena. A wave of such updating occurred during the 1990s, following the collapse of Communism; and another wave is occurring now in the face of the collapse of the U. S. financial system. China has played an especially ambiguous role in the updating of economic viewpoints. I propose to address the significance of the Chinese experience by first looking at the most common ways that people have interpreted that experience. I am less concerned with analytic insight at the beginning, but rather with the formation of various "folk wisdoms", the relatively simple ways that people have incorporated China into existing world views while partially revising and updating those views.

When we examine China's impact in this way, we discover that there is no agreement about the meaning of the Chinese experience, but that the prevailing folk wisdom does sort into two clusters, into, as it were, two big baskets of lessons. There is certainly no "Beijing Consensus". Ironically, it is difficult to identify a single point on which something like consensus might exist. [1] Nevertheless, the prevailing folk wisdom does sort into two big baskets: two clusters of lessons, each of which is "comfortable" in the sense that it brings together many sharp insights that are compatible with each other. However, the two baskets do not comfortably co-exist, and indeed clash on many important points. Some insights can be drawn from the clash of their incompatible viewpoints.

▪ Two Versions of the Chinese Experience

Of the two primary sets of folk wisdom circulating about the Chinese experience, the first begins with the political implications. It stresses the

---

1 Ramo (2004) suggested the term "Beijing Consensus", which is an impressionistic canvas of imaginative description.

need for an active and decisive national leadership, and emphasizes that this is compatible with economic growth and may be good for it. In order to sharpen the contours of this version I link it to the observed political processes in the developing world today that have been called "authoritarian upgrading" (Heydemann, 2007), or "Authoritarianism 2.0" (Spector and Krickovic, 2008). This is the area in which the Chinese experience is set off most starkly against the prevailing ideas and policies seen as being promoted by the US, and reflecting US interests. It is therefore probably the most *influential* of the various lessons circulating, although it has limited appeal in the US and other developed countries. In this version, the central element of the Chinese experience is seen as the success China's leaders have achieved in moving from an authoritarian system in disarray and creating a dramatically revised, but still authoritarian, system that achieved success in increasing economic benefit and distributing those benefits to a large swathe of the population. We might label this a consultative, growth-driven authoritarianism.

The adaptation of the Chinese experience in "authoritarian upgrading" can be summarized in several key points[2]:

1. A paramount emphasis on national sovereignty as an essential precondition that allows states to pursue domestic economic reforms without succumbing either to outside domination or international instability. (Thus, this version tilts against interpretations of globalization that emphasize the dominance of international economic forces and the reduced importance or maneuvering room of national governments.)

2. Maintaining control over core parts of the economy, while liberalizing the market economy overall. Markets are the basis of all allocative decisions, but government ownership or ownership by close client or ruling groups dominates sectors with natural or policy-based entry barriers.

3. Create a consultative apparatus while limiting the autonomy of civil society and opposition groups. Establish formal procedures for social groups to influence policy, but on the condition that influence on acceptance of the regime-dictated framework. Work hard to understand competing social

---

2 I have adapted these points from Heilmann (2008b); Heydemann (2007); and Spector and Krickovic (2008), who each give slightly different but consistent versions. My apologies to these authors for occasionally oversimplifying their analysis.

agendas and actively pre-empt them. Manage political contestation by introduction elements of competition for lower offices.

4. Government-sponsored infrastructure development and technological upgrading. Key importance is given to building telecommunications systems, even while allowing a modest, fragmented "blogosphere".

5. Promote international economic and political linkages.

This version of the Chinese lesson has spread broadly in the developing world. By this definition, Russia is now following the China model, and so are Egypt and Kazakhstan. The model is broadly influential in Africa and in some parts of Latin America, such as Venezuela, Bolivia, Ecuador, Nicaragua, although it is impossible to say that any single country exemplifies the application of this model.

At the core of this folk wisdom is the conviction that successful economic growth gives a regime the resources it needs to maintain power and stability. By capturing the benefits of economic reforms and growth and spreading them reasonably widely among the population, a regime can survive and stabilize itself. This can work only because it turns out that both the regime and civil society are willing to compromise. The regime must be willing to reign in its inclination to arbitrary and capricious rule; having promised influence in return for obedience, it must now actually listen to broader elements of the population and adapt policy to their interests as well. Civil society accepts limits on its activity in return for improved economic conditions and a degree of personal security and property rights. Of course, the bargain is not symmetrical, because the regime has much greater ability to police the compact, and it is difficult for civil society groups to police government misbehavior.

The contrasting interpretation of the Chinese experience is primarily economic, and it has also coalesced into a kind of folk wisdom. This interpretation places its focus on a very different set of phenomena:

1. A paramount emphasis on the gradual expansion of market forces as the essential precondition that allows accelerated economic growth. Expansion of market forces is generally seen as a consequence of the steady withdrawal of direct government control over the economy.

2. Government policy toward the economy is marked by caution and pragmatism. Flexibility and the experimental approach are linked to "gradualism", often by invoking the Chinese expression "crossing the river

by groping for stepping stones".

3. Opening to the outside world, and adopting policies to facilitate foreign direct investment, particularly in export industries. Special economic zones are used to accelerate the process.

4. Strong and consistent government emphasis on economic growth, and on investment as a means to achieving economic growth.

5. Sequencing: A preference for market opening, even if partial; entry should proceed rapidly, market regulation can follow. Dual track systems of plan and market can co-exist. Product market liberalization precedes factor market liberalization. Technically more difficult reforms such as privatization and capital account liberalization can be deferred for longer periods, measured in decades.

At the core of this folk wisdom is the conviction that government withdrawal from markets is essential to driving successful economic growth. The economics folk wisdom and the political folk wisdom direct their attention to very different parts of the Chinese experience; indeed, we could say that they face in opposite directions, and reach almost opposite conclusions about what the meaning of the Chinese experience is.

What do these two conceptions have to do with each other? Of course, a smart analyst can reconcile them. It could be argued that they don't engage at all, that they deal with different aspects of the transition process, one political, one economic, and are thus essentially orthogonal. Or it could be argued that they are essentially complementary: A government that withdraws enough from the market economy creates prosperity, which can then be translated into political stability and national autonomy. China's developmental success then represents a kind of dialectical compromise between the political and economic sides of the model, and the particular political form of the government—the shape of the political capital created—is an arbitrary choice reflecting political and social endowments. These views are plausible, but they overlook the more fundamental conflicts between these interpretations. In fact, I argue that there are two important contradictions between the two versions of the Chinese experience, and that understanding those contradictions can give us a better insight into the shortcomings of each folk wisdom.

In the first place, the authoritarian upgrading interpretation implies significant revision in the goals of development, both in terms of what is desirable and what is feasible. It directly challenges electoral democracy and unfettered market operation, asserting a crucial role for government control in creating stability, maintaining national autonomy, and thereby boosting other developmental goals. By contrast, the economists' folk model does not require revising anything about the goals of development. It is consistent with the view that development will ultimately bring about prosperous societies accompanied by a democratic, regulated market economy. This distinction is important in informing attitudes that people have about the Chinese experience, whether it is positive and whether replication of the Chinese experience would be a good thing to contemplate. In developing countries, the rough consensus in favor of democracy and a market economy that emerged in the 1990s has weakened substantially, and not just among authoritarian leaders. Some see this as threatening[3], and we should be aware that differences in evaluation criteria shape different understandings of the Chinese experience.

It is the second area of contrast between the political and economic folk models, though, that is the focus of attention here. This is that the political model emphasizes the conscious and intentional modification of the structures and institutions of the authoritarian regime. In the political model, the authoritarian government is seen as having been under pressure, and as a result having tried out new policies and organizational models in order to shore up its longevity. In other words, the regime is organizationally entrepreneurial. The economic model, in its folk form, ignores purposeful modification and institutional creativity altogether. In the economic model, the government retreats, and the market rises. If political changes are discussed at all, they are equated with democratization, and they are regarded as having been deferred.

The thirtieth anniversary of China's reform process (1978 to 2008) has given many commentators an opportunity to reflect on overall patterns, so

---

3 "As developing nations watch the convulsions in world financial markets, they may well decide that China's model of a kind of centrally controlled capitalism is more attractive than the American model of unfettered capitalism. ... The danger now is that developing nations could turn instead to the Chinese model of government, with managed mercantilism as the favored approach" (Seib, 2008).

we see many recent examples of the economic folk wisdom:

> Yet the process by which these astonishing changes have occurred owes as much
> to accident and experiment as to grand design. Deng likened his non-ideological,
> gradualist approach to "crossing the river by feeling for the stones". Many of the
> so-called market reforms were little more than giving space—often by turning a
> blind eye—to what China's entrepreneurial citizens were already doing... The
> Communist party appears to have brought 30 years of spectacularly smooth
> growth... But that obscures often desperate flailing as the party cranks this lever
> and that to produce the economic progress on which its survival ultimately
> depends. (Pilling, 2008)

Pilling's comment exemplifies the economics folk wisdom, perhaps in a
somewhat exaggerated form (but see also *Economist*, 2008; Huang, 2008).
It gives all the attention to the expansion of the market arena (indeed,
attributing it to things Chinese citizens were already doing!), and
characterizes official policy-making as "desperate flailing", as if maintaining
macroeconomic stability, carrying out tax reform, and engaging in massive
infrastructure construction were merely incidental things that all developing
economies carried out as a matter of course. Curiously, the economics folk
wisdom is very good at seeing that Chinese policy-makers learned as they
went; that they tried out many policies and retained only a sub-set; and did
not launch the transition process with a grand design. Yet they do not seem
interested in, or able to encompass, the actual process of learning and
discovery that may have gone into the policy process. Neither transformation
of institutions nor policy experimentation plays much of a role in the
economic folk wisdom, which is extremely unfortunate. [4]

The "authoritarian upgrading" model seems to give China's leadership
too much credit for institutional changes and developmental success; in this
model, the Chinese Communist Party's self-serving narrative about correct
decision-making is accepted at face value. But ironically, by under-
emphasizing the unprecedented nature of the challenges China has faced,
and the experimental, exploratory aspects of policy, this version actually
gives too little credit to the Chinese policy process. The wholesale recasting

---

4 Of course, there are much more sophisticated versions of the Chinese transition policy process,
whose insights do not get picked up in the various folk models.

of development strategy to conform with China's factor endowment (Lin, 2007) doesn't receive adequate attention, and as a result the political model seriously underestimates the uniqueness of China, in terms of size, developmental stage, and readiness for growth. Oddly enough, the political model doesn't give Chinese policy-makers *enough* credit for the sheer canniness of their economic policy-making.

By contrast, the economic model accepts an overly restricted version of the institutions at play in the Chinese transition and development experience. In the face of the extraordinary complexity of the Chinese institutional setup (itself perhaps a function of size: compare with India), many observers simply throw up their hands and say, in essence, the process has been in the direction of market forces. As a result, the process of institutional innovation and discovery that is at the heart of the political model gets neglected. This means that the economics folk wisdom has forgotten one of the key lessons of the classic analysis in Stiglitz (1999): that conserving scarce organizational capital through institutional adaptation is one of the key advantages of a gradual transition path. But what institutional innovations made in the course of Chinese transition could potentially serve as models for other developing economies?

■ Are There Any Chinese Institutional Innovations That are Potentially Replicable?

The Chinese development experience has been marked by an extraordinary institutional creativity. A number of unique Chinese institutions and terms have gradually seeped into the awareness of those concerned with international economics: township and village enterprises (TVEs), dual-track system, and "growing out of the plan". Specific Chinese organizations such as SASAC (State Asset Supervision and Administration Commission), and NDRC (National Development & Reform Commission), have gained some name recognition. Yet if we ask which of these institutions can be recommended for imitation by other developing economies, the answer has to be, "none". That is, among all the remarkable institutional improvisations in China, among all the institutional solutions that China devised to tricky transitional problems, there is none that is so successful, and so robust to context, that we would feel comfortable recommending it to other countries. Of course, posing the question in this way means framing the question about the replicability of the Chinese experience in a particularly narrow fashion: What Chinese institutions can we recommend for adoption by other developing or transitional economies? By asking a narrow question we obtain a refreshingly clear and straightforward answer: None.

Before proceeding, we must deal with one apparent exception. Hasn't the Chinese policy of Special Economic Zones (SEZs) been replicated around the world? This is the exception that proves the rule. It is true that Chinese SEZs have been an inspiration in many countries, including most strikingly India, with its SEZ policy of 2000 and SEZ law of 2005. But of course China did not originate the SEZ, which came from Ireland (after 1958) and Taiwan (1966). Indeed, ironically, India even had its own unsuccessful Export Processing Zone at Kandla in 1965, though it was not successful. So while China may well have emboldened policy-makers in India and elsewhere to give new priority to SEZs, this can hardly be considered a Chinese innovation. [5] Indeed, what is most innovative about Chinese SEZs (aside from their sheer incongruity in the Chinese planned economy of the early 1980s) is size, multi-functional use as a laboratory of multiple types of reforms, and openness to the domestic economy (Naughton, 2007, pp. 408 – 410). India has taken note of some of these, for example, requiring new SEZs to be over 10 km^2, but overall Indian SEZs are much more like standard Asian Export Processing Zones than like Chinese SEZs. Nothing exceptional about Chinese SEZs has been imitated in the outside world. Chinese SEZs are not a good candidate for replication.

Why, then, are there no Chinese institutional innovations that travel well? In fact, this is because the most important Chinese institutional innovations represented careful compromises between the pre-existing institutional framework and the innovations necessary to support economic growth. Innovation was carefully adapted to the existing institutional landscape. We can illustrate this point through three examples.

---

5 "The prime mover of the (Indian SEZ) proposal, the Commerce and Industry Minister, Mr. Murasoli Maran, has been highly impressed by the stunning success of the Chinese SEZs. " Ashok Kundra (Chairman of the Indian Tariff Commission), "SEZs: How Well Will They Perform?", *The Hindu*, August 16, 2001, accessed at http://www. hindu. com/thehindu/2001/08/16/ stories/06160001. htm; see also Ministry of Commerce and Industry, "Introduction to India's SEZs", at www. sezindia. nic. in.

The first example is that of township and village enterprises (TVEs), arguably the most distinctive and certainly the best-analyzed element of China's success. TVEs combined local public ownership with freedom to enter and profit from entrepreneurial skills. As many analysts have recognized, giving a stake in the entrepreneurial start-up to the local government was an effective second-best approach to overcome bureaucratic obstructionism (Chang and Wang, 1994; Che and Qian, 1999; Rodrik, 2008). TVEs were dependent on a unique compromise about property rights. What has been underemphasized it that to make this compromise possible within the framework of China's existing administrative hierarchy it was necessary to repeatedly adapt that hierarchy to make it compatible with the new institution. Budgetary arrangements were relaxed so that TVEs and their local government owners could retain large shares of increased revenues; and superiors with personnel authority agreed to keep successful managers and village officials in place for long periods, giving them appropriate time horizons for the task of long-run economic growth. The existing administrative hierarchy, in other words, was repeatedly adapted to provide appropriate incentives and continued enforcement of government policy. At the same time, revisions accommodated the existing distribution of power. Local government officials had power: TVE governance rules were restructured in ways that acknowledged that power, but shifted the incentives for the types of behavior that would be rewarded. This type of "fiddling" within the existing institutional structure continues on to the present, although the vast bulk of TVEs have been privatized for a decade or more. Even more dramatic changes in budgetary rules have occurred in the past 3-4 years, as agricultural taxes have been abolished and a system of inter-governmental transfers set in place; even as restless changes have taken place in the degree of village democracy. Most villages elect their own leaders. TVEs are sometimes regarded as "informal" institutional adaptations, but this is not correct. Although regulations were complex, they were clear to market participants. TVEs became important within a hierarchical institutional context that was constantly being adapted to meet the needs of economic growth and institutional innovation.

The second example is the dual-track economic system. While this term is sometimes used to cover a wide variety of phenomena, the most striking and thus paradigmatic application was its use within the state-owned enterprise (SOEs) sector. While the average TVE never had a compulsory output plan, virtually all SOEs did. A key innovation was allowing SOEs to buy and sell at market prices, on the condition that they fulfill their annual compulsory output and purchase plan. This gave firms access to market prices "on the margin" and got them started on the many changes in orientation and operations needed to adapt to a market economy. After operating the dual track system for a decade, the transition was so smooth that when the compulsory plan was abolished at the end of 1993, there was scarcely an economic ripple. Yet again, this dual track was not the result if a simple withdrawal of the planned economy. At least three active policy measures were required to make it work. First, the compulsory output plan had to be set at a slack level, or frozen, in order to ensure that individual firms had sufficient capacity to produce for the market. Second, firm managers had to have a financial interest in increasing profit, and experimentation with financial incentive systems (in the early and mid-1980s) was an essential precondition of the widespread adoption of the dual-tack system (during the mid to late-1980s). Third, and least recognized, is that the administrative hierarchy itself had to be restructured and given a new set of incentives to make it compatible with this kind of profit-oriented activity. In fact, during the 1980s and 1990s, China adopted massive reforms of its hierarchical system (Naughton, 2008). Those reforms completely threw out the old set of incentives and career paths, and replaced them with a set of incentives that were much more explicit, much more high-powered, much more focused on economic growth, and were made consistent with newly restructured career paths that were much more predictable as well. These changes re-focused the attention and behavior of bureaucrats in the hierarchy in a way that was highly compatible with the incentives of SOE managers, and allowed the dual-track system to take root, and ultimately led the economy to grow out of the plan. The hierarchical institutions, again, have been continuously adapted to meet the needs of economic growth and institutional innovation.

For a third example, we may take the complex of institutional measures taken to create China's super-high domestic saving and investment rate. As it is known, China for the past several years has invested over 40% of GDP in new fixed capital, and along with a current account surplus—that soared to 8% of GDP in 2007—domestic saving was almost 50% of GDP over the past few years. The Commission on Growth and Development (2008, pp. 34 – 37) gives first priority to high investment in their list of policies associated with rapid growth. They note approvingly that China invests even more than the 5% -7% of GDP that they recommend for physical infrastructure investment. What many do not realize, however, is that this substantial investment effort has not been a consistent characteristic of China's reform era. For more than a decade after reforms began, China under-invested in infrastructure as it gave the economy a breathing space after decades of extravagant socialist investment plans. As late as 1990— 1992, China was investing only 4% of GDP on physical infrastructure (narrowly defined as transport, communications and electricity). The extraordinary saver and investor we know today only emerged after the mid-1990s, after almost 20 years of successful reforms. China's investment in (narrow) physical infrastructure jumped above 6% of GDP in 1993— 1997, and then jumped again to 8% of GDP and above after 1998. What did China do to achieve this remarkable investment effort?

In essence, China subordinated most institutional issues to the quest for a high and adequate investment effort. A high investment effort and a rapid growth rate have been consensus objectives of Chinese leaders for the past fifty years. [6] The leadership was alarmed at the under-investment of the early 1990s, and worried broadly about the declining effectiveness of the national government. As a result, they focused institutional development on measures that would strengthen the government and restore its ability to lead investment programs. Since the beginning of reforms, China had maintained a positive rate of return to savers. Inflationary episodes had occurred but had generally been controlled with 18-24 months, and depositors had been protected with inflation supplements. As a result, household saving rates had increased at the beginning of transition and stayed high. There had never been an expropriation of saving balances such as happened in other transitional economies.

Nevertheless, the investment effort was deemed inadequate. In order to address this issue, China began a massive series of institutional reforms:

6　The Growth Commission notes the importance of national leadership in generating growth (pp. xx-yy), and it is certainly true that leadership consensus on this issue strongly characterizes China.

—The tax system was overhauled in 1994, giving China a much broader tax base, and substantially increasing the central government's share of the total tax take.

—State enterprises that dominated infrastructure provision were allowed to retain all after-tax profits, providing a dedicated financial source for some infrastructure investment.

—Key infrastructure sectors were restructured to reinforce state domination but provide oligopolistic competition between 2 or 3 main providers: this was true of telecom, electricity, and airlines, while railroad remained a de facto monopoly. Entry barriers kept profitability high while rivalry ensured that re-investment would also be high in these sectors.

—Policy banks were set up within the state banking system to systematically channel funds to infrastructure investment.

—After 1998, central government infrastructure bonds were issued to add another financial source.

Yet all these innovations were complementary to a fundamental, ongoing characteristic of China's institutional set-up. Local government officials have long had a strong incentive to invest in both infrastructure and productive (revenue-generating) investment projects. In part, this is due to soft budget constraints—the asymmetric structure of risk and return in projects, an asymmetry that characterizes bureaucratic decision-making in most places. In part, the strengthening of incentives to expand revenue-generating activity that was referred to in the description of the dual-track system may have further increased local official's incentives to invest. In either case, local officials have strong incentives to invest so long as they can gain access to funding. Nor is this a transitory characteristic of the Chinese system. On November 10, 2008, the Chinese government announced a fiscal stimulus plan to respond to the global financial crisis, envisaging a 1.18 trillion RMB increment to central government investment spending, designed to elicit more than 2 trillion RMB in additional local government investment. In fact, within two weeks, local governments proposed an astonishing total of 18 trillion RMB (about US $2.5 trillion and 60% of GDP) of local projects. Clearly, local governments still see the possibility of soft budget constraints when it comes to investment spending.

What do these three examples show? They show very strongly that Chinese gradual marketization cannot remotely be described as a simple withdrawal of the state and revival of an autonomous market sphere. Instead, marketization has always been accompanied with a process of institutional adaptation and innovation. That institutional adaptation has been closely tied to specific characteristics of the Chinese environment—of course—but more concretely to the chains of authority and delegation that cross over from the economic to the governmental side of the economy. These institutional adaptations are therefore obviously unsuitable for imitation by other economies that have totally different institutional characteristics. It is not that China is unique, it's that all economies are unique and vary substantially in institutional context and endowment.

Each of these institutional adaptations involves messy trade-offs and obvious costs as well as benefits. Each institutional innovation involves a compromise with existing power-holders that would not be at all desirable, except that the co-optation of existing power-holders is part of what has ensured the success of the innovation. None of these institutional innovations are "best practice", because all involve accepting and perpetuating significant market distortions, while failing to permanently lock in unambiguous property rights and new arms-length regulation. Indeed, even the essential "flexibility" and "pragmatism" of the Chinese approach turns out, on closer inspection, to be deeply intertwined with the institutional peculiarities of the Chinese system. Heilmann (2008a) shows that China's experiments were embedded within the political system and characterizes it as "experimentation under the shadow of hierarchy". This is realistic, and a far cry from the implicit model of open-minded empiricism that is sometimes imputed to Chinese reformers.

■ Features of Institutional Change in China

Since we will search in vain for a specific Chinese institution that should be replicated in other developing economies, we must re-frame the questions about the replicability of the Chinese experience and the lessons to be learned. First, what does the Chinese experience tell us about the way we conceive of institutions? We looked at Chinese institutional innovation as being fundamentally adaptive: How does this adaptable institution view compare with the way that institutions are generally viewed in economics? Institutional economics has certainly been flourishing in economics in recent years, but in terms of economic growth, most of the work has focused on the causal relationship between "high quality" institutions and economic growth. In this work, institutions are generally taken as exogenous. Institutional innovations that strengthen property rights, lengthen their time horizons, and give individuals stronger and more reliable rewards for economically productive behavior elicit a response. Better institutions lead to more productive activity, increase investment and ultimately create economic growth. There is much in the Chinese experience that conforms to this interpretation. The *outcome* of individuals responding to better incentives clearly fits. Incentives for saving, investment and entrepreneurship in China have been dramatically strengthened. From the top to the bottom of the society, individuals have responded to these incentives with a dramatic increase in productive behavior. This is the truth at the core of the marketization narrative.

However, institutional economics provides surprisingly little guidance in explaining what types of institutional innovation have been adopted in China. Clearly, institutional mechanisms and institutional quality are not exogenous to the Chinese institutional environment or political system. Nor does it seem that those reforms were adopted first which promised the biggest efficiency gains. Instead, institutional innovations are adopted only when they both promised efficiency improvements and were acceptable to existing power-holders. We can discern some important patterns in the way institutional innovations have been adopted.

First, existing institutions have been widely "repurposed". We have almost never seen in China a case in which completely new people have been brought in to staff a new administrative function. Instead, existing organizations have been given incentives to shift their mission in a more compatible with a market economy. Promotion patterns within the existing organization change to reflect new qualifications for the new mission, and over time a new generation brings organizational ethos to the top. This is assuredly a gradual pattern of institutional change, and it allows the transition process to reap the huge advantages of "preserving ' lumps' of social and organizational capital" (Stiglitz, 1999). It has the cost that old ways of doing things only gradually die out, as an elder generation passes from the scene. This organizational persistence may also inhibit the adoption of certain kinds of transplanted institutions.

Second, partly due to the above, many institutional innovations have the character of a bargain, or contract, between the existing power-holders and the needs of a more efficient, growth-oriented policy. That is, institutional changes succeed because vested interest groups are brought into the new institutional set-up. Their interests are protected up to a certain extent. We see this, for example, in the way that bureaucrats are brought into new corporations *and* new regulatory institutions. In a broader sense, it is possible to argue that the whole transition process fits into such a pattern, since Communist Party leaders have been given a stake in the marketization process, and became reasonably confident that marketization would benefit themselves and their families. If one imagines the Chinese reform process as a Coasian bargain between growth-oriented reformers and vested interest groups, one can capture almost all of the key dynamics. Economic nationalism provides a common language for the various groups to communicate, and an expanding economy the resources to consummate the bargain.

Third, there is an enormous amount of institutional innovation in the system, most of which fails. Institutional innovation rewards entrepreneurship. Entrepreneurs find the opportunity for gain in the discovery of a new way of doing things. The system is set up in such a way that political entrepreneurship is rewarded. In that sense, the political system resembles the economic system: investment and entrepreneurship are rewarded, while the costs of failure are dispersed over the system as a whole. Local government officials have plenty of opportunities to exercise their "animal spirits", by promoting local programs that might get them noticed in Beijing, and ultimately promoted. This generates a lot of wasteful activity, but it also succeeds in generating a lot of institutional innovation. It is crucial that China's size and quasi-federal governmental structure provides an opportunity for innovators to fail without causing enormous systemic damage. As Heilmann shows, local experimentation occurs under the shadow of hierarchy, so that experiments are frequently limited or cancelled when they appear to be failing, or running out of control.

Fourth, because experimentation is constantly occurring within an overall institutional context that is fairly well understood and monitored, there are rarely catastrophic failures of institutional implementation. In other words, there are usually not huge divergences between new rules as promulgated and their enforcement in practice, or, more accurately, when such divergences occur they are usually corrected reasonably quickly. Periods of uncertainty during rapid institutional turn-over are rare. Those episodes when market participants are uncertain what the new rules are, and daring but illegal behavior promises outsized gains, occur relatively infrequently. We can see this most clearly in the process of financial reform. Through the 1990s, China adopted program after program of financial sector reform, most of which failed. Investment trust companies, hothouse stock markets, and a wide array of bond-like fund-raising instruments were tried, but none fully succeeded and many ultimately collapsed. In many cases, individuals benefited from the failed experiments, and in all cases, the ultimate costs showed up on bank balance sheets as non-performing loans. Put together, these efforts could be described as a financial debacle, and they contributed to the ultimate write-off of more than a third of GDP in non-performing loans in the late 1990s-early 2000s (Naughton, 2007, pp. 462 – 463). Enormous real costs were involved in this failed experimentation, but the system was able to absorb the costs without a catastrophic financial crisis or breakdown. As Stiglitz (1999) points out, it is precisely in the financial sector where the agency chains are longest that we should expect the most difficulty in establishing a new functioning system. Chinese experience certainly bears this out: we are only today witnessing a halfway credible attempt to get a functioning modern financial system up and running. The Chinese experience was not in avoiding the costs of financial experimentation and failure, but rather in containing those costs such that other developmental processes could go forward.

Fifth, there is constant discussion and debate about growth, the institutional set-up, and proper strategic decisions. The debate about economic choices in China comprises at least as broad a range of alternatives as similar discussions in the US and Europe. The discussion is extraordinary lively and encompasses a range of options. Moreover, discussion is often future-oriented and accompanied by "planning". An enormous amount of planning takes place in China, and has since the very beginning of economic transition thirty years ago. A great deal of this planning is unrealistic, or suffers from an immense disjunction between goals and instruments. Indeed, much of this planning is difficult for outsiders to understand, since it seems unrealistic and anachronistic. But these planning exercises do mean that policy-makers are forced to be explicit about their expectations and objectives. As a result, failure is relatively evident. Although the political system mutes the publicity given to failure, it is fairly obvious to insiders. Policy is therefore subject to continuous appraisal and reappraisal, and regular midcourse adjustments. The quality of debate has been high, as stressed by the Commission on Growth and Development (2008, pp. 67-68).

In other words, what the Chinese experience tells us is that institutional innovation is not exogenous, but rather emerges from a national institutional framework. Perhaps it is not unreasonable to make an analogy between national institutional innovation system and the more orthodox "national innovation system", as in Nelson (1993) and much subsequent literature. The analogy is not exact because a national innovation system includes organizations whose primary function is to produce technological innovations. There are no such organizations in the Chinese institutional innovation system. But the overall environment that generates and evaluates institutional innovations in China is relatively robust. If there is anything about China's developmental experience that can be usefully studied and adapted by other developing countries it is the generally supportive environment created for institutional innovation.

■ Lessons and Conclusions

Examination of the Chinese experience leads first to some insights about the nature of institutions and institutional change, and subsequently to some tentative suggestions for the practical lessons for other developing economies. The process of institutional change in China shows the enormous role played by institutional "repurposing". This shows clearly that many different institutional forms are functional substitutes and that, as Rodrik (2007) stresses, there is no one-to-one mapping between institutional forms and institutional functions. There are many more-or-less good institutional forms that can be harnessed to provide long-run incentives that are compatible with economic growth.

This brings the endogeneity of institutional innovation into sharp focus. Institutional innovations in China have typically been compromises between the desire to reward productive behavior and the reluctance to surrender control over resources. That is, a closer look at institutional innovation reveals the extent to which it is interwoven with political systems and struggles over power and resources that are inevitable, but may not be pretty. However, this is true of all institutional innovation, so it doesn't make sense to ignore it in our discussion of specific cases. The interweaving of institutional choice and power and implementation means that there is limited usefulness in treating institutional analysis as a form of comparative statics. It is not very useful to treat the movement from centrally planned to market economy as a comparative static problem, in which the objective is to move from one equilibrium to another. It may be true that there is a long-run trend to convergence in relatively similar capitalist market systems, but this process seems to unfold only over the very long run. Indeed, even the American variant of this developed and regulated market system seems still to be very much a work in progress, and how much more true is this of developing economy variants.

Although the Chinese system is very good at generating indigenous institutional innovation, it has a decidedly mixed record of adopting outside institutions. Indeed, since the mid-1990s, China has adopted the whole panoply of "best practice" corporate institutions, at least in theory. The modern corporate organization has been adopted, even in state-owned firms, along with regulatory institutions that are, in theory, independent. But most observers would agree that the adoption of these transplant institutions has been decided slow and uneven. Most importantly, the transplanted institutions do not seem to have really taken on the institutional functions they originally evolved to take on. Instead, they robe traditional administrative hierarchies, giving bureaucrats new procedures and tools for decision-making, but not altering the traditional distribution of authority. This imperfect transplantation may be concomitant to China's strong record of generating domestic innovation. The conservation of social and organization capital and the compromise with existing power structures may liberate indigenous innovation but retard the adaptation of transplanted institutions.

For most developing countries, the question will be whether they can replicate some aspects of the Chinese experience. The analysis presented here suggests that the most important benefit would come from imitating some of the institutional entrepreneurship that underpins Chinese transition success. Of course, it is meaningless to copy the Chinese "national institutional innovation system", but there are some aspects of the overall Chinese intellectual and institutional environment that could usefully be replicated:

First, the overwhelming consensus in China in favor of economic growth can be usefully transplanted to other developing economies. National governments can demonstrate both the overall "future orientation" and the conscious choice of growth as an "overarching goal" of the nation, as recommended by the Commission on Growth and Development. But obviously this will not be done by having governments make grandiose statements about growth, which will lack credibility. In fact, it can only be done by having pervasive planning processes, where planning involves articulating objectives; describing scenarios; and setting benchmarks. The failed process of trying to achieve a single, centralized national plan has given planning a bad name; more plans, including more failed plans, can contribute to a shared future orientation and jump-start the process of institutional change necessary to achieve accelerated growth.

Second, institutional innovation needs to be focused on raising infrastructure investment rates. Many countries today are rolling out infrastructure investment programs to serve as stimulus packages in the face of the gathering world recession. China is among them. While it is reasonable to worry about the cost of poorly designed and built infrastructure, this trend is basically positive and should be encouraged. Developing countries should subordinate other legitimate concerns to the need to accelerate infrastructure construction. The pendulum has swung too far away from this kind of policy. At the same time, a stress on local institutional innovation may make it possible to expand infrastructure investment with less waste than in the past; home-grown mechanisms to provide proper incentives to maintain infrastructure in a sustainable fashion are quite feasible.

Third, a vigorous environment of economic debate and policy contention is essential. Although China is far from being a democracy, it enjoys a vigorous and robust discussion about nearly every aspect of economic policy. In part, this is simply one of the advantages of size: China's intellectual community is large because the population of concerned citizens is enormous. Robust evaluation and criticism can be achieved in many environments, and this helps to make institutional innovation possible by limiting some of the down-side risks.

Fourth, the good news is that a virtuous circle is involved in the process of growth and institutional innovation. As growth accelerates, people begin to shift their orientation, and it becomes easier to coordinate expectations about the future. Planning becomes more important and the quality of planning increases. Moreover, as income increases, the Coasian bargains needed to elicit acceptance of new institution become easier to strike. Short-term and long-term institutional solutions become easier to conceive, and the process of change is eased. Chinese experience certainly abundantly demonstrates this fact.

Overall, developing economies may gain by increasing the importance they attach to institutional innovation. Growth as a goal requires support for institutional change; the greater the extent to which institutional change can be locally grown, the more smoothly a developing economy is likely to move to a more rapid growth path. Today, few question the intrinsic benefits of gradualism in large-scale policy reform, if it can be achieved. However, we are still short of concrete advice that can assist countries in generating indigenous institutional change; strengthening overall system robustness against chaos; and harmoniously adopting growth-supporting institutional change. We face the odd conundrum that everybody talks about the Chinese model—and some even talk about a "Beijing Consensus", even though there is not a single plank of this so-called consensus that commands significant agreement. The Chinese experience strongly enforces a general principle, that economic growth takes place when market and non-market elements of an economic system are in a healthy inter-dependent relationship with each other. But the Chinese experience equally supports the assertion that the specific nature of this inter-dependent relationship is indeterminate. There is no single or any simple correct way to handle this relationship.

As a result, there is no specific feature of Chinese institutional innovation that can be replicated. However, these will always be a demand for a few key simplifications of the Chinese experience that give others guide to action. As social scientists, and as China scholars, our responsibility is to provide those lessons where possible, but also to insist on the irreducible complexity of economic and social development.

■ References

Chun Chang, and Yijiang Wang, "The Nature of the Township-Village Enterprise", *Journal of Comparative Economics*, No. 19, 1994, pp. 434 – 452.

J. Che, and Qian Yingyi, "Insecure Property Rights and Government Ownership of Firms", *Quarterly Journal of Economics*, Vol. 113, No. 2, 1998, pp. 467 – 496.

Commission on Growth and Development, *The Growth Report: Strategies for Sustained Growth and Inclusive Development*, Washington, D. C. : World Bank, 2008, accessed at http://www. growthcommission. org/index. php? option = com_ content&task = view&i d = 96&Itemid = 169.

Simeon Djankov, Edward Glaeser, Rafael La Porta, Florencio Lopez-de-Silanes and Andrei Shleifer, "The New Comparative Economics", *Journal of Comparative Economics*, No. 31, 2003, pp. 595-619.

Economist, "China's Reforms: The Second Long March", *The Economist*, Dec. 11th, 2008, accessed at http://www. economist. com/world/asia/displayStory. cfm? story id = 1275 8848&sou rce = most commented.

Ricardo Hausmann, Dani Rodrik, and Andrés Velasco, "Getting the Diagnosis Right", *Finance and Development*, No. 43, March 2006, p. 1.

Sebastian Heilmann, "Policy Experimentation in China's Economic Rise", *Studies in Comparative International Development*, Vol. 43, No. 1, March 2008, pp. 1 – 26.

Sebastian Heilmann, "Authoritarian Upgrading? The Innovative Potential of China's Economic Governance", Paper prepared for the conference "Three Decades of Reform and Opening: Where is China Headed?", Boston University, December 8, 2008.

Stephan Heydemann, "Upgrading Authoritarianism in the Arab World", Brookings Institution, Saban Center for Middle East Policy, Analysis Paper No. 13, October 2007, accessed at http://www. brookings. edu/ ~ /media/Files/rc/papers/2007/ 10arabworld/10arabworl d. pdf.

Yasheng Huang, *Capitalism with Chinese Characteristics: Entrepreneurship and the State*, New York: Cambridge University Press, 2008.

Joshua Kurlantzick, *Charm Offensive: How China's Soft Power Is Transforming the World*, New Haven: Yale University Press, 2007.

John McMillan, and Barry Naughton, "How to Reform a Planned Economy: Lessons from China", *Oxford Review of Economic Policy*, Vol. 8, No. 1, Spring 1992.

Barry Naughton, *The Chinese Economy: Transitions and Growth*, Cambridge, Massachusetts: MIT Press, 2007.

Barry Naughton, "Market Economy, Hierarchy and Single Party Rule", in Janos Kornai and Yingyi Qian (ed.), *Market and Socialism Reconsidered (with Particular Reference to China and Vietnam)*, London: Macmillan, for the International Economic Association, pp. 135 – 161.

Richard Nelson (ed.), *National Innovation Systems: A Comparative Analysis*, New York: Oxford University Press, 1993.

David Pilling, "China's 'warp-speed' industrial revolution", *Financial Times*, December 17, 2008, http://www.ft.com/cms/s/0/db443b20-cc5b-11dd-9c43-000077b07658.html.

Yingyi Qian and Barry Weingast, "Federalism as a Commitment to Preserving Market Incentives", *Journal of Economic Perspectives*, Vol. 11, No. 4, Fall 1997, pp. 83 – 92.

Qiany, Yingyi and Chenggang Xu, "Why China's Economic Reforms Differ: The M-Form Hierarchy and Entry/Expansion of the Non-State Sector", *The Economics of Transition*, Vol. 1, No. 2, June 1993, pp. 135 – 170.

Joshua Cooper Ramo, "The Beijing Consensus", London: The Foreign Policy Centre, May 2004.

Dani Rodrik, *One Economics, Many Recipes: Globalization, Institutions, and Economic Growth*, Princeton: Princeton University Press, 2007.

Ruan Qi, "Difang guding zichan touzi shuzi pengzhang; 18 wanyi shiju wuli fudan" (Local fixed investment figures are soaring; 18 trillion is impossible to actually bear), *Shanghai Zhengzhuanbao*, November 26, 2008, accessed at http://business.sohu.com/20081126/n260848416.shtml.

Gerald Seib, "U. S. Woes Open Door for China", *Wall Street Journal*, December 23, 2008, p. A2.

Regine A Spector, and Andrej Krickovic, "Authoritarianism 2. 0: Non-Democratic Regimes are Upgrading and Integrating Globally", Paper Presented at the 49th Annual International Studies Association Conference, San Francisco, CA. March 26, 2008, accessed at http://www.allacademic.com//meta/p_ mla_ apa_ research_ citation/2/5/3/0/9/pages253098/p253098-1.php.

Joseph Stiglitz, "Whither Reform? Ten Years of the Transition", Washington, D. C. : Annual World Bank Conference on Development Economics.

Thirty Years of Chinese Reform and Economic Growth: Challenges and How It Has Changed World Development

Ross Garnaut [*]

On 22 December 1978, the Eleventh Central Committee of the Chinese Communist Party completed its third plenary meeting. There was no contemporary recognition in the West of the significance of the meeting.

Now we are recognising the thirtieth anniversary of the Third Plenum. In the intervening years, China, the lives of its people, its relations with the rest of the world, and to some extent the economic lives of people in the rest of the world have been transformed. China's output has increased proportionately more than ever before over three decades in a substantial economy. The consumption levels of what had been about half of the world's people in poverty have increased beyond the usual ambitions for development. The United Nations "millennium goals" for reduction of global poverty are being met in aggregate mainly through what has been happening in this one country. An isolated, autarchic economy thirty years ago, China since the early 1990s has absorbed around half of the direct foreign investment going to developing countries. In some years in the early twenty-first century, China's exports or imports have accounted for around half of the growth in world trade and its output for around half the growth in world production. China has contributed the majority of growth in demand for some industrial raw materials in the century so far. China was the East Asian region's anchor of growth when financial crisis hit its

---

[*] Ross Garnaut is a Distinguished Professor of Economics at the Australian National University and both a Vice-Chancellor´s Fellow and Professorial Fellow of Economics at The University of Melbourne. He has held senior roles in universities, business, government and other Australian and international institutions. In December 2009, he was awarded the degree of Doctor of Letters, *honoris causa*, from the Australian National University. From 1995 to 2010 he was Chairman of Lihir Gold Limited, and now is Chairman of the Papua New Guinea Sustainable Development Program Limited.

neighbours in the late 1990s. Analysts everywhere, and nowhere more than in my own country, are waiting anxiously to see if China will be the anchor of global growth as the whole world is hit by a United States-centred financial crisis in 2008.

There is another side of the coin. The stress of economic growth without large efforts to reconcile it with environmental amenity have had negative effects on many aspects of Chinese life. Emissions of greenhouse gases have come to exceed those of any other country, and as a result, the world is moving towards high risks of dangerous climate change faster than had been understood by the scientists and economists working within the Inter-governmental Panel on Climate Change (IPCC) only a few years ago. In the absence of new policies to break the established nexus between greenhouse gas emissions and economic growth, China will account for over one third of total emissions by 2030, three times as large as any other country (Garnaut, 2008, Chapter 3).

While the beginnings of Chinese reform doesn't seem so long ago for some of us, we are talking about a fairly long period in modern Chinese history. The reform era is now longer than the period of Communist Party rule within the paradigm of central planning that preceded it. The total span of Communist Party rule now covers more years than passed between the fracture of Imperial authority in the first Opium War and its humiliation in the invasion following the Boxer rebellion. It now covers more years than passed between the Boxer Rebellion through the formation of the Republic to the coming to power of the Chinese Communist Party. We are talking about a period that is long enough for historic transformations.

Through the reform period, there has been a transformation of the Chinese mind. Hundreds of millions of Chinese are now part of an international community of ideas and information. Many threads have been woven to produce this result. One was the audacious scale of the early promotion of studying abroad. This was carried through in explicit recognition that many students would not return, and on the basis that enough would return or in other ways contribute to Chinese development for studying abroad to provide a net gain for the country. Another was the unequivocal early commitment to opening the economy to foreign trade and investment, and its requirement of open movement of business and professional people in and out of China. A third was largely autonomous to

Chinese reform decisions: the extraordinary increase in the power and reduction in cost of international information flows, with technological improvements including the Internet.

Amongst much else, the transformation of the Chinese mind included the development of a modern economics profession, familiar with the theory and techniques of economics in the West, and increasingly confident in the exchange of economic ideas. Leading members of China's economics profession are now contributing to the critique and expansion of received wisdom about economic development, and to the distillation of lessons from the Chinese experience of development into the understanding of the global profession (Lin, 2007, 2008; Fan, 2007). This has been an important and fascinating element of the reform process involving deliberate efforts of the Chinese state, external institutions (with the Ford Foundation's role being noteworthy) and Chinese intellectual entrepreneurs (with the establishment of the China Center for Economic Research building on contributions from each of these sources).

As important as any other element of the transformation of the Chinese mind was the acceptance of major roles for impersonal markets as important instruments for allocating resources and distributing incomes. This was a change not only from central planning since the revolution, but from patterns of imperial power extending far back into Chinese history.

Through these changes, personal economic security is now provided significantly through the value of people's labour and produce in the market place, in the stead of an intrusive and overwhelming state. This personal security has been enhanced in recent years as labour has become scarce and valuable in a way that has no parallel in Chinese history, as coastal China unambiguously and inland China to a considerable extent experiences the rising wage rates that come with what Minami called the turning point of economic development (Minami, 1971; Garnaut, 2006; Cai Feng, 2007).

Reform in China has not and could never be a smooth or painless process. There have been challenges at every step, some bumps in the road, detours and dead ends.

As it happens, the three biggest challenges have coincided with the decennial anniversaries: the inflationary boom of 1988, which established the conditions for the one political crisis of the reform era in 1989; the East Asian financial crisis of 1998; and the global financial crisis of 2008. More of these later.

▪ The Distance Travelled in Three Decades

Ideas and Policy

Thirty years ago, at the Third Plenum, Deng Xiaoping and his supporters took decisive control of the Chinese Communist Party. This ended what Deng once described in my presence as two years of indecisive policy after the death of Mao Zedong. During those two years, policies embodying pragmatic acceptance of a large role for domestic and international market exchange had been in continuing contest with Maoist commitments to local and national autarchy, central planning, state-owned enterprises in the cities and the People's Communes in the countryside.

During the time of indecisive policy, important steps were taken to lay a base for future growth. The awesome denial of formal education during the Cultural Revolution ended, with the return of competitive entry into the great universities in 1978. China's state enterprises experimented with the purchase of exotic technologies from abroad. But there were cross-currents and counter-currents, continued ideological contests over high policy, and uncertainty about continuity of policy as subordinate leaders watched for the emergence of a clear national direction.

Since December 1978, there has been no turning back.

It is not that Deng and his supporters obtained endorsement at the Third Plenum for an elaborate, comprehensive new economic policy or plan. There was no blueprint for China's economic reform and internationalisation—even less than there had been in Taiwan and Korea at the beginnings of their sustained rapid economic growth in the early 1960s.

But after the 1978 Plenum, there was acceptance that domestic and international exchange through markets was a necessary and acceptable component of a national development strategy. There was pragmatic acceptance that institutions and policies that raised national economic output had a valid place in China, even if they were difficult to reconcile with established ideas about what was appropriate in old perceptions of socialist China. This was summed up in Deng's rehabilitation of an early Maoist exhortation to "seek truth from facts". These strands were drawn together

in the 1987 Thirteenth Party Congress's acceptance of General Secretary
Zhao Ziyang's definition of China as a backward country in the "primary
stage of socialism" in which the first national objective was strengthening of
the national economy.

The new political environment after 1978 saw foreign trade, direct
foreign investment, and the utilisation of foreign technical assistance and
capital in all forms become acceptable components of national policy. Local
experiments with new forms of organisation of agricultural production were
given legitimacy, leading within six years to the virtually complete
replacement of the People's Communes with the immensely more
productive household responsibility system. Markets became important for
exchange for the rapidly increasing agricultural production.

The absence of a comprehensive reform strategy, the eclectic character
of economic policy and the gradualism of change have been noted and
often criticised by foreign observers from time to time over the past three
decades. Over the first two decades, China was a "neither this nor that
economy", a "mixture of half-plan, half-market; pretend-socialism,
pretend-capitalism" (Prybla, 1986). Raby (2001) noted the aptness of this
description but also remarked upon the functional strengths of this approach
to development strategy.

The absence of a comprehensive blueprint was inevitable in China's
circumstances, and the associated flexibility in response to changing
circumstance and opportunity a virtue in practice.

It was inevitable because there was no conceptual basis for a market-
oriented economy in China in the 1980s. A few leaders, and a few
intellectuals involved in the policy process, Du Runsheng the most
important amongst them, had understood the power of the market in
economic development from experience in the liberated areas before 1949,
from experience in socialist China before the push to state and collective
ownership in the late fifties, and from the high-growth interregnum of the
early 1960s between the Great Leap Forward and the Cultural Revolution.
Some had drawn lessons from observation of the powerful experiences of
other East Asian economies, including those of Chinese communities in
Hong Kong and Taiwan. But the main understanding followed the
commencement of reform, emerging from observation of the new pattern
of Chinese development and increasing contact with foreign experience and

ideas.

The absence of a blueprint was a virtue because any theoretical model of reform of the centrally planned economy in China would have been deeply flawed. The international economics profession knows much more clearly now, after the end of socialism in Eastern Europe more than a decade later, than it did at the beginning of Chinese reform, that the rapid unwinding of a centrally planned economy is fraught with risk of massive dislocation. A blueprint that won the plaudits of the international economics profession in 1978 would have been as ill-judged and as dangerous as the advice presented to Russia and Eastern Europe after the collapse of the former Soviet Union.

Some of the great sources of strength of the Chinese economy in the era of reform came as surprises to Chinese and foreign observers alike. These would have been given an inadequate place in a program of reform built upon received theory and the experience of others. First amongst the surprises was the ease and speed of successive ownership transformations: the emergence of the household responsibility system in agriculture in the early 1980s; the extraordinary dynamism and scale of activity within the township and village enterprises which grew from the remnants of the disintegrating People's Communes; and the growth to dominance of private ownership in the late 1990s and early twenty-first century. Neither the business forms nor the sequence and timing of their adoption and eclipse would have been prescribed in a blueprint inspired by received wisdom.

Deng Xiaoping used to describe economic reform in China as crossing the river by feeling for stones at each step. General Secretary Hu Yaobang in late 1986 described reform in a letter to Australian Prime Minister Bob Hawke as an "experiment without precedent". In the uncertain months after the dismissal of Hu Yaobang from his office as General Secretary in January 1987, Deng Xiaoping alluded uncharacteristically to the Chinese classics. He compared the path of reform to the mission of Guan Yu, who had to cross five passes and cut down six generals to achieve his noble objective.

These metaphors contain important insights. Chinese reform required transformation in ideology, in ideas about policy, in law and regulatory systems and in economic institutions. Above all, it required the accumulation of new knowledge in Chinese minds, as the Chinese people learned to do new things, and old things in different ways, in an economic and social world that was fundamentally changed.

These transformations in ideology, ideas, knowledge, policy, institutions, law, and experience occurred alongside each other. They reinforced each other, until new ways of interpreting the world around had formed and been rendered coherent within Chinese minds.

At some time in the third decade of growth, China ceased to be a "neither this nor that economy". It had become a large market economy. Deep integration into international trade and investment had been reinforced by acceptance of far-reaching commitments on entry to the World Trade Organisation in November 2001. The considerable remaining limits on the use of markets were similar in extent and kind to those in many market economies across the world, shaped by the usual anxieties and realities of a market economy, and by political economy constraints with no public policy purpose. The East Asian financial crisis had made China cautious about the extent and speed of external financial liberalisation. This provided inoculation from contagion out of the United States-led financial crisis of 2007—2008. While there was a genuflection to socialism—or reluctance to surrender major areas of patronage and control—in the reluctance to cut the final strands of state control from the large businesses in heavy industry and financial services, the growth in business ownership was increasingly and overwhelmingly private.

Three Crises

The first decennial crisis saw the largest departure from strong growth of the reform era so far and was the most threatening to continued reform and sustained growth. It began as the most virulent of the periodic inflationary episodes, with rapid monetary expansion driven by apparently insatiable investment demand from state-owned enterprises. There were no market-based mechanisms for constraining credit growth. Partial liberalisation of prices within the dual price system was creating opportunities for arbitrage between controlled and free markets, and opportunities for public officials to raise private incomes through the arbitrage. Within the dual price system, shortages of materials led to exaggerated price increases in the free markets.

Concerns about inflation and corruption through the early months of

1989 melded with expressions of wider political concerns. The major reconstruction of the senior personnel of Party and State in early June led to a period of political and economic retrenchment. The Western reaction to events in Tiananmen interacted with domestic political developments and contributed to the strongest doubts within the wider political leadership about reform of the three decades.

The economic retrenchment was secured through reimposition of direct central controls on investment by state enterprises and on other expenditures. This ended inflation, but at high cost to efficiency, growth and reform momentum.

This was the one period during which reform was suspended and in doubt. That it was followed by recommitment to acceleration of reform and internationalisation of the economy, alongside the maintenance of political stability through the coercive powers of the state, was determined by Deng Xiaoping himself. The outcome was not endogenous to the process of reform and growth.

This first decennial crisis was overwhelmingly domestic in origin, although its political manifestations developed foreign dimensions. The second and third were apparently entirely foreign in origin, although we will need to examine whether China contributed to the current crisis.

The Asian financial crisis began with speculative pressure against the Thai baht in May and June 1997. By July there was irresistible capital outflow, and there was massive baht devaluation within a new floating exchange rate regime. Over the next six months, the contagion forced reversals of immense capital inflows into immense outflows. The consequence was a collapse of values in all financial asset markets, currency depreciation, and shrinkage of domestic investment and then economic activity in one after another of the market economies of East Asia.

China's fixed exchange rate against the United States dollar meant that the falls in other East Asian currencies generated large real appreciation of the RMB. This coincided with reduced domestic demand in China's major trading partners. Exports fell to East Asia and stopped growing to the world as a whole. Direct foreign investment fell in China. Speculative capital outflow became important in both Hong Kong and the mainland of China, despite the inhibiting influence of controls on the capital account of the balance of payments. The Chinese currency came under strong pressure for devaluation.

China adopted a bold response to the crisis all around it. The Chinese authorities took two risky decisions. They decided to defend the value of the yuan against the United States dollar. And they decided to seek to maintain rapid economic growth—depressed by the cessation of export growth and the decline in direct foreign investment—through strong fiscal expansion.

The decisions were risky in relation to the exchange rate for two reasons. First, no one could be sure that the authorities could indefinitely resist the pressures for currency depreciation. It would depend on how long the crisis remained and how deep it became elsewhere in East Asia. Second, the large real appreciation that was occurring against all other East Asian currencies except the US-pegged Hong Kong dollar were increasing the recessionary pressure on Chinese economic activity, and this could not be sustained indefinitely if domestic sources of demand growth continued to decline.

The holding of the dollar peg seemed to contradict a lesson of crisis elsewhere in East Asia, that rigid exchange rates increased the risks of crisis because sooner or later they would need to be abandoned, and late abandonment increased the inevitable eventual adjustment costs. The financial collapses elsewhere in East Asia were partly a reflection of structural weakness in financial institutions and governance, and Chinese banks and their governance seemed to be as weak as any.

The fiscal expansion exacerbated pressures on the exchange rate and brought forward the day when the authorities might have to yield on the currency peg. The whole strategy depended on the judgement that financial stabilisation and growth would return to East Asia before China was forced by external financial pressures and decline in domestic growth to abandon either fiscal expansion or the fixed exchange rate.

The Chinese "Keynesian" strategy through the East Asian financial crisis had a chance of working because China entered the crisis in a strong macro-economic position, with low inflation, high growth momentum in exports, investment and output, and reasonably large external reserves. That it worked in reality owed much to good judgement and to the steadiness of policy and its articulation. That in turn depended on what in retrospect was a remarkable period of leadership stability, built around Jiang

Zemin as General Secretary and Zhu Rongji as Premier.

China avoided becoming part of the East Asian crisis, and its strategy helped to shorten the crisis elsewhere.

The East Asian financial crisis left a legacy of Chinese confidence in the country's capacity to maintain growth through adverse external circumstances that is important in 2008. It also entrenched the role of state-owned businesses in heavy industry, including mining, minerals and energy processing, transport and communications, and the financial sector, and indirectly to the huge surplus savings of the early twenty-first century.

Like the second, the third crisis of the reform period had external origins. Or mainly external: near its heart are all of the causes of the massive current payments imbalances between the United States and East Asia in which Chinese patterns of savings have played a part.

At first sight, the current financial crisis looks like a global version of the East Asian financial crisis. China has entered this crisis in a much stronger external payments and reserves position than it had in 1998, so can implement a massive fiscal expansion with a firm exchange rate with greater confidence than in 1998.

Having severed the rigid link between the yuan and the United States dollar in July 2005, and appreciated from 8.3 to less than 6.8 yuan to the dollar over two years or so, the Chinese authorities no longer have an established peg to defend. The yuan value in US dollars is now slightly below the peak. China is in a better position to sustain a growth-oriented strategy based on fiscal expansion of any dimension through the current crisis than it was at an equivalent stage of the financial crisis. The focus on expanded public expenditure on development of rural and inland regions in recent official policy statements, including by General Secretary Hu Jintao and Premier Wen Jiabao, suggest a better developed base for productive fiscal expansion than was present in 1998.

At first sight, the global financial crisis of 2008 calls for a larger version of the strategic response of 1998. At first sight, China is in a position to follow that approach with less risk than a decade earlier.

Deeper down, this global crisis has some more difficult dimensions affecting China's policy. The 2008 global financial crisis may end up having a much larger impact on the Chinese economy, sustained for longer, than the Asian financial crisis.

While it is early days, and the early, vigorous and concerted policy action by many countries will have beneficial effects, it is likely that the weighted average downturn in China's export markets will be even greater than the decline of export growth to zero in the late 1990s. It may be much greater.

The export share of the Chinese economy is now much larger: a downturn in exports has greater leverage over Chinese growth.

China is now a much more market-oriented economy. It is subject to greater fluctuations through the ebb and flow of private business sentiment. Many of its enterprises and state investment vehicles, even those which are majority-owned by the state, have lost large amounts of capital in the collapse of United States and other financial institutions and asset values. Their behaviour will be affected more than the loss of financial capacity alone would suggest.

For all of these reasons, China will have to sustain larger fiscal expansion for longer through the current crisis than it did through the Asian financial crisis, if it is to maintain strong growth in output. It will need all of the increase in capacity that is provided by a degree of exchange rate flexibility, huge foreign exchange reserves and current account surplus at the starting point, and the policy confidence that comes from having done something like it successfully once before.

There is one other issue, arising from China's much larger role in the global economy in 2008. China represents now a high proportion of global savings, and a higher proportion still of the pool of surplus savings over domestic investment that is available for international investment. There is a sense in which the huge flow of surplus savings from China to the United States has funded the near-zero interest rates, the household and public budget deficits and more generally the financial imbalances that have been the source of the contemporary crisis.

The correction of the domestic recessionary pressures in China through massive domestic demand expansion will reduce the amount of surplus savings available for international investment. Something similar will be happening in other East Asian surplus economies. This will coincide with the reductions in surpluses in oil exporting countries deriving from large falls in the oil price.

The total pool of global savings could diminish to an extent that has material effects on global real interest rates. This would be offset for a while by lower investment rates in recession or lower growth in many countries. It would become more important as recovery gets under way and investment rises. In these circumstances, permanently lower Chinese surplus savings could, in the absence of corresponding structural change in America behaviour to raise the rate of savings and reduce the current account deficit, contribute to early increases in the real global interest rate. The subsequent recovery could be weaker and shorter than might be anticipated from historical experience. We all have a strong interest in the changes in United States official and household savings behaviour that could avoid this outcome.

The Crises That Didn't Happen

The crises that didn't happen through the reform period are just as important and just as interesting.

The scale and the unusual institutional setting of Chinese reform and growth have stretched Chinese and foreign capacities for comprehension. The unfamiliar settings have always seemed to threaten the continuation of market-oriented reform and growth. The perceptions of threat have sometimes related to challenges of ideology and policy, sometimes of political resistance to change, and sometimes prosaic problems of economic management in a rapidly growing and changing economy.

In the first decade after 1978, there was widespread incredulity about the continuation of market-oriented reform beyond each step as it was revealed. Often the successful steps were revealed after they had been successfully implemented in many places. Sometimes the successful steps evolved independently of policy, so that their absorption into development strategy took the form of pragmatic acceptance of fait accompli.

In that first decade of reform, I recall the confidence with which commentators announced that the residual role of ideology would block the emergence of a labour market in China. That barrier to the emergence of a market economy melted away when the melting served an essential development purpose. There was confident expectation that the limits to ownership reform of enterprises would eventually constrain growth. Rural Chinese ingenuity flowed around the blockage, and a new form of collective ownership, the township and village enterprise, was observed to be playing a crucial role in the industrialisation of the countryside. It was

not long before flaws in the institutional structures of township and village
enterprises were being held up as a reason why the rapid growth to which
they were contributing exceptionally would come to an end. Before that
end came, the large-scale removal of "red hats" revealed a transformation in
favour of private ownership.

I recall the confident pronouncements that it would be politically
impossible to unwind the cradle-to-grave protections associated with
employment in state enterprises, or to substantially liberalise foreign trade in
agricultural products, or to rely mainly on international markets for important
industrial raw materials. Here the confidence was based on the experience
of other countries, supported by knowledge of a Chinese reality. As it
turned out, the constraints were removed when the economic value of
doing so became large enough.

The more prosaic barriers to continued economic growth had been
daunting in the first decade of reform. There were long debates about
whether it was better first to change the basis of price formation, or to
change enterprise ownership and control. Successful urban reform required
both, but there were many barriers to doing them together, and to start
with either one raised many difficult issues of economic stability. The
outcome was inelegant, pragmatic and for a while destabilising.

The problem of macro-economic stabilisation policy in a partially
reformed economy was especially difficult. How to control monetary
expansion when major enterprises still had state-like command over financial
resources, but were less and less under the control of the central monetary
authorities? The increasing amplitude of successive business cycles through
the reform period raised doubts about the longevity of strong growth.

All of these ideological and policy, political and economic management
challenges to reform and growth came together in the inflationary and then
political crisis of 1988—1989.

The crises that didn't end reform and growth over the second decade
1988—1998, were increasingly of conventional economic and political
kinds, familiar from development experience in many contexts. The slump
in economic growth in 1989 and 1990 ended the raging inflation that had
emerged in 1988. It did this partly by slowing greatly for a while domestic
and foreign interest in Chinese investment. To the extent that the deflation
was engineered by the authorities, it was through the application of crude

controls on expenditure and especially investment by state-owned enterprises. These controls had all of the costs to growth of resource allocation within the planned economy. Deng's declaration in 1991 that reform and opening to the outside world were to accelerate and expand unleashed a new and virulent inflationary episode. The Deng boom coincided at first with the developed country recession of 1991—1992. The China boom of the early 1990s eased the impact of OECD recession on growth in smaller East Asian economies—the first of several episodes in which Chinese expansion offset the East Asian growth impacts of downturns in economic activity elsewhere.

This was the decade in which the ownership issues were resolved in favour of widespread private roles, with state-owned enterprises remaining prominent in heavy industry and the financial sector. It was the decade in which critical decisions were taken on deepening Chinese integration into the international economy, with commitments being made to secure membership of the World Trade Organisation. It was the decade in which the increasing amplitude of the business cycle was tamed, with more effective discipline on bank lending and the development of more sophisticated instruments for financial management.

The second reform decade ended with the uncertainty of the East Asian financial crisis.

At the time of the twentieth anniversary of the Third Plenum, the risks that China would become a victim of the crisis were high.

The downturn during the financial crisis left a heavy shadow. Growth, while remaining high by the standards of the rest of the world, around 7%, was lower than in any other part of the reform period except 1989—1990. Huge and sustained fiscal expansion left the state much larger than the leaders of reform had judged to be desirable. Much expenditure was allocated poorly for growth. Part of the growth in output found its way into huge stocks of unwanted goods, leading to cynicism about the reality of growth performance.

This macro-economic episode and the strategic response to it left lingering concerns about the quality of the financial system, and questions about whether its evident weaknesses would one day generate China's own financial crisis. Now, with the global financial system in crisis, China is vulnerable from the weaknesses of Western financial institutions that have invested in its own institutions.

Throughout the reform era, there has been a persistent question about whether the Chinese political system would change enough and sufficiently fast to accommodate the immense changes in the society and economy that inevitably accompany economic expansion and structural change. There has been a persistent question about whether the Chinese political system would change enough and fast enough to maintain political stability.

Chinese reform governments have not responded to pressures for political change along lines suggested by conventional Western analysis. There have nevertheless been responses. In the third decade of reform, they have included changes in governance arrangements at a local level, and more overt concern for development in poor regions and for incomes and living standards amongst people who were not early beneficiaries of the growth process. Through the third decade of reform, disruption of growth as a result of political unrest is another crisis that has not happened. At least, not yet.

▪ Where is Growth Going and Where Will It End

China's reform and development have a long way to go, but the directions are clearer to Chinese and to foreigners than ever before. At the beginning of reform, few spoke of the end point being an economy with living standards in the range of the countries that were then developed. The numbers were too large to contemplate. That would mean the addition to global output of an amount well in excess of the sum of production in all of the developed and transitional economies together. This would place great strain on every world market, producing the goods and services in which Chinese resources were deficient, and in which China had or would develop international comparative advantage. It would place great strain on the Chinese and global physical environments.

In 1986, I asked Deng Xiaoping where growth would have taken China by the middle of the twenty-first century. He said that by the middle of what was then the next century, the Chinese people would enjoy average living standards comparable with those of the newly industrialised economies of Asia at the time of our conversation. He added that he hoped that the Chinese people would be satisfied by that.

It is now clear that the only resting place for rapid growth is Chinese living standards and per capita output and consumption that are close to the global frontiers. At that place, China's people will have demanded and received the quantum of security against poverty and in other ways that is usual in advanced industrial societies. At that resting place, China will be contributing more or less its proportionate population share of the developed world's ideas and productive innovation—which itself requires considerable political liberalisation. It will be generating more or less its proportionate share of the developed world's environment hazards, including greenhouse gases. At that time, there is no prospect of being a successful international community unless China is producing more or less its proportionate share of global public goods, including leadership of economic and environmental stabilisation, and peace and good order.

Increasingly, the new agenda of Chinese government under the twenty-first century leadership of Hu Jintao and Wen Jiabao has involved the spreading of Chinese growth into areas and amongst people that been only slightly touched by its beneficent processes.

Increasingly, the new agenda has involved China playing a larger role in leadership of the global economic and political systems. There is an inevitable lag between the reality of the expansion of China's weight in the global community, and domestic and international recognition of that weight. Successful management of all of the international challenges of the early twenty-first century requires us all to shorten that lag, because there will be no provision of the international public goods that are necessary for sustainable growth, peace and environmental amenity without Chinese leadership playing a major role.

▪ How China Has Changed Perceptions of Global Development

There is one overarching lesson for global development from the success of thirty years of Chinese reform. The beneficent processes of modern economic growth that began in Western Europe, its offshore settlements and Japan in the nineteenth century, and which spread to small East Asian economies in the third quarter of the twentieth century, are available for much of humanity. They are not restricted to a small proportion of people, with narrowly particular histories and cultural backgrounds. Chinese success more than doubled the beneficiaries of sustained, rapid, internationally-oriented modern economic growth. It has since been followed by success in other populous countries, whose experience together with that of China suggests that the necessary conditions for growth can be met in many economies in many cultural and historical circumstances.

The Chinese experience confirms old knowledge about the necessary conditions for sustained modern economic growth. Sustained rapid growth requires widespread acceptance in the community that economic growth and the associated rise in living standards has primacy amongst policy objectives. Economic growth is disruptive. It changes the distribution of income and wealth, transforms basic institutions and churns elites. All of this generates resistance, and no government will want to confront resistance unless there is broadly based support for change within society. Even where there is sufficiently widespread political support, there must be an effective state, capable of applying growth-oriented policies against the inevitable resistance from the many interests that believe that they are damaged by them.

Sustained rapid growth requires a large role for markets in the allocation of resources and the distribution of incomes. This is necessary for efficiency in resource allocation and also for flexibility in resource use in response to changes in the economic value of various activities, including in response to economic growth itself. The demands on flexibility increase as incomes rise, and economic activity becomes more complex.

Sustained rapid growth requires a high degree of international orientation in markets for goods, services, capital, technology and ideas. Again, this requirement expands with the complexity of the economy as incomes grow.

Sustained economic growth requires high levels of investment. For this to provide a stable basis for long-term growth, it needs to be supported by high rates of domestic savings. The experience of many countries, now including China and India, is that high savings rates are to a considerable extent endogenous to sustained rapid growth, so that this becomes an easier condition to meet once strong growth that has been established.

Education—investment in human knowledge and skills—is a necessary component in the high levels of investment. This becomes a more and more critical condition as incomes rise in the process of growth.

One piece of good news from the Chinese and other experience, is that rapid growth is reasonably tolerant of imperfect provision of its necessary conditions. If the conditions are present in reasonable degree, strong results can be achieved.

These are the general lessons of the Chinese experience with reform and growth, when Chinese reality is read alongside the successful development outcomes of others, earlier and later. There are some more specific lessons.

One specific lesson from Chinese experience is that there are advantages in starting reform and growth from agriculture and more generally from the countryside. The wide dispersion of the benefits of growth that came with the early success of agriculture galvanised political support for market-oriented reform. Here the outstanding contrast is with India, where the apparent exclusion of agricultural communities from the benefits of accelerated growth has been an important focus of political resistance. The large early gains in agriculture also laid the basis for the industrialisation of the countryside of coastal China, which itself had many advantages for sustained rapid growth in the country as a whole.

A second specific lesson is a corollary to the general lesson confirming the importance of free trade. Chinese experience reveals that rapid, internationally-oriented growth is possible in a big country. The General Secretary of the Chinese Communist Party, Zhao Ziyang, began to articulate the "coastal strategy" in 1987, based on growth in exports of labour-intensive products from the coastal provinces. One reaction of some Western economists was to say that China cannot be an export-oriented economy on the pattern of Taiwan, South Korea, Hong Kong and Singapore. China was too big. It would turn the terms of trade against itself. The requirements of structural change in importing countries would generate unmanageable protectionist reactions.

We now know that China was not too big for export expansion, and the associated opportunities associated with specialisation according to comparative advantage, to play major roles in development. To be sure, Chinese export prices fell relative to imports—to the great advantage of countries, like many developing countries and like my own, whose comparative advantage in foreign trade was complementary to that of

China's. But the loss in the terms of trade was small compared with increased gains from more efficient resource allocation and related dynamic advantages. To be sure, there were protectionist reactions—but not so large as to block rapid expansion of total Chinese exports over the next twenty years. To be sure, to sustain rapid export growth, China had to diversify exports into more capital-intensive and technologically more sophisticated products at an earlier stage of development than had been the case in the smaller East Asian countries which had followed strategies of export-oriented growth.

But China was not too big. The lesson here is a strong one. If China is not too big for an internationally-oriented growth strategy with strong initial specialisation in line with comparative advantage on exports of labour-intensive products, neither is India, nor Indonesia, nor any other developing country.

A third specific lesson is that there are advantages in gradual change. This is an important insight from the analysis of Lin and his colleagues at the China Center for Economic Research (Lin, 2007, 2008). This is an important antidote to mistaken views of influential parts of the Western economics profession. Many foreign analysts have underestimated the importance of institutions in economic development, and the inevitably gradual nature of successful institutional change. The development of the institutional basis of a market economy in particular, with its requirements of education, accretion of new cultural norms, and the development of regulatory frameworks and the people to manage them, takes time. Chinese reform gradualism gave them time.

There are two closely related lessons related to reform culture. One is to give a major role to experiment. There are many inevitable risks in reform. These can be reduced by proceeding in moderate steps, expanding on reform measures that have been successful. This helps to build confidence in the reform process, and avoids periodic setbacks when large steps have surprising and adverse consequences. A second is to take steps towards greater use of markets and deeper integration into international markets when you can, and not to wait until ideal circumstances have emerged. It is a lesson of Chinese development experience that you can get a long way on the good. There is no need to make the best the enemy of the good.

Post-Socialism Revisited: Reflections on "Socialism with Chinese Characteristics", Its Past, Present and Future

Arif Dirlik [*]

On this occasion of the sixtieth anniversary of the founding of the People's Republic of China(also the thirtieth anniversary of "Reform and Opening"), I would like to reflect on some issues I raised in an essay published two decades ago, "Postsocialism? Reflections on Socialism with Chinese Characteristics"[1]. That essay was written in the midst of uncertainties concerning both socialism and the future of the PRC. The present is also a time of uncertainty, this time concerning the future of the capitalist world-system, as well as of the PRC which is now an integral part of that system, but with continued insistence on commitment to a socialist future. In 1989, socialism appeared as a residue of a fading past. China's integration into a globalizing capitalist economy over the last two decades demanded the erasure of the last residues of an earlier revolutionary socialism, making official claims to socialism less convincing than ever before. With "capitalism in ruins", as a recent newspaper headline put it, those claims need to be reconsidered—especially for the historical experience that continues to

---

[*] Arif Dirlik is a historian most known for his works about 20th century Chinese history. From 1971 to 2001, he stayed as a member of the History faculty at Duke University. In 2001, he moved to the University of Oregon as Knight Professor of History and Anthropology where also was appointed Director of the Center for Critical Theory and Transnational Studies. He retired from Oregon in 2006. He was a Visiting Professor in Summer 2006 at the Central Bureau for Compilation and Translation in Beijing, a Senior Fellow at the International Institute for Asian Studies in the Netherlands, and Distinguished Visiting Professor at the Peter Wall Institute for Advanced Studies at the University of British Columbia.

The author is grateful to Olivia Bina, Ann Huss, Roxann Prazniak, QS Tong, and Aihe Wang for taking the time to read and comment on this essay. They are not responsible in any way for the views expressed here.

[1] Arif Dirlik, "Postsocialism? Reflections on Socialism with Chinese Characteristics", in Arif Dirlik and Maurice Meisner (ed.), *Marxism and the Chinese Experience*, Armonk, NY: M. E. Sharpe, 1989, pp. 362 – 384.

inform them despite the repudiation of the revolutionary past, and for the important part past legacies may have to play in confronting challenges thrown up by the current crisis. Postsocialism offers a fruitful point of departure for such reconsideration.

▪ Postsocialism

"Postsocialism" was written in response to simplistic (and ideological) readings of "reform and opening" in the 1980s: predictions of imminent restoration of capitalism, on the one hand, and an unproblematic affirmation of socialism, on the other hand. Opponents of socialism hailed Deng Xiaoping as a revolutionary leader who was prepared to return China to the capitalist path. Friends of Chinese socialism, ready to follow whatever line the leadership proposed, pretended that despite its repudiation of the revolutionary past, "reform and opening" did not imply any significant retreat from socialism.

In my reading at the time, "reform and opening" signaled the end of the revolution, and reopened the question of socialism with regard both to goals and the strategy of achieving them. The years 1956—1978(from the Eighth Party Congress to the end of the Cultural Revolution) witnessed a failed revolutionary attempt to secure the transition to socialism. In its economic and political policies, "reform and opening" was reminiscent of the policies of New Democracy that had brought the Communist Party to power, and guided the changes of the initial years of the People's Republic. But those policies acquired a new significance with the abandonment of hope in revolutionary transition to socialism, and required reorientation in response to changes in the world situation. In short, they required rethinking of socialism. The Cultural Revolution had been inspired in part by the rethinking of Soviet-style socialism. This time around, it was the Chinese revolutionary experience with socialism that required rethinking, reopening the whole question of socialism. Any reading of the situation in the 1980s had to take this rethinking as its point of departure.

"Postsocialism" represented a conceptual effort at grasping this situation. It was informed by... a historical situation where (a) socialism has lost its coherence as a metatheory of politics because of the attenuation of the socialist vision in its historical unfolding; partly because of a perceived need on the part of socialist states to articulate "actually existing socialism" to the demands of a capitalist world order, but also because of the vernacularization of socialism in its absorption into different national contexts;

(b) the articulation of socialism to capitalism is conditioned by the structure of "actually existing socialism" in any particular context which is the historical premise of all such articulation; and (c) this premise stands guard over the process of articulation to ensure that it does not result in the restoration of capitalism. Postsocialism is of necessity also postcapitalist, not in the classical Marxist sense of socialism as a phase in historical development that is anterior to capitalism, but in the sense of a socialism that represents a response to the experience of capitalism and an attempt to overcome the deficiencies of capitalist development. Its own deficiencies and efforts to correct them by resorting to capitalist methods of development are conditioned by this awareness of the deficiencies of capitalism in history. Hence postsocialism seeks to avoid a return to capitalism, no matter how much it may draw upon the latter to improve the performance of "actually existing socialism". For this reason, and also to legitimize the structure of "actually existing socialism", it strives to keep alive a vague vision of future socialism as the common goal of humankind while denying to it any immanent role in the determination of present social policy. [2]

The "post" in the term postsocialist carried two meanings, referring to the ambiguities in the situation: "Chinese society today is postsocialist because its claims to a socialist future no longer derive their force from socialism as an immanent idea. On the other hand, it is also postsocialist because socialism, as its structural context, remains as a possible option to which it can return if circumstances so demand (this is what distinguishes it from a capitalist or even a postcapitalist society where such options as collectivization, socially, and a socialist culture, ideologically, are foreclosed). "[3] To stress the capitalist elements and assume that China must develop into a capitalist society would be erroneous "because it remains to be seen what the incorporation of socialist systems into the capitalist world order will imply for capitalism itself"[4]. Rather than signaling the end of socialism, "postsocialism" offered "the possibility in the midst of a crisis in socialism of rethinking socialism in new, more creative ways... Freed of the

---

2 Ibid. , p. 231.
3 Ibid. , p. 244.
4 Ibid. , p. 246.

commitment to…. an inexorable future, socialism may be conceived in a new way: as a [re] source for imagining future possibilities that derive their inspiration not from a congealed utopia, which postpones to the future problems that await resolution today, but from the impulses to liberation that represent present responses to problems of oppression and inequality"[5].

▪ China and Global Capitalism

Two decades later, there is seemingly greater clarity over the status of socialism in the PRC. The economy has experienced enormous growth. While the PRC has resisted neoliberal policies emanating from the US, its contribution to the global economy has done much to legitimize those policies. The consequence of integration into the global economy, economic development has made China into a major force and advocate of globalization. China has become the strategic center of the "global factory" that produces the commodities consumed globally, above all in the centers of global capitalism. It has emerged as a major player in the global economy to the point where many look to it to save the global economy from the crisis brought about by irresponsible neo-liberal policies. Predictions abound as to its recovering the position once held by imperial China during the Ming Dynasty as the focal point of global economic activity.[6] Economic power has brought with it political inclusion in the councils capital. Those who would manage the capitalist world economy no longer can afford to ignore the counsel of Chinese leaders and, reluctantly or not, make room for their voices in any serious consideration of the world's problems.

The globalization of the Chinese economy also has produced significant social changes. Cities such as Guangzhou, Shanghai and Beijing have joined the urban hubs of the global economy. Chinese society has been integrated with societies elsewhere through the motions of its citizens and cultural products, not least through the interactive possibilities offered by

---

5 Ibid. , p. 247. This reconceptualization of socialism bears a close resemblance to a statement by the Indian Marxist Aijaz Ahmad shortly after the fall of the Soviet Union that "socialism is the determinate name for [the] negation of capitalism's fundamental systemic contradictions and cruelties, and the necessity of this negation will remain, regardless of the fate of the Soviet Union as such". Aijaz Ahmad, *In Theory: Classes, Nations, Literatures*, London: Verso, 1992, p. 316.

6 I am referring here to such works as Andre Gunder Frank, *Re-Orient: Global Economy in the Asian Age*, Berkeley, CA: University of California Press, 1998, and Giovanni Arrighi, *Adam Smith in Beijing: Lineages of the 21st Century*, London: Verso, 2007.

the new communications and information technologies. The standard of living of the population as a whole has gone up significantly. Economic development has created a new entrepreneurial class that is active not just in China but globally. A growing urban middle class has joined its counterparts elsewhere as a consumer of material and cultural commodities. Significant portions of rural society have risen above official thresholds of poverty as they venture out of agrarian into other forms of economic activity. Any visitor to China is likely to be impressed by the social vitality and restlessness against which older centers of capitalism appear as quaint and sleepy residues of development gone dormant. Chinese society is no longer merely a recipient of Euro/American cultural and intellectual products, but a consumer of global exotica, as well as a major exporter of cultural artifacts of its own. As it flexes its muscles in expression of newfound political and military power, it seeks also to demonstrate its "soft power" in the global projection of native ideologies and culture, including language.

The issue of culture is especially pertinent to the question of socialism. In the midst of economic and cultural (and to some extent, social) globalization, the last two decades also have witnessed a revival of cultural traditions, most notably Confucianism, that the Chinese Revolution sought to sweep into the proverbial "dustbin of history" for nearly a century. The vocabulary of Confucianism has infused the language of socialism, Confucianism has been officially sanctioned as a marker of Chinese identity, and it is under the cover of Confucianism, not socialism, that Chinese "soft power" is projected globally ("Confucius Institutes"). Social and cultural globalization, ironically, has been accompanied at the popular level by a turn to things "Chinese" that in their very consumption nourish cultural nativism. The pursuit of TOEFL, ironically, goes hand in hand with a stubborn insistence on loyalty to a past that the revolution had sought to overcome, if not to erase.

Yet, despite this evidence of economic, social, cultural and ideological incorporation in global capitalism, or nativistic revivals at the official and the popular level, fundamental ambiguities remain in the Communist self-image, and images of China's relationship to the world both within and without the PRC. The Communist Party refuses to let go of its socialist commitments, or the ideological legacy of the revolution, which now includes Deng Xiaoping's legacy of "reform and opening", as enshrined in the slogan, "Marxism-Leninism, Mao Zedong Thought, Deng Xiaoping

Theory". This self-image in practice is at least partly responsible for the ambivalent relationship to the capitalist world. In spite of the powerful position the PRC holds in the contemporary global economy, it is possible to argue that it is at once inside and outside that economy: inside as a major player within it, outside in its insistence on keeping capitalism at arm's length(which is reciprocated by continued suspicion of the PRC among major capitalist powers). And so it is with regard to the Global South. The Chinese revolution all along had a double character as a socialist revolution and as a national liberation struggle of a country suffering from semi-colonial domination, which gave it a sense of kinship with the Third World. This ambiguity persists presently in the status of the PRC as a developing country which nevertheless has come to hold a powerful position vis-à-vis developed capitalist societies. This double identity accounts for both a sense of kinship with the Global South (the earlier Third World) and suspicions of imperialist exploitation of the South's resources(see below for further discussion).

Given these ambiguities, there is much to be gained from thinking of China as a postsocialist, rather than simply a socialist, capitalist or neo-Confucian society. The leadership's insistence on its socialism may be dismissed as political expediency, as the Communist Party ultimately derives its legitimacy from the revolution that brought it to power. What endows the claims with plausibility lies elsewhere: in their readiness to draw upon the legacies of the socialist revolution that distinguishes their response to contemporary challenges from leaders elsewhere. Those legacies, moreover, need to be understood not in terms of a generic socialism that lends itself to an unchanging definition regardless of time and place, but as an idea that needs to be reworked in response to concrete historical circumstances, in this case, the century-long revolutionary process in China which was informed by a socialist vision but also has repeatedly redefined both the vision, and the means for its realization.

Socialism as it was understood earlier, even in the ambivalent days of Deng Xiaoping, may be over, but it would be a mistake to assume therefore that its legacies are no longer alive. I am not referring here simply to the perpetuation of a centralized, closely regulated economy, which might distinguish this socialism from neo-liberal fantasies about unregulated market economy, but is not sufficient to endow it with a vision that transcends the horizon of capitalism. By that measure, moreover, the whole world, including the United States, might be said presently to be on the verge of socialism in their response to the crisis created by a permissive neoliberalism, governments worldwide are in haste to regulate the operations of capital, and establish control if not ownership over its institutional apparatus. This obviously does not make any sense, contrary to the protestations of unreconstructed neoliberal utopians to whom any interference in the market represents a move toward socialism.

What is more important is the continued urge to find an alternative to capitalism that has remained alive even as the Chinese economy has been integrated to global capitalism. The persistence of this vision may account for some of the contradictions that puzzle, if not annoy, those who would wish socialism away. It also presents Chinese leaders with challenges as they seek to reconcile the demands of the vision with the practical realities of incorporation in global capitalism.

▪ Revolutionary Legacies

The legacy of the Chinese revolution may be understood in two senses. One sense, the more straightforward one, is that of revolution as a storehouse of values, aspirations and policies that are available for inspiration and example in the formulation of present policy. In this sense, moreover, the revolutionary past is part of a larger past that also includes the imperial and the pre-imperial past in China, as well as non-Chinese histories. In spite of allegations of Chinese close-mindedness, Chinese leaders and thinkers since the twentieth century have been remarkably open to drawing upon different pasts in dealing with problems of the present. This is as true of the present leadership as it was of earliest leaders such as Mao Zedong. That different leaders or thinkers drew upon different pasts is only an indication of different perceptions of contemporary problems, and different aspirations for the future. The demotion of revolutionary history to one past among others implies a retreat from revolution, to be sure, but it suggests neither the denial of revolution nor a conservative escape to a pre-revolutionary Confucian past, as ideologues of Confucianism in and out of China would like to think. Rather, that past is itself viewed now through the lens of revolutionary history. It represents, on the one hand, an affirmation of the pre-revolutionary past against its Eurocentric denials by Chinese and non-Chinese alike. On the other hand, it places that past in the service of aspirations that are very much products of the revolution itself.

The second sense of revolutionary legacy is related to the first but is much more complex, and must remain abstract by its very nature. It refers to a mode of thinking that was the product of the revolutionary process in China, especially the Communist revolution as a protracted guerilla struggle. A guerilla struggle almost by definition involves experimentation with revolution, and one of the most remarkable things about the Communist Revolution in China from the 1930s to the present is its openness to experimentation with policy—from the flexible social and economic policies of the 1930s to the New Democracy of the "long 1940s" to the Great Leap Forward and the Cultural Revolution to "reform and opening" since the 1980s. Mao Zedong—with his openly admitted policies of trial-and-error, and slogans such as "two steps forward, one step backward"— was the "great experimenter", but he was by no means the only one. Deng Xiaoping was equally committed to trying out policies to see what proved to be workable, and so have been his successors. Indeed, this commitment to experimentation has been visible over the years in the trial of policies in a restricted way in certain locations in the country to test their workability before finally deciding on policy shifts. Indeed, it may be plausibly argued that the history of the socialist revolution in China is a history of experimentation with socialism and revolution.

Theoretically speaking, such experimentation was not open-ended but limited by the commonly shared goal of creating a socialist society (inextricably entangled in the goal of a strong China). Except during the height of the Cultural Revolution, however, this goal was not allowed to congeal into a rigid utopia. Stated somewhat differently, in contrast to the religious utopianism of the Cultural Revolution (which also endowed Mao with supernatural qualities), utopianism in the Communist Revolution most of the time has been a secular utopianism, with a future vision to guide the present, but with the present playing an equally important part in the formulation of what the vision might ultimately contain—so long as it retained the basic commitment to national goals of development and independence as filtered through socialist aspirations of equality and justice (or the other way around, depending on ideological priorities).

The relationship between present activity and future goals is ultimately homologous to the relationship between theory and practice in Chinese Marxism, which would find its most articulate expression in Mao Zedong's "sinicization" of Marxism, or making Marxism Chinese: integrating "the universal truths of Marxism with the concrete realities of Chinese society". Regardless of the fate of particular policies associated with Mao at different times, Mao Zedong Thought remains a central component of Communist ideology, partly because it represented not just Mao's thought but the collective experience of the Party, but more importantly because of the continued significance of the impulse that lies at its core: the integration of Marxism with the Chinese experience. For the same reason, I would like to suggest here, the integration of Marxism and the Chinese experience in Mao Zedong Thought offers one important theoretical tool for reading post-Mao ideological transformations.

Mao articulated the philosophical premises of his Marxism in the processand as an integral part of the sinicization of Marxism. His two essays "On practice" and "On Contradiction" were delivered as speeches in July and August 1937 respectively, coinciding with his call for a shift in Communist revolutionary strategy in response to Japan's fullscale invasion of China in July 1937. At its most fundamental level of vernacularization (translating Marxism into a Chinese idiom) , the sinicization of Marxism was a product of revolutionary problems (especially the problem of a Marxist revolution in agrarian China, which theory was illprepared to contain) ; some of the key ingredients that were to go into the making of a "sinicized" Marxism had been enunciated earlier in response to these problems, which were quite independent of the national problem.[7] The national problem as a problem in Marxism was also a subject for intensive discussion in Chinese

---

7 Indeed, some of the earliest and most important discussions on the need to translate Marxism into the language of the masses were provided not by Mao, or Maoists, but by Qu Qiubai, an earlier secretary of the party and a literary theorist. For a discussion of his ideas, see Paul Pickowicz, *Marxist Literary Thought in China: The Influence of Ch'u Ch'iupai*, Berkeley: University of California Press, 1981. A more direct discussion of Qu's (and the party's) efforts to accomplish this through literary means in the early part of the agrarian revolution is to be found in Ellen Judd, "Revolutionary Drama and Song in the Jiangxi Soviet", *Modern China*, Vol. 9, No. 1, January 1983, pp. 127 – 160. Early practice is most readily (and comprehensively) apparent in a recently (1982) published account of a local investigation he conducted in 1930, which has just become available in English. See Mao Zedong, *Report from Xunwu*, ed. with an Introduction by Roger R. Thompson, Stanford, CA: Stanford University Press, 1990. This essay has justified some Chinese authors in carrying Mao's "sinicization" of Marxism past the war years back to 1930. See Shu Riping, "Shinian lai Mao Zedong zhexue sixiang yanjiu shuping"(A Critique of Research on Mao Zedong's Philosophical Thought Over the Last Decade), *Mao Zedong zhexue sixiang yanjiu* (Research in Mao Zedong's Philosophical Thought), No. 5, 1989, pp. 4 – 10...

intellectual circles as early as 1936.[8] Nevertheless, the project of sinicization
was clearly formulated and realized only between 1937 and 1940: there was
a direct line connecting the theoretical formulations of Mao's philosophy in
these two essays and the reasoning underlying the sinicized Marxist strategy
that Mao was to enunciate in his "On New Democracy" in 1940. Eminently
practical and tactical in intention, the two essays nevertheless sought to ground
the problems of the Chinese Revolution within Marxist theory, in the process
offering Mao's fullest and most comprehensive statement on the philosophical
considerations underlying his reformulation of Marxist theory.

The concept of contradiction is central to Mao Zedong Thought. The
centrality the concept assumed in Mao's original presentation was a direct
product of the reformulation of Marxism to account for China's historical
situation, which was defined structurally by the contradictoriness of its various
moments, and the articulation of this contradictoriness as a contradiction
between theory and practice. While the contradiction between national and
social revolutionary needs is the most obvious, the problem went deeper
into the very practice of revolution in a social situation that was not
anticipated in theory: an agrarian society in which a socialist revolution had
to be engineered out of components that theory did not account for; in
which the revolutionaries themselves were outsiders to the social situation
(and, therefore, in contradiction to it). Beyond the level of the national
struggle, it was this social situation that made the "sinicization" of Marxism
into a total theoretical project, and called for the reformulation of theory in
terms of the multitude of contradictions that revolution faced at the level of
practice.

"The law of contradiction in things, that is the law of the unity of
opposites, is the basic law of materialist dialectics."[9] Thus began Mao's

---

8 These discussions were published under the title of *Xian jieduande Zhongguo sixiang yundong*(The
Chinese Thought Movement of the Present), Shanghai: Yiban shudian, 1937.

9 *Selected Works of Mao Tse-tung*(hereafter, SWMTT), 1965—1967, Vol. 1, Beijing: Foreign
Languages Press, p. 311. The parenthetical references in the text will all be to this translation,
pp. 311 – 347. Nick Knight has demonstrated that this text is an edited version of the pre-liberation
text of "On Contradiction" (which contained additional passages which were edited out after
1949), but has not otherwise questioned what is given in this translation. See Nick Knight, "Mao
Zedong's On Contradiction and On Practise: Pre-liberation Texts", *China Quarterly*, No. 84,
1980, pp. 641-668.

discussion of "Contradiction". He continued:

> As opposed to the metaphysical world outlook, the world outlook of materialist
> dialectics holds that in order to understand the development of a thing we should
> study it internally and its relations with other things; in other words, the
> development of things should be seen as their internal and necessary self-
> movement, while each thing in its movement is interrelated with and interacts
> with the things around it. (p. 313)

"On Contradiction" depicts a world (and a mode of grasping it) in which not "things" but relationships are the central data. Such relationships are relationships of mutual opposition as well as transformation, difference as well as identity. These relationships do not coexist haphazardly, moreover, but constitute a totality structured by their many interactions, a totality that is nevertheless in a constant state of transformation because the relationships between the whole and the parts that constitute it, no less than the relationships between the parts, are not merely functional but also (and more importantly) oppositional. The idea of "contradiction" encompasses both functionality and opposition ("unity of opposites"); "contradiction" as a constitutive principle of the world (and the cosmos) produces a totality where everything (the parts no less than the whole) contains everything else, and yet nothing is therefore reducible to anything else. As Mao puts it later on in the essay:

> Since the particular is united with the universal and since the universality as well
> as the particularity of contradiction is inherent in everything, universality
> residing in particularity, we should, when studying an object, try to discover
> both the particular and the universal and their interconnection, to discover both
> particularity and universality and also their interconnections of this object with
> the many objects outside it. (p. 329)

As a philosophical essay, "On contradiction" is devoted to an elaboration of the characteristics of "contradictions" in which these general ideas are embedded. These may be summarized (using Mao's own wording) as follows:

Contradiction is Universal:

> The universality or absoluteness of contradiction has a twofold meaning. One is
> that contradiction exists in the process of development of all things, and the

other is that in the process of development of each thing a movement of
opposites exists from beginning to end…There is nothing that does not contain
contradiction; without contradiction nothing would exist. (p. 316)

Contradiction is also Particular:

Every form of motion contains within itself its own particular contradiction. This
particular contradiction constitutes the particular essence which distinguishes one
thing from another (p. 320) …Only after man knows the particular essence of
many different things can he proceed to generalization and know the common
essence of things. When man attains the knowledge of this common essence, he
uses it as a guide and proceeds to study various concrete things which have not
yet been studied, or studied thoroughly, and to discover the particular essence of
each… Qualitatively different contradictions can only be resolved by qualitatively
different methods (p. 321) … contradictions [in Chinese society] cannot be
treated in the same way since each has its own particularity…We who are
engaged in the Chinese revolution should not only understand the particularity of
these contradictions in their totality, that is, in their interconnectedness, but
should also study the two aspects of each contradiction as the only means of
understanding the totality. (pp. 322 – 323)

Principal Contradiction and the Principal Aspect
of a Contradiction:

There are many contradictions in the process of development of a complex thing,
and one of them is necessarily the principal contradiction whose existence and
development determine or influence the existence and development of the other
contradictions (p. 331)… In any contradiction the development of the contradictory
aspects is uneven (p. 333) … The nature of a thing is determined mainly by the
principal aspect of a contradiction, the aspect which has gained the dominant
position. But this situation is not static; the principal and the nonprincipal
aspects of a contradiction transform themselves into each other and the nature of
things changes accordingly. (p. 333)

Identity and Struggle of the Aspects of a Contradiction:

Identity, unity, coincidence, interpenetration, interpermeation, interdependence
(or mutual dependence for existence), interconnection or mutual cooperation all
these different terms mean the same thing and refer to the following two points:
first, the existence of each of the two aspects of a contradiction in the process of
development of a thing presupposes the existence of the other aspect, and both
aspects coexist in a single entity; second, in given conditions, each of the
contradictory aspects transforms itself into its opposite. (p. 337) How then can

one speak of identity or unity? The fact is that no contradictory aspect can exist in isolation. Without its opposite aspect, each loses the condition for its existence (p. 338) ... the unity of opposites is conditional, temporary and relative, while the struggle of mutually exclusive opposites is absolute. (p. 342)

Antagonism in Contradiction:

Antagonism is one form, but not the only form, of a struggle of opposites. In human history, antagonism between classes exists as a particular manifestation of the struggle of opposites (p. 343) ... Contradiction and struggle are universal and absolute, but the methods of resolving contradictions, that is, the forms of struggle, differ according to the differences in the nature of contradictions. Some contradictions are characterized by open antagonism, others are not. (p. 344)

"On Contradiction" is a revolutionary hermeneutics; an interpretative strategy, in other words, the premise of which is "making revolution". While it is revealing of a life outlook that may include native philosophical elements in addition to Marxism, all these elements are subsumed under, and refracted through, this basic problem.

At one level, it is possible to read the essay simply as a statement in the abstract of specific problems of revolution in the immediate circumstances of Chinese society in 1937. The statements above are interspersed with observations on contemporary developments in China's historical situation that are used in illustration of Mao's various abstractions. [10] A fundamental

---

10　Textual analyses by Schram and Knight have revealed (contrary to earlier opinions) that "On Contradiction" and "On Practice, " along with "Lecture Notes on Dialectical Materialism", were composed in 1936—1937, and together represented "a single intellectual enterprise". Op. cit. , Knight, See also, Stuart Scram, *The Political Thought of Mao Tse*-tung, New York: Praeger Publishers, 1971. Mao's philosophical effort at the time was part of the struggles for leadership within the Communist Party, as an endeavor to demonstrate his qualification for leadership against theoretically much betterinformed opponents. Indeed, Wylie has argued that the "sinicization of Marxism" was a product of organizational struggles against "dogmatists" within the party. See Raymond Wylie, *The Emergence of Maoism: Mao Tse-tung, Ch'en Po-ta and the Search for Chinese Theory, 1937—1945,* Stanford, CA: Stanford University Press, 1980. While this view has much virtue, it needs to be placed within the broader context of the problem of revolution. I focus on the first two essays, because unlike the "Lecture Notes on Dialectical Materialism", which were mainly copied from other sources, "On Contradiction" and "On Practice" represent original contributions by Mao. While these essays were part of an ongoing philosophical effort that preceded Japan's invasion of China, moreover, they were still rooted in practical considerations, and the texts we have are explicitly devoted to the legitimation of change in political policy in response to the "new situation".

goal of the essay is to provide a theoretical justification for change in revolutionary policy in response to the Japanese invasion of China (which shifted the "primary" contradiction from class struggle to national struggle). This also explains why the major part of the essay is devoted to discussion of the "particularity" of contradiction (which includes discussion of primary/secondary contradictions, as well as the discussion of its primary/secondary aspects). It is in the process of this legitimation of change in policy that Mao articulates the priority of practice to theory. As he put it:

> The dogmatists... do not understand that conditions differ in different kinds of revolution and so do not understand that different methods should be used to resolve different contradictions; on the contrary, they invariably adopt what they imagine to be an unalterable formula and arbitrarily apply it everywhere, which only causes setbacks to the revolution or makes a sorry mess of what was originally well done. (p. 322)

In spite of the priority of practical questions in Mao's thinking, however, it would be reductionist to read the essay simply as a discussion of practical questions, and ignore the consequences for theory of Mao's theoretical justification of practice. The French Marxist theorist Louis Althusser grasped the significance of this problem when he wrote of "On Contradiction":

> Mao's essay, inspired by his struggle against dogmatism in the Chinese Party, remains generally *descriptive*, and in consequence it is in certain respects *abstract*. Descriptive: his concepts correspond to concrete experiences. In part abstract: the concepts, though new and rich in promise, are represented as specifications of the *dialectic* in general rather than as *necessary implications* of the Marxist conception of society and history. [11] (italics in the original)

What Althusser tells us is that while Mao's theoretical formulations remain under-theorized, they are nevertheless path-breaking and significant (and are not therefore reducible to descriptive abstractions). The former is evident. While Mao sought in the essay to theorize the particularity of revolutionary practice, he consciously demoted theory: "in the contradiction between theory and practice, practice is the principal aspect" (p. 335).

---

11 Op. cit., Althusser, p. 94n.

This demotion of theory was also to lead to a restatement of the role of theory: Mao conceived of theory primarily as an abstraction of concrete revolutionary practice, and only secondarily as an abstract formulation of "laws" of social movement. Mao did not repudiate theory, or the necessity of understanding it. On one occasion, responding to an imaginary audience which held that those who were "instinctively" dialectical in their activity did not need to read books to understand theory, he reaffirmed the importance of studying theory because, without such study, there was no possibility of synthesizing the multifaceted phenomena that the revolutionary faced. [12] "Without revolutionary theory", he believed with Lenin, "there can be no revolutionary movement. "[13] Indeed, given his revolutionary hermeneutics, theory was to reappear in Mao's thinking as an essential guide to the revolutionary in determining the direction of revolution.

The priority that Mao assigned to practice meant that, unlike Althusser, he was only marginally interested in theorizing his abstract formulations. It is even possible to suggest that "On Contradiction" was only "in part abstract" because Mao's historicism (by which I mean his emphasis on concreteness and particularity) did not allow theorization beyond a certain point. What it did produce was a hermeneutic: revolutionary practice was no longer predictable from theory; rather, the latter became a guide to "reading" historical situations in the activity of making revolution. Mao's appreciation of theory was itself "contradictory" in the double meaning he assigned to it as at once guide and instrument: "guide" in the longterm direction of revolution, "instrument" in immediate analysis. Theory, in other words, was part of the very contradictions that it was intended to unravel and to resolve. This was the key to Mao's restructuring of theory.

The world of "On Contradiction" is a world of ceaseless and endless confrontation and conflict, where unity itself may be understood only in terms of the contradictoriness of its moments, where no entity is a constant because it has no existence outside its contradictions or a place of its own other than in its relationship to other contradictions. It may be that all

---

12 Mao, "Bianzhengfa weiwulun" (Dialectical materialism), in *Mao Zedong ji, Vol. VI,* (Mao Zedong Collection, 10 Vols.), by Takeuchi Minoru ed. , Hong Kong: Bowen Book Co. , 1976, pp. 265 – 305, 302 – 303.
13 Mao quotes Lenin in both essays. See *SWMTT, Vol. I,* p. 304, 336.

Marxism is a conflictbased conceptualization of the world. But however differently Marxists may have structured conflict or organized the structure of society, conflict in most interpretations of Marxism is conceived of in terms of a limited number of social categories (production, relations of production, politics, ideology, etc.), and there has been an urge to hierarchize these categories in terms ⁻of their effectivity in the social structure. Mao's multitude of contradictions resist such hierarchization and, more significantly, reduction to a limited number of categories. Some contradictions are obviously more significant than others in determining social structure or historical direction, but Mao refuses to deny a role in social dynamics to what seem to be the most trivial contradictions (and, therefore, to dissolve them into broader categories) or to hierarchize them except on a temporary basis, for in their interactions they are in a constant state of flux as regards their place in the structure. What he says of the primary categories of Marxist theory is revealing:

> For instance, in the contradiction between the productive forces and the relations of production, the productive forces are the principal aspect; in the contradiction between theory and practice, practice is the principal aspect; in the contradiction between the economic base and the superstructure, the economic base is the principal aspect; and there is no change in their respective positions. This is the mechanical materialist concept, not the dialectical materialist conception. True, the productive forces, practice and the economic base generally play the principal and decisive role; whoever denies this is not a materialist. But it must also be admitted that in certain conditions, such aspects as the relations of production, theory and the superstructure in turn manifest themselves in the principal and decisive role. (pp. 335 − 336)

Causation here is conjunctural and overdetermined: social and historical events are products of the conjuncture of multiple contradictions. Essential to Mao's idea of contradiction was the role of the revolutionary subject. In the first place, an "overdetermined conjuncture" points to a revolutionary alternative as one possibility among others, because such a situation is of its very nature openended; in other words, open to interpretation. It is up to the revolutionary to interpret it in accordance with revolutionary goals. This is also where the importance of abstract theory as guide to action comes in; because without the aid of theory, the revolutionary will be at a loss to make choices consistent with longterm goals. Second, while itself a product of contradictions, revolutionary practice is part of the structure of contradictions, and effective in aligning the contradictions in a manner most consistent with revolutionary goals. The role of revolutionary struggle in converting an unfavorable to a favorable situation was part of Mao's analysis of contradiction (see above); it appears most prominently in other places in the context of his discussions of the military strategy of revolutionary struggle. [14]

Mao's companion essay, "On Practice" offers in epistemological form a more direct statement on interpretation as an essential component of revolutionary activity (or, if I may overstate the point, on revolutionary activity as interpretative activity). On the surface, the epistemology which "On Practice" offers is an empiricist one. As he presents it, cognition begins with perceptual cognition, which is "the stage" of "sense perceptions and impressions". [15] As sense perceptions are repeated and accumulate, "a sudden change (leap) takes place in the brain in the process of cognition, and concepts are formed. Concepts are no longer phenomena, the separate aspects and the external relations of things; they grasp the essence, the totality and the internal relations of things" (p. 298). (Mao also describes this as "the stage of rational knowledge".) The knowledge thus acquired is then tested for its validity in actual practice, which leads to further perceptions, conceptual modifications, back to practice in an ongoing cycle of perception→conception→practice→perception.

If Mao's epistemology is empiricist, however, it is the empiricism of an activist who constructs knowledge in the process of reconstructing the world with revolutionary goals. Mao begins his discussion of cognition at the stage of perception, but this does not imply that the mind is a blank sheet of paper upon which perceptions rewrite themselves into conceptions, because the mind already has a conceptual apparatus for organizing perceptions (implicit in the class character of knowledge), and a theoretical apparatus (dialectical materialism) for articulating them. His epistemology, furthermore, elevates certain activities over others in the acquisition of knowledge (the struggle for production and class struggle) (p. 296, 300),

---

14 See, for instance, "On Tactics Against Japanese Imperialism", in *SWMTT*, *Vol. I*, 1935, pp. 152 – 254.

15 *SWMTT*, *Vol. I*, p. 297. References in the text will be to this translation, pp. 295 – 309.

and knowledge has a clear goal: "making revolution". Most important is the place of practice, which Mao consistently used in the sense of praxis: activity to change the world. The goal of "On Practice" is not to argue for a vulgar empiricism ("seeking truth from facts"), but to assert the priority of practice in cognition against a theoretical dogmatism oblivious to concrete circumstances of revolution. Quoting Stalin, Mao observes: "Theory becomes purposeless if it is not connected with revolutionary practice; just as practice gropes in the dark if its path is not illumined by revolutionary theory." (p. 305)

"On Practice" may be viewed as a call for the revolutionary hermeneutic which Mao would elaborate a month later in "On Contradiction". Composed as parts of a single project, the two discussions illuminate each other in their intertextuality. Mao's understanding of knowledge as interpretation, as well as his unwillingness to view it just as interpretation, is expressed in the following statement:

> Fully to reflect a thing in its totality, to reflect its essence, to reflect its inherent laws, it is necessary through the exercise of thought to reconstruct the rich data of sense perception discarding the dross and selecting the essential, eliminating the false and retaining the true proceeding from the one to the other and from the outside to the inside, in order to form a system of concepts and theoriesit is necessary to make a leap from perceptual to rational knowledge. Such reconstructed knowledge is not more empty or more unreliable [than empiricism]; on the contrary, whatever has been scientifically reconstructed in the process of cognition, on the basis of practice, reflects objective reality. (p. 303)

There is a profound contradiction in Mao's thinking. As a Marxist materialist, Mao believes that there is an "objective reality" against which to judge the validity of competing forms of knowledge; hence his repeated references to cognition as a "reflection" of the world in the mind. At the same time, as the essay "On Contradiction" leaves little doubt, Mao views objective reality (or the context of thought) itself to be a product of contradictions; which renders it into an object of interpretation and "reconstruction". His foray into the discussion of "truth" is revealing of this contradiction in its simultaneous assertion of the "relativity" of truth, even of revolutionary truth, and his conviction of the possibility of an "absolute truth":

> Marxists recognize that in the absolute and general process of development in the universe, the development of each particular process is relative, and that hence, in the endless flow of absolute truth, man's knowledge of a particular process at any given stage of development is only relative truth. The sum total of innumerable relative truths constitutes absolute truth. Marxism-Leninism has in no way exhausted truth but ceaselessly opens up roads to the knowledge of truth in the course of practice. (pp. 307 – 308)

The contradiction between absolute and relative truth presents an unresolvable contradiction which is to be overcome by resorting to practice as "the criterion of truth" (p. 305). Practice as activity to change the world is bound up in Mao's thinking with the notion of contradiction: that is, changing the world is a process of resolving contradictions, which leads to new contradictions, which leads to new practices and so on in an endless process. This itself is problematic, however, because, as the discussion of "contradiction" tells us, practice in and of itself does not provide a direction to history, or any judgment of validity other than "what works, works". The assumption of an "absolute truth", in other words, serves as an ideological closure upon a fluid reality that is hardly an "objective reality", but is itself the product of human activity, which constructs its understanding of the world in the process of reconstructing the world:

> The struggle of the proletariat and the revolutionary people to change the world comprises the fulfillment of the following tasks: to change the objective world and, at the same time, their own subjective world to change their cognitive ability and change the relations between the subjective and the objective world. (p. 308)

This very representation of the world as ongoing revolutionary interpretation and construction is disruptive of the ideological closure, and exposes the latter as a contradiction between theory and practice, and absolute and relative truth, which, in its openendedness, may be resolved only through revolutionary intervention. Mao's own Marxism could in the end restore a direction to history only through revolutionary will and suppression of alternative interpretations.

▪ The Past in the Present

While it was a powerful instrument of revolutionary practise of which it

was a product, the rendering of theory into a hermeneutic in Mao Zedong
Thought presented two problems of lasting significance. First, any
situation, revolutionary or not, could lend itself to more than one
interpretation (or "reading" of contradictions). If the validity of
interpretation could be judged only by its results, there was no a priori way
of determining the correctness of any one interpretation. In such a case,
the clash of interpretations might easily degenerate into endless conflict or
forceful suppression of alternatives. Secondly, for the same reason, there
was no telling what choice best pointed to the long term goal of socialism,
especially as socialism as utopian end was secularized and historicized. The
freedom gained by opening up theory to experimentation exacted a price in
uncertainties over the meaning of socialism and the way to get there.

The role assigned to contradiction in Mao Zedong Thought suggested a
world-view (and even a cosmology) that elevated conflict to a pervasive
universal. Ironically, the immediate goal within its historical context was to
justify putting an end to the conflict with the Guomindang (class struggle)
to establish an alliance against Japanese imperialism, which made the
interpretation readily acceptable to many, if not to all, especially the more
orthodox adherents of Marxism in the Party who did not approve of the
tampering with theory. Conflict over interpretations would assume much
greater severity in ensuing years, especially after 1956, when the post-
revolutionary leadership was faced with the necessity of making decisions
concerning the most appropriate way to proceed to socialism. The choice
seemed to be between rapid development of the forces of production to
establish an economic basis for socialism, and deepening the revolution by
further transformation of the relations of production, and overcoming the
contradictions that had been created by the developmental policies pursued
in the early years of the PRC. This, it was hoped, would also contribute
to the development of the forces of production. The choice was not
between development and revolution, as is sometimes suggested, but
different paths to development: the technological versus the political. Both
choices, moreover, were justifiable in terms of theory.

The choice of the political over the technological would dictate policy
over the next two decades. Disagreements over this choice were resolved
in the end by the elevation of conflict to a metaphysical principle that
infused everyday existence, the utopianization of revolution itself, and the

assertion of revolutionary will over the demands of collective wisdom and organizational prudence. This time around, the experiment would take a heavy toll on society, in the process discrediting the interpretation which had informed it.

The launching of "reform and opening" after 1978 was justified by the alternative that had been rejected in 1956: rapid development of the forces of production. The choice was accompanied by a repudiation of further social conflict—especially class struggle—as a necessity of progress toward socialism. To put it somewhat crudely, the immediate task appeared to be the completion of the bourgeois revolution that had been aborted by the Cultural Revolution. Within the Chinese context, this meant a return to the policies of New Democracy that had guided the policies of the early 1950s, with an emphasis on class alliance and the encouragement of private initiative in economic development, which also seemed to require the dismantling of the collective institutions established earlier.

Equally radical was "opening", which meant the repudiation of the autarkic policies pursued during the previous two decades. "Opening" in China coincided with important shifts in economic practices world-wide—especially in Eastern Asia—from import-substitution to export-orientation, which by the 1990s would culminate in neo-liberal globalization. Effective opening—the need to attract foreign capital—introduced pressures toward further erosion of the collective institutions associated with socialism. By the 1990s, when the hesitant opening of the 1980s gave way to full-scale integration into global capitalism, the "globalization" of the Chinese economy would be on its way.

Present-day China is the product of these policies, and is perceived largely within and without China as a continuation and fulfillment of the policies initiated in 1978. Nevertheless, as a recent study has suggested, we need a more nuanced understanding of the post-1978 period than that which portrays the last three decades as an inevitable progress(or decline, depending on political position) to capitalism and incorporation into the global capitalist economy. The author suggests a periodization of the period that proceeds from the ambivalent openings of the 1980s (that the concept of "postsocialism" sought to capture) to full scale opening of the 1990s to the return during the last decade of concerns about the future of socialism. [16] These concerns are products of the ecological and social problems created by the rapid developmental policies of the previous decade which, if unchecked, threaten not only further development but also the socialist claims from which they have derived at least some of their legitimacy. To be sure, development has alleviated poverty for large numbers of people, and brought enormous national prestige and power with it. But it has also created immense social and regional inequalities, wrought havoc on the environment, and nourished a popular culture (similar to elsewhere under global capitalism) of consumerism, indifference to public issues, and seemingly endless tolerance of inequality and injustice that also has created an enormous gap between the revolutionary culture the leadership continues to claim as its own and the general public, especially the urban public. In 1956, in his "On the Ten Great Relationships", Mao Zedong had offered an analysis of contradictions in Chinese society that he thought obstructed any progress toward socialism. [17] The developments of the last three decades have once again brought to the fore many of these contradictions, albeit with somewhat different characteristics than in the 1950s. As the current leadership is quite ready to admit, the resolution of these contradictions is a major challenge of the present. Interestingly, however, the interpretation of these contradictions and of their resolution are still conditioned by the same two alternatives as in the past: that they are products of backwardness that will go away with further development or that they are products of the development policies and need social and political transformation for their resolution.

What distinguishes China from other societies with comparable problems, and justifies the perspective afforded by the concept of "postsocialism", is the

16 Lin Chun, *The Transformation of Chinese Socialism*, Durham, NC: Duke University Press, 2006.

17 The "ten relationships" were: 1. —The relationship between industry and agriculture, and between heavy industry and light industry. 2. —The relationship between industry in the coastal regions and industry in the interior. 3. —The relationship between economic construction and defence construction. 4. —The relationship between the state, the units of production and the individual producers. 5. —The relationship between the Centre and the regions. 6. —The relationship between the Han nationality and the national minorities. 7. —The relationship between Party and non-Party. 8. —The relationship between revolutionary and counter-revolutionary. 9. —The relationship between right and wrong. 10. —The relationship between China and other countries.

continued willingness in Chinese politics and intellectual debate to entertain the necessity of social and political transformation in the resolution of these contradictions. There may be no agreement on what such transformations may entail. The possibilities under consideration also have proliferated with opening up to the world and to the past, but the consideration is itself significant in revealing the persistence of the legacies of the socialist revolution. Socialism itself has acquired new dimensions in the proliferation of terminology that seeks to keep alive an idealist commitment to transcending the past and the present without being trapped in the language of orthodoxy: "Small-Welfare society" (*xiaokang shehui*), "Harmonious Society"(*hexie shehui*), "Ecological Civilization"(*shengtai wenming*), etc. Innovations at the conceptual level are accompanied by experimentation with new forms of governance. And the leadership has by no means given up on its theoretical commitments to Marxism, as is indicated by renewed efforts to rejuvenate Marxism by reinterpreting it in response to a changed world situation, supported by President Hu Jintao himself.

Contemporary experimentation with political theory and organization is no doubt reformist, and incremental, to cite one of its theorists. [18] This also presupposes a recognition of socialism not as a utopian beacon but as an uncharted frontier, where what may lay ahead is far less certain than what needs to be overcome at the present: what I have described above as a secular in contrast to a religious utopianism. Analysis of the contradictions of Chinese society presently is even more complicated than in the past, due to the integration to global capitalism, and so are the possibilities of reading contradictions—and the predicament of determining what reading may be most consistent with long-term aspirations. One solution to the predicament is to replace the teleology of a distant utopia by a succession of short-term goals toward a desirable future, while taking care not to allow the solution of present contingencies to create obstacles to its realization.

■ To the Future—If There is One

I will conclude here with a few observations on the contradictions that

---

18   Yu Keping, "Toward an Incremental Democracy and Governance: Chinese Theories and Assessment Criteria", in Yu Keping, *Globalization and Changes in China's Governance*, Leiden: EJ Brill, 2008, Chapter 9.

need to be overcome to this end. I would like to begin with an explanation
of the sub-title, "if there is one". The ecological and resource crisis of the
present is so serious that it is possible to wonder if humanity has a future.
This also makes it seem that it is pointless to talk about socialism, or any
other "ism", as political causes appear trivial in the perspective of the far
greater problem of the human relationship to nature. On the contrary, I
think, that very problem makes it more important than ever to speak to
political issues, and the kind of political system that may best contribute to
human survival and welfare.

Over the last sixty years, Chinese socialism has been driven by the
related goals of achieving national wealth and security, on the one hand,
and distributive justice, on the other hand. In the early years in the 1950s,
priority was given to building up a heavy industrial base, along with
collectivization in agriculture both to increase production and to bring
greater equality to rural society. The following twenty years witnessed a
shift of emphasis to radical egalitarianism, accompanied by the
encouragement of self-reliance both at all levels of society, including the
national level, which meant as little interaction as possible with the outside
world. The policies pursued were reminiscent of a war economy driven by
an excessive concern for security, and a puritanical control of consumption
through self-sacrifice for the greater collective good. Changes in the world
situation—both economic and political—beginning in the 1980s made
possible the policies of "reform and opening", which aligned the direction
of development with contemporary changes in the capitalist world
economy. The concern for national welfare and security was still
paramount, but the search for equality now placed priority on the
alleviation of poverty through the rapid development of production. In the
process, there was an attenuation of distributive justice, which pushed the
achievement of socialism farther and farther to an unspecified future.

This change in direction was to create its own contradictions. I have
already pointed to the political, social and cultural dimensions of these
contradictions. These are all recognized by the leadership and Chinese
intellectuals. One problem that has not received sufficient attention,
however, is the idea of "development" itself. The program suggested by

"the scientific outlook on development", for instance has noted the importance of making adjustments in development policies to alleviate the ecological and social problems created by development-moving toward more "sustainable" development, but it does not question the idea of development itself. In other words, a fundamental question that faces China and the world presently is whether or not development as it has been understood since the nineteenth century, but especially since 1945, is sustainable. This, I think, should be the point of departure presently for all discussion, including the present and future of socialism.

In outlining "the scientific outlook on development", President Hu stated that "humans (ren) are the point of departure for and the end of development". This is in many ways what socialism has been about in theory if not in practice: to establish a society in which humans can live in welfare, justice and dignity. But is this what contemporary development is about? If not, can we hope ever to even come close to a socialist society through developmental programs that negate these goals? Furthermore, how must we understand these goals, and the way to achieve them, when we are made painfully aware by natural destruction that there are ecological limits to what we call development?

These limits have been there all along. They have become threateningly visible with the globalization of capital, and the spread globally of its productive and consumptive practices. The destruction of nature did not begin with capitalism, but the same technologies of capital that enabled humans "to conquer" nature, and expand the material horizon of human development, also unleashed forces of unprecedented power in human destructiveness. These forces have been intensified with the globalization of capital, and its promise of limitless material progress.

I have argued elsewhere that socialism, beginning with Karl Marx, has shared in the developmentalist assumptions of capitalism. [19] Marx was quite aware of the destructiveness of capitalism. He nevertheless was fascinated with the human creativity and the productive forces unleashed by

---

19　Arif Dirlik, *After the Revolution: Waking to Global Capitalism,* Hanover, NH: Wesleyan University Press, 1993.

capitalism, and saw in them the means to fulfilling human needs that must be the basis for socialism. The rendering of capitalism into the prerequisite for socialism would subsequently justify the argument that the transition to socialism must await the full development of the forces of production— though it remains unclear how much development constitutes full development, and whether a fully developed capitalist society would lend itself to socialist transformation. It is equally unclear at what point in the development of the forces of production new relations of production would emerge to signal the coming of socialism.

Capitalist societies, on the other hand, have been able to sustain the myth of limitless and universal development by the evidence of the wealth they have created, the promise of the ability of technological creativity to overcome human problems, including the problems created by its own development, and even the fairer distribution of social wealth they had achieved—at least until recently. The myth has drawn additional plausibility from the conscious representation as poverty the condition not only of the hopelessly needy, but also of those who did not have access to the products of capital, and did not need to do so for their survival. [20] Capitalism, in other words, has depended for its expansion not only on the production of goods to satisfy human needs but also the production of the need to make those goods indispensable to human life. In the process, it has concealed inequalities in access to its products by the promise of their availability to all successful players in its operations. Such inequality in access to the products of capital both within and between nations, we might add, has been one factor among others for the invisibility of ecological limits to development, which have become far more visible as the globalization of capital has opened up production and consumption to those formerly excluded from it. Beyond contingent factors, including outsight instances of theft and plunder, it remains to be seen how much the current crisis of the capitalist

---

20 How development policy was based on arguments of poverty is analyzed in Arturo Escobar, *Encountering Development: The Making and Unmaking of the Third World*, Princeton, NJ: Princeton University Press, 1994. The question of the need to distinguish different kinds and levels of poverty is analyzed in Albert Tevoedjre, *Poverty: Wealth of Mankind*, Oxford, UK: Pergamon Press, 1979.

world economy is due to overproduction brought about by competition among nations to join the capitalist market. Such competition also has added to pressures on the environment and resources.

If these arguments have any plausibility at all, it follows (in answer to the question I posed above) that developmental policies associated with the globalization of capitalism are not sustainable—even with so-called "sustainable development" which seek to bring an ecological dimension to development without addressing the most fundamental questions it raises, which requires reconsideration not only of what is meant by development but also of poverty. Such reconsideration cannot be undertaken on a nation by nation basis, as the problems that call it forth are products of globalization. But some nations, by virtue of the part they have played in globalization, are strategically better placed than others in taking the lead.

The PRC is one such nation. Not just because of its contemporary importance in the global economy, but also because of its experience with efforts to formulate an alternative to the capitalist world system. The idealism that is the legacy of the revolution is still visible in the leadership's affirmation of humans as the goal of development. No less important is the willingness to rename past efforts to accord with new circumstances. Ideals expressed through concepts such as "harmonious society" or "ecological civilization" draw upon past visions of socialism, among other legacies, but also promise to shed the intellectual and political baggage associated with them. Above all, they offer signs of continued willingness to experiment with alternatives to the present, which provides an interesting contrast to the reluctance even of the more progressive leaders in Europe, North America and elsewhere to question the fundamental assumptions of capitalist society.

It remains to be seen whether or not the idealism that has characterized the current leadership's programmatic statements will be fulfilled in reality, or have lasting power beyond the present. For the time being, China's ambivalent relationship to global capitalism—both inside and outside—also may facilitate a leadership role in the search for alternatives to the present. While the globalization of the economy has had an impact on all parts of Chinese society, large sections of the population have not benefited from it even as they have suffered from its consequences. The current leadership is deeply aware of this problem, and already has begun to address it. The global economic crisis, ironically, has provided further stimulus for investment in the improvement of the lives of the Chinese people, especially the rural population in the interior. Stemming the dislocation of the rural population, strengthening rural reconstruction, and distributing internally the benefits of globalization may go a long way towards overcoming some of the inequalities created by globalization, and establishing the basis for an economy that gives priority to the needs of the population over the demands of a global economy abstracted from human life.

This by no means implies a return to economic isolation. The "off-grounding" of the economy under the sign of globalization has come close to realization of basic premises of the capitalist economy to valorize exchange over local need, separate the consumer from the direct producer, and subject both to the demands of financial accumulation. The wealth thus created has benefited a fraction of the world's population, while leaving the great majority at the mercy of the motions of capital which has grown ever more vulnerable to unscrupulous manipulation as it has been liberated from everyday production, consumption and exchange. The task now is to re-ground the economy by turning to the satisfaction of domestic needs—and the creation of a domestic economy which, while it is not to be isolated from the world, nevertheless gives priority to the needs of the people and the creation of a sustainable future.

The challenge is not just economic but political and ecological as well. The re-grounding of the economy is also to give a closer hearing to the needs of the people, rather than to manipulate them with illusory dreams of endless consumption, which must be a necessary point of departure for any kind of democratic governance. The issue of democracy is complex and controversial in China as it is elsewhere. It is rendered more complex by its use for political purposes by those such as former President of the US, George W. Bush, who advocated it abroad but did not hesitate to curb it at home. Well-intentioned intellectuals in the PRC and elsewhere have raised serious questions about universalizing democratic practices as they have evolved in Europe and North America. [21] Democratic governance must take different forms not only in different societies but even within the same society where conditions differ from one location to another. On the other hand, democracy also serves an essential function in opening up channels of communication between governors and the governed, and has an important part to play in curtailing corruption and arbitrary use of power, which is an important consideration especially under circumstances of bureaucratic capitalism. It may also be a precondition of any radical transformation in development policy as a means of mobilizing the population in favor of such transformation—not as its passive objects but as active participants whose everyday experiences need to serve as a resource in the formulation of policy if development policy is to do more than pay lip service to local needs and experience. Giving priority to everyday life over abstract promise is also to bring into play ecological considerations not as economic calculation but as a condition of survival.

Given the strategic part the Chinese economy has come to play in the global economy, any shift in the Chinese economy will have significant repercussions globally. We frequently hear these days that China has a major part to play in countering the current global recession. The usual

---

21   See the discussion by Yu Keping in his collection of essays, *Democracy is a Good Thing* (op. cit.), especially the title essay. See also his preface to his recent book, *Rang minzhu zaofu Zhongguo* (Make Democracy Serve China) (Beijing: Zhongyang bianyi chuban she, 2009). Whether or not the Chinese people are ready for democracy is raised in a recent discussion by the distinguished writer, Han Shaogong, in his "Democracy: A Lyrical Poem or a Construction Drawing", unpublished essay, tr. by Xie Shaobo. This question, in relationship to the possibilities of socialism, is also taken up in an interview by Barbara Foley with Wang Fengzhen and Xie Shaobo, "Crossroads: China's Future Under Debate", published in *Science and Society*, Vol. 73, No. 2, 2009, pp. 193 – 210. For a thoughtful discussion by a distinguished Indian intellectual, Harbans Mukhia, see "Liberal Democracy for Asia and the World: Problems and Prospects", Valedictory Speech to the 20th Anniversary Meeting of the International Association of Historians of Asia, Jawaharlal Nehru University, Delhi (November 14-17, 2008). I am grateful to Harbans Mukhia, Shaobo Xie and Han Shaogong for sharing their unpublished pieces with me. For examples of experimentation with local governance, see *Zhongguo difang zhengfu chuangxin* (Innovations and Excellence in Chinese Local Governance, 2005—2006)(Beijing: China Center for Comparative Politics and Economics, 2007). While it is important to recognize that forms of governance and democratic practices, to be effective, need to respond not just to national but local circumstances, it is equally important to remind ourselves at all times, as many a Chinese intellectual has argued over the past century, that the best school for democracy may be the practice of democracy itself.

implication is that China may help return the global economy to where it
had been before the recession: to an unsustainable global capitalism. We
may suggest, to the contrary, that China may have a significant part to play
in effecting a change of direction in economic practices globally: in re-
grounding the global economy. China has benefited from globalization in
its emergence of an economic power. It has also contributed to
globalization in its service as a "global factory", as well as providing the
credits that have made possible the continued illusion of endless
consumption not just in advanced capitalist societies but even in the Global
South. Any significant shift in economic practices in China is likely to force
a much needed re-thinking of development in these other societies.
Especially important in this regard may be the leadership role China can
play in Africa and Latin America. There has been some ambivalence
concerning intensified Chinese activity in the Global South in recent years.
We may easily dismiss charges of Chinese colonialism by representatives of
former colonial powers who resent intrusion in their former colonies. But
the resentment goes beyond them to native populations who justifiably
perceive in Chinese activity the colonialism of an emergent world power
that is concerned primarily with the extraction of resources without any
heed for economic and ecological consequences, the creation of markets for
its cheaper and shoddier commodities, and the separation of economic
activity from political consequence that enables business with unscrupulous
dictators. Overcoming these perceptions requires, among other things,
greater control of corporations, some of which would seem to be as
oblivious to the social and economic damage they inflict on populations
elsewhere as they are within China itself.

On the other hand, China is also a developing country which provides a
sense of kinship with other societies of the Global South. No less important
are shared memories of oppression and exploitation by European
colonialism, and an earlier identification as Third World societies. These
commonalities provide a basis for cooperation, and the formulation of
alternative development strategies that respond to the particular needs of
different societies. Sensitivity to difference and particularity has been a
hallmark of Chinese conceptions of development against the one-size-fits all
philosophy that has guided modernization strategies inspired by capitalism

(and followed in the past by socialist societies as well) .[22]

The redefinition of development in China and the Global South, however, may have the greatest consequences for the US and Europe, especially the former. Advanced capitalist societies continue directly and indirectly to consume the greater part of the world's resources, and make the greatest contribution to the degradation of the environment. The export of production to locations in the Global South, including China and India, has meant that resource depletion and environmental degradation in these societies, too, is due at least partly due to the role these societies have assumed in servicing the consumption needs of advanced capitalist societies. Not least is the important part these societies have played as models and exporters of unsustainable economic practices.

One of the most difficult things to face up to in these societies may be the necessity of a lowering of the living standards to which they have been accustomed if the world economy is to be sustainable. Whether in developed or developing societies, or in international fora, attention in discussions of development is focused almost invariably on raising standards of living—of the poor nationally, and of poor nations, globally. Given the Euromodern faith in development which has gone global since World War II, it seems inadmissible to acknowledge not only that it may be physically and socially impossible to raise the living standards of world's populations to the levels of the middle classes (not to speak of the wealthy) in advanced capitalist societies, but that middle classes in advanced societies will have to lower their standards of living as pressures on resources intensify globally. There is already some evidence that this is happening. Admitting it in development thinking and policy would be to overcome a major ideological hurdle to the rethinking of development.

Here, too, China could play a leadership role as a developing country, where it may still be possible to distinguish the alleviation of poverty from

---

22　For a discussion of some of these possibilities, see Edward Friedman, "How Economic Superpower China Could Transform Africa", *Journal of Chinese Political Science*, No. 14, 2009, pp. 1 – 20. For a useful survey of Chinese activities in Africa, with interviews with African leaders, see the series of reports 2008—2009 by Richard Behar in www. fastcompany. com, an Internet publication of the Harvard Business School. As the reports suggest, some of this activity is a direct product of globalization: the search for resources to sustain production in China for consumption in the US and Europe.

the mimicking of middle class life in advanced capitalist societies. To do so, however, it is necessary to question not only the illusions of globalism, but also legacies of past notions of socialism that mortgaged socialist possibilities to capitalist developmentalism. At this particular conjuncture in human history, it seems that socialism, while it continues to draw its poetry from the future, as Marx put it, must also search in the past for clues to making the future possible.

Post-Socialist States and the Evolution of
a New Development Model:
Russia and China Compared

*Peter Rutland**

■ Introduction

The onset of globalization in the 1980s—1990s coincided with the shift in China and Russia from autarkic central planning to trade-driven market economies. The Chinese leadership consciously embraced globalization, and saw it as an opportunity rather than a threat. The reaction in Russia has been quite different, since during the 1990s Russia seemed to be suffering from the impact of globalization. Some observers even argue that globalization was itself one of the causes of the collapse of the Soviet state. However, the picture has changed over the past decade, as Russia has regained political stability and experienced rapid and sustained economic growth while continuing a policy of greater integration with the global economy.

Both Russia and China have emerged from the transition to global capitalism as stronger and more stable states. Yet neither of them has fully embraced the values and institutions of the "Washington Consensus"—the belief that the best economic policy is one of free trade, freely floating currencies, the lifting of government regulation, and the privatization of state-owned industries. Nor do they confirm the "Washington Hypothesis"— the idea that globalization promotes democratization. [1] The Russian and Chinese development model combines an acceptance of market forces and

---

* Peter Rutland is professor of government at Wesleyan University. He is the author of *The Politics of Economic Stagnation in the Soviet Union: The Role of Local Political Organs in Economic Management*, and forthcoming, *Moscow Rules: The Politics of the Post-Soviet State*. His current research interests include Russian foreign policy, the oil and gas industry, and the dynamics of nationalism.

1 Nita Rudra, "Globalization and the Strengthening of Democracy in the Developing World", *American Journal of Political Science*, Vol. 49, No. 4, October 2005, pp. 704 – 730.

global integration with a rejection of neoliberal economics and liberal democracy, and the reaffirmation of nationalism and sovereignty.

The first section of this article compares and contrasts the evolution of the Chinese and Russian economic systems over the past two decades. We find some many sharp differences and a few points of similarity. One important debate is the extent to which it was initial conditions or leadership policy choices which determined the outcome of the transition. A third factor—the external economic environment—must also be taken into account. The final section of the article summarizes the common features that have emerged as of 2008, and speculates as to whether this convergence amounts to the emergence of a new development model—one that could even contribute to the evolution of a new type of international economic order.

▪ A Tale of Two Transitions

Russia and China are large autonomous countries with strong state traditions. They both turned their backs on the global capitalist system in the 20th century, and adopted communist systems. Prior to that, they had emerged historically as land empires in the center of Eurasia. This left them with a legacy of a strong central state with a distinct identity and legitimacy. Correspondingly they had weak traditions of civil society. The state acted as a gatekeeper for their interactions with the outside world, which was seen as hostile and threatening. Both had been subject to military defeats in the 19th—20th centuries and subsequent loss of territory, and had then emerged bloodied but victorious from World War Two. Both Russia and China have distinct cultures, tracing their roots and maintaining their identities *outside* of European culture. However, Russia's interactions with Europe were much more intense, so Russia is a hybrid with strong European elements, unlike China. Both countries' elites currently see themselves—and have long seen themselves—as economically backward compared to the West (since the early 19th century in the case of China, since the 16th century in the case of Russia). "Modernization" is a term that Chinese and Russian leaders still use when discussing their goals.

Under communist rule, their state-owned, centrally-planned economies had many common features and stood in stark contrast to the Western model of democratic capitalism. But in the 1990s, both countries abandoned many elements of their model. At first, they seemed to be headed in opposite directions: Russia towards Western integration and market democracy, while China strove to preserve its authoritarian rule alongside limited opening to foreign trade and investment. Russia experienced rapid political liberalization under General Secretary Mikhail Gorbachev, followed by *system collapse* and the break-up of the Soviet Union. China embarked on a *managed transition* that involved the step-by-step introduction of elements of capitalism while the Chinese Communist Party (CCP) retained a monopoly of political power. The Tiananmen events in 1989 led some to believe that Communist China was experiencing the same profound contradictions that were sundering the Soviet system. However, the Chinese political system remains intact, and expectations that the introduction of capitalism must inevitably lead to the introduction of democracy have eroded. [2]

China's transition away from state socialism is generally considered a success, while Russia's is generally considered a failure. China has doubled its GDP every decade, and has lifted 400 million people out of absolute poverty—perhaps the largest single increase in human welfare in world history. In key development indicators such as phone lines, Internet usage, life expectancy, and high-tech exports, it has closed the gap with Russia. (Table 1) These economic achievements have translated into a substantial rise in China's global status, a process symbolized by the success of the 2008 Olympic Games. In contrast, the Soviet state lost half its territory and population, and the Russian Federation has struggled to maintain its status as a great power. Although the implosion of the Soviet Union was shocking enough to Chinese leaders, equally disturbing was the collapse of Russian society that occurred *after* 1991—economic recession, an upsurge in crime and lawlessness, a falling birth rate rise and rising death rate, and the war in Chechnya. The Chinese leadership tried to learn from Moscow's mistakes. They scrutinized developments in the Soviet Union very closely, and adjusted their policies accordingly. [3] They concluded not only that they must be willing to use repression, but also that reforms were needed to

---

2   Andrew Nathan, "Authoritarian resilience", *Journal of Democracy*, Vol. 14, No. 1, 2003, pp. 6 – 17.

increase the state's capacity to rule, and to bolster the regime's legitimacy in the eyes of the people. In contrast, there is little evidence that Russian leaders have made any serious effort to draw lessons from China's success.

Table 1 *Development Indicators, 2006*

	China	Russia
Life expectancy (years)	72	66
Fertility (births per woman)	1.8	1.3
Infant mortality (per 1000 births)	24	16
GNI per capita (Atlas, $)	2,010	5,800
GNI per capita (PPP, $)	4,700	12,810
Agriculture as % of GDP	12	5
Inflation (%)	3.3	15.7
Gross domestic capital formation as % of GNI	44	21
Phone subscribers (per 100 people)	63	137
Internet users (per 100 people)	10.4	18.0
High tech as % of manufacturing exports	30	9
Merchandise trade as % of GNI	66	47
Government revenue as % of GDP	9.6	28.7
Foreign direct investment (net inflow, $ bn)	78	12.5
Exports as % of GNI	40	34

Source: World Development Indicators, www. worldbank. org, accessed 20 October, 2008.

a) Initial Conditions

The initial conditions at the onset of transition in Russia and China were very different. Moreover, the political leadership of the two countries pursued radically different transition strategies. Despite starting in different places and heading in different directions, the two countries are now converging on a similar model of state-led development in the face of common global challenges and opportunities.

By the late 1980s Russia was a mature industrial economy with an educated, urban labor force. It was a military superpower equal to the United States that still saw itself as a world leader in science and technology. At the onset of its transition in the late 1970s China was still overwhelmingly agricultural (80%

---

3 Christopher Marsh, *Unparalleled Reforms: China's Rise, Russia's Fall and the Interdependence of Transition*, Lexington Books, 2005.

peasants, compared to 15% in Russia), with a small and uncompetitive industrial base and minimal scientific capacity. China struggled with the problem of excess population relative to the available land, but at least this meant it had a pool of cheap labor. Russia faced a declining population and chronic labor shortage, but was resource rich, while China was relatively resource poor.

Not only were the economic conditions quite different, but the political evolution of the two countries prior to 1980 was also very distinct—although both Chinese and Russian elites saw the need for reform. The Chinese Communist Party was rebuilding in the wake of the Cultural Revolution (1966—1976) which had seriously damaged its organized coherence, governing capacity, and popular legitimacy. The Soviet Union had experienced 20 years of stability under General Secretary Leonid Brezhnev—but this period had produced rising corruption, bureaucratic ossification, economic stagnation, and a number of costly foreign policy adventures (notably, the invasion of Afghanistan, and a renewed arms race with the US).

An obvious difference is that while China is ethnically homogenous (90% Han), the Soviet Union was ethnically diverse. Ethnic Russians made up only 53% of the Soviet population, and 80% of the Russian Federation. It might be argued that this ethnic homogeneity should have made it easier for Beijing to introduce democracy. But Chinese leaders had other reasons to fear democratic contestation—there are strong regional differences in their vast country, and there is a huge pool of desperately poor peasants.

b) Different Paths

Not only were the initial conditions different in the two countries, but the respective national leaderships chose divergent development strategies. It is often said that the key difference between Russia and China was the *sequencing* of reform. The argument goes that Gorbachev's big mistake was to opt for political liberalization first and economic reform second. Clearly, the Chinese leadership cannot be accused of committing that error. In Gorbachev's defense, however, it can be argued that economic reform without political reform had been tried by a succession of Soviet leaders since the 1950s—and was attempted again by Gorbachev in 1985—1987.

It was the failure of these earlier economic reforms in the face of bureaucratic intransigence that forced Gorbachev to embrace political reform.

Western scholars had predicted that political liberalization would cause problems for economic reform in the socialist bloc. Subsequent events proved them right—but they got the political mechanism wrong. In an influential 1991 book Adam Przeworksi argued that democratization in Eastern Europe would empower the workers, who would mobilize to protect their state-guaranteed jobs. [4] Thus political reform would enable the interest groups created by the socialist economy to block radical economic reform.

As it turned out, this did not happen. It was nationalism, not worker unrest, that sealed the fate of the Communist states in Europe. In Poland, the workers were swept up in the nationalist project of getting out from under Soviet influence by joining the West—which meant embracing capitalism. In Russia, the political turmoil that the country experienced in 1989—1993 was so severe that the workers were politically neutralized and were unable to prevent President Boris Yeltsin's embrace of liberal market reforms. What happened next was equally unexpected: the emergence as if from nowhere of a small group of powerful oligarchs, who helped to keep Yeltsin in power, while blocking the second wave of reforms that liberals had hoped for.

Second, there is the contrast in *pace* of reform. The conventional wisdom is that China followed a gradual path while Russia embraced shock therapy in 1992. The Chinese were burned by a century of failed efforts at radical change and were thus philosophically committed to incrementalism. [5] In contrast, Moscow had grown tired of decades of incremental change, and the crisis conditions of early 1992 seemed to leave Yeltsin with no option but to embrace radical reform. [6] It also reflected his advisors' conviction that the only way to break with central planning was to enforce hard budget constraints and market-clearing prices as part of an integrated package. The

---

4   Adam Przeworksi, *Democracy and the Market: Political and Economic Reforms in Eastern Europe and Latin America*, Cambridge University Press, 1991.

5   Joseph Fewsmith, *China Since Tiananmen: The Politics of Transition*, Cambridge University Press, 2001, pp. 80 – 83.

6   Yegor Gaidar, *Days of Defeat and Victory*, University of Washington Press, 1999.

reformers also made a Przeworksi-type argument about a political window of opportunity: that Yeltsin had to capitalize on his power in early 1992 before anti-reform forces rallied and used the democratic process to unseat him. Freed from the threat of a democratic turnover of power to reactionaries, the CCP leadership could afford to take a more gradual reform path.

The Politics of Transition

In retrospect, it was neither the sequencing nor the pace of reform that was the crux of the problem. The key question is more basic—the need to maintain political power and state capacity. Putting economic reform first allowed the Chinese state to maintain the political capacity to manage the process, correcting for mistakes and imbalances as they arose. In a more negative light, Minxin Pei argues that it gave the political elite the resources they needed to maintain their repressive system of rule.[7] In contrast, Gorbachev threw out the very tools with which he hoped to promote economic reform. Gorbachev's reforms disrupted the organization cohesion of the Communist Party apparatus and directly undermined its ideological legitimacy.[8] His reforms destroyed the party and then the Soviet state itself. In their struggle to hold onto power, both Gorbachev and Yeltsin used divide-and-rule strategies that split the elite and fragmented political institutions.

Chinese leaders seem to have managed to avoid such divisions, despite— or perhaps because of—the fact that the CCP leadership was historically much more ridden by factionalism than its Soviet counterpart. The Chinese learned their lesson from the Cultural Revolution and from the Soviet break-up. Despite deep disagreements over policy (such as over Tiananmen[9]) they have managed to preserve a united front in the public arena. They have also undergone two relatively smooth transitions in the top leader position (from Deng Xiaoping to Jiang Zemin in 1997, and

---

7 Minxin Pei, *China's Trapped Transition*, Harvard University Press, 2006, p. 19.
8 Shiping Hua, "The Deng Reforms and the Gorbachev Reforms Revisited", *Problems in Post-Communist Politics*, Vol. 53, No. 3, May 2006, pp. 3 – 16.
9 Liang Zhang, Andrew Nathan and Perry Link (eds.), *The Tiananmen Papers*, Public Affairs, 2001.

then to Hu Jintao in 2002) without experiencing a political crisis. [10] This is something Russia has not managed. Yeltsin's nomination of Putin as his successor in December 1999 was a fairly smooth transition, though it was accompanied by the second war in Chechnya. The transition from Putin to Dmitry Medvedev is not yet a clean break.

Looking back, one sees a surprising pattern. In both Russia and China, the highest level of democratic debate occurred in the late 1980s, during the early experimental period when various reform paths were being debated by the national leadership. Over time, as the economic reforms eventually took over, the scope for political dissent actually shrank. This is the opposite of what one would expect from modernization theory, which expects socio-economic development to produce new constituencies (workers, the middle class and businessmen) that demand a say in decision-making. [11]

In the wake of the Tiananmen events, in China oppositionists were jailed or driven from the country; reformists were purged from the CCP leadership; and intellectuals lost their faith in the possibility of the "fifth modernization"—democracy. Nevertheless, Deng Xiaoping in his 1992 tour of the south made the historic decision to accelerate economic reform—in a bid to build a new basis for CCP legitimacy, and thereby prevent a repeat of 1989. This danger was magnified by the dramatic implosion of the Soviet state at the end of 1991. The failure of the August 1991 coup attempt by Soviet hardliners was a blow to CCP leftists who thought that repression was a sufficient basis for rule. Subsequent political reforms in China have been limited to the spread of electoral competition at village level, introduced in 1988; a strengthening of the oversight role of national and local legislatures; and steps to bolster the rule of law and fight corruption. [12] None of these measures have been allowed to infringe on the authority of the CCP. The CCP has undergone some organizational reforms to maintain its

---

10 Op. cit., Nathan, 2003.

11 Minxin Pei, "China: Can Economic Growth Continue without Political Reform?", *Strategic Asia 2006*, National Bureau for Asian Research, 2006, pp. 303 – 332.

12 Ibid., Pei, ch. 2; Ibid. Fewsmith., Even so, the Standing Committee of the National People's Congress only rejected government-proposed bills three times in 28 years. A more positive statistic is that 21% of lawsuits filed against government officials succeeded in 2002. Ibid., Pei, p. 60, 67.

effectiveness post-Mao—most notably, the 2002 decision to allow private entrepreneurs to become CCP members. [13]

Ironically, the quality of Russian democracy arguably peaked in 1990—1991, the last year of the Soviet Union. In 1992—1996 politics settled down into an ugly standoff between a reformist president and an opposition-dominated parliament, and after 1996 the level of competition steadily eroded from election to election.

The most well-known democracy index is that compiled by Freedom House, grading the level of political rights (PR) and civil liberties (CL) on a 1-7 scale, with 1-2 being "free" and 6-7 "unfree". Freedom House regarded the new Russian Republic as "partly free", ranking it 3 for PR and 4 for CL from 1993 through 1997. Russia's grade slipped to 4/5 in 1999 and 5/5 in 2000—2003. In 2004 Russia was relegated to the category "unfree", with a 6 for PR and 5 for CL, which has stayed its rating through 2008. [14]

There has been much less variation in the political climate in China, especially since 1989. Freedom House scored China a 7/7 from 1972 through 1977, when it jumped to 6/6. In 1989 it slipped back into 7/7 and stayed there until 1998, when it rose to 6 for civil liberties and 7 for political rights. Freedom House has kept that score for China through 2008.

In both countries, the traditions of one-party rule have created a culture inimical to pluralism, in which politics is seen as a "winner takes all" game. The key liberal argument for pluralism is that you cannot always be sure of being a winner, so it is better to share power and grant rights to all political actors. But in neither country has the political elite accepted this idea. Both countries have preserved one-party systems based on clientilistic networks in which particularism rather than pluralism is the structuring principle of political life.

13　Bruce Dickinson, "Threats to Party Supremacy", *Journal of Democracy*, Vol. 14, No. 1, 2003, pp. 25 –35. 20% of entrepreneurs are members, but the CCP has branches in less than 1% of the 1.5 million private enterprises.

14　Robert W. Orttung, "Russia", *Nations in Transit 2005*, Freedom House, 2005, at http://www.freedomhouse.org. That puts Russia's political system *below* that of Afghanistan, Bahrain or Burkina Faso.

The Economics of Transition

There are many differences between the Russian and Chinese economic reform strategies. Russia's government unleashed a hastily-assembled package of radical reforms in 1992. Beijing's reforms were middle-up rather than top down—the center encouraged and tolerated initiative from below, and local entrepreneurs and politicians responded to the challenge. The operative metaphor in China was "feeling the stones as you cross the river"[15], while in Russia one of the reformers' favorite sayings was that "you cannot cross a chasm in two jumps"[16]. Crucially, the CCP preserved the capacity to monitor the implementation of the reforms, and adjust them when necessary. While the Chinese talked about "growing out of the plan", Russia was effectively "falling" out of the plan. [17]

Russia launched "shock therapy" in 1992, but the government was unable to control monetary and fiscal deficits, which meant that high inflation and macroeconomic instability prevailed until stabilization was finally achieved in 1999. The privatization program was hijacked by a small group of well-connected insiders, leaving the Russian public feeling cheated and the state treasury empty. Foreign investors were largely shut out from the "crown jewels" of the economy—oil, gas and metals. Although the basic structures of a market economy had emerged by 1999, free entry was still limited, oligopolistic rents were high, and the incentives to efficiency and investment were low. By 2001, the country's 23 largest firms accounted for 30% of Russia's GDP, and these firms were effectively controlled by a mere 37 individuals. [18] In addition to the national oligarchs, many regional markets were controlled by local monopolists.

After Putin was elected president in March 2000, he started an energetic campaign to strip the oligarchs of their political influence. Putin both consolidated and rolled back the market reforms. On one hand, he created

---

15 Op. cit. , Fewsmith, p. 83.

16 George Taber, "Rx for Russia: Shock therapy", *Time Magazine*, 27 January, 1992. Taber writes that the well-known advisor Jeffrey Sachs "frequently cites the old Russian maxim that you cannot cross a chasm in two jumps".

17 Barry Naughton, *Growing Out of the Plan: Chinese Economic Reform, 1978—1993*, Cambridge University Press, 1995.

18 World Bank, *From Transition to Development*, April 2004, www. worldbank. org. ru.

a more robust legal infrastructure, increased taxation, and oversaw eight years of economic growth averaging 6% a year. On the other hand, he strengthened state control over key industries, and a new system of state corporatism took shape. The post-Soviet state bureaucracy, spearheaded by a team of ex-KGB officials, had asserted its dominance over the newly-minted capitalist oligarchs.

China started in 1978 by freeing peasant farmers from plan controls through the household responsibility system. This boosted output and also started released labor for factory work. Then local state authorities were allowed to set up profit-seeking town and village enterprises (TVEs). State owned enterprises (SOEs) were likewise freed to7 become more entrepreneurial. The seventh five year plan that began in 1986 encouraged coastal regions to engage in manufacturing assembly for foreign markets. Between 1978 and 2003, China recorded an annual growth rate of 9.4%, while per capita income rose from $150 in 1978 to $1,700 in 2005. China maintained the state industry sector with its social guarantees, initially through budget subsidies and then through soft credits via the four state-controlled banks. The rapid growth of the private sector meant that the state sector's share of the industrial labor force fell from 80% to 29% in 1978—2000. [19] Small and medium SOEs began to be privatized in 1994—though the government avoided using that term, instead talking of restructuring and asset transfers. In 1997 a major program of restructuring SOEs was launched, leading to wage arrears and layoffs. The government softened the blow by introducing severance pay at 60% of the previous wage for three years. Overall, the state planners showed caution and flexibility in introducing these reforms. For example, price controls on grain were lifted in 1993, but restored in 1995 after the move triggered shortages and price gouging. In 2001 controls were once again eased in grain consuming regions. [20]

While agriculture was the initial driver of the Chinese, in Russia the organization of farm production was largely untouched by the reforms. There was a divergence in the pace of change in the opposition direction in

---

19 Op. cit., Pei, 2006, p. 3. SOE share of industrial output fell from 78% to 41%.

20 Op. cit., Pei, 2006, pp. 97 – 102.

the case of banking. The Chinese state kept firm control over the banking system, while in Russia the lifting of controls led to the sprouting of 1, 500 private banks, many of which collapsed in the August 1998 financial crisis. Russia's mass privatization program converted state firms into legally independent corporations, in line with Western theory stressing the importance of creating clear property rights in a rule of law system. China pursued a very different path: no mass privatization, but the evolution of a hybrid model of SOEs and TVEs behaving as profit-seeking entities with unclear property rights. These Chinese enterprises were also deeply embedded in strong local and even family networks. [21] One important step was the 1998 decision ordering the CCP and army to divest themselves of businesses. In practice, the Russian approach failed to generate the transparent and secure property rights that the reformers claimed as their goal. There were hundreds of cases of organized crime groups seizing control of enterprises by force, and dozens of cases of state officials seizing firms through manipulation of tax arrears and other instruments. Putin's expropriation of the leading private oil company Yukos in 2003—2005 and Shell's forced sale of its majority stake in Sakhalin II in December 2006 are two striking examples of the political contingency of property rights.

So at the end of the day the weakness of property rights is something that unites rather than divides the Russian and Chinese cases. And in neither Russia nor China has the state given up control over key strategic sectors such as telecommunications or power generation. [22] Small steps have been taken in both countries to promote competition in these sectors and create a modern regulatory framework, but in practice political dirigisme is still decisive. Another similarity is that in both countries the tax-gathering capacity of the central state shrank and then recovered in the course of the reforms. In China central government revenues fell from 31% of GDP in 1978 to 10.7% in 1995, rebounding to 17.1% in 2001. [23] Similarly, Russian federal revenues fell to 9.2% of GDP in 1998, recovering to

21 Shu-Yun Ma, "Understanding China's Reform", *World Politics*, Vol. 52, No. 4, 2000, pp. 586-603.

22 Margaret Pearson, "Institutions and Norms of the Emerging Regulatory State: The Business of Governing Business in China", *World Politics*, Vol. 57, No. 2, 2005, pp. 296 – 322.

23 Dali Yang, "State Capacity on the Rebound", *Journal of Democracy*, Vol. 14, Vol. 1, 2003, pp. 43 – 50.

17. 1% in 2001.[24] But after 2001, the two countries drew apart, with China's state revenues shrinking to 10% while Russia's grew to 28%, thanks to the oil boom.

Regional and social inequalities sharply increased in both countries as a result of the reforms. In Russia the Gini coefficient rose from 0. 29 in 1992 to 0. 40 in 1997, where it stayed through 2008, while in China it went from 0. 28 to around 0. 45 in 1978—2000.[25] In Russia there was a more extreme concentration of wealth in the hands of the new oligarchs than in China. This was a result of the more uncontrolled nature of the privatization; the weakness of law enforcement agencies; and the resource-based character of the economy. By 2006 *Forbes* magazine was reporting 33 dollar billionaires in Russia, but "only" eight in China.[26] Their ranks had risen to 87 by 2008, putting Russia in second place after the US. In contrast to the Russian oligarchs, who were in effective control of the political system between 1993 and 2000, Chinese tycoons stayed in the political shadows, colluding with regional political bosses but avoiding anything like a direct challenge to the national state.[27]

Corruption is a debilitating problem for both countries; a drag on efficiency and a turn-off for foreign investors.[28] Its practice is so commonplace at both high and low levels that bribery and clientilism seem to be the glue holding the political system together.[29] The character of corruption in China shifted after 1992 as marketization took root and the

---

24 OECD, *Economic Survey: Russian Federation 2004*, OECD, 2004.

25 Rosstat, www. gks. ru; Op. cit. , Pei, 2006.

26 India was listed with 23 billionaires. *Forbes*, April 2006, at http://www. forbes. com/billionaires/.

27 For example, they are absent from the national legislature, in contrast to the Russian case—Margaret Pearson, *China's New Business Elite: The Political Consequences of Economic Reform*, University of California Press, 1997, p. 111; Bruce Dickson, *Red Capitalists in China: The Party, Private Entrepreneurs, and Prospects for Political Change*, Cambridge University Press, 2003.

28 Transparency International's Corruption Perceptions Index, based on surveys of international businessmen, rates Russia 126th out of 159 countries surveyed in 2005, with a score of 2. 4 out of 10, while China is seen as less corrupt, ranked 78th with 3. 2. The situation is unchanged since 1998, when Russia ranked 52nd (out of 85) with 2. 4, and China 76th with 3. 5, www. transparency. org.

29 Op. cit. , Pei, *Transitions*, 2006, ch. 4; Yan Sun, *Corruption and Market in Contemporary China*, Cornell University Press, 2004.

role of "connections" (*guanxi*) diminished. [30] Leaders in both Moscow and Beijing claim that battling corruption is a top priority, but their actions have barely made a dent in the problem. China has seen the arrest of thousands of top officials, even including a Beijing mayor and two governors. [31] Russia has been less decisive: Putin's anti-corruption campaigns have taken down a few top private businessmen and some police generals, but it was not until 2006 that a sitting governor was arrested.

c) External Integration

Both countries relied on external integration as a key driver of their economic transition. But here, again, their experiences diverged. China's trade tripled in every decade, raising its share in world trade from 0.8% in 1978 to 7.7% in 2005. Because of the 1990s slump and the breakdown of the Comecon trading bloc, Russia's share of world trade fell from 3.4% in 1990 to 1.5% in 2000, recovering slightly to 1.8% in 2005. [32] China's economic regeneration was led by an explosion of manufacturing assembly plants in coastal locations, importing components and raw materials and exporting manufactured goods to foreign markets, and tapping into its seemingly limitless supply of cheap labor. [33] Russia had neither the labor reserves; nor the ports close to global shipping routes; nor the entrepreneurial spirit; nor the political will to embrace this kind of export manufacturing-led growth path.

Unlike Russia, the Chinese relied on an influx of foreign direct investment (FDI), while keeping portfolio investors at arm's length. China attracted an annual average of $12 billion FDI 1985—1995, rising to $78

---

30 Ibid., Sun. Sun's data suggest that the number of cases did not substantially increase in the 1990s, although the author herself does not highlight this point. Table 1.2 shows the number of economic crimes fell from 65,000 in 1992 to 35,000 in 1999, and Table 1.8 shows the number officials investigated rose from 150,000 in 1992 to 175,000 in 2001.

31 Yan Sun provides a list of 21 such officials 1986—2004. Ibid., p. 49.

32 Martin Wolf, "China Should Risk Bolder Trials", *Financial Times*, 6 June, 2006; Giorgio Navaretti, "Patterns of Trade and Protection", World Bank, May 2004; WTO, "World Trade 2005", 11 April, 2006.

33 Shang-jin Wei (ed.), *The Globalization of the Chinese Economy*, Edward Elgar, 2002; Peter Nolan, *Transforming China: Globalization, Transition, and Development*, Cambridge University Press, 2004; Nicholas Lardy, *Integrating China into the Global Economy*, Brookings Institution, 2001. By 2007 wage costs were rising, providing a constraint on growth in the coastal region.

billion in 2006.[34] Russia averaged only $1.3 billion FDI per year 1985—1995 and $12.5 billion in 2006, while experiencing an annual outflow of capital far in excess of those figures. By 2006 China had accumulated a net stock of $207 billion FDI (15% of all capital), while Russia had only $17 billion.[35] To facilitate this inflow of capital China created Special Economic Zones with favorable tax and regulatory conditions. This process was greatly facilitated by the existence of Chinese capitalist exclaves in Hong Kong and Taiwan, part of the 50 million-strong Chinese diaspora.[36] Though foreign investors were encouraged, they were typically forced into joint ventures with their own stake capped at 50%.

China preserved tight controls on capital flows. The RMB is convertible on current account but not on capital account, and was pegged to the dollar after 1995, at a rate equal to about 25% of purchasing power parity (PPP). (In July 2005 the peg was switched to a basket of currencies.) Thanks to these controls, China has maintained its cheap labor advantage, and has prevented the speculative capital inflows and outflows that have devastated other developing economies. They rode out the 1997 Asian financial crisis largely unscathed.

In contrast, Russian reformers largely followed Western advice to pursue external liberalization—in part because IMF credits were conditional on such policies.[37] Russia lifted many capital controls in 1992—1994 and dollars flooded in, forming a parallel currency for most of the 1990s. $40 billion of speculative capital entered the country—mainly to cover the government's yawning fiscal deficit. This reckless borrowing led to the August 1998 financial crash, which was triggered by the slump in the price of oil following the 1997 Asian crisis. August 1998 saw a 75% devaluation of the ruble, a default on foreign loans, and the destruction of the assets of most of the financial oligarchs. The crisis ironically cleared the decks for an economic recovery by making Russian food and manufactures more competitive with imports. More importantly, it enabled a renaissance of

---

34 UNCTAD, *World Investment Report 2005*, www. unctad. org.

35 Yasheng Huang, *Selling China: Foreign Direct Investment during the Reform Era*, Cambridge UP, 2003.

36 Brunson McKinley, "Migration is Here to Stay, So Get Used to It", *International Herald Tribune*, 24 June, 2005.

37 Randall Stone, *Lending Credibility*, Cornell University Press, 2004.

state power by fatally weakening the oligarchs, financially and politically.

d) Future Prospects: Stability or Instability?

According to conventional Western assumptions about the congruence of political and economic liberalism, the current situation in Russia and China is unsustainable. In both countries, the economic system is significantly more market-driven and hence pluralist than the political system. "The market's irresistible force is meeting the party's immovable object. At some point, one of them must surely give."[38] Liberals assume that a breakthrough to democracy is still possible and necessary in both countries. Pessimists expect the state to take more steps to rein in the market—jailing businessmen, nationalizing private companies, erecting protectionist barriers.

Moves by the CCP to broaden the political elite to include businessmen have exposed the contradictions within a regime that embraces capitalism while maintaining Marxism-Leninism as its official creed. The dismantling of the Maoist-era social safety nets, and the never-ending battles with corruption, also raise doubts about the long-term viability of the Chinese model. The country is highly vulnerable to cyclical and exogenous shocks—the bursting of the property bubble; the collapse of the pyramid of bad loans to loss-making SOEs; a slump in demand for China's manufacturing exports; health crises and ecological disasters.[39] This all leads Pei to conclude that without democratic reform, economic growth will stagnate and regime will be faced a series of mounting internal challenges[40], though his pessimism is not shared by all China watchers.[41] The international climate that was so favorable for China's export-led growth cannot continue indefinitely: the 2008 global financial crisis may well mean the end of growth driven by US consumers with money borrowed from China, Japan and the petro-states.

But in a world replete with failed and failing states, the Chinese state still

---

38   Martin Wolf, "An Autocracy of Bureaucrats Can Only Crush China's Growth", *Financial Times*, 31 May, 2006.

39   Gordon Change, *The Coming Collapse of China*, Random House, 2001.

40   Op. cit. , Pei, forthcoming 2006.

41   Andrew Nathan, "Present at the Stagnation", review in *Foreign Affairs*, Vol. 85, No. 4, July 2006, pp. 177 – 182.

looks fairly effective. It is still able to identity problems and deal with them, to complete massive projects such as the Three River Gorges dam or the building of pipelines from Kazakhstan. Even their ability to create a system to effectively censor the Internet is something of a technological and political achievement.[42] On the other hand, the dismal failure of regulatory agencies to prevent the tainted milk scandal in 2008, and the thousands of protests each year surrounding illicit land seizures, are persisting challenges to state capacity.

There are also plausible crisis scenarios in Russia's near future. Russia gained little from its political and economic opening in the 1990s. Not until the commodities boom that saw the oil price rise from $12 a barrel in 1997 to $60 in 2005, did Russia enjoy a clear benefit from global integration. During the years 2000—2008, oil and gas alone were accounting for 60% of export earnings and one third of government revenues. The bursting of the financial bubble and global economic slowdown inn 2008 caused the world oil price to fall from a peak of $147 in July to below $80 in October, which bodes ill for Russia's future growth prospects.

■ The "Regulated Market" Consensus

The differing trajectories of Russia and China underline the point that the impact of globalization on individual states is unpredictable. Despite the common pressures brought by global economic competition, leadership choices and the contingencies of historical evolution still matter. Both China and Russia present a common lesson for theorists of globalization: that the world is not "flat", and that strong states can find a niche role in the new global economic order.

Both countries now seem to be converging on a regulated market model in which elements of market pluralism are embedded in post-communist, authoritarian institutions and practices.[43] (This is sometimes called the

---

42 Op. cit. , Pei, 2006, pp. 84 – 88.

43 See Wei-Wei Zhang, "The Allure of the Chinese Model", *International Herald Tribune*, 1 November, 2006; and the debate between Professor Wu Shuqing and Cheng Enfu, "Washington Consensus and Beijing Consensus", *People's Daily*, 18 June, 2005 (online). Harley Balzer uses a more neutral term, "Managed Pluralism", to describe the Russian-Chinese convergence, "China in Comparative Perspective", ch. 12 in Peter Hays Gries and Stanley Rosen (eds.), *State and Society in* 21*st-century China*, Routledge, 2004.

"Beijing Consensus"[44].) What are the elements of this new "regulated market" model?

(1) The leaders are committed to preserving the integrity of **state sovereignty and national identity.** This means preventing foreign leaders and institutions from forcing political or economic decisions on the government of Russia or China. Participation in international economic integration must not require a trade-off of national sovereignty. Critics argue that this insistence on sovereignty is merely a façade to justify the leaders' grip on power. Defenders would say it is a principled stance, based on a concern for the welfare of their people, whose histories have shown the dire consequences of allowing foreigners to infringe on the country's territory.

Nationalism is part of the leaders' rhetoric, but they do not want to allow it to get out of control, lest it ignite a destabilizing mass movement, and/or threaten relations with important trading partners. [45] Still, it seems clear that nationalism has been strengthened in both Russia and China as they opened up to international market forces, contrary to the argument that globalization necessarily produces "the continuing fragmentation of identities and institutions"[46].

(2) The leaders are focused on **economic growth** as a major goal— something that is good for national security and good for boosting the popular legitimacy of the regime—at a time when other ideological justifications are eroding. Growth also expands the opportunities for personal enrichment by political cadres—while regrettably taking their attention away from human development issues.

(3) The **market mechanism** is the most effective tool for economic growth, both domestically and internationally. International trade is a win-

---

44　The term "Beijing Consensus" was coined by Goldman Sachs advisor Joshua Cooper Ramo, in his article "The Beijing Consensus", Foreign Policy Center, UK, May 2004. http://fpc. org. uk/fsblob/244. pdf. Ramo focuses on China's embrace of the neo-liberal paradigm, and he arguably overlooks the distinctive political features of China's policies which are outlined in this section.

45　Peter Hays Gries, "Popular Nationalism and State Legitimation in China", in Gries and Rosen, ibid. , ch. 9.

46　Philip G. Cerny, "Globalization and the Erosion of Democracy", *European Journal of Political Research*, Vol. 36, No. 5, 1999, pp. 1 - 26, 20.

win situation for all participants. [47] The country must find the most appropriate place in the international division of labor, by accepting the logic of comparative advantage. In China, that means exploiting the country's pool of cheap labor, through export-oriented manufacturing. In Russia, it means selling off the country's mineral resources. But in each case, the leaders want to move up the food chain by developing more capital and technology-intensive industries. China has outpaced Russia in accepting the logic of globalization. Beijing is even more committed to lowering trade barriers than the old US ally Japan. [48]

(4) The **market has its limits,** which must be policed by the state (see point 1). Market forces that erode state legitimacy and capacity, that unleash uncontrollable social protests, must be corrected. The state must step in to provide public goods, from investment in infrastructure to compensation for the reform losers, to the creation of a regulatory framework. The political elite is uncomfortable with the idea of economic actors beyond their control. So the political economy that emerges is one characterized by the hybridity of political and economic power. This may be less efficient than a separation of politics from economics, but it has the advantage (for the leaders) of ensuring the indispensability of the political class.

(5) **Liberal democracy is inappropriate** or unnecessary, and open public contestation between rival members of the ruling political elite is to be kept to a minimum. The Chinese leadership unequivocally rejects the liberal-democratic paradigm: as Andrew Nathan puts it, "The argument that democratization, freedom, and human rights would lead to a truer kind of stability—as convincing as it may be to the democrats of the world—holds no appeal for these men"[49]. They even have the audacity to issue a report critical of human rights in the US in response to the State

---

47 *China's Peaceful Development Road*, State Council Information Office, 22 December, 2005, http://www. chinadaily. com. cn/english/doc/2005-12/22/content_ 505678. htm.

48 William H. Overholt, RAND Corporation, "China and Globalization", testimony to the U. S. - China Economic and Security Review Commission, 19 May, 2005, http://www. rand. org/ pubs/testimonies/CT244/.

49 Nathan, 2003, p. 16.

Department's report on China's human rights record. [50] The Russian position is more nuanced: the leadership officially embraces democratic values, and they are enshrined in the 1993 Constitution. But Russian practice diverges markedly from democratic theory. In partial recognition of this, Kremlin ideologists have floated notions of "managed democracy" and "sovereign democracy" to try to bridge the gap between Russian practice and Western ideas. [51]

(6) The **new middle class** that the economic boom has produced serves as a social basis for the regulated market regimes. This is contrary to the expectations of Western liberals, who traditionally saw the middle class as the trusted standard bearers for democracy. Fewsmith writes that the basis of the post-1989 social contract in China is "economic prosperity in exchange for political quiescence" (p. 103). Ed Freidman argues that "the new middle class in urban China tends to imagine democracy as a system that would empower the majority who are the rural poor"[52]. The Chinese middle class were also frightened by the chaos that followed the Soviet collapse and were thus more willing to support a technocratic authoritarian leadership. [53]

In Russia, professionals were traumatized by the economic shocks of the 1990s and welcomed the stability brought by Putin's firm hand, as is evidenced by opinion surveys and election results. In both countries the middle classes have embraced consumerism and "bourgeois individualism" with a vengeance, fusing it with politics in what Wang Hui has called "consumer nationalism"[54].

▪ Conclusion

Does this "regulated market" approach really amount to a coherent

50　"The Human Rights Record of the United States in 2004", issued by the State Council of the People's Republic of China, *People's* Daily, 3 March, 2005, http://english.people.com.cn/200503/03/eng20050303_175406.html.

51　Vladislav Surkov, "Nationalization of the Future", *Ekspert*, 20 November, 2006.

52　Ed Friedman, *The Rise of China and Its Impact on the World*, International Political Science Association, Fukouka Japan, July 2006.

53　Gongqin Xiao, "The Rise of the Technocrats", *Journal of Democracy*, Vol. 14, No. 1, 2003, pp. 60-65.

54　Wang Hui, *China's New Order: Society, Politics, and Economy in Transition*, Harvard University Press, 2006.

paradigm, intellectually and practically? Or is it a contradictory mixture of ideas and policies, a temporary coincidence of diverse trends that will pull apart within a few years?

The previous wave of authoritarian developmentalism of the 1960s—1980s, from Brazil to East Asia, fell apart in the 1990s. The context of that previous wave was quite different. There was a real anti-capitalist threat, both internationally (global communism) and domestically (powerful labor unions). So the state needed to defend the market from its adversaries. When those adversaries were weakened by the end of the Cold War, the rationale for authoritarianism dissolved. But the regulated market model is rooted in a different world order, that of globalization, which is not likely to vanish any time soon. The state's role is seen as providing the political stability for market forces to do their work, and the regulatory interventions needed to ensure that international trade and investment benefits the host countries and not just foreign partners. The regulated market seems to represent a viable organizational response to the exigencies of life in the post-Cold War world for these two large, ex-socialist powers.

This phenomenon opens the door to a new phase of global development in which the rules of the game may not be dictated by the established Western powers. Russia and China want to be rule-makers and not just rule-takers on the international stage. But is the development path of the two respective countries sustainable? And if so, will they be able to forge a consensus with the other leading powers on a new set of values, different from those currently in force, which will shape the global political and economic institutions of the next decade? Countries such as Brazil, India, South Africa, Mexico, and Indonesia are also experiencing rapid growth having embraced international integration—but unlike Russia and China they are robust democracies. So, the globalized world is not "flat": there is a broad and diverse range of viable models that have emerged in response to its challenges.

Figure 1 *Contrasting Reform Paths*

	Sequence	Pace	Initiative	Spirit	Western advice
Russia	Politics First	Rapid	Top-down	Shock therapy	Strong influence
China	Economy first	Gradual	Middle-up	Controlled transition	No influence

China and India: The Institutional Roots of Differential Performance

Ashwani Saith *

■ At the Races

Ever since Independence in India in 1947, and Liberation in China in 1949, there has been intense interest in the comparative economic performance of the two Asian giants. China showcased revolutionary socialism to be constructed under the central command of the communist party; India aspired to a "socialistic pattern of society" and boasted a parliamentary democracy. Who would win? In the charged post-colonial era of the Cold War, on the dawn of the release from the last century of colonialism, the eyes of the world's nations and peoples were on this race. The two great powers were also in the stands, with more than just a gambling stake or voyeuristic interest in the outcome—it was no ordinary day at the races.

Following his trip to Asia in 1953, John Foster Dulles, the US Secretary of State, shared his thoughts on India and China: "There is occurring between these two countries a competition as to whether ways of freedom or police state methods can achieve better social progress. This competition affects directly 800 million people in these two countries. In the long run, the outcome will affect all of humanity, including ourselves. " (Bowles, 1954, p. 229, cited in Ghosh, 2002) The Indian Prime Minister Jawaharlal Nehru, writing in 1954, was equally forthright: "The most

* Ashwani Saith is Professor of Rural Economics at the Institute of Social Studies; Visiting Professor at the London School of Economics & Political Science, UK; and Visiting Professor at the Institute for Human Development, New Delhi.

An earlier version of this paper formed the Silver Jubilee Lecture at the Centre for Social and Economic Studies, Hyderabad, on 27 March, 2006; a shorter adapted text was presented at the Symposium in honour of Professor Ajit Singh at Queens' College, Cambridge, on 15 September, 2007. I am grateful to participants at both events, and to the reviewers of the paper, for their feedback.

exciting countries for me today are India and China. We differ, of course, in our political and economic structures, yet the problems we face are essentially the same. The future will show which country and which structure of government yields greater results in every way. " (Frankel, 1978, p. 120, cited in Ghosh, 2002)

Half a century later, Nehru's question of the future was given an answer by India's current Prime Minister, Dr Manmohan Singh, in his Independence Day Address to the Nation:

> It is almost sixty years since Independence. It is but a brief period in the history of an ancient civilization. But, it is a long time in the life of a young nation. In these sixty years, the world has been transformed beyond recognition. The empires of Europe have faded away. New powers have emerged in Asia. Look at where Japan was and where it is today. Look at where China was and where it is today. When I see them, I wonder whether we are living up to our full potential or not. (Singh, 2006)

Behind the polite protocol of good-neighbourly coexistence and a shared rhetoric of anti-imperialism, the economic and political rivalry between the two countries has been tense and intense, both regionally and internationally. Both countries wanted to modernize their systems and achieve rapid long-term growth with equity. However, it is arguable that in their own perceptions, the two horses were running different, independent, races. India mostly compared its performance with its own past, demonstrating the achievements of the new proud independent nation relative to the stagnation and mass deprivation of the colonial era. Against a stationary object, this was not a particularly difficult race to win. A second yardstick was the internal comparison with its own adopted plan targets— had they been achieved, and usually, of course, they had not. China, on the other hand, never seriously compared its own performance with its Himalayan neighbour. Doing better than India was not the issue: the challenge was to catch up with the West. In 1958, the Chinese Communist Party launched the campaign to "Catch up with Great Britain in Fifteen Years" (Selden, 1979, p. 78). China had set itself targets on a truly Himalayan scale.

The life cycle of the fluctuating relationship between the two neighbours traverses several phases. They started off together, both flush with the national and social pride of independence and liberation and the adoption of high agendas of structural transformation. This was the stage of the slogan of brotherhood, "Indo-Chini, *Bhai-Bhai!* ", where the would-be siblings emphasized what they had shared up to that historical conjuncture. Zhou Enlai visited India in the winter of 1956, at which point the brotherliness was at its peak. This was reversed dramatically in the next few years, when the inheritance of colonialism in the form of contested borders surfaced as friction, acrimony and eventually as war in 1962. In India, China the brother was suddenly transformed into China the dragon, ushering in an extended period of the siblings falling out and growing apart—"Indo-Chini, Bye-Bye! ". It took tumultuous changes in both economies and societies, and two generations before Rajiv Gandhi, Nehru' s grandson, visited China in 1988 taking a first step towards normalization and to a resolution of the longstanding conflict. Several exchanges of visits by leaders—Premier Li Peng to India in January 2001 and Prime Minister Vajpayee to China in 2003—alongside the emergence of regimes in both countries which highlight market-led, state managed capitalist growth have created a similarity of ideological orientation. Both countries share similar powerful national aspirations, consumer-driven economies characterized by a toleration of high degrees of inequality. This ushered in the current phase in the relationship, possibly involving reconciliation, one we might characterize by the slogan "Indo-Chini, Buy-Buy! ".

Starting together in terms of similar initial conditions and levels of development, the two economies grew apart, with China pulling ahead across the entire broad front of development indicators. In the last decade, there has been an acceleration in the macro-economic performance of the Indian economy, generating much triumphalism amongst the Indian elite and inducing speculation as to whether India is catching up with China, if the two economies are converging, with the seriously optimistic daring to ask if India might soon overtake China. [1]

---

[1] See for instance, Goldman Sachs, 2003; Huang, 2006; Huang and Khanna, 2003; Poddar and Yi, 2007.

▪ Matched Competitors?

Could the outcome of the race not have been pre-determined by a high initial level of inequality between the competitors? Were the contenders fairly matched at the starting line?

Colonial Legacies and Systemic Features

A meaningful comparison cannot be reduced to a single economic axis of comparison; also pertinent are other initial conditions, specific colonial legacies and systemic features.

There were many broad similarities. Both systems inherited economies characterized by mass rural poverty under feudal modes of production in the countryside. Walter Mallory, R. H. Tawney and John Lossing Buck testify to the structural vulnerabilities of the Chinese peasantry, just as Dadabhai Naoroji, William Digby, Romesh Dutt and other early anti-colonial stalwarts attest to the endemic state of rural destitution in India. Both societies displayed acute, embedded forms of patriarchy with its flagrant manifestations of gender violence and oppressions: female infanticide, foot-binding, child marriage and so forth.

But alongside this, there is evidence that both systems had maturing non-agricultural economies involving comparatively developed systems of technology. Radha Sinha and Mark Elvin advance the notion of the high-level equilibrium trap for explaining Chinese economic stagnation in pre-Liberation China; variously, many historians, including Irfan Habib, Tapan Raychaudhuri, Amiya Bagchi and Bipin Chandra, have argued that deindustrialization under colonialism interrupted an embryonic, potentially viable process of capitalist economic development. By the time of independence, both countries had distressed agricultural systems, high inequalities with not insignificant potential economic surplus, but without an institutional framework of economic mechanisms for utilizing these productively for modern economic growth.

In spite of these similarities, there were also some crucial differences. One prime contrast lies in the realm of society and culture. China, as a nation state and society, is characterized by the overwhelming dominance of the Han ethnic group; numerically it constitutes roughly 90% of the population. There is just one dominant language which functions effectively as a *lingua franca* across the entire nation. Such cultural homogeneity provided a crucial, actively enabling environment for the specific needs of Chinese development. It provided the basis of a broad acceptance and legitimation of state authority structures; for a commonality of socio-cultural orientations and interests; and it contributed crucially to the viability of what I call the *mass mobilizational mode of transformation*. The contrast with India could not be wider, with the latter's mosaic of languages and cultures; its frictional cellular structures of caste and class divisions and its fractious religious diversity. [2] It is the former feature that allowed China to so radically transform its institutions and economy in such a short frame of time; it is the latter complexity that perhaps made rapid Indian change more contested and difficult.

In both cases, the colonial experience had a profound impact on the shaping of the future state and its transformative development imperatives and agendas. Yet there were also some profound differences, the implications of which carry through and account for some important contrasts in their subsequent development trajectories.

While both post-independent governments inherited a tired and tawdry agriculture with most surplus squeezed out by a rapacious and non-investing class of landlords, there was one telling difference. While the landowning class had lost out in the socialist revolution in China, it effectively remained powerful in India as an integral part of the winning coalition of classes that gained independence, protected by and well ensconced in the ruling political party, and able to thwart any further redistributive or collectivist agrarian reforms.

Colonial penetration was never so deep and total in China, even on the coast, as in India. The British colonial regime governed India through direct mechanisms as well as through arrangements and settlements imposed

---

2   A recent national ethnographic profile identified 4,694 communities (Singh, 2000). In 2001, 13 languages were each spoken by more than ten million persons, 29 by more than a million persons, and 122 by at least 10,000, and only ten of twenty-eight states had accepted Hindi as their official language. For good measure, about a dozen different major scripts are used. There are eight major religions. In the context of affirmative action programmes, 3,743 castes were identified within the "other backward classes" category alone, and non-Hindu groups have their own internal caste hierarchies and divisions.

on local rulers, using an administrative machine manned largely by Indians educated with this very role in mind, as expressed in the colonial policy vision of Wood and Macaulay. A new middle class of bureaucratic and usually comprador functionaries emerged who, in Macaulay's famous terminology, were English in all respects but the colour of their skin. This was later to form an important bulwark of the Indian Congress Party, the precursor of the embryonic Indian state. Much later, this inheritance of a massive middle class, educated well in English, combined with the Nehruvian emphasis on modern scientific education (as through the formation of the now much-vaunted family of the Indian Institutes of Technology) and the slow-growing Indian economy to generate an infinite supply of highly skilled labour at a low wage. This serendipitous conjuncture of factors at least partially forms the initial basis of the Indian information technology (IT) software explosion that has spearheaded recent services-led accelerated growth. In contrast, it is the relative reduction of the unit cost of labour, alongside a relatively high level of human development that created the Lewisian-type situation for the manufacturing sector-led development in China.

The vital difference lay in the constitution of state power in the two systems, and that was itself a product of the political forces and processes that achieved independence from colonialism. In China, power emerged in the hands of a revolutionary communist party based on peasants and workers: effectively, state power was in the hands of the poor and their direct representatives. In the terminology of Perkins (1975), the poor were placed in command. The mass acceptance of this revolutionary power, alongside the high degree of cultural homogeneity, formed the basis for the mass mobilization mode of production certainly in the period up to, and partially beyond, the reforms of 1978. Earlier exclusionary power structures were swept away in the revolutionary struggles involving military action against colonials and indigenous class oppositions.

In India, by contrast, the control of the independence movement remained fundamentally in the hands of the middle and upper classes and castes, and thus the structures that emerged with independence, including the state, while being nationalist in language and some substance, remained primarily the instruments of the broad class/caste interests of the propertied sections that formed the backbone of the Indian Congress Party at the time.

Gandhian non-violence, while intrinsically laudable, was also opportunistically used at key conjunctures to prevent the leadership and control of potential mass movements from slipping away from the indigenous elite, (in) famously, for instance, during the spontaneous, grassroots Eka (or "unity") movement in the 1920s. [3] The direct violence of Japanese colonialism further radicalized and hastened the Chinese revolution, whereas the sophisticated cunning of the British rulers was mindful that post-independence power should remain in the hands of the Indian elite with which it could continue, in due course, to do business.

Initial Conditions: Similar Economic Structures, 1950

Despite all the specificities, in 1950, India and China had remarkably strong structural similarities. Weisskopf (1980, pp. 81 - 82) estimates a per capita GDP (in US $ at 1960 prices) of 65 for China, and 62 for India. In the labour force, the share of agriculture was 77% in China and 72% in India; in industry 7% in China and 11% in India; and in other sectors 16% in China and 17% in India. In China in 1952, the share of agriculture in total output was 48%; in India in 1950, it was 51%; large-scale manufacturing and utilities generated 9% of the total output in China, and 6% in India; small-scale manufacturing and construction accounted for 9% in China and 10% in India.

The competitors were clearly well matched at the starting line. At the outset, the structures of economy and society shared strong similarities. But there were equally striking differences in the domains of institutions and polity. The outcome of the race, and also the margin and manner of its winning, then highlight the role of some of these differentiating features.

▪ Who Is Ahead?

What has happened thus far? It is not necessary to track each lap in this marathon of giants. The bottom line is clear and unambiguous. In terms of comparative performance since 1950 with respect to a full range of material, economic and social indicators, there can be no argument that

---

3   For a contextual analysis of the conditions leading up to it, see Saith, 1978, Ch. 2; for a skilful deconstruction, see Amin, 1995; for a powerful indictment in 1939, see Kosambi, 1957.

China has performed emphatically better than India.[4] Starting from a virtually identical position in 1950, China's per capita income stood at twice the Indian level in 2003; it has a much lower incidence of headcount poverty regardless of the specific methodologies used; at seventy-one, its life expectancy is six years more than that of the average Indian; its adult literacy rate is 91% compared to 65% for India; it has more than twice as many physicians per head of population as India; only 8% of its under-fives are moderately underweight and none are severely so, whereas for India, as many as 47% are moderately or severely underweight; only 14% of children suffer from moderate or severe stunting in China, but as many as 46% do in India.

At the outset, while China had less arable land per capita[5], this was cultivated more intensively and with higher physical yields, so that per capita agricultural output was not much different from the Indian level. By 1978, clearly discernible differences in the conditions of the agricultural sector had emerged and distances in social indicators had magnified dramatically in favour of superior Chinese performance; by the turn of the millennium, the gaps in productivity indicators had become chiasmic. In terms of agricultural yields (in kilograms per hectare) for the 2003—2005 period, wheat stood at 2,688 in India against 4,155 in China; rape/mustard was 909 in India and nearly twice that level, at 1,778 in China; and rice in India was 3,034, and more than twice as much, at 6,233, in China. The annual growth rates for yields during the 1990—2005 period for rape/mustard were 0.6% in India and 3% in China; and those for rice, 1.0% in India and 2.1% in China. Not only are the levels higher, but they are also diverging for some of the main crops.

On other comparisons, electricity consumption per capita—a crucial indicator—is 893 kwh in China, compared with just 379 in India; cement production is 650 m. tons per year in China, and 109 in India; steel production amounts to 163 m. tons in China and 29 m. tons in India. In China, as much as 53% of GDP comes from industry; in India only 26%.

---

4 The data in this section refer variously to the 2002—2005 period and are assembled from a variety of official national and international statistical sources, including SSB (various issues).

5 In 1965, arable land per head of agricultural population was 0.18 hectares in China, but 0.46 hectares in India (Saith, 1995b, p.34, Table 4).

Of course, in comparison, India obtains 52% of its GDP from services, while the percentage for China is only 32—though it is questionable if this comparison fully reflects a mature, or a partially residual services sector. Regardless of this, the Chinese growth rates in agriculture, industry and services are all above the Indian ones.

For those who might point to the sterling performance of India's IT sector, it is worth noting that, per 1, 000 persons, fixed line and mobile phone subscribers in China numbered 424 in 2003, as against just 71 in India; Internet users in China were 63 against 17 in India, and personal computers totalled 28 in China (in 2002) compared with 7 in India. Yet others might wish to dwell on the merchandise bilateral trade surplus in India's favour, as trade burgeons between them; but they would do well to scrutinize the pattern of trade and reflect on the sobering finding that more than 50% of India's exports to China were made up of iron ore, while the largest imports from China into India were machinery.

Already a Gap at the Mid-way Point

Most often, observers point to the growth-unleashing impact of the Chinese economic reforms after 1978, and to the fact that neoliberal reforms started rather later in India, where the dating of the switch-point varies between 1980 and 1990. [6] Regardless of this, however, a crucial fact is that the differential performance was already observable in substantial measure by 1978.

The annual growth rate of Indian GDP during 1960—1980 was 3. 6% ; during 1970—1990, it was 4. 7% ; and for the period 1985—1990, it rose further to 6. 2% . This acceleration was accompanied by rising investment rates and declining incremental capital—output ratios (Saith, 1995b, p. 31, Table 1). Between 1961 and 1970, the average annual growth rate of agricultural production per capita was 0. 4% in India, and 3. 7% in China; for the decade 1971—1980, the rates were 0. 4% and 1. 5% , respectively. (see

---

6　The issue of the timing of the switch point in Indian economic performance is a topic in itself. It would be overly simplistic to date it from 1990; this would conflate its timing with the fanfare of the switch in official orientation of Indian economic policy, as incumbent government economists and politicians are wont to do. However, there is considerable evidence that the neoliberal reform process began during the 1980s.

Saith, 1995b, Table 5 and sources cited therein).

By 1980, the share of GDP from industry had exploded to 48. 5% in China, but was only 21. 9% in India; for 2003, the figures were 53% and 26% respectively. This wide gap had opened up, significantly, by 1980, and has persisted since then. On the other hand, the share of agriculture in GDP had, by 1980, dropped in China to 30. 1% (compared to 42. 8% for India); and fell further to just 15% by 2003 (23% for India). India showed a much higher share for services throughout; being 35. 3% in 1980 (21. 4% for China); and 52% in 2003 (32% for China). (Weisskopf, 1980) It is this sort of comparison that has prompted many to regard China as the world's factory, and India as the world's office.

Thus, from the same starting point around 1950, China had outpaced India dramatically in the first three decades of planned development, notably also in the rural sector, and pulled away discernibly further (on most material and human development indicators) in the second market-led phase of the race to the present. The answer to the question, who won the race, is not much in doubt. Indeed the margin of the victory, after the first sixty years, is quite astonishing; it is one that might have alarmed Nehru should he have seen it, and one that could well explain the touch of ruefulness in Manmohan Singh's implicit acknowledgement of economic defeat.

▪ Why?

Since wide differentials were already apparent by the mid-way point, it is appropriate to seek explanations through the operation of factors active prior to that point, highlighting the contrasts between the two.[7] For China, this also calls for a careful assessment of the contribution of the collectivist development period to post-1978 economic performance.

An Overview

There are close similarities between the early Indian and Chinese

---

7　For this reason, the following treatment pays greater attention to the rural than to the formal industrial sector.

development strategies at the level of idea and intent, if not in terms of ground realities of implementation and of outcomes. In the context of the seminal Indian Second Five Year Plan, Mahalanobis—the pioneering theoretician of Indian planning—had argued the case for a land reform and for a land army that would provide universal employment to the rural landless for the purpose of constructing rural infrastructure; he conceptualized the need for a rural or traditional small-scale industrial sector that would be given some protection and which would balance the anticipated deficit of the employment equation for the modern industrial sector. The key differences lay not just in other aspects of the planned strategy, such as agriculture, but in the nature of the economy, society, polity and the character of the state, that is, structural aspects of the realities within which the ideas were meant to be realized.

This comparative parallel needs to be drawn out further. In both economies, the state-led, public sector based industrialization process was the key driver. In neither case did the central government invest heavily in rural development. While the Indian process wound up protecting or subsidizing the rural elite, the Chinese actually drew surplus from agriculture and the peasantry in favour of modern industrialization. Yet, the rural sector and the peasantry did remarkably better in China than in India. Why? How? The significance of the Chinese collectivist strategy lies in not jettisoning the peasantry and the rural sector after squeezing it of its surplus contributions for modern industrialization; rather, it has remained within the national frame, even if inter-sectoral inequalities have widened with the acceleration of the pace of industrialization.

It is argued here that the answer lies in the distinctive institutional configuration of the two economies, especially in the rural sector. In China, rural collectives worked as engines of accumulation in large parts of China, through ensuring an integration of agriculture and rural industry; through creating the incentives and the self-financing basis for vast labour accumulation that raised the productivity of land and generated forward and backward linkages to rural industry; and through supporting a strong upward trend in levels of human development. This in turn led to a more mature, generically skilled work force that was relatively well fed and provided for, and yet remained competitive in conventional unit cost terms. [8] The motive power underlying these developments was what I have labelled the mass mobilization mode of transformation that relied on massive inputs of human labour; this passes the baton of explanation to the ideological and motivational factors that released such committed labour investments. The Chinese rural masses all stood to gain directly from their own labour, since the benefits accrued to them as owners of the collective. None of these conditions were operational in the Indian countryside. Similarly designed macro-economic strategies then lead to widely divergent outcomes in the rural sector. In a later phase, this difference could mean that while the Chinese growth acceleration will find increasing space in a widening domestic market, the Indian path might find sustainability potentially choked by the sluggish home market in the rural sector, suggesting that the growth process is likely to be more exclusionary than in the Chinese case.

The Institutional Factor: Enabling or Constraining Change?

The two trajectories are clearly products of complex forces, and not easily reducible to simplistic explanations. Here, I wish to stress the significance of selected institutional and policy factors; in particular, that in many crucial respects the trajectories of the two economies had been set on structurally distinct foundations before 1978. In this, the role of the rural sector was critical; it is here that some of the greatest contrasts in institutions, growth and distributional outcomes are visible between the two systems. While the institutional framework served as a contextual rigidity and as a development constraint in India, in contrast, the Chinese socialist development state was able to address the institutional framework as a prime target variable, to be refashioned instrumentally as deemed functionally optimal with respect to accelerating the growth process. This dimension provides an underlying unifying leitmotiv over the entire period since 1949 in China.

The term institutional is used here in its broadest sense, covering personal, public and commercial domains, embracing value, belief and

---

8 For a fuller discussion, see Saith, 1995b, pp. 15 – 21.

faith systems; received and mediated norms and notions of the good life; norms guiding behaviour; lived culture as embedded in social structures and organizational forms; civil codes, penal systems, religious codes; and all these as embedded in social structures and organizational forms and relations and networks, such as family, marriage, households, communities, collectivities, companies, occupational class and caste constituencies, and neighbourhoods, ethnic and religious groups, nations, global or cosmopolitan ethical, i. e. , local, national and global civil society.[9] Usually, these institutional dimensions, which underpin and stabilize socio-economic and political transactions and societal arrangements, are the cement that binds units and provides the parameters of dynamic evolutions, often with a high degree of path dependence, clay-clay stickiness, and a high degree of inertial ballast to the system as a whole. Continuity is thus written into the script, not discontinuous change; evolutionary trends,

rather than revolutionary breaks. It was perhaps the cumulative force of the inherited institutional dimension, fashioned and reproduced over centuries, that inspired such formulations as the Hindu rate of growth, or the depiction of India as an elephant, large, slow moving, with a long memory. No doubt old China could have been similarly regarded. But the Chinese revolution broke the inherited feudal mould, and forced the construction of an institutional frame that was functional to the accelerated construction of a socialist economy and society.

In India the institutional framework specifies the context and constraints for policy formulation; in China, the institutional framework is itself a prime target variable, an object of policy. In India, the institutional framework is realistically taken as the constant, sticky, unchanging context, a constraint, within the straitjacket of which development occurs. It is subject to change, but only in evolutionary, reluctant terms. In China, in contrast, the institutional framework has formed not the contextual constraint, but a policy-amenable instrumental catalyst of the development strategy. Traditional institutional frameworks have been swept aside; new ones designed and constructed in acutely compressed time

---

9 However, in order not to lose explanatory power, in what follows, institutional dimensions are identified and used with greater particularity in context and process specific arguments.

frames, and then again dumped for yet other institutional templates deemed more appropriate for the national development strategy. Kojima (1982) astutely described this as the perennial Chinese search for institutions that seek out, release and exploit new potential sources of accumulation and growth, irrespective of the ideological lexicon of the time. The continuity is provided by the underlying foundational consensus and motivation of sustained material advancement and national strength.

Handling the Ricardian Constraint: A Comparison of the Land Reform Processes

As early as the Second Five Year Plan, various economists, including Dobb (1951) and Kalecki (1964/1976), had pointed to the need to resolve the Ricardian constraint that would otherwise hold back Indian growth. The need for meaningful land reforms, which catered both to equity and efficiency considerations, was paramount. No such resolution took place. Indian agrarian reforms have a long history. There was a tortuous pre-independence period that cut down the lands and power of the old *zamindars* and *taluqdars.* [10] This process culminated in North India, in the Zamindari Abolition Act that provided firm ownership rights to a class of superior tenants who formed the first land-operating layer under the *zamindars* and *taluqdars.* These beneficiaries were strongly represented in the Congress Party, and this has much to do with the subsequent loss of all momentum for further redistributive or radical land reforms in the direction of co-operatives. The few reforms that have occurred since then have focused on the consolidation of holdings, and on the registration of tenants' rights as in West Bengal. Most land reform interventions have languished in courts, and the agrarian structure has shown acute signs of disaggregation through the progressive sub-division of owned holdings under conditions of a turgid and blocked land market. The result is that there is endemic (near) landlessness, a dominance of uneconomic marginal, fragmented holdings, with the vast majority being below a scale which can

---

10 For a discussion of this, see Saith, 1978, Ch. 2. Stokes (1975) provides an empirical depiction
   of this secular trend towards the disaggregation of the agrarian structure between 1860 and 1948.

guarantee a reasonable level of living. In such scenarios, the small islands of commercial agriculture do not have any compensatory capacity for employment generation, and general production-oriented strategies structurally fail to reach the poor sections of the rural population. After over a century since the institution of the first serious land acts in Uttar Pradesh, the structural situation is perhaps more acute than it ever was, with few indications that the foreseeable future is likely to witness any reversal of direction. The Indian economic story might have been radically different in several crucial respects, not least in terms of superior distributional outcomes laying the basis for more sustainable longer term growth, had the Indian land reform process been deeper and been enacted around the time of the launching of the new development process. It is worth recording that each of the successful East Asian cases has incorporated such a powerful egalitarian land reform virtually as an initial pre-condition. [11]

The Chinese case provides a complete contrast. Starting from a roughly equivalent agrarian structure displaying similar features of acute fragmentation and distress (Riskin, 1975), the development strategy effectively overcame the Ricardian constraint through the replacement of the inefficient and inequitable feudal agrarian formation by dynamic and egalitarian, growth-oriented People's Communes. The impressive sequence of reforms dramatically outdoes and outpaces the foot-dragging minimalist Indian case. The initial land reforms of 1949—1952 left substantial residual asset inequalities; these were addressed through the subsequent creation of elementary and then advanced producer co-operatives, culminating in the formation of the first, problematic, type of large People's Communes covering 98% of the countryside by September 1958. The final stages of the transition had taken less than three years (Selden, 1979, p. 79, Table 6). Re-modelled, smaller, three-tier communes provided the rural

---

11 The role of cooperative and collective rural institutional arrangements has been widely emphasized, including for instance by Joan Robinson (1979, p. 135): "Some kind of cooperative or collective property in land and in means of production is necessary to provide a frame in which modernisation can go on without polarisation between wealth and misery which it is bringing about all over the Third World today."

institutional template from 1962 until de-collectivization. The structural characteristics of these People's Communes have been extensively scrutinized. Their institutional attributes enabled the dynamic mass mobilization mode of transformation; schemes of labour accumulation; the industrialization of the countryside; the pre-emption of distress out-migration of peasants following the traditional well-beaten paths to the towns; exploitation of economies of scale and scope; and potential for the effective universal social provisioning of health, education and food security as a common right.

The second reform was as dramatically precipitous. The Chinese authorities experimented quietly with prototypical forms of decollectivization in chosen locations with various alternative contractual systems: *bao chan dao zu; bao chan dao hu; bao gan dao hu*. The objective was to establish the preferred configuration that would displace the People's Commune on a national scale. Once the decision was made, the institutional transition displayed characteristically amazing rapidity. Until 1978, the commune system was essentially intact. In January 1980, only 0. 02% —that is, virtually none—of the basic accounting units were employing the *bao gan dao hu* contract that came to be known as the household production responsibility system. By the end of 1980, this figure stood at just 5% , but it had risen to 38% by October 1981; and to 70% by December 1982, with another 22% covered by the other two contractual reform systems on trial. In a country as vast as China, the revolutionary collectivist reforms had been virtually reversed to peasant holdings in the breathless space of just two years.

The sweeping abolition of the People's Communes, while providing each household with the universal land endowment which served as a cushion and insurance against the vicissitudes of the new strategy, also created the need for such insurance by cutting off the direct access that peasants had earlier enjoyed to the jobs and economic surpluses generated by the dynamic commune and brigade-run enterprises. The balance sheet of the second land reform is complex. But what it demonstrates again is the ability of the system to reshape its basic institutions to make them functional to the perceived needs of any reorientations in the development strategy. The contrast with the Indian scenario could not be more extreme.

Chinese Collective Labour Accumulation versus Indian Rural Public Works

It is instructive to look inside the rural People's Communes in China's period of high collectivism, 1962—1978.[12] With his characteristic ideological ingenuity, Mao introduced the notion of labour accumulation, in contra-distinction to capital accumulation. Essentially, he argued that in a populous, poor agrarian economy, there was an opportunity to create rural land-related infrastructure through an investment of this peasant labour into accumulation projects—hence, labour accumulation (LA). Such labour was dramatically mobilized across China, and formed one of the twin engines of rural development—all this in a period when it is acknowledged that the pattern of inter-sectoral resource flows was tilted against the rural sector by State policy. Such LA had a major impact on agricultural productivity in large parts of rural China, and provided synergetic demand and supply side impulses that triggered off a dynamic growth process within the communes.[13]

The other engine was rural industrialization within the commune: this also used surplus labour from within the collective, and generated high financial surpluses, which went into four major uses: further diversification of the unit's non-farm portfolio of activities; significantly, into projects of agricultural development; into providing a social consumption floor to all the members of the unit; and into further strengthening the capacity of local government. Peasants contributed higher productivity labour in rural non-farm activities, or hard manual labour into LA projects, but were paid in work points at an implicit wage rate that was linked to the average consumption level of the peasant households of the unit concerned. As a result, financial surpluses earned by the rural non-farm (RNF) enterprises accumulated almost automatically and were recycled with their dynamic

---

12 For a detailed analysis of the Chinese experience before and after the Reforms, see Saith (1987, 1993, 1995a, 2001, pp. 90 – 94).

13 The role of labour accumulation in the period of high collectivism, and its decline in the post-reform period is discussed in Saith (1995a, pp. 212 – 217). Earlier treatments confirming the extensive, though occasionally problematic, contribution of labour accumulation to rural development are to be found in the work of Minquan (1991), Nickum (1978), Raj (1983/2006, pp. 265 – 266) and Vermeer (1977).

multipliers generating locally egalitarian growth.

LA has been criticized, naively, by many as an example of *corvee*, or coerced, unpaid labour. This is patently incorrect, since the labour investment of households in any one year on a productive project earned its returns once the project's benefits came on line after completion, and these benefits accrued to all members of the collectively owned unit. While there were some white elephants, and while admittedly many unsound schemes might have wasted some effort, no serious scholar or field observer of rural China of the period could fail to register the remarkable impact of such a vast country-wide bootstraps-type of operation. It catalysed and launched the rural development process. From the point of view of rural households, this was additional work for additional income, not just from the LA project, but also from the indirect returns that came from the rural industrialization that it enabled. Within this, mechanization was undertaken when it contributed to overall productivity, and labour displacement was not an issue, again, since the benefits were shared out. This mass mobilization mode of transformation was essentially fired by ideological zeal and commitment though, as mentioned, within the micro-level collectivist units there were well thought out co-operative payment systems with a robust economic logic for that stage of development. The process was both sustainable for an extended period and capable of nation-wide replication, since it was essentially locally self-financing and therefore free of the usually throttling constraint of pre-financing of such investments by the government.

It would be unthinkable to imagine that this scale of rural investment and transformation could have been initiated by state withdrawal and simple open market signals within an inegalitarian agrarian structure. This is, in fact, what the dismal experience of rural South Asia confirms. The current discussions over the alleged financial constraint to the acceptance of any universal employment guarantee scheme in India provides a good example. The schemes have to be pre-financed. There has never really been a hard enough look taken at their productivity. Even when the infrastructure created by the scheme is productive, the government is unable to include the incremental benefits in its resource mobilization net. So the financial hurdle exists in the real sense that there is no automatic internal circuit which recycles the benefit streams into payments for past labour, and investments for future expansion. When such employment-generating rural public works (RPW) schemes are launched, they need fiscal allocations from the state. This severely limits their scope and coverage.

Careful scrutiny is also necessary of how these schemes (do not) function as forms of anti-poverty interventions. There are fundamental blind-spots in the manner in which such interventions are evaluated and validated, leading to serious misinterpretations of their development impact. RPWs are intended to raise agricultural productivity and generate related multiplier effects. Most of these are trapped, both during the construction and especially the operational phase of these projects, by local non-target, landowning groups.

In the evaluation methodology applied to such schemes the criterion for targeting efficiency is concerned with the percentage of target group *beneficiaries* in the *construction* phase of the scheme, and so would overlook the pattern of incidence of the stream of direct benefits generated by the scheme in subsequent years for the target as against the non-target groups. Data from a study in Bangladesh[14] provide an insight into the dramatic extent to which such a methodology hides the reality and the identities of the true beneficiaries of the public investments made for the rural poor. The bottom line of overall ratio of benefits from the schemes showed that three-quarters of the total benefits generated went to the non-target groups as windfalls! This is a shocking result; all the more so since such schemes are launched in the name of the poor.

The wage benefits accruing to the poor from these schemes are far from adequate: they are sporadic, shifting and not sustainable livelihood sources for even those households that can participate in them. But the total stream of benefits, including those to non-target groups, could be quite considerable, especially if the schemes are productive. The question is: how can the poor tap into this wider river, instead of being restricted to the fitful trickle-down flows that come their way? As it is, the dice are loaded against the poor working on such schemes. The caloric value of the returns per day for performing hard manual labour on these schemes is much lower, possibly as low as about one-half, than the energy expended in earning these returns. It has also been demonstrated that even with the assumption of full employment at legal minimum wages set for rural India,

---

14   For a more detailed discussion and sources, see Saith, 1992, Ch. 4.

the average agricultural labour household would not be able to obtain the equivalent of the poverty line income (Kannan, 2005, pp. 2 – 3).

Clearly new forms of institutional contracts are needed through which the working poor who create these public assets can also claim some version of ownership or lease rights which give them a rightful claim to the non-wage component of the value-added generated by the infrastructure. Such institutional arrangements have to be supplemented with direct and indirect financial instruments and devices that enable charges to be levied and recovered, either locally or through more indirect higher-level fiscal circuits, from the landowner or other groups which have thus far been receiving windfalls. In turn, this requires new kinds of contracts between stakeholders. The existing arrangements lead to low and low-quality assets, but suit everyone: the politician who gets publicity, the contractor who gets the money for low quality construction, the civil servant, the landowners who get something for nothing, and the poor, who at least get something out of it. That the quality and the longevity of the scheme do not bother any one of the stakeholders too seriously is then hardly a matter of surprise. Resources disappear into a black hole of expediency. But other ways are possible. [15] There are regular reports of endemic corruption in the implementation of the RPW schemes associated with the recently adopted Indian National Rural Employment Guarantee Act (NREGA) inviting the question as to whether these rural employment interventions for poverty reduction should be called schemes or scams. [16]

---

15 It is technically possible, as the Chinese have shown, to make good use of the idle time of the cultivators (once they have enough to eat all the year round) to improve irrigation, check erosion, build roads, and so on, but individual property in land is an impediment to such schemes because of the problem of who is to get the benefit from them (Robinson and Eatwell, 1973, p. 328).

16 A substantial body of empirical evidence testifies to extensive leakages in the targeting of various anti-poverty programmes, see Saith, 2005. Investigative media reports regularly highlight endemic corruption and mal-governance in NREGA projects. The cumulative weight of these findings has prompted an official audit of the national portfolio of NREGA projects. The official report is a devastating catalogue of acts of omission and commission, and makes depressing reading. Virtually every level of formal requirement was found to be widely violated in a significant number of states, districts or gram panchayats. The overall coverage was also dismal: 38. 1 million households registered under the scheme; only 55% of these received any employment; and a miniscule 2. 2 million, or 5. 8%, of the registered households received their full entitlement of 100 days of employment per household (GOI, 2007, p. 9). Further, investigators from civil society organizations frequently suffer violence at the hands of the local political mafia.

The Productivity versus Employment Trade-off

Two examples demonstrate how this vexatious and ubiquitous trade-off was institutionally resolved in rural China, but took its toll in the Indian countryside.

The power of collective institutional arrangements with regard to land ownership is demonstrated by the case of labour-displacing but productivity-enhancing technological change. This could take the form of the mechanization of various otherwise labour-intensive operations, extending from land preparation, to planting, irrigation, harvesting and threshing. In the Indian case, this leads to labour displacement and the loss of wages for the laid off workers. In the Chinese case, the productivity gains are shared by all workers, who now acquire some time released for other productive, or leisure, activities. Thus, while both India and China had acute problems of surplus labour, China adopted extensive rural mechanization even while stressing labour accumulation projects in parallel. The gap between private and social profitability of mechanization was not relevant in the Chinese collective, but was wide in the Indian case, taking the form of the loss of incomes of displaced agricultural workers.

Another powerful example of the importance of institutional change laying the basis for rural modernization in China is provided by rural industrial enterprises (Saith, 1987, 1996). At the time of the formation of the People's Communes, the scattered traditional low productivity and low technology rural crafts and manufacturing activities were centralized within the co-operative structure and were then rationalized and modernized as co-operative ventures. There was no danger of the familiar story of the destitution of the uncompetitive rural handicrafts sector, since here the displaced persons could be absorbed in the agricultural sector if necessary. The growth of rural demand, in any event, limited the need for such relocations. Also, these enterprises were located within the commune and were thus owned by the peasants, not by rich landlords. Thus, the process and product upgrading and modernization using mechanized labour-displacing methods in these rural handicraft enterprises could be managed without creating the classic flow of impoverished expelled rural artisans. The conflict, so characteristic of capitalist systems, between higher productivity through labour displacement on the one side, and employment generation and distributional outcomes on the other, was pre-empted, with institutional change converting the nature of the game.

These rural industrial enterprises, which were stimulated by the forward and backward linkages of successful processes of labour accumulation, themselves constituted engines of rural investment and growth. It was akin to the workings of an intra-rural sector Lewisian process of accumulation and growth working within the collectivist institutional framework of the People's Commune. Peasants working on the rural enterprises owned by their collective earned work points which were cashed back in their agricultural teams at conversion rates roughly equivalent to the average distributed income per peasant. The productivity gap between the farm and the enterprise was retained by the enterprise and then used according to an agreed formula, with a significant share going back into agricultural investment. Peasant consumption levels were more linked to the productivity of the farm sector than the incomes earned in the non-farm units of the collective. In regions where non-farm enterprises could thrive, the collectives became powerful internal agents of rural accumulation so obviously lacking in other parts of the developing world, including rural India.

Field investigations in Cheng Dong People's Commune on the outskirts of Shanghai provided a microcosmic demonstration, in 1978, of the dynamic transformative power of the model. Of its gross income, more than three-quarters came from above the team level, nearly half at the commune level; of its total accumulation, 83% came above the team level, over half at the commune level; at the team level, 12% of the net income was accumulated, but at the commune level, 50% of the net income was accumulated. As growth and development occurred, the share of the higher levels increased steadily (Griffin and Saith, 1981, pp. 75 − 77, Tables 5. 1-3). The commune resembled a modern small-scale industrial estate, but one owned by the peasants who had thereby also managed to invest a substantial part of the surplus back into agriculture, infrastructure and social development. It was typical of the strong people's commune, its strength deriving essentially from favourable location in an agriculturally and industrially prosperous area. It was communes such as Cheng Dong that initially opposed the Second Land Reform of 1978.

In contrast, in India, rural artisans and handicrafts have suffered steady erosion through unsustainable competition with modern manufactures. Over the decades, the outcome has been the virtual disappearance of the traditional manufacturing sector from village India, with only non-tradable goods and services surviving in pockets. The share of incomes of villagers that is earned from activities located in the village have steadily declined, being replaced by various forms of labour, and poverty-propelled participation in unskilled self-employment activities. Even when there are profitable rural enterprises, their surpluses do not get re-channelled into rural development, poverty reduction, infrastructure or further accumulation within the rural sector. The owners tend to invest in urban trade and property, leading to a further atrophying of the rural sector, thus intensifying the pressure to migrate. [17]

Overcoming the Information Dichotomy

The strategic value of cultural homogeneity and of the widespread acceptance of the leadership and authority of the socialist state are realized to great effect in the re-orientation of the economy and its institutions. The Chinese government used the new institutional and organizational structures created in the countryside to overcome the phenomenon of informational dichotomy, in which the central planners and leaders have a superior overall awareness of the objectives of development and the trade-offs between them, while the dispersed local units retain the downstream knowledge of their appropriateness, applicability, costs and constraints, at the disaggregated, micro level. National policies, with all their necessary local variations, could then be finalized through iterative information flows. It was through this type of interaction between the centre and the people's commune—which constituted the lowest rung of government— and then between the commune leadership and peasant households through the collective layers of the production brigades and teams, that policies could be rapidly formulated, re-oriented or fine-tuned. Two examples demonstrate how the institutional dichotomy was bypassed in rural China: one pertains to the generation and diffusion of new technology, and the

---

17 No doubt, there are regional variations, and possibly some exceptions, to this general trend. For an analytical overview, at macro and village levels, see Saith, 2001.

other to fashioning appropriate institutional change.

While much is made of the unchanged nature of agricultural technology in India and China in the hundred or more years before 1950, this was followed by dramatic changes in a short span of time. While the green revolution ushered in new technological packages for the larger landowning classes, large parts of the Indian peasantry were not its prime movers or main beneficiaries. The process of its diffusion was fitful and far from universal. This contrasts with the experience of China, where specific institutional features could be utilized for a rapid and up-scaled dissemination and adoption of new techniques on a significantly wider scale. The American delegation that visited rural China in 1977 to study agricultural technology and rural industry (ARSID, 1977) reported that prize competitions took place in various parts of rural China for the identification of the rice transplanting and harvesting technologies that were most suited to local conditions. This stimulated local, regional and national innovations. The designs were carefully selected after extensive scientific evaluations and then diffused on a national scale through the pyramid structure of government characterized by rapid two-way flows of information, of queries and responses, of instruction and action.

The second, generic case applies to institutional experiments. Should grain be distributed according to family size and structure, or according to the work points earned? What might be the optimal policy for the use of the household private plot allotment under socialism? How should the work point system be reformed? After the dissolution of the people's commune, what kind of tenurial and contractual system might be optimal? What parameters might be appropriate for the population control policy at the local level? How should different units relate to the process of labour accumulation, viz., rural infrastructure development, and what incentives or rules should guide the behaviour and decision of peasant households, production teams and other units? Perhaps the most powerful demonstration of this was the dramatically fast diffusion of the household production responsibility system, *bao gan dao hu*, during the early 1980s following the demise of the people's commune.

The institutional framework thus became a powerful instrument not just for the design and implementation of national policies, or the diffusion of innovations, but also for experimentation and redesigning of the institutional framework itself. Such institutional flexibility assured the functionality of the structures with respect to the needs of rapid growth within a socialist framework. Again, the contrast with the sticky, stagnant rural institutional framework in the Indian countryside is acute. The only meaningful experiment is Panchayati Raj, and this form of "local" village government most often merely tends to reflect and reproduce the inherited hierarchical, inegalitarian ownership and power structure. Of course, India abounds with non-governmental, civil society and activist development organizations, and there is an enormous cumulative experience including perhaps a compendium-sized potential list of "good practice" interventions. However, these tend to collapse at the first hurdle of up-scaling or diffusion to a regional, let alone the national, level. Meanwhile, the dominant role of state resources in rural programmes, especially poverty reduction schemes, is manifested through the local state, where local elites predictably and disproportionately capture the process and the outcomes.

The Mass Mobilization Mode (MMM) of Transformation

In the early years of Indo-Chinese co-operation, at the invitation of Madame Sun Yat Sen who visited India in 1955, a high-level Indian delegation visited China (and Japan) the following year to study the role of agrarian cooperatives in development and carry back transferable lessons applicable in the Indian rural landscape. The ensuing report (GOI, 1956) bears testimony to the explosion of collective energy in rural China:

> The phenomenal success achieved by the Chinese in the formation of agrarian cooperatives has astonished all, both inside China and outside it. To a visiting team from India, such as ours, who are used to individual cultivation, the Chinese success appeared no less than a miracle. Naturally, the first question that strikes anybody is, how was all this achieved in such a short period? (GOI, 1956, p. 86)

Perkins (1980, p. 127) rightly emphasizes the role of labour based transformation within the collective:

> In China, in contrast [to other LDCs, such as India], both urban and rural populations are hard at work throughout the entire year. Much of this activity is an occupation of very low productivity. Peasants carrying dirt from a nearby mountainside to build a dam or a small addition to the cultivated acreage are

doing back-breaking labor in exchange for often only modest increases in farm output. Many rural people, one suspects, would choose leisure time if they were free to do so. Whether voluntarily or not, China has succeeded in mobilizing billions of man-days of labor from a labor pool that in most less developed nations would have remained idle.

But how was such mass mobilization achieved? In Mao-speak, the answer lay "in releasing the enthusiasm of the masses". Anti-socialists tend to query, if not dismiss altogether, any claims of voluntarism in such transformations. It is interesting, then, to read the contemporary reactions of the visiting Indian team of bureaucrats and politicians on this issue:

> Coercion is the negation of enthusiasm. The enthusiastic outburst of energy which we saw could not be expected from a people who had been coerced into cooperatives. We noticed among them a great patriotic fervour which reminded us of the great patriotic zeal which had seized our own people in their fight for freedom in the thirties and forties of the century. To the peasants in China, increased income and better living was only one aspect of the producers' cooperatives. We were repeatedly told that in joining cooperatives, they were working for the development of the country and towards a Socialist transformation of Society. (GOI, 1956, p. 95)

One key instrumental mechanism in the MMM was the campaign, responding to a slogan launched by the Party. The campaign could involve a political action against perceived enemies of the revolution; or be an intervention to modify group behaviour whether in the cultural or economic domains; or an action to catalyse particular forms of investment, development or environmental change. [18] Often, there would be a successful role model held up for emulation, as for instance in the case of the development of Dazhai brigade where sheer peasant labour was pitted against extreme natural odds to demonstrate the socialist capacity to mould and wrest its own future even in the face of highly adverse natural circumstances. Other powerful campaigns involved the development of the five small rural industries within the collective framework; yet another was the Four Pests campaign of the 1950s against mosquitoes, flies, rats and

---

18 The "campaign" as a political form pre-dates the Chinese revolution. Lu Caizhen (2008, Appendix 2) provides an inventory of sixty-six campaigns in China since the mid-1930s.

sparrows. Vast amounts of labour were enthusiastically mobilized and expended. When they succeeded, they were phenomenal; when sometimes they were failures, the scale of replication could also be alarming. The latter was demonstrated in the case of the elimination of sparrows in the countryside, and the subsequent discovery that they had been crucial for protecting the crops from various insects; another failure was the case of rural small-scale chemical and fertilizer plants that wound up severely polluting local water bodies. However, these problems, which remained the exception rather than the rule, could be acknowledged and addressed, as far as possible, as they were encountered.

Several latent and active factors combined to form the preconditions for the successful exploitation of the mass mobilization mode of transformation. First, the existence of cultural homogeneity on a near-national scale; second, a powerful sense of ownership of the state by the masses and a strong sense of identification with it; third, the mass appeal of many major rural policy interventions made by the state, such as land reforms, rural industries and rural socio-economic security policies; fourth, an efficient organizational framework for enabling two-way flows of information; fifth, a powerful, unified command structure; sixth, the use of instruments for the ideological motivation of the rural masses; finally, success itself was the lubricant for sustaining the process—the benefits of economic achievements were widely shared and there for most to experience, and this made the hard work seem right and worthwhile.

A spectacular illustration of the capacity for and the power of mass mobilization is provided by the Haicheng earthquake in the winter of 1975. Chinese officials ordered the evacuation of the entire population of one million, and saved possibly a few hundred thousand lives that would otherwise have been lost in the powerful earthquake—7.3 on the Richter scale—that struck soon after, on 4 February. How had the Chinese anticipated this with such precision? The prediction was based on a painstaking and systematic collation of vast amounts of information provided in the form of reports and feedback from members of the public, reporting odd occurrences such as sudden changes in land elevation, inexplicable variations in ground water levels; peculiar animal behaviour. This along with evidence of seismic activity led to the prediction. At the time, this was heralded as another demonstration of the power of the people to attain impossible heights under the GPCR. However, the devastating 7.6 magnitude earthquake that struck Tangshan, a similar sized city, on 28 July, 1976, went unpredicted, and cost over 250,000 deaths, thereby undermining the power of participatory prediction methods. Nevertheless, what was undoubtedly demonstrated was the mass mobilizational capacity, readiness and willingness of the people.

The Dignity of Labour: Old and New

Maoist collective doctrine also emphasized the need for economic development to be directly reflected first in the living standards of the peasantry, though socialist surplus extraction was an unavoidable reality in the early phase of industrialization. Attacking inherited forms of exploitation and alienation, there was a sustained drive to develop a new socialist identity and dignity for socialist labour and work. Poster campaigns, films, music, the opera, all fashioned a new culture of the dignity of socialist labour: the socialist worker and the socialist peasant were revolutionary heroes; and the soldiers of the People's Liberation Army also farmed land. No labour within the collective was deemed intrinsically demeaning. The burden of handling the daily bucket of human excreta, traditionally "delegated" to women, was increasingly shared by the males of households. Production teams near towns would acquire contracts for the collection of night soil from urban facilities and process it for plant nutrition back in the villages. India and Indians, hidebound by casteism and elitism and the encyclopaedic forms of social exclusion that these reflect and reproduce, also equally strongly emphasize the dignity of labour, but with one small difference—the dignity is captured and retained as the privilege of some, while raw labour is delegated to and demanded from others as an obligation.

Structural Outcomes

Some version of an industrialization-led trickle-down process was embedded in the development strategies of both countries in the first decades of development, with the rural small-scale sector ascribed the role of meeting the employment gaps anticipated from the capital-intensive industrialization process. While this succeeded on the whole in rural China, it did not in India.

Most economic observers of India are so mesmerized by the so-called convergence in the overall growth rates, that they tend to ignore the plight of the rural sector. In virtually every respect, this sector has steadily fallen further behind the levels attained in China, whether in terms of indicators of positive structural change, employment generation, output growth, input use and productivity, or exports and investment. In India, between 1996—1997 and 2003—2004, the growth rate of the output of the crop sector fell to an abysmal 0. 6% per year, with that for cereals actually registering an annual decline of 0. 1%. In the decade 1984—1985 to 1995—1996, the trend growth rate of net state domestic product from agriculture was 3. 62%; it dropped to 1. 85% for the following decade during which non-agricultural growth rates peaked, and in this period, as many as fifteen states recorded growth rates of under 2% per annum. Rural capital investment fell in real terms. Rural employment suffered. Rural income poverty rates fell, officially, though no plausible pathology could be demonstrated for this outcome to be credible, other than a faulty poverty-line methodology. There are signs of enclaves of commercialization and capitalization in agriculture, with the entry of corporates, MNCs and financial companies into rural markets. But profitable as these enterprises might be for the corporate share-owners, there is little in it for the rural masses, and in any event these are tiny, even if growing, islands of capitalist intervention. The prospects appear sobering, in the light of the recent decline in the terms of trade for a range of commercial crops, rising imports and competition often from heavily subsidized OECD countries. Rural poverty is being exported increasingly into the urban sector for lack of options. Close observers of Indian agriculture refer to a state of agrarian crisis, manifest in the suicide of over 100, 000 farmers over the past decade in a range of states, including Maharashtra and Punjab, two of the richest in India. It is clear that the rural sector lacks the capacity of serving as a residual employment or livelihoods sink for the rural masses.

But worryingly, there are few signs that the high growth rates of the nonagricultural economy are translating into a significantly increased capacity for labour absorption. The high growth rates here have created few jobs in manufacturing. Services have no doubt boomed, but more in output terms than in employment. In service-sector job creation, it is unclear what proportion comprises poverty-driven, survival-oriented activities of the poor obstinately scratching out a living, as against dynamic high-productivity jobs. The information technology boom has not created jobs for the poor, except through relatively limited indirect effects. The Lewisian process of transfer of labour has stalled. The inexorable process of sub-division of owned holdings in agriculture now shows that only a tiny fraction of rural households own enough land to make a poverty line income from agriculture alone. This suggests that there is only limited room for a conventional redistributive land reform as a general solution. If anything, the land rights of the rural population are further under threat from the expansion of nonagricultural activities, from urbanization, and from the de facto and formal privatization of previously commonly held property and environmental resources. Rising health and education bills, as privatization proceeds, add to the burden of survival. In terms of averages, the rural sector in India has seriously underperformed; when the process of rural polarization is factored into this, it becomes plain that the conditions of the majority are even worse than those implied by the averages. It is for this reason that both discourse and policy seem to have shifted towards fiscally redistributive mechanisms at the secondary level.

China provides a contrast. The higher growth rates in the non-agricultural sector are based on manufacturing, including small and medium sized enterprises (SMEs), which is far more labour absorbing; there is a massive construction boom that also serves as a powerful employment generator. On the other side of the equation, the rural sector, with its legacy of an egalitarian household-based land reform, provides a socio-economic cushion in terms of livelihoods. No doubt there are regional and sub-regional stories that vary, but the overall sectoral scenario provides a dramatic contrast to the Indian case, despite the rural sector and its population falling continuously further behind the urban beneficiaries of China's explosive growth. Indeed, there is some speculation at present, based on recent survey data on rural incomes, that China might well be approaching the Lewisian turning point in labour markets. After a period of widening intra-rural income inequalities, there are findings of a more recent reduction in rural inequalities primarily sourced in a reduced gap in wage incomes, in the receipt of transfer incomes (mainly migrants' remittances) and progressive fiscal transfers (implying some role for state policy) (Khan,

2005). Rural China does need the Chinese government to act effectively and quickly in some important areas of economic and social policy; but this notwithstanding, the overall story is one of outstanding success. This bears little resemblance to the experience of the overwhelming majority of the rural population in India.

Is India Catching Up?

In the past decade, the Indian economy has posted high growth rates, sparking the question: is India catching up with China? There is much Indian talk of this, but is it just premature triumphalism voicing the good times of the emerging new elites? There is an unambiguous bottom-line answer to the question in terms of growth rates, but the comparison has other relevant dimensions.

Persisting Divergence

There are indications of persisting gaps in some key areas. India continues to significantly lag behind with respect to agricultural performance; employment generation and poverty reduction. Both economies maintain their respective relative positions with regard to the dominance of manufacturing or services as a driver of growth, though there is more evidence of China catching up on services than there is of India making up ground in manufacturing. Hunger, on the whole, is a faded memory in China, though it remains a daily reality for very many in India. China's lack of liberal political democracy survives intact; so does the rich-man's version of Indian parliamentary democracy that keeps coming up trumps for the middle and upper classes. Chinese socialism has not yielded liberal political rights; and neither has India's socialistic nor its neoliberal path delivered adequate material and human development benefits to the masses. No osmotic convergence is in evidence in either system in this regard.

Some Convergence

Are there indications of positive convergence? The rates of change are indeed getting closer, but the level has remained consistently higher for China, implying that in terms of *absolute* levels of achievement, there is little likelihood of India catching up, or overtaking China, except hypothetically in the Keynesian long term, that is, when we are all dead. India is projected to have a per capita income in 2050 that is still only 55% that for China, although Indian GDP per capita growth rates are projected to exceed Chinese rates by 2020—2025 (Goldman Sachs, 2003).

Much is made of the so-called demographic premium arising from a younger Indian population with falling dependency ratios, with the opposite holding true in China as a (well-predicted and anticipated) consequence of its one-child-family policy. However, this is a debatable matter. Whether a larger population constitutes an economic opportunity or a burden depends crucially on its quality, and on whether the system is capable of generating matching employment for the new entrants into the work force. With persistent low incomes, low human development levels, qualifications and skills, India could as easily encounter the downside of these demographic trends on both the demand and the supply sides, unless there are some substantive reversals in ongoing processes and policies. This undermines the potential strength and automaticity of such a hypothetical demographic premium as a mechanism for convergence.

Of course, there is bound to be a convergence in some aspects, such as literacy and education, as both economies approach maximum coverage in the future for primary and secondary education. But even here, other indicators focusing on quality or on resources per student might fail to converge. Likewise, the absolute gap in longevity might decrease as diminishing returns set in and make each additional life year more difficult and expensive to achieve; but the quality of health care might well continue to show diverging trends alongside this, and dramatically so, as and when the Chinese government finally accepts the responsibility for universally affordable high quality health care insurance systems. But there are also signs that some traditional Indian advantages might have begun to wear out. The Chinese educational system is placing a high emphasis on languages and the English language premium enjoyed by India might soon be at an end. How far India can retain its early-bird advantage in the IT sector also remains an open question. In most other dimensions, where India is doing much better than before, China was and is doing even better still, so that there could well be a continued divergence, and not a positive convergence.

Much "Pervergence"

By "pervergence", I mean a perverse convergence, where the two economies and societies catch up on each other's negative features. There is indeed a steady flow of qualitative and quantitative evidence testifying to such pervergence, arising mainly from China beginning to display some of the negative socio-economic and political governance features of the Indian system. This is evident in a wide spectrum of phenomena: the status of women, including the return of strong gender disadvantage, prostitution, terrible sex ratios at birth; the state of the environment; the spectacular rise in corruption; the endemic expansion of socio-economic insecurity in the countryside as health and education become increasingly inaccessible to a significant section of the rural population on account of unaffordable user charges levied as part of the reforms; and the spectacular rise in inequalities in both systems, with China going downhill much faster here and perhaps overtaking India in some undesirable respects. Those who use the preservation of democratic institutions and values as a reason, excuse, or alibi for India's poorer economic performance, need to take note of the continual attritional deterioration in the quality of public life in the country, including especially the flagrant penetration of corruption, criminality and communalism into the body politic. In this perverse sense, the two countries are indeed converging, and it is difficult to say if the loss of the values of socialist community has been greater and more devastating than the loss of democratic and "socialistic" norms and ways of being in India. In both systems, the public good has been thoroughly privatized. This raises the question if too much attention has been focused on the wrong race.

China's achievements with regard to poverty reduction have been undermined by the recent dramatic rise in the socio-economic vulnerability of the rural population, predominantly on account of their inability to access increasingly expensive health and education systems. It is arguable that post-reform education policies are creating significant educational and social exclusion, and leading to the widespread emergence of child labour, thus laying the foundations for the creation of a new underclass of underprivileged, undereducated people in China. The trends in health policy are similarly regressive. While the levels of Chinese health-related indicators remain well ahead of their Indian equivalents, there are distressing signs of shrinkage in the scope and quality of access to health services for a significant proportion of the population. From a near universal coverage system, albeit with varying quality levels, the last two decades display a trend of atrophy. The Third Chinese National Health Service Survey of 2003 reveals that:

> about 49% of citizens in China that should have sought medical treatment had not done so—up from 36% in 1993; around 44% of in-patients were discharged from hospitals even when they had not fully recovered, as they were mostly unable to afford the medical costs; 75% of farmers for economic reasons, were not hospitalized when they should have been—up from 64% in 1993; and about 33% of the farmers became impoverished because of ill-health—up from 22% in 1993. (Chen and Shiva Kumar, 2007, p. 164)

While the overall sex ratios are rather similar, in the dismal range of 930–945 females per 1000 males, what is alarming is the recent trend and level of the sex ratio at birth. Both countries show despicable outcomes, testifying to the fact that patriarchal biases in India are alive and well even if many a girl child to be is not; and in China that a generation of revolutionary gains in the domain of gender appear to have been casually reversed in the spate of half that time, with a relapse into the traditional attitudes of patriarchal dominance within families, with strong son preference, and an exalted role for the male head of the household. Pervergence here is distressingly dramatic and occurring in double-quick time. In China, some of these strands inter-weave: rural poverty and exclusion, the feminization of agriculture, and rising male domination perhaps account for the high rates of female and farmer suicides in rural China, a phenomenon with obvious resonance to the unabated wave of farmer suicides in the Indian countryside in the recent past.

Governance issues are becoming increasingly important, epitomized by high levels of corruption. Transparency International's Corruption Perception Index sees both China and India displaying deteriorating performances, and while India has always been bad, China, as a new entrant, has fast caught up with India. For India, political parties, the judiciary, the police, and parliament and legislature get the worst scores on the corruption index; this says something about the quality of democracy, beyond simply the issue of its formal existence. For China, the entry of big business into the upper echelons of the communist party and leadership at all levels of government perhaps obviates the need for businessmen to try to influence politicians with bribes; this tendency of the cosying up of the party and business provides a new dimension to the notion of embedded government. Orwellian imagery from Animal Farm inevitably pervades the mind (Orwell, 1945).

Finally, inequality, which was traditionally moderately high in India and rather low in China, has spiralled in China at dramatic rates and seems to have overtaken India in some respects. [19] For instance, over the 1992—2002 decade in India, the bottom 40% had 21% of household income, and the top 20% had 42% of household income. The corresponding shares for China were 14% and 52% for the 1993—2003 decade. In both systems, inequality at the upper end is extreme and vulgar, and cannot remotely be justified in terms of any hypothesized functionality with respect to incentives for investment and growth. These income and wealth inequalities are paralleled by equivalent exclusions in the new labour processes emerging in China, both in rural and urban areas. These are highlighted in the cases of migrants and workers in Special Economic Zones, and also for many other categories of labour—including child labour—and in the extension of working life into old age beyond the earlier norm for retirement.

In terms of regional inequality, too, post-Reform Chinese trends have taken a sharp turn for the worse. China has always displayed wide interregional and inter-provincial disparities arising from structural, geo-natural features. In the period to the early 1970s, regional disparities in urban consumption per capita declined, reflecting the industrial location policy that favoured provinces away from the coast. Very noticeably since 1978, both rural and urban inequalities have widened in regional terms (Saith, 1993, Table 1). Since the reforms, all evidence points to a sharp acceleration in the degree of regional inequality. This is accounted for partly by the cumulative effects of educational differentials, and partly by the longer term dis-equalizing

---

19　For a review of the evidence on trends in inequalities in India, see Pal and Ghosh, 2007; for an analysis of Chinese trends, see Wan Guanghua, 2008.

impact of rural industrialization (which favoured the better endowed and located regions); but in the main it has been driven by the extreme concentration of foreign direct investment in the coastal regions. India displays disturbing evidence of a similar widening of the gulf between the advanced and the backward states since the onset of reforms.

No single conclusion is thus possible on the issue of convergence: there is evidence of some positive convergence, primarily in the form of a rise in the Indian growth rate approaching Chinese levels. There is still a differential, however, and even if this were to be bridged, there would remain a chasm separating the overall absolute levels of development for most relevant indicators. On the other hand, there is a far more dramatic pervergence, that is, a coming together in terms of the negative aspects of growth, with China increasingly displaying the undesirable socio-economic features typical of the Indian system, with rising levels of inequality and exclusion, gender bias, environmental stress and governance deficits.

▪ Significance of the Race

Indian Democracy: How Many Cheers?

What, then, of the *kohinoor* of the Indian experience, its special distinguishing feature, its democracy? Has Indian democracy constrained Indian performance, or has it merely provided an eternal alibi and convenient excuse for coming a distant second in this race? Consider how Swamy (1973, p. 1) poses the conundrum.

> In the context of the China—India comparison… if it turns out that the Chinese growth rate is only 0.5% age point higher than India's rate, one may ask: is this half percent worth the costs of social regimentation that the Chinese pay? Alternatively, if the Indian rate is half percent higher, is it worth the cost of the gross inequality that is permitted in India?

While Swamy confesses that he "cannot answer this question in any definite sense", a current, gung-ho view of Indian reforms and their outcomes is less reticent: "Yes, democracy does slow us down… If it came to a trade-off, however, I don't think anyone in India would give up our democracy for a two-percentage point higher growth rate. We have waited 3000 years for this moment to wipe out poverty, and if needed we will wait another twenty years and do it with democracy" (Das, 2007).

Such modes of argumentation trivialize the issue; democracy cannot be defined naively as a simple variable which can be scaled on one axis against the rate of growth of GDP on the other. Some might favour definitions of democracy that do actually deliver on the guiding principles of the constitution within half a century; the poor and the excluded might well think of it as a periodic *tamasha* full of sound and fury signifying precious little change in their lives; hence also the so-called "incumbency factor" in Indian elections, where the party holding power is almost invariably thrown out, suggesting that perhaps there is more nominal than real choice of substantive options offered to the electorate.

There have been vicissitudes in the idea of democracy as a positive contributor to economic growth. While the initial billing and expectation, in the context of the competition with socialist China, was positive, the early realized development experience was sobering. This induced a quiet U-turn with various forms of hypotheses arguing that there was a price to pay for the virtues of democracy in terms of a slower pace of growth. [20] In turn, this received, or "old", view of a trade-off between democracy and development ran into difficulty with the recent acceleration in the Indian growth rate: after all, India had been as democratic and "hindu" before the growth spurt as it was afterwards, and this was incompatible with notions of the "hindu" growth rate, or other forms of the negative trade-off. Not surprisingly, this brought about another *volte face* amongst reductionist theorizing on democracy and development. [21] This "new" thinking of a

---

20 Notions of the "soft state" from Gunnar Myrdal, the "intermediate regime" from Michal Kalecki and K. N. Raj, the "cruel trade-off" between democracy and development *a la* Bhagwati, the so-called "hindu rate of growth" from Raj Krishna, or the "hindu equilibrium" from Deepak Lal, are contrasted with the aggressive "developmental state" governing the growth process in East Asia. This alleged trade-off then becomes a default explanation for differences between the economic performance of India and China.

21 Jagdish Bhagwati introduced a "new" thinking on development based on the possibility of a virtuous synergy between democracy and development "in the right circumstances". Amartya Sen cited India's "functioning democracy" and its "free press" as the reason for not experiencing famines; Atul Kohli had argued earlier that Indian democracy provides some benefits for the poor through poverty reduction programmes triggered by incumbent governments at tactically optimal points prior to the next election; while Pranab Bardhan and T. N. Srinivasan have separately argued that Indian democracy enables the resolution of endemic political conflicts and that China lags far behind India in this regard.

positive, synergetic relationship also underpins the recent upbeat projections by global consultancies and international development agencies showing that India could soon be performing better than China. In doing so, it highlights the institutional trinity of the judiciary, the executive and the legislature, and also superior corporate and financial governance, including the stock exchange. [22] However, there remain grave methodological and empirical reasons for maintaining considerable scepticism over each of these reductionist, often tautological, "hypotheses".

The default position being argued here is certainly not one that condones regimentation or totalitarianism, but one that demands a little more of Indian democracy than just evergreen good times for the fat (and increasingly obese) Indian elite. It remains plausibly arguable that the Indian masses have experienced neither the benefits of development, nor the rights of democracy, in an intrinsically meaningful manner. Expressions of Indian triumphalism, whether over recent economic performance, or on the ascribed virtues of Indian democracy as-is, come mainly from India's new flamboyant transnational elite; the majority constituting the other India, however, still remain expectant onlookers, waiting for the breeze of benefits to touch their lives.

Chinese Socialism: Pioneer of Capitalism?

A comparative reflection on the development experience of these two great civilizations cannot really be reduced to a multiple-choice balance sheet, or be treated as laboratory evidence for the "superiority" of capitalism vis à-vis socialism. In focusing exclusively on the numerics of the economic race, one loses sight of deeper implications and clues about the large and complex evolutionary processes of societal dynamics, and the historical significance of Indian democracy and Chinese socialism as catalysts of such transformations.

After lengthy eras of feudal and colonial experience, both countries broke away at the same historical moment. They also detached, to different degrees, from the world system and adopted autonomous, though not

---

22 See Goldman Sachs, 2003; Huang, 2006; Huang and Khanna, 2003 and Poddar and Yi, 2007, amongst others. Dwight Perkins and Martin Wolf lend support to this emerging new consensus (cited in Srinivasan, 2006, p. 38, 41).

autarkic, planned strategies for rapid, egalitarian development to overcome the inertia and deficits inherited from the colonial era. This break could be described in Toynbee' s terminology of challenge and response, or in terms of Gerschenkron's analysis of the role of the state as an agent of transformation overcoming historical backwardness, or in Marxian categories and dynamics in terms of modes of production. While each approach highlights the discontinuous nature of this change, none can satisfactorily explain its timing, nor predict its subsequent course, its permanence or its dissipation. Both represented oppositional projects to market-based capitalist change, though each used a distinct lexicon, with profound differences of substance partially disguised by the radical vocabulary of early Indian planning discourse. The Chinese path was a full-blooded socialist one, whereas the Indian one was euphemistically described as being "socialistic". Oskar Lange described it as an example of a "national revolutionary pattern" of change. The Indian state, regardless of its propertied class base, spoke of controlling the commanding heights of the Indian economy, of re-directing a state-led development process towards achieving social objectives. Underlying it implicitly was an imagined community and nation reflecting the aspirations set down in the constitution. It is interesting to note that in both countries this initial trans-formative project, based on such a reality (in China) or a notion (in India) of shared community values, lasted only three decades before the new era of reforms ushered in capitalist growth, albeit with variations, in both countries. In this current phase, while both emphasize economic modernization, there is an atrophying of the initial socialist or socialistic aspirations that provided the social motivation and *raison d'etre* of the first independent governments.

Now, both countries have re-entered the global capitalist order, but on dramatically revised terms—not as basket cases but as dynamos of global growth. The oppositional project has yielded to its anti-thesis. This raises the question of the historical significance of the state-led non-capitalist or socialist interventions in each country. Are these to be understood as systemic, revolutionary, corrections to the evolutionary accumulation of inefficiencies in economic institutions and the extreme inequalities in material consumption, status and political power? Viewed thus, China has clearly emerged with a historic, massively successful correction in terms of economic and human development; and an agenda of political democratization dominates the future. For India, the corrections are far less dramatic, and the emergent economy and nation still retain the extreme inequalities and exclusions that it set out to overcome. Its politically democratic system has on the whole failed to deliver inclusive economically democratic outcomes thus far. With its superior fiscal strength, and its much more culturally cohesive socio-cultural fabric and strong central state, China would appear to be rather better placed to enact further socially progressive corrections than might be extracted by the excluded in the Indian political configuration, where new and old elites dominate state and society and successfully resist attempts at any significant forms of redistribution other than the periodic handouts induced by fear and the imperative to win elections every few years.

In the long sweep of historical change, mutations of socialism in China and planned development in India have served as far more effective pioneers of capitalism in the two countries than imperialism or colonialism ever did. Just as the other India is made to wait on its political democracy to deliver sustainable growth that is inclusive and egalitarian, the other China waits to add meaningful political rights to its considerable economic gains. The clock ticks impatiently on how long either people will be held back.

▪ References

American Rural Small-scale Industry Delegation (ARSID), *Rural Small-Scale Industry in the People's Republic of China*, Berkeley, CA: University of California Press, 1977.

Shahid Amin, *Chauri Chaura, 1922—1992: Event, Metaphor, Memory*, Berkeley, CA: University of California Press, 1995.

Chester Bowles, *Ambassador's Report*, London: Gollancz, 1954.

Lincoln C. Chen, and A. K. Shiva Kumar "Turnaround in China's Health Policies?", *Indian Journal of Human Development*, Vol. 1, No. 1, 2007, pp. 161 – 168.

Gurcharan Das, "Preface", in Guy Sorman, *Year of the Rooster*, New Delhi: Global Full Circle, 2007, http://ccs. in/gdas/?pagejd = 72.

M. H. Dobb, "Some Aspects of Economic Development: Three Lectures", Occasional Paper, 1951, Delhi: Delhi School of Economics: University of Delhi.

Francine Frankel, *India's Political Economy, 1947—1977: The Gradual Revolution*, Princeton, NJ: Princeton University Press, 1978.

Suniti Kumar Ghosh, *The Himalayan Adventure: India—China War of 1962—Causes and Consequences*, Bombay: Rajani X. Desai for the Research Unit for Political Economy, 2002.

GOI, "Agrarian Cooperatives in China and Japan: Report of an Indian Visiting Delegation", New Delhi: Government of India Planning Commission, 1956.

GOI, "Performance Audit of Implementation of National Rural Employment Guarantee Act, 2005", Draft Report, NREGA, Office of the Principal Director of Audit, Economic and Service Ministries, New Delhi: Government of India, 2007.

Goldman Sachs, "Dreaming with BRICs: The Path to 2050", Global Economics Research Paper No. 99, 2003, http://www 2. goldmansachs. com/ideas/brics/book/ 99-dreaming. pdf.

K. B. Griffin, and Ashwani Saith, *Growth and Equality in Rural China*, Singapore: Maruzen, 1981.

Huang Yasheng, "China Could Learn from India's Slow and Quiet Rise", *The Financial Times,* 27 January, 2006.

Huang Yasheng and Tarun Khanna, "Can India Overtake China?", *Foreign Policy,* No. 137, July-August 2003, pp. 74 – 81.

M. Kalecki, "Financial Problems of the Third Plan: Some Observations", in M. Kalecki, *Essays on Developing Economies,* pp. 147 – 156, Hassocks: The Harvester Press, 1976 (Originally published 1964).

K. P. Kannan, "Linking Employment Guarantee with Human Development", Paper presented at the international conference on "Employment and Income Security in India", New Delhi: Insitute for Human Development, 6-8 April, 2005.

A. R. Khan, "Inequality and Poverty in China in the Post-Reform Period: An Overview", 2005, http://www. azizkhan. net/ChinaBagchiFest. pdf.

Kòjima Reiitsu, "Accumulation, Technology and China's Economic Development", in M. Selden and V. Lippit (eds.), *The Transition to Socialism in China*, New York: M. E. Sharpe, 1982, pp. 238 – 265.

D. D. Kosambi, *Exasperating Essays: Exercises in Dialectical Method*, Poona: People's Book House, 1957.

Lu Caizhen, "Who is Poor in China? A Comparison of Alternative Approaches in Rural Yunnan", PhD project, Institute of Social Studies, The Hague, 2008.

Liu Minquan, "Commune, Responsibility System, and China's Agriculture", Paper presented at the Rural Development Research Seminar Series, Institute of Social Studies, The Hague, 20 February, 1991.

James E. Nickum, "Labour Accumulation in China and Its Role since the Cultural Revolution", *Cambridge Journal of Economics,* Vol. 2, No. 3, 1978, pp. 273 – 286.

George Orwell, *Animal Farm,* London: Secker and Warburg, 1945.

Parthapratim Pal, and Jayati Ghosh, "Inequality in India: A Survey of Recent Trends", DESA Working Paper No. 45, ST/ESA/2007/DWP/45, New York: United Nations, 2007.

Dwight H. Perkins (ed.), *China's Modern Economy in Historical Perspective,* Stanford, CA: Stanford University Press, 1975.

Dwight H. Perkins, "The Central Features of China's Economic Development", in Robert F. Dernberger (ed.), *China's Development Experience in Comparative Perspective,* Cambridge, MA: Harvard University Press, 1980, pp. 120 – 152.

Tushar Poddar, and Eva Yi, "India's Rising Growth Potential", Goldman Sachs Global Economics Paper No. 152, http://portal. gs. com.

K. N. Raj, "Agricultural Growth in China and India: Role of Price and Non-price Factors", re-published in Ashoka Mody (ed.), *Inclusive Growth: K. N. Raj on Economic Development,* Hyderabad: Orient Longman, 1983/2006, pp. 255 – 272.

Carl Riskin, "Surplus and Stagnationin Modern China", in Dwight F. Perkins (ed.), *China's Modern Economy in Historical Perspective,* Stanford, CA: Stanford University Press, 1975, pp. 49 – 84.

Joan Robinson, *Aspects of Development and Underdevelopment,* Cambridge: Cambridge University Press, 1979.

Joan Robinson, and John Eatwell, *An Introduction to Modern Economics,* London: McGraw-Hill, 1973.

Ashwani Saith, "Agrarian Structure, Technology and Marketed Surplus in the Indian Economy", PhD dissertation, University of Cambridge, UK, 1978.

Ashwani Saith, "Contrasting Experiences of Rural Industrialisation: Are the East Asian Successes Transferable?", in R. Islam (ed.), *Rural Industrialisation and Employment* in Asia, New Delhi: ILO/ARTEP, 1987, pp. 241 − 304.

Ashwani Saith, *The Rural Non-Farm Economy: Processes and Policies*, Geneva: ILO, 1992.

Ashwani Saith, "Chinese Rural Industrialisation: Some Lessons for Reforming and Developing Economies", ARTEP-ILO Working Paper, New Delhi: ILO, 1993.

Ashwani Saith, "From Collectives to Markets: Restructured Agriculture—Industry Linkages in Rural China, Some Micro-level Evidence", *Journal of Peasant Studies*, Vol. 22, No. 2, 1995a, pp. 201 − 260.

Ashwani Saith, "Reflections on South Asian Prospects in East Asian Perspective", Issues in Development Discussion Paper 7, Development and Technical Co-operation Department, Geneva: ILO, 1995b.

Ashwani Saith, "Chinese Rural Industrialisation: Policy Perspectives and Emerging Problems", in G. K. Chadha and Ashwani Saith, *Rural Industrialisation in Post-Reform China: Issues and Policy Perspectives*, New Delhi: ILO-SAAT, 1996, pp. 29 − 59.

Ashwani Saith, "From Village Artisans to Industrial Clusters: Agendas and Policy Gaps in Indian Rural Industrialisation", *Journal of Agrarian Change*, Vol. 1, No. 1, 2001, pp. 81 − 123.

Ashwani Saith, "Poverty and Anti-Poverty: Troubling Tendencies and Quarrelsome Questions", *Joan Robinson Memorial Lecture*, Thiruvanthapuram, Kerala: Centre for Development Studies, 2005.

Mark Selden, *The People's Republic of China: A Documentary History*, New York: Monthly Review Press, 1979.

Kumar Suresh Singh, "A Perspective on the Anthropological Survey of India", Seminar 495, 2000, http://www. india-seminar. com/2000/495/495% 20k. % 20suresh% 20singh. htm.

Manmohan Singh, "Independence Day Address to the Nation", 15 August, 2006, http://www. hindu. com. nic/independence. htm.

T. N. Srinivasan, "China, India and the World Economy", Working Paper No. 286, Stanford, CA: Stanford University, Center for International Development, 2006.

SSB (various annual issues), *Statistical Yearbook of China*, Beijing: State Statistical Bureau, People's Republic of China.

Eric Stokes, "The Structure of Landholding in Uttar Pradesh", *Indian Economic and*

Social History Review, Vol. 12, No. 2, 1975. Reprinted in Eric Stokes, *The Peasant and the Raj: Studies in Agrarian Society and Peasant Rebellion in Colonial India,* Cambridge: Cambridge University Press, 1978, pp. 205 – 227.

Subramanian Swamy, "Economic Growth in China and India, 1952—1970", *Economic Development and Cultural Change,* Vol. 21, No. 4, 1973, Part II, pp. 1 – 84.

E. B. Vermeer, *Water Conservancy and Irrigation in China: Social, Economic and Agrotechnical Aspects,* Leiden: Leiden University Press, 1977.

Wan Guanghua (ed.), *Understanding Inequality and Poverty in China,* Basingstoke: Palgrave-Macmillan, 2008.

Thomas Weisskopf, "Patterns of Economic Development in India, Pakistan and Indonesia", in Robert F. Dernberger (ed.), *China's Development Experience in Comparative Perspective,* Cambridge, MA: Harvard University Press, 1980, pp. 38 – 90.

Economic Reform and Performance: A Comparative Study of China and Vietnam

Khuong M. Vu [*]

■ Introduction

Over the past five decades, East Asia has emerged as a region with several spectacular stories of catch-up development. The World Bank identified the eight highest-performing Asian economies (HPAEs) as Japan, the "Four Asian Tigers" (Hong Kong, Singapore, South Korea and Taiwan) and the three newly industrialised economies (NIEs) —Indonesia, Malaysia and Thailand. [1] While the "Four Asian Tigers" and the NIEs have made impressive achievements in economic growth and development, gaps in the pace and efficiency of their growth have been substantial. [2] Furthermore, the slower recovery from the 1997 Asian financial crisis of the NIEs relative to that of the "Four Asian Tigers" suggests that these two groups have some significant disparities in the fundamental factors underlying their economic performance. [3]

China and Vietnam have achieved remarkable economic growth since the launch of their economic reforms (China in 1978 and Vietnam in 1986). However, the two countries have also experienced a divergence that resembles that of the Four Tigers versus the NIEs. Figure 1, which plots the relationship between per capita GDP and GDP growth rate, shows that China and Vietnam have followed very similar growth patterns, but

[*] Khuong M. Vu is Assistant Professor at the Lee Kuan Yew School of Public Policy, National University of Singapore. He received his PhD in Public Policy from Harvard University. His research interests include the determinants of economic growth and competitiveness, impact of information technology on development and global best practices for enhancing good governance. The author is grateful to Danny Quah, Dwight Perkins, John Wong, Henry Wan and Matthew Beckwith, as well as two anonymous referees, for very helpful suggestions, and to Stevenson You for research assistance.

[1] World Bank, "The East Asian Miracle: Economic Growth and Public Policy", *A Policy Research Report*, New York: Oxford University Press, Washington, D. C., 1993.

[2] According to World Bank over the period 1960—1985, the "Four Asian Tigers" significantly outperformed the NIEs' average GDP and TFP growth. See World Bank, "The East Asian Miracle: Economic Growth and Public Policy", p. 29, 61.

[3] GDP in 2000 relative to 1996 was 125% for Taiwan and 116% for Korea, but only 97% for Thailand and 96% for Indonesia. See Asian Development Bank, "Key Indicators 2001", ADB, 2001.

Vietnam's growth has been below China's by a notable margin. [4]

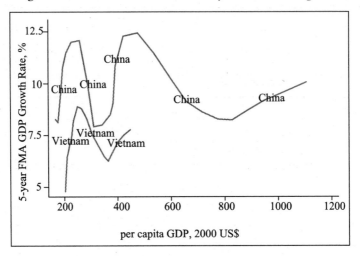

Figure 1   *Pattern of Economic Growth during Reform*
Period: China vs. Vietnam
Note: FMA is Forward Moving Average.
Source: WDI.

Furthermore, Vietnam's per capita GDP growth path appears to follow Indonesia's (from the $200 level) and Thailand's (from the $400 level), while China's shows a decisive deviation from these patterns (Figures 2A and 2B).

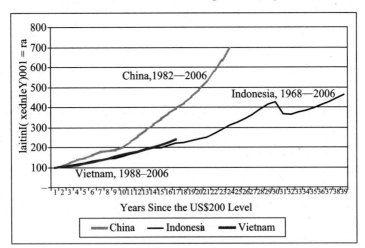

Figure 2A   *Per Capita GDP Growth Paths: China, Indonesia and Vietnam*

---

4   The 5-year forward moving average (FMA) growth rate is used to smooth out short-term fluctuations and capture the growth trend.

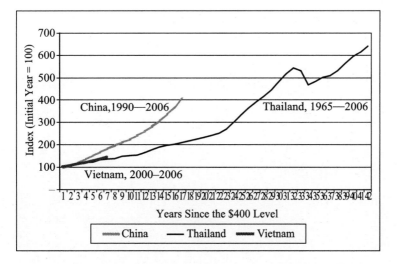

Figure 2B *Per Capita GDP Growth Paths: China, Thailand and Vietnam*
Source: WDI.

Apart from China, it is important to note that India, which has achieved accelerated economic growth since its launch of reforms in 1991, has outperformed Vietnam since 2004, and both India and China are expected to be notably more resilient than Vietnam in this current global economic crisis (Figure 3).

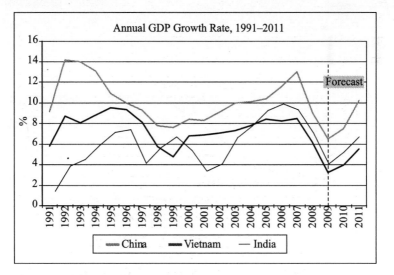

Figure 3 *Economic Growth since 1990: China, Vietnam and India in Comparison*
Source: IMF.

These observations suggest that the gap in economic performance between China and Vietnam is something more serious than a simple quantitative difference in economic growth over a given period.[5] This paper aims to gain insights into the gap in economic performance and the main factors behind it.

■ Economic Reform in Vietnam and China: Similarities and Dissimilarities

China started building its socialist economy in 1949, while the construction of the socialist economy in Vietnam began in 1954 for North Vietnam and in 1975 for the unified country. Both China and Vietnam began their economic development from economies dominated by agriculture, and in both cases, their attempts to build a Soviet-style economy failed during their pre-reform periods.

In December 1978, the Third Plenary Session of the 11th Central Committee, in which Deng Xiaoping became the "core" of the Communist Party of China's leadership, initiated China's economic reform. Eight years later, in December 1986, the Sixth Congress of the Communist Party of Vietnam (CPV) launched Vietnam's economic reform, known as "*Doi Moi*" (Renovation) .

Although economic reforms in the two countries were launched nearly a decade apart, they have strikingly similar features. These similarities lay in the circumstances leading to reform, the initial socio-economic development conditions and the approaches to reform and economic management.

---

5 Regarding Vietnam's rapid economic growth, see Brian Van Arcadias, and Raymond Mallon, *Vietnam: A Transition Tiger?* Canberra: Asia Pacific Press, 2003, p. 8. They point out the potential impact of "powerful exogenous factors" such as "Vietnam's regional location and the trajectory of the regional economy, the timing of natural resource (oil) exploitation, the entrepreneurial vitality of the Vietnamese, access to a sizeable and dynamic emigrant community, and the onset of peace". On the other hand, Dollars observed, "Vietnam is one of the fastest growing economies in the world in the 1990s, yet by many conventional measures, it has poor economic policies". See David Dollar, "Reform, Growth, and Poverty in Vietnam", World Bank Policy Research Working Paper No. 2837, 2002, p. 1. These observations suggest that comparing Vietnam's economic growth to that of China can shed valuable insights into the factors underlying the economic performance of the two countries.

Similarities in the Factors Leading to Economic Reform

The economic reforms in both China and Vietnam were initiated under
circumstances that provided three critical factors for change: receptivity,
crisis and opportunity.

Receptivity: During their pre-reform periods (China: 1949—1978;
Vietnam: 1954—1986), the two countries made extraordinary efforts to
build their socialist economies, but they experienced failure rather than
success. China was impoverished by the catastrophic Great Leap Forward
and Cultural Revolution, while the Vietnamese economy was ruined by
the collectivisation of land, nationalisation of privately-owned industrial and
trading establishments and socialist ideology-driven initiatives.

After nearly 30 years of economic development with an annual growth
rate of 2.7%, China's per capita GDP in 1978 was only US $164
(Table 1).[6] Nathan describes the beginning of China's reform as a time
when "agriculture was stagnant, industrial production was low, and the
people's living standards had not increased in twenty years"[7]. In 1986,
Vietnam was listed among the poorest countries in the world, with per
capita GDP at $203. The per capita GDP growth rate was only 1.4%
over the 10 years following the country's official reunification in 1976 and
the country was heavily reliant on the Soviet Union for economic aid.[8]

These frustrating economic development patterns caused the Chinese and
Vietnamese people to long desperately for the government to change the
way it managed the economy. For Vietnam in 1986, the receptivity to
change was even greater due to the initial success of the economic reforms
in China.

Crisis: The two countries faced critical difficulties that made their reforms
even more urgent. China's agricultural sector shrank by 1.8% in 1976 and
2.2% in 1977.[9] Vietnam suffered severe food shortages, hyperinflation and
aid reduction. The annual per capita food output fell from 304 kilograms

---

6 Computed from the Penn World Table (PWT) dataset for the period 1952—1978.
7 Andrew J. Nathan, *China's Crisis*, New York: Columbia University Press, 1990, p. 200.
8 General Statistics Office, *Statistical Yearbook 1996*, Hanoi: Statistical Publishing House, 1997.
9 All the data used in this paper, unless otherwise specified, are from the *World Bank Development Indicators* (WDI) online dataset.

(of paddy rice equivalent) in 1985 to 301 kg in 1986 and to 281 kg in 1987. [10] The inflation rate was extremely high: 90% in 1985, 455% in 1986, 361% in 1987 and 374% in 1988. [11] The annual aid per capita received by Vietnam dropped by more than 50%, from $6 during 1978—1982 to $2.6 during 1983—1987.

Opportunity: Reforms in the two countries became possible thanks to internal and external factors. For China, the death of Chairman Mao Zedong in 1976 paved the way for Deng Xiaoping to rise to the core of the party's leadership. For Vietnam, the radical reform programmes launched by Mikhail Gorbachev in 1985 in the Soviet Union—which was then Vietnam's model for economic development as well as its main provider of aid—to some extent were an inspiration for the Vietnamese leadership. Furthermore, the death of Party General Secretary Le Duan in 1986, who had dominated the political system for decades, facilitated the transition of Vietnam into its reform stage marked by the Sixth Party Congress in December 1986.

The similar circumstances leading to reforms in China and Vietnam, as presented above, are behind the fact that the reforms in both countries were "more economic than political" as observed by Fforde and Vylder. [12]

Similarities in the Development Conditions at the Launch of Reforms

At the launch of their economic reforms, China and Vietnam were at similar developmental positions in many areas, including basic human capital, economy and infrastructure, as depicted in Table 1.

Table 1 *Developmental Conditions in China and Vietnam at the Launch of Their Reforms*

Indicator	China (1978)	Vietnam (1986)
Human capital *		
Adult literacy (% of total)	67.1	89.2

---

10   General Statistics Office, *Statistical Yearbook 1996.*
11   See *IMF World Economic Outlook* Database [15 Oct., 2008].
12   Adam Fforde and Stefan De Vylder, *From Plan to Market: The Economic Transition in Vietnam,* Boulder: Westview Press, 1996, p. 304.

	(*Cont'd*)	
Indicator	**China** (1978)	**Vietnam** (1986)
Young adult literacy (% of total)	91. 3	93. 6
Calorie supply (kcal/day)	2, 328	2, 300
Median age	22. 1	19. 5
Life expectancy at birth, years	67	63
GDP per capita		
In 2000 US $	165	203
In 2000 PPP $	685	1, 031
GDP structure, %		
Agriculture	28. 1	38. 1
Industry	48. 2	28. 9
Services	23. 7	33. 1
Rural economy		
Share of rural population (%)	81. 3	80. 3
Cereal yield (kg per hectare)	2, 802	2, 715
Openness		
Exports of goods and services (% of GDP)	6. 6	6. 6
Imports of goods and services (% of GDP)	7. 1	16. 6
Infrastructure		
Main line telephones per 1, 000 people	2. 0	1. 3

Note: ∗ For human capital, the data is from 1980 for China and 1985 for Vietnam.

Sources: WDI; Data on human capital except for life expectancy is from the UN (2006).

With regard to human capital, the two countries had comparable levels of literacy and nutrition. While life expectancy was somewhat higher in China, Vietnam had a slight edge in terms of adult literacy rate and the average age of the population. The Chinese and Vietnamese economies at the launch of reform were underdeveloped, with per capita GDP at $165 for China and $203 for Vietnam. [13] Pertaining to the GDP structure, the industrial sector was dominant for China (48. 2%), while for Vietnam, agriculture was the largest sector (38. 1%). This difference between the two countries posed both advantages and disadvantages for each in its early stages of economic reform. For China, the large industrial sector, which

---

13 Measured in constant 2000 US $.

was mainly state-owned, provided a stronger base for industrialisation, but its serious inefficiency, overstaffing and lack of market orientation would require costly efforts and strong political will to reform. [14] For Vietnam, the larger agricultural sector could allow it to "leap frog" with new industrial development projects. However, its smaller industrial sector also meant that the country would have difficulty in acquiring skilled labour and building a network of supporting industries at the beginning of its industrialisation.

With respect to the rural economy, 80% of the population in both countries lived in rural areas, and the two countries had a similar level of cereal yield per hectare (2,802 kg for China and 2,715 kg for Vietnam). Both China and Vietnam had a very low level of openness as well as severely inadequate infrastructure. The export share of GDP was 6.6% for both countries. Telephone penetration (per 1,000 inhabitants) was 1.3 for Vietnam and 2.0 for China. [15]

Similarities in Reform Approach and Implementation

While the reforms in China and Vietnam were initiated under the pressure of economic despair and the critical need to find a new way to build the economy, the paramount concern of the leadership in both countries was to maintain political stability and the absolute power of the Communist Party. As a result, to justify the legitimacy of the political system, both countries chose a "gradualist" approach to reform with a special focus on economic growth.

Table 2, which lists the reform milestones and major initiatives undertaken by China and Vietnam over their reform periods, shows some striking similarities:

- The launch of reforms was a landmark decision of the Communist Party led by a new leadership team.
- Unshackling the agricultural sector (which accounted for over 80% of the labour force in each country): both countries introduced the "household

---

14 Export-oriented, labour-intensive manufacturing in China developed largely independently of the industrial base laid down in the earlier period. This implies that the initial industrial base is not a precondition for successful export-oriented industrialisation. See J. Riedel, "Vietnam: On the Trail of the Tigers", *World Economy*, Vol. 16, No. 4, 1993, pp. 401–422.

15 For comparison, the figure was 8.2 for the Philippines in 1978.

contract responsibility system". This step turned households into production units, giving farmers the incentive to maximise their efforts. This officially took place in China in 1980 and in Vietnam in 1988, that is, about two years after the launch of the reforms in each country.

Table 2 *Reform Milestones: Comparison of Vietnam and China*

| Reform Initiatives | Major Events, Policy Documents and Timeframe | | Time Lag VN-CN |
	China (CN)	Vietnam (VN)	
Reform Launching	The Third Plenary Session of the 11th Central Committee of the CPC, in which Deng Xiaoping became the core of the party leadership and announced the official launch of the Four Modernisations, the drivers of China's reform, Dec. 1978	The Sixth Congress of the CPV elected a new leadership with a liberal reputation and launched Vietnam's economic reform, dubbed as "Renewal", Dec. 1986	8 years

I. Fundamental Changes

Nation-wide introduction of the "household contract responsibility system"	Circular on further strengthening and improving the rural responding system, 1980	Resolution 10-NQ/TW of the CPV Politburo on agricultural sector management reform, 1988	8 years
Legalising the development of the private sector	Constitutional amendments making the private economy a "supplement to the socialist economy", 1982	"The law on private enterprises", 1990	8 years

II. State-owned Enterprise (SOE) and "Level Playing Field" Reforms

Phase 1: Giving SOEs increasing autonomy through eradication of the command economic system; implementing experimental privatisation	**1979—1984**	**1987—1993**	8 years

Table 2 (*Con'd*)

Reform Initiatives	Major Events, Policy Documents and Timeframe		Time Lag VN-CN
	China (CN)	Vietnam (VN)	
Phase 2: Restructuring SOEs, establishing the legal framework for SOEs to operate in a market economy	**1985—1993** "Interim regulations on revitalisation of large and medium-sized state owned enterprises" (State Council), 1985	**1994—1998** "Transformation of selected SOEs into Joint-Stock Companies" (Government Decree No. 28 − CP), 1996	10-11 years
	"Regulations on deepening reform and invigorating state owned enterprises" (State Council), 1986	The first SOE Law, 1995	7 years
	The first SOE Law, 1988		

II. State-owned Enterprise (SOE) and "Level Playing Field" Reforms

Phase 3: Levelling the playing fieldand speeding up privatisation	**1994** *onwards* The first Company Law, 1994	**1999 onwards** The first Enterprise Law, 1999	5 years
	The revised Company Law, 2005, taking effect on 1 Jan. 2006	The revised Enterprise Law, 2005, taking effect on 1 Jan. 2006	0 years
	NA	Investment law, 2005, taking effect on 1 July 2006	NA

III. Embracing Globalisation

Attracting FDI	Law on Sino-foreign joint ventures, 1979	Foreign Investment Law, 1987	8 years
		Law on Industrial Zone and Export-Processing Zone, 1994	
Bilateral trade agreement with the US	1979	2000	21 years
Admitted to the WTO	2001	2006	5 years

Table 2 *(Cont'd)*

| Reform Initiatives | Major Events, Policy Documents and Timeframe | | Time Lag |
	China (CN)	Vietnam (VN)	VN-CN
IV. Financial Reforms			
Banking sector reform	"Decision of State Council on Reform of the Financial System", 1993	"Law on Value-added Tax", 1997	4 years
Introduction of VAT	"The Provisional Regulation of the People's Republic of China on Value-added Tax", 1993	"Law on Value-added Tax", 1997	4 years
IV. Financial Reforms			
Unifying the corporate income tax code for all sectors and reducing the corporate tax rate to 25%	"(New) Corporate Income Tax Law", 2007, taking effect on 1 Jan. 2008	Introduced in 2008	1 year
Opening of the stock market	Establishment of the Shanghai Stock Exchange (SSE), 1990	Establishment of Ho Chi Minh City Stock Exchange (HOSE), 2000	10 years
The first major state-owned bank is listed on the stock market	Industrial and Commercial Bank of China (ICBC), 2006	Vietnam Commercial Bank (Vietcombank), 2007	1 year

- Legalising the formation and growth of the private sector. This step was taken by China in 1982 through a constitutional amendment, placing the private sector as a "supplement to the socialist economy". Vietnam followed suit in 1990 with the introduction of the "Private Business Law".
- SOE and "level playing field" reforms were conducted in three phases. The first phase (1979—1984 for China and 1987—1994 for Vietnam) focused on giving SOEs more autonomy and making them more commerce-oriented while eradicating the command economy. The second phase (1985—1993 for China and 1994—1998 for Vietnam) aimed to restructure SOEs while establishing a legal framework for SOEs to operate in a market economy. The third phase (1994 onwards for China and 1999 for Vietnam) sought to level the playing field for all players in the economy and speed up privatisation.
- Embracing globalisation, promoting FDI and exports. Both countries have

proactively embraced globalisation, making great efforts to attract FDI and promote exports. The *two* countries also introduced laws for attracting FDI shortly after the launch of reforms (China in 1979; Vietnam in 1987).

- Financial reforms. Both countries started with banking sector reform, separating the specialised major state-owned commercial banks from the central bank and putting them on a more strictly commercial footing with newly established joint stock and private banks. It took each country more than a decade from the launch of their reforms to establish their first stock market exchanges (China in 1990; Vietnam in 2000).

Table 2 also indicates that Vietnam has accelerated the pace of its reforms to catch up with China. The time lag for similar reform milestones/ initiatives has decreased over time. For example, Vietnam legalised the private sector in 1990, eight years after China, but it levelled the business playing field with a unified enterprise law in 1999, only five years after China, and it revised this law at the same time as China did in 2006. Vietnam also passed its investment law in 2005, which fundamentally created a level playing field for the business sector, while no similar law has been passed in China. This observation suggests that Vietnam has become increasingly proactive and independent in fostering its economic reforms, especially in the legal framework area. The key difference between the two countries, therefore, lies not in a willingness to carry out reforms, but likely in other leadership-related factors such as vision, commitment and the effectiveness of implementation.

Dissimilarities

The two countries have notable dissimilarities, such as population scale, historical characteristics and effectiveness of leadership. The scale and historical factors give each country certain advantages, which are expected to have a significant impact on economic performance. The sheer size of China makes it remarkably attractive as a market as well as a source of skilled and unskilled labour. China's longer period of peaceful development makes its political system less preoccupied with war legacies and more accountable for the country's developmental progress.

On the other hand, Vietnam's smaller size perhaps makes it more nimble. In addition, Vietnam has a "latecomer" advantage that allows it to study and learn from China's reform experiences without having to pay for the costs of experimentation. The rise of China has also made Vietnam a highly attractive place for FDI as foreign investors try to diversify their investments with the formula "China plus one".

As such, each country can leverage some significant advantages from its own characteristics to foster economic performance. However, the effectiveness of leadership has appeared to be critical in a country's ability to exploit its endowed advantages and turn them into superior performance.

▪ Divergence in Economic Performance

As Vietnam's economic reforms extend back 20 years and China's 30 years, comparative analyses of growth for the two countries can be based on a broad timeframe. The first timeframe for analysis is the initial 20 years of reform (1978—1998 for China and 1986—2006 for Vietnam), during which the two countries underwent similar stages of reform and development. The second timeframe is the past 20 years (1986—2006), during which both China and Vietnam were exposed to the same external environment.

To analyse the growth patterns of the two countries, the episodes of sustained growth accelerations for each country or the episodes of growth divergence between the two are identified.

Sustained Growth Acceleration Episode (SGAE)[16]

Concerning the growth pattern of a country, a period $[t, t+k]$ (from year t to year $t+k$) is defined as an SGAE if it meets the following conditions:

- $k \geqslant 5$; the SGAE must last at least five years.
- $g_{t-1} > 0$; the growth in year $t-1$, the year before the SGAE, is positive.
- $g_{t+1} > g_{t-1} + a$ for $0 \leqslant i \leqslant k$ and $a \geqslant 2.0\%$; the growth rate in any year during the period $[t, t+k]$ is higher than the growth rate in the year just before the episode by at least one percent. This period is called a *moderate* SGAE if, and a *rapid* SGAE if $2.0\% \leqslant a \leqslant 3.0\%$, and a *rapid* SGAE if $a \geqslant 3.0\%$.

Growth Divergence Episode (GDE)

Concerning the growth patterns of two countries X and Y, a period $[t, t+k]$ is defined as a GDE led by country X if the following conditions are met:

- $k \geqslant 5$; the GDE must last at least five years.

---

16 This definition is inspired by Hausmann, Pritchett and Rodrik. See Ricardo Hausman, Lant Pritchett and Dani Rodrik, "Growth Accelerations", *Journal of Economic Growth*, No. 10, 2005, pp. 303 – 329.

- $g_{t-1}^{X} \leqslant g_{t-1}^{Y}$; the growth rate of country X is not higher than that of country Y in year $t-1$, the year just before the GDE.
- $gX_{t+1} \geqslant gY_{t+1}$ for $0 \leqslant i \leqslant k$ and the strict inequality $gX_{t+1} > gY_{t+1}$ takes place in at least $(k-1)$ years.

The patterns and sources of economic growth experienced by Vietnam and China during the two 20-year timeframes are captured in Figures 4A, 4B and Table 3.

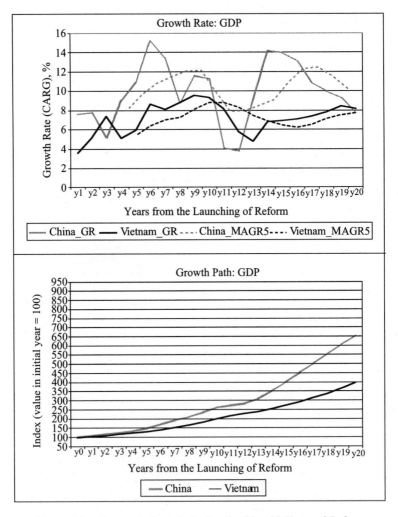

Figure 4A *Economic Growth during the First 20 Years of Reform*
(China: 1978—1998; Vietnam: 1986—2006)

Note: MAGR5 means 5-year moving average growth rate.

Source: WDI.

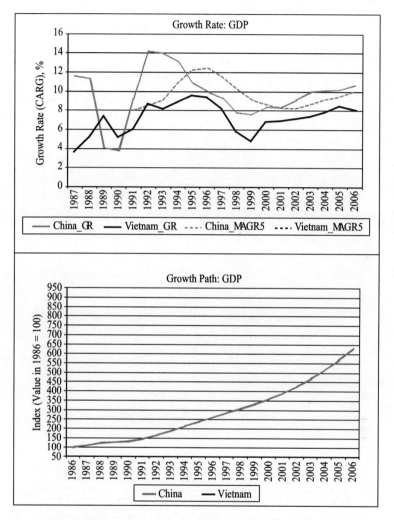

Figure 4B *Economic Growth during the Period 1986—2006*

Note: MAGR5 means 5-year moving average growth rate.

Source: WDI.

Table 3 *Economic Growth Patterns*

	Period GDP Growth Rate (CAGR), %				
	0-5	**5-10**	**10-15**	**15-20**	**0-20**
The first 20 years of reform					
China (1978—1998) (CN1)	8.1	12.1	9.0	10.2	9.8
Vietnam (1986—2006) (VN)	5.4	8.9	6.5	7.8	7.1
Growth Gap (CN1-VN)	**2.7**	**3.2**	**2.5**	**2.4**	**2.7**

(*Cont'd*)

	Period GDP Growth Rate (CAGR), %				
	0-5	**5-10**	**10-15**	**15-20**	**0-20**
The past 20 years of reform					
China (1986—2006) (CN2)	7.9	12.4	8.3	10.0	9.7
Vietnam (1986—2006) (VN)	5.4	8.9	6.5	7.8	7.1
Growth Gap (CN2-VN)	**2.5**	**3.5**	**1.8**	**2.3**	**2.6**

Source: Author's calculation based on data from WDI.

The First 20 Years of Reform (Vietnam: 1986—2006; China: 1978—1998)

In the first 20 years of reform, Vietnam experienced two moderate SGAEs. One was from year 6 to year 11, denoted as [y6 ÷y11] and the other was [y14 ÷y20]. At the same time, China underwent two rapid SGAEs. One was [y4 ÷y10] and the other was [y13 ÷y20] (Figure 4A, Upper panel).

The two SGAEs for Vietnam and China were rather similar in timing. The first SGAE, which started after a few years of reform, was enabled mainly by unshackling resources mismanaged in the old system for more efficient uses driven by market forces. The second SGAE, which started only after 13-14 years of reform, was the result of new investments made during the reform period. Therefore, the magnitude of the first SGAE depended on the severity of previous mismanagement and the decisiveness of the reformist leadership, while the second SGAE was determined by the depth and consistency of reform, which laid the foundation for longer term growth.

Interestingly, the two SGAEs, [y6 ÷ y11] and [y14 ÷ y20] for Vietnam, and [y4 ÷y10] and [y13 ÷y20] for China, nearly coincided with the two GDEs [y4 ÷ y10] and [y13 ÷ y19], during which the growth divergence in favour of China occurred. This means that the growth divergence between Vietnam and China occurred not during the period of Vietnam's growth slowdown, but when both countries enjoyed accelerated growth. In fact, Vietnam's growth increased but did so at a slower pace than China's. This observation implies that the growth divergence between these two countries could be even more pronounced in good times than bad.

The two GDEs have enabled China to far outperform Vietnam in growth during the first 20 years of the reform timeframe. The 5-year moving average of China's GDP growth rate curve is well above Vietnam's, except for year 12 (year 1990 for China), when China suffered the consequences of the Tiananmen Square Incident. This curve ranges between 8.0% and 12.5% for China and moves in a lower range of 5.0% to 8.5% for Vietnam (Figure 4A, Upper panel).

More specifically, China's average GDP growth rate over the 20-year reform timeframe was 9.8%, exceeding Vietnam's 7.1% by 2.7% and there existed a notable gap between the two countries in each of the four 5-year sub-periods of the first 20-year reform timeframe (Table 3). After the first 20 years of reform, China's GDP expanded 6.5 times, while Vietnam's rose only 4.0 times (Figure 4A, Lower panel).

The Past 20 Years, 1986—2006

Over the 20-year period from 1986 to 2006, China enjoyed a rapid SGAE [1991 ÷06] over nearly the entire 20-year period, while Vietnam underwent two moderate SGAEs, [1991 ÷ 97] and [2000 ÷ 06]. Furthermore, the SGAE [1991 ÷06] is also a GDE, throughout which China's growth rate was well above Vietnam's (Figure 4B, Upper panel). As a result, since 1992, China's GDP growth path has taken off relative to that of Vietnam's (Figure 4B, Lower panel). In fact, 1992 was the critical year marking a remarkable takeoff in China. This is discussed further below.

Averaged over 1986—2006, China's GDP growth rate was 9.7%, exceeding Vietnam's 7.1% by a gap of 2.6% and there was a significant gap between the two countries' growth for each of the five-year sub-periods (Table 3). Over the period 1986 to 2006, China's GDP rose nearly six times, while Vietnam's increased only four times (Figure 4B, Lower panel).

Gaps in Efficiency of Growth

Vietnam has lagged behind China not only quantitatively but also in qualitative terms. This is manifested in the gap in total factor productivity (TFP) growth, the agricultural sector's productivity growth and selected development indicators as discussed below.

TFP Growth

China's TFP growth was significantly higher than Vietnam's, as shown in Table 4 for the period 1986 to 2006. It is important to note that TFP growth for Vietnam during the sub-period 1986 to 1996, when the country was in the first phase of reform, was quite high (4. 4%), close to that in China (5. 6%). However, TFP growth slowed sharply to 1. 8% from 1996 to 2006 for Vietnam while remaining high at 4. 5% for China. The slowdown in TFP growth and the widening gap between Vietnam and China suggests that the efficiency of Vietnam's economic growth notably deteriorated.

Table 4   Sources of GDP Growth, 1986—2006

| | China | | | | Vietnam | | | |
| | | Growth Contribution | | | | Growth Contribution | | |
Period	GDP Growth	Capital	Labour	TFP	GDP Growth	Capital	Labour	TFP
1986—1996	10. 2	3. 7	0. 9	5. 6	7. 2	1. 8	1. 0	4. 4
1996—2006	9. 2	4. 0	0. 7	4. 5	7. 1	3. 6	1. 7	1. 8
1986—2006	**9. 7**	**3. 8**	**0. 8**	**5. 1**	**7. 1**	**2. 7**	**1. 3**	**3. 1**

Note: The key assumptions for this calculation exercise include: (i) capital stock is estimated based on the Perpetual Inventory Method (PIM) with the depreciation of aggregate capital at 7%; and (ii) the share of input in GDP is 0. 35 for capital and 0. 65 for labour.

Source: Author's calculation based on WDI.

The Agricultural Sector's Productivity Growth

The agricultural sectors in China and Vietnam were very similar at the beginning of their reforms, especially in terms of the sectors' share of employment and the yield per arable hectare.

The agricultural sector of both countries enjoyed high growth during the reforms. However, their growth patterns varied in efficiency. With regard to production output, Vietnam outperformed China in both timeframes (Figures 5A and 5B, Upper panel), implying that Vietnam potentially has a distinct competitive advantage in this sector. However, in terms of the agricultural sector's productivity, measured as value added per worker, China grew significantly faster than Vietnam in both timeframes (Figures 5A and 5B, Lower panel).

The sharp contrast between the two countries in the growth performance of crop production (led by Vietnam) and productivity (led by China) shows a notable gap in the efficiency of growth between the two countries.

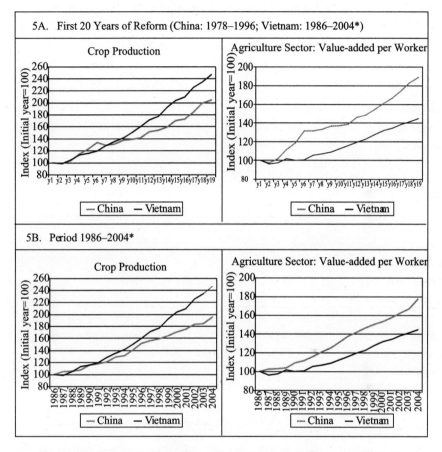

Figure 5 *Agricultural Sector Growth: Production Output vs. Productivity*
    Note: * The period 1986—2004 instead of 1986—2006 is examined because the data for later years is not available.
    Source: WDI.

Contrasts in Development Indicators

Comparing China and Vietnam on social development indicators reveals a mixed picture. Vietnam appears highly competitive with China in terms of the basic measures of human development. However, Vietnam pales beside China with respect to other indicators such as research productivity, AIDS prevalence and traffic accidents.

Basic Human Capital Indicators

Vietnam has caught up with China in life expectancy and school enrolment while markedly surpassing China in terms of child mortality (since 2000), Internet penetration (since 2004) and rate of students studying in the US (since 2006) (Table 5).

Table 5 *Human Capital: Basic Indicators*

Indicator	China	Vietnam
Life expectancy at birth (years)		
1990	69	65
2000	70	69
2005	72	71
Child mortality rate under 5 (per 1,000)		
1990	49	53
2000	41	30
2005	27	19
Literacy of adults (%)		
1989—1990	77.8	87.6
1999—2000	90.9	90.3
School enrolment, primary		
1991	125.9	106.7
2001	117.4	103.5
2006	111.2	90.3
School enrolment, secondary		
1990—1991	48.7	32.2
2000—2001	62.9	64.6
2005	74.3	75.8
School enrolment, tertiary		
1991	3.0	1.9
2000	7.6	9.5
2005	20.3	16.0
Students studying in the US (per 100,000 population) *		
2005	4.8	5.5
2006	5.2	7.2
Internet penetration per 1,000 population		
1996	0.13	0.001
2000	17.8	2.6
Life expectancy at birth (years)		
2004	72.5	77.3
2006	104.4	174.6

Note: * Institute of International Education (IIE) at < http://opendoors. iienetwork. org/?p =28633 >.
Sources: WDI.

Research Productivity

The research productivity of a country can be assessed on the basis of such indicators as the rates of patent applications filed to the local and American patent offices and the rate of published scientific and technical journal articles.

As shown in Table 6, Vietnam is far behind China in these measures in both magnitude and growth. For example, the rate (per one million residents) of patents filed to the local patent office in China rose from 6.4 in 1991 to 20.1 in 2000 and to 71.4 in 2005, while for Vietnam it was 0.55 in 1991 and 0.44 in 2000.[17] The gap in the rate (per one million residents) of published scientific and technical journal articles between China and Vietnam was also large and widening, from 5.4 vs. 1.0 (5.4 times) in 1991 to 31.9 vs. 2.7 (11.8 times) in 2005.

Table 6 *Research Productivity*

Units: rate per one million people

| Year | No. of Applications filed by residents to | | | | No. of Scientific and Technical Journal Articles | |
| | Local Patent Office | | US Patent Office | | | |
	China	Vietnam	China	Vietnam	China	Vietnam
1991	6.41	0.55	0.10	0.0	5.4	1.0
1992	8.60	0.49	0.11	0.0	6.0	1.1
1993	10.25	0.45	0.11	0.0	6.4	1.0
1994	9.39	0.31	0.10	0.01	6.6	0.9
1995	8.31	0.32	0.13	0.0	7.5	1.4
1996	9.55	0.50	0.21	0.01	8.6	1.6
1997	10.30	0.40	0.18	0.03	9.9	1.6
1998	11.05	NA	0.23	0.01	11.1	1.3
1999	12.44	0.48	0.22	0.01	12.5	1.4
2000	20.07	0.44	0.35	0.01	14.6	1.9
2001	23.62	NA	0.55	0.06	16.6	2.0
2002	31.09	NA	0.75	0.01	18.2	1.8
2003	44.06	NA	0.96	0.01	22.3	2.5
2004	50.60	NA	1.32	0.04	26.9	2.0
2005	71.4	NA	1.79	0.07	31.9	2.7

Sources: Author's computation; data from WIPO (for the number of applications filed

---

17   The data in WDI for Vietnam is missing from 2001 onwards.

to the US Patent office) and WDI (for the number of applications filed to the local patent office and the number of scientific and technical journal articles).

Rates of Death Caused by AIDS and Traffic Accidents[18]

As shown in Table 7, the rates of death (per 100,000 people) caused by AIDS and traffic accidents were much higher and grew more rapidly in Vietnam than China. It is worth noting that the difference in these rates must be judged with caution because the two countries are vastly different in size and geography. However, the widening of the differences between the two countries on these rates should be taken seriously because it reflects a gap in government effectiveness.

- The rate of deaths caused by AIDS jumped from 10.9 (per 100,000 people) in 2003 to 15.7 in 2005 (a 44% increase) for Vietnam, while these figures were 2.0 and 2.4 for China, respectively. Vietnam's death rate caused by AIDS was 5.5 times higher than China's in 2003 and 6.5 times higher in 2005.
- The rate of fatal traffic accidents rose 176% in Vietnam from 7.9 in 1998 to 13.9 in 2003, while this growth was 131% in China, from 6.2 in 1998 to 8.1 in 2003. Vietnam's rate of fatal traffic accidents was 1.3 times higher than China's in 1998 and 1.7 times in 2003.

Table 7 *Death Rates (per 100,000 people) caused by AIDS and Traffic Accidents*

	Deaths Caused by AIDS			Deaths Caused by Traffic Accidents		
	2003	2005	2005/2003	1998	2003	2003/1998
China	2	2.4	120%	6.2	8.1	131%
Vietnam	10.9	15.7	144%	7.9	13.9	176%
Vietnam/China	5.5	6.5	1.2	1.3	1.7	1.3

Source: Computed from WHO (2006) and World Bank (2006).

▪ Explaining the Growth Divergence Using the Determinants of Growth Model

The growth literature initiated by the seminal work of Barro sheds light

---

18　The data are available only for the periods reported in Table 7.

on the factors explaining the variations in economic growth performance across countries. [19] These can be grouped into four interrelated categories.

- The initial level of income is expected to have a negative effect on growth. That is, a country with a lower income tends to grow faster than a country with a higher income, all else being equal. This is called the conditional convergence effect. [20]

- Basic human capital is proxied by various variables such as education (e. g., school enrolment, years of schooling) and health (e. g., life expectancy at birth). These factors have a positive impact on growth. [21]

- The variables capturing the quality of institutions include rule of law[22], property rights[23], corruption[24] and political instability[25]. According to these studies, better maintenance of the rule of law and property rights has a positive effect, while corruption and political instability have a negative effect on growth.

- Government-related factors include an array of aspects, ranging from the leadership's commitment to reform to government effectiveness. Hausman, Pritchett and Rodrik analysed the growth acceleration patterns of 110 countries over 36 years (1957—1992) and the factors underlying those patterns, and found that the most important determinant of sustained acceleration in economic growth is "a major change in economic policy"[26]. Their findings suggest that for

19 Robert J. Barro, "Economic Growth in a Cross Section of Countries", *The Quarterly Journal of Economics,* Vol, 106, No. 22, 1991, pp. 407 – 443.

20 Barro, "Economic Growth in a Cross Section of Countries"; and R. Barro and Salai-Martin, *Economic Growth,* New York: McGraw-Hill, 1995.

21 Barro, "Economic Growth in a Cross Section of Countries"; and Robert J. Barro, *Determinants of Economic Growth: A Cross-Country Empirical Study,* Cambridge, MA: MIT Press, 1997.

22 Barro, "Economic Growth in a Cross Section of Countries"; and Dani Rodrik, Arvind Subramanian and Trebbi Francesco, "Institutions Rule: The Primacy of Institutions Over Geography and Integration in Economic Development", *Journal of Economic Growth,* Vol. 9, No. 2, 2004, pp. 131 – 165.

23 Stijn Claessens and Luc Laeven, "Financial Development, Property Rights, and Growth", *The Journal of Finance,* Vol. 58, No. 6, 2003, pp. 2401 – 2436.

24 Paolo Mauro, "Corruption and Growth", *The Quarterly Journal of Economics,* Vol. 110, No. 3, 1995, pp. 681 – 712.

25 John Luke Gallup, Jeffrey Sachs and Andrew Mellinger, "Geography and Economic Development", NBER Working Paper No. W6849, 1998.

26 Hausman, Pritchett and Rodrik, "Growth Accelerations", pp. 303 – 329.

transitional economies such as Vietnam and China, the leadership's decisiveness, pioneering and commitment in making strategic shifts to deepen economic reform, as well as the government's effectiveness in executing reform policies, play a crucial role in boosting and sustaining the country's high performance.

Initial Level of Income

Vietnam's per capita income in 1986 was lower than China's by 20% to 30% (Vietnam: US $203, purchasing power parity $1,031; China: US $311, purchasing power parity $1,289).[27] This means that the initial level of income or conditional convergence effect is in favour of Vietnam, and is hence not a factor in explaining China's faster growth performance.

Basic Human Capital

While basic human capital is influenced by policy, it is more fundamentally shaped by social legacies. Vietnam and China have striking similarities in human capital endowment due to their closeness in geography, culture and history.[28] In fact, as presented above, Vietnam is highly competitive with China on the basic measures of human capital, namely educational attainment, health care and information technology penetration. This implies that basic human capital is not a factor causing the growth divergence between China and Vietnam.

Institutions

The differences between China and Vietnam in institutions are based on a set of variables that includes political stability, voice and accountability (an indicator of democracy), rule of law and regulatory quality, as provided by the World Bank Governance Indicators, composed by Kaufmann et al.[29]

---

27 See *World Bank Development Indicators Database* [15 Oct., 2008].

28 Brantly Womack, *China and Vietnam: The Politics of Asymmetry*, Cambridge: Cambridge University Press, 2006.

29 This dataset covers 212 countries and six dimensions of governance: (i) Voice and Accountability; (ii) Political Stability; (iii) Government Effectiveness; (iv) Regulatory Quality; (v) Rule of Law and (vi) Control of Corruption. Each index ranges from −2.5 to +2.5 (higher is better). The data for 1996—2006 is available at < http://www.govindicators.org > [10 Oct., 2008]. See Daniel Kaufmann, Aart Kraay and Massimo Mastruzzi, "Governance Matters VI: Governance Indicators for 1996—2006", World Bank Policy Research Working Paper No. 4280, 2007.

The mean and median of each of these indicators for China and Vietnam are compared to reveal which country has an advantage over the other (see Table 8). [30]

Table 8 *Institutional Indices for China and Vietnam*

Factors	Effect on Growth	China	Vietnam	Advantage
Governance indices *				
Political Stability	+	−0.23(−0.24)	0.29 (0.31)	V
Rule of Law	+	−0.40(−0.40)	−0.54 (−0.53)	C
Regulatory Quality	+	−0.27(−0.29)	−0.57 (−0.58)	C
Voice and Accountability	+/?	−1.52(−1.53)	−1.45 (−1.47)	V

Note: * Each indicator is averaged for 1996—2006, the period for which the data is available. Numbers in parentheses are the median.

Source: World Bank Governance Indicators.

Political Stability

Political stability was defined by Kaufmann *et al.* as "the likelihood that the government will not be destabilised by unconstitutional or violent means, including terrorism"[31]. Vietnam is clearly better positioned in this regard than China. Vietnam is comfortably in the positive zone with the mean score (over time) of +0.29, while China is in the negative zone (−0.23). As political stability has a solid impact on investment and growth, this factor should be considered a plus for Vietnam compared to China in its effect on economic growth.

Democracy

Democracy or "voice and accountability" was defined by Kaufmann *et al.* as "the extent to which a country's citizens are able to participate in selecting their government as well as freedom of expression, freedom of association, and a media"[32]. For this measure, both China and Vietnam are very weak, as their indexes are far below 0. China (−1.52) is a bit weaker than Vietnam (−1.45). On the other hand, Barro points out that

---

30　The data for these indicators is available for only the 1996—2006 period.
31　Kaufmann *et al.*, "Governance Matters VI: Governance Indicators for 1996—2006".
32　Ibid.

"one cannot conclude [from empirical evidence] that more or less democracy is a critical element for economic growth "[33]. That is, democracy is not a factor explaining the divergence between China and Vietnam during their economic reforms.

Rule of Law

Rule of law was defined by Kaufmann *et al.* as "the extent to which agents have confidence in and abide by the rules of society, including the quality of contract enforcement, property rights, the police and the courts, as well as the likelihood of crime and violence"[34]. Both China and Vietnam are in the negative zone (below the average country) and Vietnam is slightly weaker than China in this measure (-0.54 vs. -0.40). As "rule of law" has a strong impact on growth, this factor should have some effect on the gap in growth performance between China and Vietnam.

Regulatory Quality

As defined by Kaufmann *et al.*, regulatory quality is "the ability of the government to provide sound policies and regulations that enable and promote private sector development"[35]. On this measure, both countries are weak, falling in the negative zone. However, China is significantly stronger than Vietnam (-0.27 vs. -0.57). This observation suggests that regulatory quality, to some extent, is a factor causing the China-Vietnam divergence in growth performance.

In summary, the gaps in regulatory quality and to a lesser extent, rule of law are the two institutional factors in which China has some advantage over Vietnam. Vietnam, however, has a clear advantage over China in terms of political stability. Due to these trade-offs, institutions seem not to be the decisive factor explaining the divergence between the two countries.

Leadership and Government Effectiveness

The gap in leadership commitment to reform is measured on the basis of two pieces of evidence: decisiveness in making strategic decisions at critical

---

33 Barro, *Determinants of Economic Growth: A Cross-Country Empirical Study.*
34 Kaufmann *et al.*, "Governance Matters VI: Governance Indicators for 1996— 2006".
35 Ibid.

junctures of economic reform and efforts made to streamline the bureaucracy.

Decisiveness in Making Strategic Decisions at Critical Junctures

As noted above, there were moments marking notable divergences between China and Vietnam in growth, especially in the industry and service sectors. The critical moments were an uptick in growth in China in 1991 and a slowdown in Vietnam's growth in 1999 (Figures 4A and 4B, Lower panel).

After the first ten years of reform, both China and Vietnam had been able to escape from economic hardship and enter a more comfortable stage of development, but a stage in which it was harder to make decisive and difficult decisions. The economic reforms have made China and Vietnam deviate farther from their ideology of socialism. This may have seriously upset some influential members of the leadership, whose power was based on loyalty to the past rather than future achievements.

The two forces mentioned had put China (in the early 1990s) as well as Vietnam (in the late 1990s) at risk of falling into political deadlock and indecisiveness in making strategic decisions. In this situation, the leadership-related factors such as vision, decisiveness and execution capability played a critical role in decisively moving the economic reforms forward.

For China in 1991, Chen Yun, the most powerful leader after Deng Xiaoping in post-Tiananmen China, along with his allies launched a series of attacks against reform, including a call for abolishing special economic zones. [36] Facing these critical challenges, Deng Xiaoping did not compromise, and instead decided to undertake a pre-emptive step by launching a trip to southern China in January 1992 to rally support for accelerating reforms.

Deng's trip is believed to have "produced both short-term and long-term effects on China's political and economic development", although "the economic effects are far more clear-cut". [37] Economic growth surged from 9% from 1978 to 1991 to 12% from 1991 to 1996, while total FDI flows

---

36 Suisheng Zhao, "Deng Xiaoping's Southern Tour: Elite Politics in Post-Tiananmen China",
    Asian Survey, Vol. 33, No. 8, 1993, p. 745.

37 John Wong, "The Economics of the Nanxun", Chapter 3 in *The Nanxun Legacy and China's
    Development in the Post-Deng Era*, John Wong and Zheng Yongnian (eds.), Singapore:
    Singapore University Press, 2001, p. 43.

amounted to US $ 156 billion over 1991 to 1996 compared to US $ 23. 3 billion for 1978 to 1991 (see Table 1). [38]

For Vietnam, a slowdown in reform efforts was observed some time after 1995, which cumulated in Vietnam's refusal to sign a trade agreement with the United States in 1999. As a US trade official involved in this process noted, "When you compare this to the effort put forward by China during trade negotiations, [...] it shows how Vietnam is simply not convinced about opening up"[39]. Perkins stated:

> Vietnam's initial refusal to sign a trade agreement with the United States, an agreement that its own officials had negotiated, is clear evidence of the reluctance of many officials, even in the top leadership, to accept the kind of industrial policy that is likely to be the most appropriate for their country. [40]

However, it is important to note that Vietnam signed the trade agreement in July 2000, just less than one year after its initial refusal. Also in 1999, Vietnam passed the enterprise law, only five years after China's own passing of its enterprise law (Table 2), which marked a prominent change in the creation of a level playing field for Vietnam's business sector. These examples reveal that the Vietnamese leadership, while lacking foresight and decisiveness in making strategic decisions, was willing and able to make significant changes once they became obviously necessary.

Streamlining the Bureaucracy

China and Vietnam are both burdened with a large and overstaffed public sector, which is among the main causes of red tape, corruption, incompetence and inefficiency. Therefore, streamlining the public sector is a good indicator of the depth of a country's commitment to reform. In this endeavour, China and Vietnam have gone in opposite directions. As shown in Table 9, China consistently and drastically reduced its public sector's share of

---

38 Ibid, p. 44.

39 Thomas Crampton, "Politburo Is Hesitating on Pact, Official Says: U. S. Aide Is Pessimistic On Hanoi Trade Accord". See *Herald Tribune* at < http: //www. iht. com/articles/1999/09/1 1/ viet. 2. t_ 0. php > [11 Sept. , 1999].

40 Dwight Perkins, "Industrial and Financial Policy in China and Vietnam", in *Rethinking the East Asian Miracle* (World Bank Publication), Joseph E. Stiglitz and Shahid Yusuf (eds.), World Bank and Oxford University Press, 2001.

employment relative to the entire economy by 27% between 1995 and 2000 and by 22% from 2000 to 2005, while Vietnam increased its public sector's share of employment relative to the economy by 1.3% over 1995 to 2000 and 9.3% from 2000 to 2005.

Table 9 Employment Growth, 1995—2000 and 2000—2005 for Vietnam vs. China

Sector	China		Vietnam	
	1995—2000	2000—2005	1995—2000	2000—2005
The Economy (E), %	5.9	5.2	13.9	13.6
The Public Sector (Government, Party, and SOEs) (P), %	−21.1	−17.0	15.2	22.9
Public sector expansion (+) or reduction (−) relative to the economy (P-E), %	−27.0	−22.2	+1 −3	+9 −3

Sources: Author's calculation based on national statistical data, Vietnam: *Statistical Yearbooks,* 2001—2006, *Establishment Census,* 2002; China: *Statistical Yearbooks,* 2005 and 2006.

Government Effectiveness

In addition to the leadership's commitment to reform, government effectiveness is critical to the performance of a country. Vietnam is notably below China in terms of the World Bank measure of government effectiveness, as shown in Figure 6 (Upper panel) for the period 1996—2007. More alarmingly, this gap has been widening since 2005, with China on the rise and Vietnam on the decline. [41]

The gap in government effectiveness between the two countries can also be seen in the pace of SOE sector reforms, control of corruption, pattern of energy consumption and efficacy of openness.

Pace of SOE Sector Reforms

The SOE sector has been problematic for both China and Vietnam, but Vietnam has been far behind China in reforming it. Perkins pointed out

---

41 World Bank notes that "[Vietnam has a] reputation for slow decision making and inefficient transparency". See World Bank, "Vietnam—Implementing Reforms for Growth and Poverty Reduction", *Country Development Report,* 2002, p. 6.

that Vietnam was much less reliant on market forces than was China in reforming the SOE sector. [42]

Both China and Vietnam have experimented with a shareholding system [...]. In Vietnam, as of 1998, only a dozen state firms were corporatized, while the number in China was in the many thousands. Shareholding could become the vehicle for creating boards of directors who would ensure that plant managers

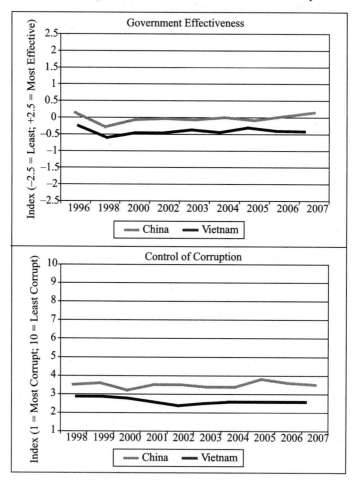

Figure 6 *The Gap in Government Effectiveness*

Sources: World Bank Governance Indicators (for government effectiveness) and Transparency International (for control of corruption).

---

42 Perkins, "Industrial and Financial Policy in China and Vietnam".

concentrated mainly on making profits rather than on pleasing their government and party superiors. [43]

and

> The mergers and acquisitions process in China, therefore, has begun to take on some of the characteristics of similar processes in market economies, although the government's role remains large. [At the same time], Vietnam's government-directed approach in creating state-owned conglomerates, following the Japanese and Korean models appears to be little more than a repackaging of existing arrangements without a change in business behaviour. [...] It is hard to see what contribution these new, larger units will make to Vietnam's international competitiveness. [44]

With regard to privatisation, China has also been more effective than Vietnam. As shown in Table 10, as a percentage of GDP in 2000, the total value of proceeds from privatisation over the period 1990 to 2005 was 4. 8% and the average size of each transaction was $ 252 million, comparable to figures for neighbouring countries such as Thailand, Indonesia, Malaysia and the Philippines. These figures are much smaller for Vietnam, which are only 1% and 3 million, respectively.

Table 10 *Privatisation Transactions over the Period 1990—2005*

| Country | Total Number of Transactions | Total Proceeds | | Average Transaction Size (US $ millions) |
		(US $ millions)	Relative to GDP in 2000, %	
China	229	57, 706	4. 8	252. 0
Vietnam	107	318	1. 0	3. 0
Indonesia	35	8, 418	5. 1	240. 5
Malaysia	50	12, 394	13. 7	247. 9
Philippines	79	4, 180	5. 5	52. 9
Thailand	23	5, 946	4. 8	258. 5

Sources: Author's calculation from the World Bank's Privatisation Transactions database; GDP data from WDI.

The Control of Corruption

Institutions (such as transparency, democracy) and government

---

43   Zhao, "Deng Xiaoping's Southern Tour: Elite Politics in Post-Tiananmen China", p. 269.
44   Ibid. , p. 272.

effectiveness (such as strong leadership, execution capability) have a major impact on the control of corruption. As discussed above, institutions in both China and Vietnam remain weak. As a result, corruption is a serious problem in both countries and their success in controlling this problem remains limited. However, China has been consistently rated above Vietnam on this effort, as indicated by the gap between them in the Transparency International (TI) Index (Figure 6, lower panel). China's higher score on control of corruption is mainly due to its more effective government. In fact, China and Vietnam have handled the scandals associated with high-ranking officials very differently. In solving these cases, the Chinese leadership has demonstrated their highest level of toughness and resolution, while the Vietnamese leadership has shown a reluctance to be decisive in these efforts. The most notable evidence is Japan's decision in December 2008 to suspend development aid to Vietnam in order to press the government to take stronger measures to fight corruption. [45]

Patterns of Energy Consumption

Energy is increasingly becoming a scarce and strategic resource. Thus, reducing the energy intensity of a country's economic development implies wisdom and strategic thinking. The energy consumption patterns of the two countries indicate that China is more strategically effective than Vietnam on this issue (Table 11).

The energy intensity of China's economy, measured as kilograms of oil equivalent per US $1,000 of GDP, was 1.95 in 1990, much higher than that of Vietnam (1.62). However, China decisively reduced this intensity from 0.94 in 2000 to 0.91 in 2005 while the figures for Vietnam were 1.2 in 2000 and 1.15 in 2005 (Panel A).

Furthermore, as observed for the period 1990 to 2005, China's intensity of electric power consumption fell while Vietnam's rose. At the economy-wide level, the difference in growth rates between GDP and electric energy consumption was +0.4% for China and -6.5% for Vietnam. For the

---

45 "Vietnam Aid Loans Suspended", *Strait Times* at < http://www. straitstimes. com/Breakingper cent2BNews/Money/Story/STIStory_ 310286. html > [4 Dec. , 2008].

industry sector, this difference was + 3. 3% age points for China and
−3. 4% age points for Vietnam (Panel B).

Table 11   *Efficiency of Energy Consumption*

A. Energy Consumption per 1, 000 US $ of GDP ∗ (kg of oil equivalent)

	1990	2000	2005
Vietnam	1. 62	1. 20	1. 15
China	1. 95	0. 94	0. 91

B. Electricity Consumption for Growth, %

	1990—2005 Growth (CAGR)		Electricity Savings (II)-(I)
	Electricity Consumption (I)	Value – Added (II)	
China			
Economy	9. 7	10. 1	+0. 4
Industrial Sector	9. 3	12. 6	+3
Vietnam			
Economy	14. 1	7. 6	−6. 5
Industrial Sector	14. 3	10. 9	-3. 4

Note: ∗ The 2000 price level.

Sources: Key World Energy Statistics 2007, International Energy Agency; China's Yearbook 2006; Vietnam's Ministry of Industry and Trade (for electricity consumption by sector).

Efficacy of Openness

Openness has a significant positive impact on economic growth.[46] On the two widely-used metrics of openness—the ratio of total trade to GDP and the weighted mean of tariffs, Vietnam is more open than China.[47] Since the launch of the reforms in 1986, Vietnam has rapidly increased its openness to the world. These simple openness measures, therefore, do not explain why Vietnam has lagged behind China in growth performance.

This calls for a deeper investigation into the efficacy of openness of the two countries with respect to their integration into the world economy. It

---

46 Jeffrey Sachs and Andrew Warner, "Economic Reform and the Process of Global Integration", *Brookings Papers on Economic Activity*, Vol. 26, No. 1, Economic Studies Program, The Brookings Institution, 1995, pp. 1 – 118.

47 In 2000, the merchandise trade to GDP ratio was 87. 9% for Vietnam and 44. 6% for China, while the average tariffs were 15% and 20%, respectively.

is obvious that the two countries have achieved rapid growth in both exports and imports. However, China's exports have grown faster than its imports, while the reverse pattern was observed for Vietnam (Figure 7).

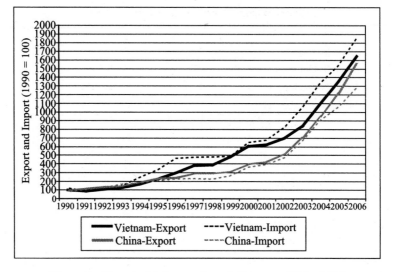

Figure 7 *Export and Import Growth Patterns, 1990—2006*
Source: WDI.

Furthermore, Vietnam was slower than China in moving up the technology ladder.[48] For Vietnam, the share of low technology and agricultural products fluctuated at 57% -58% during 2000—2005 and declined very little (by 0. 6% age points), moving from 58. 1% in 2000 to 57. 5% in 2005. At the same time, this figure for China fell sharply by 12. 9% age points, from 44. 9% in 2000 to 32% in 2005. On the other hand, the share of the high-tech industry in Vietnam's exports was small and rose little (by only 1. 8%) from 5. 8% in 2000 to 7. 8% in 2005, while this figure went up drastically for China, reaching 41. 3% in 2005 from 28. 9% in 2000, a rise of 12. 3%. In particular, China has effectively embraced the boom in the Information and Communication Technology (ICT) market for expanding its exports (the share of the ICT industry in China's exports rose by 9. 0% age points, from 15. 3% in 2000 to 24. 2% in 2005), while Vietnam's gain in these exports was modest (from 2. 8% in 2000 to 3. 9% in 2005) (Table 12).

---

48 The data is available only for the 2000—2005 period.

Table 12 *Structural Changes in Exports and Imports, 2000—2005*

Industry	2000	2005	Change
China: Export Structure, % (Total = 100%)			
HighTechnology	28. 9	41. 3	+12. 3
of which: ICT Industry	15. 3	24. 2	+9. 0
Medium–High Technology	10. 4	11. 1	+0. 7
Medium–Low Technology and Mining	15. 8	15. 7	−0. 1
Low Technology and Agriculture	44. 9	32	-12. 9
China: Import Structure, % (Total = 100%)			
High Technology	31. 3	37. 6	+6. 3
of which: ICT Industry	11. 3	13	+1. 7
Medium–High Technology	19. 3	17. 8	−1. 5
Medium–Low Technology and Mining	29	31. 6	+2. 6
Low Technology and Agriculture	20. 3	13. 1	-7. 3
Vietnam: Export Structure, % (Total = 100%)			
High Technology	5. 8	7. 6	+1. 8
of which: ICT Industry	2. 8	3. 9	+1. 0
Medium–High Technology	2. 3	3. 7	+1. 4
Medium–Low Technology and Mining	33. 8	31. 2	−2. 7
Low Technology and Agriculture	58. 1	57. 5	−0. 6
Vietnam: Import Structure, % (Total = 100%)			
High Technology	14. 3	15	+0. 6
of which: ICT Industry	5. 3	5. 4	+0. 1
Medium–High Technology	28. 3	21. 8	−6. 5
Medium–Low Technology and Mining	28. 7	36. 2	+7. 5
Low Technology and Agriculture	28. 6	27	−1. 5

Note: The classification of technology is based on OECD (2006) for manufacturing industries.

Sources: Author's calculation based on data from UNTAC.

Note also that the driver of import growth in China over the period 2000—2005 was high technology, with an increase in its share of exports of 6. 2% from 31. 3% in 2000 to 37. 6% in 2005; while for Vietnam medium-low technology and mining (oil and gas) products drove this growth, with this sector's share increasing by 7. 5% from 28. 7% in 2000 to 36. 2% in 2005.

The findings suggest that China has been more strategic than Vietnam in both exports and imports with a notable push made in moving up the technology ladder. Vietnam has been slower than many other East Asian economies in exploiting the rapid growth of the Asian market driven by China. During the period 1990—2006, Asia's share in Vietnam's total exports declined from 39.2% to 36.5%, while this share rose rapidly for Korea (from 34% to 51%), Taiwan (38.2% to 64%), Singapore (47.1% to 63.4%), Hong Kong (42.3% to 61.9%), Thailand (37.8% to 53.3%) and the Philippines (34.8% to 64.9%).[49]

The analyses reveal a significant gap in the efficacy of openness between the two countries, which is related to the effectiveness of each country's government in carrying out industrial policy. The analyses also explain why simple measures of openness, such as trade-to-GDP, are not robust predictors of the variation in growth.

▪ Conclusion

This study provides important insights into the determinants of economic growth and growth divergence in China and Vietnam. The two countries initiated their economic reforms from comparable economic and social conditions and have followed rather similar approaches to reform and economic management. Since the launch of reforms, both countries have made impressive achievements in their growth performance. However, their growth patterns have significantly diverged. China has far outperformed Vietnam in both the pace and efficiency of growth. This parallels a gap between the Asian Tigers such as Korea and Taiwan on the one hand and ASEAN economies such as Indonesia and Thailand on the other.

This study finds that the growth divergence between China and Vietnam is substantial not only quantitatively but also qualitatively, and that the gap in economic growth between the two countries enlarged during good times, when both countries accelerated their growth with China outperforming Vietnam. A key finding was that disparity in government effectiveness has been the main factor explaining the divergence in

---

49　Asian Development Bank, "Key Indicators 2007", ADB, 2007.

economic performance. This paper suggests that for a developing country where institutional quality is usually weak and takes a long time to develop, enhancing government effectiveness is a critical step in fostering economic performance and creating the necessary conditions for upgrading institutional performance.

This study also shows that while China has an advantage in government effectiveness, its institutional foundation remains weak, which is rather comparable with Vietnam. Simple indicators such as the trade-to-GDP ratio for openness or schooling for human capital are not robust predictors of variations in economic growth.

Developmental States in East Asia: A Comparison of the Japanese and Chinese Experiences

Mark Beeson *

▪ Introduction

The economies of East Asia have attracted the attention of scholars and policy makers for decades. Rightly so, although some observers may have become blasé about, if not bored with, the story of the "Asian miracle". The rise of Japan and more recently China remain remarkable, unparalleled—largely optimism—inducing events of enormous long-run, geopolitical significance. But it is not just the fact of Japan's and China's unprecedented economic expansion that has been noteworthy, it is also themanner in which it has been achieved. What has really set the most successful East Asian economies apart, and what has given them a wider significance in debates about economic development and public policy, has been the role of government. The "developmental state" pioneered by Japan, which was emulated with varying degrees of faithfulness and efficacy elsewhere in the region, became synonymous with East Asia's rapid economic expansion and emblematic of the region's distinctive approach to economic management. [1]

---

* Mark Beeson is Winthrop Professor in Political Science and International Relations at the University of Western Australia. His main publications include *Competing Capitalisms: Australia, Japan and Economic Competition in the Asia Pacific*, *Contemporary Southeast Asia: Regional Dynamics, National Differences* (ed.), *Bush and Asia: America's Evolving Relations with East Asia* (ed.), *Regionalism, Globalization and East Asia: Politics, Security and Economic Development* and *Securing Southeast Asia: The Politics of Security Sector Reform*.
Numerous people have read and commented on earlier versions of this paper. The author would like to thank Andre Broome, Adrian Leftwich, Ronen Palan, Hugo Radice, Richard Stubbs, and *Aisan Perspective*'s anonymous reviewers.

1 Alice H. Amsden, *The Rise of "The Rest": Challenges to the West from Late-Industrializing Economies*, Oxford: Oxford University Press, 2001. It should be noted that there is also an extensive literature that considers the developmental experiences of South Korea, Taiwan, Singapore, and even Southeast Asia, but this lies beyond the scope of this article. For an overview, see Mark Beeson, *Regionalism, Globalization and East Asia: Politics, Security and Economic Development*, Basingstoke: Palgrave, 2007.

The precise impact of the developmental state in actually accelerating e-
conomic growth or in "deepening" the extent of subsequent industrialization in either Japan or elsewhere remains uncertain, contentious, and
indicative of our imperfect understanding of such processes.[2] However,
even among those observers who are prepared to acknowledge that a
powerful state apparatus may have played an important role in overseeing
and directing the course of Japan's post-war economic renaissance, there is
a widely held view that in an era of growing cross-border economic
integration, such a role for the state is anachronistic at best, inimical to
further development at worst.[3] Japan's comparatively anemic economic
performance throughout the 1990s and into the new century seemed to
confirm the wisdom of such views: Not only was Japan performing
badly—especially when measured by its own lofty former standards—but it
seemed that Japanese policy makers were incapable of coming up with ways
to address the malaise. Worse still, the entire Japanese political and
bureaucratic system seemed to be contributing to the problem and came in
for extensive criticism as a consequence.[4]

In such circumstances, some observers think it unlikely that the
developmental state might persist in Japan, let alone still be emulated
elsewhere.[5] And yet that is precisely what seems to have happened: Not
only does the legacy of Japan's "interventionist" state live on and
continue—for better or worse—to shape public policy in that country[6],

---

2 Charles Kenny and David Williams, "What Do We Know about Economic Growth? Or, Why
   Don't We Know Very Much?", *World Development*, Vol. 29, No. 1, 2001, pp. 1 – 22.

3 Richard Katz, *Japan: The System That Soured*, Armonk, N. Y. : M. E. Sharpe, 1998; Edward
   J. Lincoln, *Arthritic Japan: The Slow Pace of Economic Reform in Japan*, Washington, D. C. :
   Brookings Institute Press, 2001.

4 T. J. Pempel, *Regime Shift: Comparative Dynamics of the Japanese Political Economy*, Ithaca,
   N. Y. : Cornell University Press, 1999.

5 Andrew MacIntyre and Barry Naughton, "The Decline of a Japan-led Model of East Asian
   Economy", in T. J. Pempel (ed.), *Remapping East Asia: The Construction of a Region*, Ithaca,
   N. Y. : Cornell University Press, 2005.

6 Mark Beeson, "Japan's Reluctant Reformers and the Legacy of the Developmental State", in
   Anthony Cheung and Ian Scott (eds.), *Governance and Public Sector Reform in Post-crisis Asia:
   Paradigm Shift or Business as Usual?*, London: Curzon Press, 2003; Steven K. Vogel, *Japan
   Remodeled: How Government and Industry Are Reforming Japanese Capitalism*, Ithaca, N. Y. :
   Cornell University Press, 2006.

but others have sought to replicate aspects of the "Japanese model" elsewhere. [7] By far the most important of these potential acolytes is China, which has attempted to reproduce some elements of the Japanese exemplar to accelerate and manage its own remarkable rise. [8] China consequently presents an important case study of the durability and continuing attractiveness of something approximating a developmental state in the contemporary era, especially when the neoliberal, Anglo-American alternative looks so discredited, and when some are suggesting that East Asian forms of capitalism look increasingly attractive. [9]

Given the significance of Japan and China as developmental exemplars and as pivotal economic, political, and strategic actors in East Asia and the wider international system, it is surprising how few attempts have been made to compare their respective historical experiences. [10] Doing so, however, provides important insights into the dynamics of development in East Asia and the importance of specific historical conditions. The principal conclusion that emerges from what follows is that while contingent international strategic and economic conditions may structurally constrain policy choices and developmental paths, agency matters and political elites may retain a surprising degree of autonomy if they care to try and exercise it.

In short, there are complex dialectical processes at work in East Asia that will continue to shape political and economic structures in the region, and ensure not only that it will continue to look noticeably different from Anglo-American forms of capitalism, but that something approximating the developmental state is likely to remain part of it. The first part of the discussion provides a brief conceptual introduction to the developmental state and the persistence of difference in East Asia. I suggest that whatever

---

7 Edith Terry, *How Asia Got Rich: Japan, China, and the Asian Miracle*, Armonk, N. Y. : M. E. Sharpe, 2002.

8 Seung-Wook Baek, "Does China Follow 'the East Asian Development Model'?", *Journal of Contemporary Asia*, Vol. 35, No. 4, 2005, pp. 485 – 498; David Kerr, "Has China Abandoned Self-Reliance?", *Review of International Political Economy*, Vol. 14, No. 1, 2007, pp. 77 – 104.

9 Elliott Larry, "Asian Model Should Have More Fans", *The Guardian* (London), September 8, 2008.

10 For a rare exception, see Saadia M. Pekkanen and Kellee S. Tsai (eds.), *Japan and China in the World Political Economy*, London: Routledge, 2005.

we may think about the utility or feasibility of developmental states in the current era, they are likely to persist as a consequence of path dependency, institutional "stickiness", and the interlocking patterns of political and economic power that are such a ubiquitous and distinctive part of development in East Asia. [11]

Conceptualizing Developmental States

State Capacity

The developmental state became a widely used and understood concept as a consequence of Chalmers Johnson's seminal analysis of Japan's postwar economic reconstruction. [12] In Johnson's original formulation the developmental state had a number of features—principal among which were competent state agencies and carefully calibrated industrial policies—that allowed it to play a decisive role in directing the course of Japan's economic resurrection. The key quality that made the state in Japan developmental was that it planned the development process rather than relied on market forces to determine the optimal allocation of resources. Unlike "market rational" states, which were concerned with simply establishing the rules ofthe economic game, the "plan rational" state sought to formulate and pursue "substantive social and economic goals". In Japan's case, as I explain in more detail below, there is no doubt that such goals were often achieved, thanks to a combination of domestic capacity and favorable external circumstances. [13] The unprecedented success of Japan's postwar developmental project gave it—for a while, at least—a talismanic status for

11　Mark Beeson, "The More Things Change…? Path Dependency and Convergence in East Asia", in Beeson (ed.), *Reconfiguring East Asia: Regional Institutions and Organisations after the CrisisV*, London: Routledge Curzon Press, 2002, pp. 246 - 256; Edward T. Gomez, *Political Business in East Asia*, London: Routledge, 2002; Joe Studwell, Asian Godfathers: Money and Power in Hong Kong and Southeast Asia, New York: Atlantic Monthly Press, 2007.

12　*Chalmers Johnson,* MITI and the Japanese Miracle: The Growth of Industry Policy *1925—1975*, Stanford, Calif. : Stanford University Press, 1982.

13　*William K. Tabb,* The Postwar Japanese System: Cultural Economy and Economic Transformation, New York: Oxford University Press, 1995.

other would be developers, and a special place in debates about and analysis of the rapidly expanding field of comparative political economy.

The nature of contingent circumstances determines both the quality and impact of national public policy. Differing "state capacities" are at the core of idealized depictions of the developmental state. Because Japan appears to be losing them and China has never fully developed them, it is worth spelling out what they are supposed to be. At one level state capacity is easily defined: simply a state's ability to design and implement policy. [14] However, this begs a series of further questions about the precise attributes that allow some broadly similar states to do this more or less effectively while others find it more difficult. Again, this seems superficially straightforward and a function of the degree of "stateness" or "strength" that different states may have. It was the apparent absence of such qualities that Migdal thought explained disappointing developmental outcomes in Africa, for example. [15] By contrast, it was precisely the possession of state strength, or more particularly an ability to "penetrate" and mobilize the society in which the state was embedded, which some observers claimed was the key to the rise of East Asia. [16]

The challenge has always been in achieving the right degree of what Peter Evans famously described as "embedded autonomy"[17]—in other words, bureaucratic agencies that were not only capable and coherent, but also were sufficiently close to society and economic actors to implement policy and "guide" development. The danger has always been that such agencies would become too close, "captured", and the servants of particularistic interests. It was precisely this possibility that was described as

14　Charles Polidano, "Measuring Public Sector Capacity", *World Development*, Vol. 28, No. 5, May, 2000, pp. 805 – 822.

15　Joel S. Migdal, *Strong States and Weak Societies: State-Society Relations and State Capabilities in the Third World*, Princeton, N. J. : Princeton University Press, 1988.

16　Linda Weiss and John M. Hobson, *States and Economic Development: A Comparative Historical Analysis*, Cambridge: Polity Press, 1995. For a more detailed discussion of the evolution of state "infrastructural power", or the ability to reach down into society and extract resources and implement policy, see Michael Mann, *The Sources of Social Power: The Rise of Classes and Nation States*, 1760—1914, Cambridge: Cambridge University Press, 1993.

17　Peter Evans, *Embedded Autonomy: States and Industrial Transformation*, Princeton, N. J. : Princeton University Press, 1995.

"crony capitalism", and considered by critics as part of the explanation for the East Asian financial crisis. [18]

The Developmental State

One of the advantages of comparative analyses of the sort that follows is that it illustrates the way that some of these factors are actually realized or approximated in practice. It is worth emphasizing a few general issues at the outset, though. First, the idea of the developmental state deployed here stands for a general policy orientation on the part of the state, rather than a specific set of initiatives or bureaucratic practices. The key point is that such an activist orientation is fundamentally at odds with the idealized small-state, market-centered, neoliberal model associated with the Anglo-American economies; it consequently remains a useful point of departure when thinking about broad brush distinctions between East Asia and elsewhere. Adopting a new policy paradigm inevitably creates winners and losers, something that helps to explain the continuing resistance to neoliberal reform in East Asia. [19] Second, the particular way that such an orientation will reveal itself will vary as a consequence of specific national histories and may endure even when the original "need" for such an approach has apparently passed. As Stephan Haggard points out:

> Asia proves that a variety of institutional arrangements can contribute to high growth. Understanding the diversity of institutional arrangements, however, requires an analytic strategy that differs somewhat from focusing on the functions that institutions might perform, and calls on us to dig beneath institutional arrangements to reveal the political relationships that create and support them. [20]

This is a point that has also been emphasized by Adrian Leftwich, who

---

18 The literature on the East Asian crisis and the possible role of crony capitalism is vast. Useful discussions include Joseph E. Stiglitz, *Globalization and Its Discontents*, New York: Norton, 2002; and Richard Robison, Mark Beeson, Kanishka Jayasuriya, and Hyuk-Rae Kim (eds.), *Politics and Markets in the Wake of the Asian Crisis*, London: Routledge, 2000.

19 Mark Beeson and Iyanatul Islam, "Neoliberalism and East Asia: Resisting the Washington Consensus", *Journal of Development Studies*, Vol. 41, No. 2, February 2005, pp. 197 – 219.

20 Stephan Haggard, "Institutions and Growth in East Asia", *Studies in Comparative International Development*, Vol. 38, No. 4, December 2004, p. 74.

reminds us that development "must always be understood as an inescapably political process in which the purposive interaction of people, power and resources, in diverse cultural and historical contexts, shapes the pattern and the outcomes at any given point"[21]. Both the Japanese and Chinese cases reflect this point but also suggest that, despite very different national histories, state capacities, and modes of integration into the global economy, there are sufficient commonalities in the overall patterns of economic governance in Japan and China to allow us to label them both as being in the developmental camp. There are, however, also important and enduring differences. Paradoxically, both the differences and similarities can be explained in large part by domestic politics, and the way they have been shaped by and have responded to a complex array of economic and geopolitical forces. [22]

The very different reactions of Chinese and Japanese elites during the nineteenth century in particular provide a compelling reminder that state policy makes a decisive difference in determining long-run developmental outcomes. [23] From being the center of an East Asian political order that had endured for centuries and which plainly engendered a degree of hubris and insularity, China found itself unable to respond to the economic and political expansion of Europe. By contrast, the response of Japan to Western, or more especially, American intrusion could hardly have been more different. True, Japan's elites were initially just as insular and unhappy about the prospect of adjusting to external pressure as China's were, but the forced "opening" of Japan by the United States in the middle of the nineteenth century triggered a process of profound social transformation. [24] The Meiji Restoration marked the beginning of a process

21 Adrian Leftwich, "Politics in Command: Development Studies and the Rediscovery of Social Science", *New Political Economy*, Vol. 10, No. 4, December 2005, p. 575.

22 Richard F. Doner, Bryan K. Ritchie, and Dan Slater, "Systemic Vulnerability and the Origins of Developmental States: Northeast and Southeast Asia in Comparative Perspective", *International Organization*, Vol. 59, No. 2, Spring 2005, pp. 327 – 361.

23 Frances V. Moulder, *Japan, China and the Modern World Economy*, Cambridge: Cambridge University Press, 1977.

24 Walter LaFeber, *The Clash: U. S. -Japanese Relations Throughout History*, New York: W. W. Norton, 1997.

that would see Japan completely overhaul its structures of governance, and institutionalize a powerful, centralized state at the heart of its long-run rise to prominence as an industrial and military power.[25] It is also important to recognize that the political histories and cultures of both Japan and China have made the very idea of a powerful, interventionist state much less problematic than it has in the Anglo-American economies.[26]

The durability of Japan's political and economic institutions in the face of American reformist pressures is attributable to the fact that such pressures dissipated with the onset of the cold war and the need to stabilize capitalist allies of any sort—even those that practiced the sort of centralized, neo-mercantilist interventionism that was an ideological anathema to many U. S. policy makers. Put bluntly, the imperatives of cold war rivalry and the need to consolidate Japan as a successful bulwark against possible Soviet expansion and as the centerpiece of a regional economic revival meant that the United States was forced to tolerate a largely unreconstructed Japanese developmental state.[27] The geopolitical context of the cold war also proved both a powerful external spur to development through aid and investment packages[28], and a surprisingly permissive ideological context within which to pursue state-led development strategies.[29] At least this was the case for U. S. allies.

For countries like China that were on the "wrong" side of the ideological fence, the developmental forecast was a good deal gloomier. Indeed, it is easy to forget that China's relatively isolated and intimidated "socialist developmental state" achieved substantial industrialization and modernization from a very low base and in remarkably unpropitious circumstances.[30] Moreover, as Alvin So perceptively points out, "the

---

25 W. G. Beasley, *The Rise of Modern Japan: Political, Economic, and Social Change Since 1950*, London: Weidenfeld and Nicholson, 1990.

26 I am indebted to Adrian Leftwich for this important point.

27 Michael Schaller, "Securing the Great Crescent: Occupied Japan and the Origins of Containment in Southeast Asia", *Journal of American History*, Vol. 69, No. 2, September 1982, pp. 392 – 414.

28 Richard Stubbs, *Rethinking Asia's Economic Miracle*, Basingstoke: Palgrave, 2005.

29 Beeson, *Regionalism, Globalization and East Asia*.

30 Gordon White, "Developmental States and Socialist Industrialisation in the Third World", *Journal of Development Studies*, Vol. 21, No. 1, October 1984, pp. 97 – 120.

present developmental miracle of China actually owes much to the historical heritage of the Maoist era. Despite many shortcomings, the Maoist legacy has provided China with a strong Leninist party-state, [and] a concentration of power in the communist party"[31].

Paradoxically enough, therefore, the cold war period, and the exigencies of development and even state survival in China's case, have at least partly enabled China's current state-directed integration into the global economy. But it is doing so in very different circumstances from those that confronted Japan, and without some of the advantages that Japan possessed. The next section spells out how Japan managed this process, what eventually went wrong, and why aspects of the developmental state persist.

▪ Japan: Still Developmental after All These Years?

The current conventional wisdom is that whatever the advantages Japan's developmental state may once have enjoyed, it is now associated with stasis at best, long-term decline at worst. Nevertheless, elements of the developmental state persist as a result of path dependency, institutional inertia, and because some actors continue to support them. In order to understand why, it is useful to remind ourselves of what the Japanese developmental state looked like in its heyday and why it has proved so resistant to change.

Japan's Success Story

The story of the Japanese miracle has been frequently told, so I shall simply highlight some of its key features here. Most importantly, perhaps, Japan's resurgence occurred in very different circumstances from those confronting China. Two external conditions were especially favorable as far as Japan was concerned. First, the Japanese were actively supported rather than "contained" by the now hegemonic presence of the United States. The willingness to tolerate Japan's neo-mercantilist developmental strategies

---

31   Alvin Y. So, "Guest Editor's Introduction", *Chinese Economy*, Vol. 35, No. 3, May-June 2002, p. 6. For a general discussion of the comparative significance of post-communist transition, see Andrew G. Walder, "The Decline of Communist Power-Elements of a Theory of Institutional Change", *Theory and Society*, Vol. 23, No. 2, April 1994, pp. 297 – 323.

was a crucial component of the permissive environment in which Japan prospered. This was especially important given a second factor that favored Japan. The U. S. promotion of a broadly "liberal" world order in the aftermath of World War II would eventually culminate in the greater degree of international economic integration that we now associate with "globalization". [32] For the first few decades of this process, however, Japan would enjoy the best of both worlds: It was able to take advantage of a rapidly expanding international economy and relatively unfettered access to important markets in Europe and North America, without having to open up its own markets and, crucially, while maintaining control of the domestic financial system. [33]

Japanese bureaucrats had some particular advantages in pursuing their vision of industrial rebirth. First, the idea of a powerful, interventionist state enjoyed a degree of legitimacy that it did not in the Anglo-American economies, where very different traditions of economic and political thought prevailed. [34] Moreover, the bureaucrats not only enjoyed a good deal of prestige, they also had real power: The nature of Japan's political system, in which the conventional political class is famously ineffective and preoccupied with raising money to fight elections, meant that the bureaucrats were generally allowed to get on with running the economy. [35] When the developmental state was at the height of its powers, state officials were able to exploit the sorts of "embedded autonomy" that Evans considered vital to effective policy implementation. [36] Close connections with Japan's powerful *keiretsu* business groups allowed industrial policies to be coordinated via an "old boy network" of ex-public servants who ended their careers in the board rooms of leading Japanese corporations. [37]

Such relationships were fundamental components of the old order. The very different way in which they are now viewed is emblematic of the real

---

32 Robert Latham, *The Liberal Moment: Modernity, Security, and the Making of Postwar International Order*, New York: Columbia University Press, 1997.

33 Kent E. Calder, *Strategic Capitalism: Private Business and Public Purpose in Japanese Industrial Finance*, Princeton, N. J. : Princeton University Press, 1993.

34 Beeson, *Regionalism, Globalization and East Asia*.

35 Karel van Wolferen, *The Enigma of Japanese Power: People and Politics in a Stateless Nation*, London: Papermac, 1989.

36 Evans, *Embedded Autonomy*.

37 Ulricke Schaede, "The 'Old Boy' Network and Government-Business Relationships in Japan", *Journal of Japanese Studies*, Vol. 21, No. 2, Summer 1995, pp. 293 – 317.

material changes that have overtaken Japan and of the ideological prism through which they have been refracted. But before considering these changes it is important to briefly note that the "Japanese model" had other important components that help explain its undoubted success. The *keiretsu* networks, for example, enjoyed significant competitive advantages[38], partly because they were embedded in a wider array of institutionalized social relationships that together helped Japan to "catch-up" with the rest of the industrialized world; they also gave Japan's distinctive patterns of social accommodation a good deal of stability and resilience. Not only did its industrial relations system feature "lifetime employment"[39] and a more collective commitment to corporate goals;[40] Japan's economic and social institutions were also widely thought to give it a competitive advantage over other economies.[41]

Things Fall Apart

Japan's growth record since the beginning of the 1990s has caused a major rethinking of the entire Japanese experience and about the role of the developmental state within it. While this is understandable enough, perhaps we also need to think about the wider geopolitical context in which the Japanese model appeared to founder. Of central importance in this context was the winding down of the cold war and an increased willingness on the part of the United States to pressure Japan into opening up its domestic economy. Precisely the same sorts of pressures are building up around China since it has supplanted Japan as the principal source of U. S.

---

38 What Michael Gerlach calls Japan's alliance capital benefited from stable patterns of cross-shareholding and preferential trading relations with other *keiretsu* members and access to "patient" capital for their "main banks". There is, of course, currently a debate over whether such relationships are either any longer beneficial or sustainable in the face of greater competition and external pressure, but they undoubtedly underpinned the expansion of Japanese capital domestically and overseas. See Michael L. Gerlach, *Alliance Capitalism: The Social Organization of Japanese Business*, Berkeley, Calif.: University of California Press, 1992.

39 In reality, lifetime employment only ever applied to about one third of the workforce, and much of the labor force enjoyed much less security and was often fairly ruthlessly squeezed by big business.

40 Masahiko Aoki, *Information, Incentives, and Bargaining in the Japanese Economy*, Cambridge: Cambridge University Press, 1988.

41 Ronald Dore, *Flexible Rigidities: Industrial Policy and Structural Adjustment in the Japanese Economy 1970—1980*, Stanford, Calif.: Stanford University Press, 1986.

trade deficits. They are no more likely to address the underlying problems than they were in Japan's case. Nevertheless, they do serve as a reminder of the dynamics, importance, and possible unintended consequences that flow from specific geopolitical contexts.

Many of Japan's current problems were either caused by, or manifest in, the "bubble economy" that emerged in the late 1980s. The causes and consequences of the bubble economy have already been extensively analyzed[42], so it is sufficient to simply make a few general points here. First—and something that is generally neglected in most analyses—Japan's strategic dependence on the United States and the non-negotiable nature of the security relationship meant that it was potentially vulnerable to shifts in the overarching geopolitical context.[43] The growing preoccupation of the United States with its own national economic position during the 1980s was making it increasingly unwilling to bear the costs associated with benign hegemony[44], and more demanding of allies as their strategic importance declined. When the Americans demanded that Japan cooperate in a process of managed currency realignment, Japanese policy makers had little choice but to oblige.

The so-called Plaza Accord negotiated in 1985 may have had the desired short-term impact of reducing the value of the dollar against the yen, but it set in motion a series of unforeseen and often unwelcome consequences that continue to reverberate.[45] As far as Japan was concerned, the Accord had two principal effects. First, as a consequence of a loosening of domestic monetary policy to compensate for the appreciation of the yen, speculative bubbles developed in the real estate and stock markets. The yen appreciation

---

43   Christopher W. Hughes and Akiko Fukushima, "U. S. -Japan Security Relations: Toward Bilateralism Plus?", in E. S. Krauss and T. J. Pempel (eds.), *Beyond Bilateralism: U. S. - Japan Relations in the New Asia-Pacific*, Stanford, Calif.: Stanford University Press, 2004, pp. 55 – 86.

44   Jagdish Bhagwati and Hugh T. Patrick (eds.), *Aggressive Unilateralism: America's Trade Policy and the World Trading System*, New York: Harvester Wheatsheaf, 1990. For many observers in the United States, American hegemony was seen as benign, necessary, and central to the provision of collective public goods, without which an "open" international order could not function. For an overview of competing perspectives, see Mark Beeson, "American Ascendancy: Conceptualising Contemporary Hegemony", in Mark Beeson (ed.), *Bush and Asia: America's Evolving Relations with East Asia*, London: Routledge, 2006, pp. 3 – 23.

45   R. Taggart Murphy, *The Weight of the Yen*, New York: W. W. Norton, 1997.

and the increased cost of doing business in Japan also led to a second effect: the off-shore migration of Japan's most competitive, export-oriented companies and a greater reliance on (and need to protect) the "inefficient" domestic sector. [46] In the longer term, Japan's underlying political dynamics and economic structures, which had become increasingly reliant on trade surpluses to underwrite a distinct domestic accommodation, appeared incapable of delivering continuing high growth in the face of increased international competition. This created pressure for reform from inside, and especially outside, Japan. [47]

Yet, while it is true that the liberalization of finance has begun to loosen ties between the financial and industrial sectors in Japan and undermined the policy tools available to agencies like the Ministry of Finance (MoF) [48], the reform process has been anything but a "big bang". Not only has the MoF fought to resist change—as have other key bureaucracies[49]—but it has actually sought to expand its power by managing the very reforms that were supposed to curb its influence[50]. What is especially noteworthy about Japan is that financial regulation in particular has been based on "informal relational ties linking government regulators and financial institutions and [a] reliance on discretionary rather than rules-based procedures "[51]. Consequently, transforming Japan's policy networks and the political rationality that pervaded the developmental state will require more than simply rewriting the regulatory framework.

Given that the integration and evolution of financial sector activity has

---

46 Katz, *Japan*.

47 Pempel, *Regime Shift*; Leonard J. Schoppa, *Bargaining with Japan: What American Pressure Can and Cannot Do*, New York: Columbia University Press, 1997.

48 Kent E. Calder, "Assault on the Bankers' Kingdom: Politics, Markets, and the Liberalization of Japanese Industrial Finance", in Michael Loriaux, Meredith Wu-Cummings, Kent E. Calder, Sylvia Maxfield, and Sofia A. Pérez, *Capital Ungoverned: Liberalizing Finance in Interventionist States*, Ithaca, N. Y. : Cornell University Press, 1997, pp. 17 – 56.

49 Aurelia George Mulgan, *Japan's Interventionist State: The Role of the MAFF*, London: Routledge Curzon, 2005.

50 Elizabeth Norville, "The ' Illiberal' Roots of Japanese Financial Regulatory Reform", in Lonny E. Carlile and Mark C. Tilton (eds.), *Is Japan Really Changing Its Ways? Regulatory Reform and the Japanese Economy*, Washington, D. C. : Brookings Institute, 1998, pp. 111 – 141.

51 Jennifer A. Amyx, *Japan's Financial Crisis: Institutional Rigidity and Reluctant Change*, Princeton, N. J. : Princeton University Press, 2004, p. 29.

arguably gone further than any other aspect of "globalization" and consequently might be expected to have a major impact on domestic regulatory structures, the limited extent of financial-sector reform in Japan is especially revealing. It becomes easier to understand why reform initiatives have had a modest impact elsewhere, too. As Edward Lincoln points out[52], a big chunk of Japan's population has a powerful stake in the old regime and little incentive to seek or lobby for change. As a result, the problem Japan confronts is that although the constellations of political power and social accommodation that underpinned the old model may still be largely in place, the policy tools and thus the effectiveness of the developmental state have been significantly eroded.

While it is clear that Japan's developmental state played a pivotal role in shaping its post-war recovery, it is equally apparent that it has become increasingly dysfunctional. Even in its heyday the developmental state didn't entirely manage to avoid capture by particularistic interests, as the notorious "construction state" and the astounding waste of public money with which it was associated attests.[53] The weakness and idiosyncrasies of the Japanese political system suggest that there is still little appetite or political capacity to promote major reform.[54] As a result, Japan finds itself in something of a governmental limbo. As Steven Vogel puts it, "Japan's error may not have been sticking with a model that was outmoded but abandoning a model that worked without converting to a new one."[55] Yet despite current problems with the "Japanese Model", it continues to provide something of an inspiration and a useful comparative benchmark for other East Asian states, including China.

China: Not Developmental Enough?

The central issue in what follows is whether, despite—or perhaps

---

52 Lincoln, *Arthritic Japan*.

53 Gavan McCormack, *The Emptiness of Japanese Affluence*, St. Leonards, Australia: Allen and Unwin, 1996.

54 Gerald L. Curtis, *The Logic of Japanese Politics: Leaders, Institutions, and the Limits of Change*, New York: Columbia University Press, 1999.

55 Vogel, *Japan Remodelled*, p. 34. Also see Bai Gao, *Japan's Economic Dilemma: The Institutional Origins of Prosperity and Stagnation*, Cambridge: Cambridge University Press, 2001.

because of—the profound economic and political changes that have swept through China over the last thirty years or so, it can be thought of as a developmental state in broadly the same way as Japan. Despite some significant differences, I shall suggest in what follows that it can, and it may even become more so in time. At the very least, a comparison with the Japanese experience highlights important elements of the general East Asian success story that may have enduring significance for the East Asian region and beyond.

Two general issues are worth highlighting at the outset. First, like Japan, the People's Republic of China's (PRC's) developmental project has been profoundly influenced by the wider geopolitical context in which it was embedded. In China's case, of course, this has—until relatively recently, at least—been a major disadvantage: China found itself politically and economically marginalized in an increasingly integrated international political-economy dominated by the United States. [56] In such circumstances, it is hardly surprising that China's leaders initially "leaned toward" the Soviet Union, its notional ideological ally. The second point which flows from this is that, although China's political and economic regime is very different from Japan's, the PRC government has from its inception also been a developmental state, albeit one that was initially socialist and Maoist. [57] Indeed, it could hardly have been otherwise: States can't get much more "interventionist" and directive than they do under central planning.

But the limits of China's self-reliance and the disadvantages of isolation from global economic forces became increasingly apparent during the 1950s and 1960s. This is not to say that significant development did not occur during the Mao era—it did[58]—but it was dwarfed by the rapid economic growth that was occurring elsewhere in the region, most gallingly in

---

56 John K. Fairbank, *The United States and China*, Cambridge, Mass. : Harvard University Press, 1983.

57 Gordon White, *Riding the Tiger: The Politics of Economic Reform in Post-Mao China*, Stanford, Calif. : Stanford University Press, 1993.

58 Even under Maoist central planning, China's growth was much higher than that of India's, the only country with which it could really be compared in terms of demography and developmental challenges. See Mark Selden, *The Political Economy of Chinese Development*, Armonk, N. Y. : M. E. Sharpe, 1993.

Taiwan. Even when Deng Xiaoping made the pragmatic decision to begin "opening" China and integrating with the global economy, it was not obvious whether the capitalist road and the journey from plan to market would prove successful. Equally importantly, the implications of this transition for the Chinese Communist Party (CCP) —which, despite significant changes, remains the central political force in Chinese politics— were far from clear. [59] Although there are powerful forces in Japan that have also resisted wholesale economic liberalization, in the PRC policy change has an ideological significance that potentially transcends the concerns of simple vested interests. The ability of the ruling elite to reconcile potentially competing political and economic imperatives has placed a strain on already limited state capacities.

China's Paradoxical Developmental State

Given China's unprecedented recent growth spurt, we might be forgiven for thinking that the PRC government must be doing something right. And yet many China specialists argue that China's development is either "dysfunctional"[60], or caution that "[r] eifying the PRC as a developmental state would reflect only the center's official aspirations, not the empirical reality within the party-state's own institutions"[61]. How do we reconcile this apparent contradiction? Plainly, at one level the Chinese economy must finally have been in the right place at the right time, but this still begs the question of how much credit the PRC government deserves for directing or managing this process. At the very least, Deng's decision to "open " the Chinese economy was a political initiative that merits comparison with Japan's opening a century earlier. As we have seen, in Japan's case there is a substantial consensus that whatever problems the Japanese economy may presently have, historical patterns of state intervention and direction were decisive and beneficial in the high growth period. In China's case, the lack of a similar state capacity and doubts about

---

59 Tony Saich, *Governance and Politics of China*, 2nd ed. , Basingstoke: Palgrave, 2004.

60 Shaun Breslin, "China: Developmental State or Dysfunctional Development?", *Third World Quarterly*, Vol. 17, No. 4, December 1996, p. 689.

61 Kellee S. Tsai and Sarah Cook, "Developmental Dilemmas in China: Socialist Transition and Late Liberalization", in Saadia M. Pekkanen and Kellee S. Tsai (eds.), *Japan and China in the World Political Economy*, London: Routledge, 2005, p. 61.

the state's ability to direct the course of development have led to more equivocal interpretations of the developmental process. Indeed, it has been argued that it is a lack of state capacity and the concomitant inability of government to direct or compel compliance with its initiatives that have actually made market-led development more attractive. [62]

A number of factors seem to have stopped the state in China from playing as extensive and effective a role as it did in Japan. Most obviously, of course, the fact that China was geographically and demographically massive, "socialist", impoverished, and lacking in the sort of developmental track record that led Japan to colonize China rather than vice versa, were clearly long-term handicaps. But the nature of the political relationships and economic structures that developed in the PRC meant that the course of development was shaped by contingent forces that continue to constrain policy options even in the post-Mao reform era. At the center of China's comparatively modest levels of state capacity is what Lieberthal called "fragmented authoritarianism"[63], or functionally differentiated clusters of responsibility that have made decision making contested and far less coherent than in Japan, where its bureaucrats were less constrained by rival centers of political, ideological or even military power. [64]

The ability of the central government to exercise its authority and guide development appears to have been further compromised by a process of decentralization. However, like much else in China's developmental history, there is a good deal of debate about the impact and even the reality of the decentralization process. On the one hand, some argue that decentralization had little to do with China's remarkable recent growth, claiming that the state remains highly centralized and authoritarian, and that the key reforms that underpinned recent development were in place by the

---

62 Thomas G. Moore, *China in the World Market: Chinese Industry and International Sources of Reform in the Post-Mao Era*, Cambridge: Cambridge University Press, 2002, p. 279.

63 Kenneth G. Lieberthal, "Introduction: The 'Fragmented Authoritarianism' Model and Its Limitations," in Lieberthal and David M. Lampton (eds.), *Bureaucracy, Politics, and Decision Making in Post-Mao China*, Berkeley, Calif.: University of California Press, 1992, pp. 1–30.

64 Although the People's Liberation Army (PLA) is less domestically influential than it once was, even now the PLA is part of what Susan Shirk describes as a "control cartel" of party leaders and security agencies that exercises a constraining influence over China's political elite. See Susan L. Shirk, *China: Fragile Superpower*, Oxford: Oxford University Press, 2007, p. 42.

1970s and 1980s—well before decentralization took hold. [65] On the other hand, what has been described as "federalism Chinese style" is seen as having "placed considerable limits on the discretion of the central government"[66]. A more nuanced middle ground stresses the way institutions have been reconfigured in a continuing interaction between the center and the provinces, a process that constrains but does not determine. Consequently, "local actors have exercised agency in manipulating formal institutions to their advantage"[67].

The dialectic between center and provinces continues to unfold, with no definitive outcome. [68] What is becoming apparent, however, are the distinctive problems and features of the Chinese system that distinguish it from Japan's. Although it is important to recognize that corruption and "money politics" have been endemic in Japan for decades[69], during the height of the developmental state, at least, the bureaucracy was generally uncompromised and corruption posed little direct threat to the developmental project. [70] In China, by contrast, corruption has become pervasive, a source of popular unrest, and potentially corrosive of state legitimacy. [71] Paradoxically enough, however, corruption has also been central to the acceptance and successful integration of capitalist social

---

65 Hongbin Cai and Daniel Treisman, "Did Government Decentralization Cause China's Economic Miracle?", *World Politics*, Vol. 58, No. 4, July 2006, pp. 505 – 535.

66 Gabriella Montinola, Yingyi Qian, and Barry R. Weingast, "Federalism, Chinese Style: The Political Basis for Economic Success in China", *World Politics*, Vol. 48, No. 1, October 1995, p. 50.

67 Kellee S. Tsai, "Adaptive Informal Institutions and Endogenous Institutional Change in China", *World Politics*, Vol. 59, No. 1, October 2006, p. 129.

68 Jude Howell, "Reflections on the Chinese State", *Development and Change*, Vol. 37, No. 2, 2006, pp. 273 – 297; Andrew C. Mertha, "China's 'Soft' Centralization: Shifting Tiao/Kuai Authority Relations", *China Quarterly*, Vol. 184, 2005, pp. 791 – 810.

69 Curtis, *The Logic of Japanese Politics*.

70 Indeed, the relationship between growth and corruption is not clear, but it is possible that corrupt relationships and rent-seeking activity may actually be positively correlated with economic development in some circumstances. See Paul D. Hutchcroft, "The Politics of Privilege: Assessing the Impact of Rents, Corruption, and Clientelism on Third World Development", *Political Studies*, Vol. 45, No. 3, 1997, pp. 639-658.

71 It should be noted, however, that as in Japan during its high growth period, the state in China continues to enjoy high levels of legitimacy and approval, its authoritarian government notwithstanding. See Bruce Gilley, "Legitimacy and Institutional Change: The Case of China", *Comparative Political Studies*, Vol. 41, No. 3, 2008, pp. 259 – 284.

relations.[72] The expansion and transformation of the economy and its associated incentive structures have not only made capitalism more attractive, they have also fundamentally reconfigured the position of individual cadres. The "informal privatization" processes that have seen former party officials become capitalist entrepreneurs has not only blurred ontological and class boundaries[73], it has also had an impact on the state and its role.

Two aspects of this process are especially noteworthy. First, the Chinese state has deviated from the sort of "autonomous" leadership role played in Japan, partly as a consequence of some party members' enduring "suspicion" of the private sector[74], and partly because of the entrepreneurial, profit-seeking role of elements of the state bureaucracy.[75] Put differently, where elements of the state are engaged with the new private sector they are frequently corrupted and self-serving; where they are not, they lack the channels of communication and authority to actually implement policy effectively. These potential problems are exacerbated by a second distinctive feature of the embrace of capitalism: the contradictory place of capitalists themselves.[76] The key point to make about China's expanding capitalist class is that it is not a threat to the extant ruling elite. On the contrary, in what some have described as China's corporatist political-economy, there is a growing coincidence of interests between the CCP and private capital.[77] Consequently, there is little immediate prospect of an expanding bourgeoisie playing the sort of historical role it did in

---

72 Yan Sun, "Reform, State, and Corruption: Is Corruption Less Destructive in China than in Russia?", *Comparative Politics*, Vol. 32, No. 1, October 1999, pp. 1 – 20.

73 X. L. Ding, "Informal Privatization Through Internationalization: The Rise of Nomenklatura Capitalism in China's Offshore Businesses", *British Journal of Political Science*, Vol. 30, 2000, pp. 121 – 146.

74 Howell, "Reflections on the Chinese State", p. 288.

75 Xiaobo Lu, "Booty Socialism, Bureau-Preneurs, and the State in Transition: Organizational Corruption in China", *Comparative Politics*, Vol. 32, No. 3, April 2000, pp. 273 – 243.

76 The key manifestation of the new order was the admission of capitalists into the CCP and the declining role of ideology. See Richard McGregor, "Power not Socialism is Today's Chinese Ideology", *Financial Times* (London), July 25, 2006, online at www. ft. com/cms/s/0/ e2a7539a1c02-11db-a555-0000779e2340. html?nclick_ check = 1.

77 Bruce J. Dickson, "Integrating Wealth and Power in China: The Communist Party's Embrace of the Private Sector", *China Quarterly*, Vol. 192, 2007, pp. 827 – 854; Kellee S. Tsai, *Capitalism Without Democracy: The Private Sector in Contemporary China*, Ithaca, N. Y. : Cornell University Press, 2007.

Europe. [78]

But China's distinct political accommodation has some telling differences and similarities with Japan's. Japan was also taken to be corporatist in its developmental heyday[79], and the relationship between its political and economic actors remains surprisingly impervious to "global" reformist pressures to this day. What is perhaps most noteworthy about China, however, is that unlike Japan, its ruling elites have been able to utilize foreign direct investment (FDI) to actually reinforce their political authority and control. As Mary Gallagher points out: "While foreign investment may indirectly improve the environment for future democratization, through the promotion of the rule of law, transparency, and the freer flow of information, in the short term its presence has afforded the regime more time and more political space to pursue economic reform without political liberalization."[80] The point to emphasize is that, even though China has been much more economically open and reliant on FDI than Japan was, its political elites have managed to exert a degree of control over its possible political impact, at least—its inferior state capacity notwithstanding. The question is what impact such practices have had on the quality of the developmental process and whether they will remain effective in the future.

Developmental Outcomes

Given the structure of the Chinese economy and the political constraints it generates, it is remarkable how effectively the contradictory dynamics of developmentalism have actually been managed. China's governing elite is, after all, caught between the need to prop up unprofitable and uncompetitive state-owned enterprises (SOEs)—the former stalwarts of the centrally-planned economy—and an export-oriented economy that is increasingly dominated by the private sector and/or foreign multinational

78 Dietrich Rueschemeyer, Evelyn H. Stephens, and John D. Stephens, *Capitalist Development and Democracy*, Cambridge: Polity Press, 1992.

79 T. J. Pempel and Keiichi Tsunekawa, "Corporatism Without Labour? The Japanese Anomaly", in Philippe C. Schmitter and Gerhard Lembruch (eds.), *Trends Toward Corporatist Intermediation*, Beverly Hills, Calif.: Sage, 1979, pp. 231 – 270.

80 Mary E. Gallagher, "'Reform and Openness': Why China's Economic Reforms Have Delayed Democracy", *World Politics*, Vol. 54, No. 3, April 2002, p. 368.

corporations. [81] In sharp contrast to Japan, the emergence of a competitive export sector in China has relied heavily on foreign investment, and the resultant economic activity consequently is not easily controlled or necessarily beneficial as far as long-term development and industrial deepening are concerned. For example, 60% of exports to the United States are from foreign firms. [82] More generally, the amount of value added in the production of such exports within China is "extraordinarily low", with imported components accounting for 80% of the value of the final product. [83]

As a result, one of the most common criticisms of China's developmental project has been about the quality and depth of the industrialization process, making comparisons with Southeast Asia's "ersatz capitalism" not inappropriate. As with the debate about decentralization, the evidence about China's development is mixed and often contradictory, despite the unambiguous and dramatic expansion of the Chinese economy overall. Part of the ambivalence flows from the fact that China, like Japan, has developed a "dual economy"[84]. In China's case, this "dual track" was an intentional part of the shift from plan to market[85], and it has manifested itself most obviously in the continuing prominence of the uncompetitive SOEs. Despite the rapid decline in the absolute number of SOEs and of their share in overall economic activity, the general state attitude toward the SOEs and privatization was enunciated by former Prime Minister Zhu Rongji and his strategy to *zhuada fangxiao* ("grasp the big, let go the small"). [86] The intention was to maintain control of the "commanding heights" of the economy while allowing small-scale enterprises to flourish in

81 Shahid Yusuf, Kaoru Nabeshima, and Dwight H. Perkins, *Under New Ownership: Privatizing China's State-Owned Enterprises*, Washington, D. C.: World Bank, 2006.

82 Neil C. Hughes, "A Trade War With China?", *Foreign Affairs*, Vol. 84, No. 4, July-August 2005, p. 94.

83 Shaun Breslin, "Power and Production: Rethinking China's Global Economic Role", *Review of International Studies*, Vol. 31, No. 4, 2005, p. 743 (figure updated by Breslin).

84 Shaun Breslin, *China and the Global Economy*, Basingstoke: Palgrave, 2007; Jenn-hwan Wang, "China's Dualist Model on Technological Catching up: A Comparative Perspective", *Pacific Review*, Vol. 19, No. 3, September 2006, pp. 385 – 403.

85 Naughton, *The Chinese Economy*.

86 Cited in Sameena Ahmad, "Behind the Mask: A Survey of Business in China", *The Economist*, March 20, 2004, p. 3.

an increasingly market-driven economic environment.

But whatever the merits of a Japanese-style attitude to industrial development and national security may have been, China's political elites confronted a very different international context. Not only had greater transborder economic integration become the norm in the intervening decades, the international regulatory architecture had become more influential and intrusive as well. Nowhere was this more apparent than in China's accession to the World Trade Organization (WTO). China agreed to entry terms that "far surpass[ed] those made by founding members"[87]. As a consequence, some of the potential advantages of "late" development and the catch-up strategies that were available to Japan were effectively foreclosed. As Kerr puts it, "the TRIPS and TRIMS constraints of WTO membership, and the sensitivity of other economies to China's developmental rise, mean that technological 'free-riding' is much harder for China than previous late industrializers."[88] Equally importantly, the very structure and underlying logic of international production has undergone profound changes that highlight the tensions between China's economic goals and political imperatives.

One of the more significant recent developments in the organization of international economic activity has been the modularization of manufacturing processes and the creation of new transnational networks of production.[89] Late industrializers like China must attempt to integrate themselves within such networks, which are generally dominated by established foreign multinationals with embedded ownership and organizational advantages.[90] The dilemma for Chinese policy makers is that modular production networks open up great opportunities for "China" to be incorporated into rapidly expanding, hyper-competitive corporate structures; but such processes may be difficult to control and occur on unfavorable terms. As Steinfeld points out, "networked modular production

---

87 Nicholas R. Lardy, *Integrating China into the Global Economy*, Washington, D. C.: Brookings Institute, 2002, p. 104.

88 David Kerr, "Has China Abandoned Self-Reliance?", *Review of International Political Economy*, Vol. 14, No. 1, February 2007, p. 79.

89 Timothy J. Sturgeon, "Modular Production Networks: A New American Model of Industrial Organization", *Industrial and Corporate Change*, Vol. 11, No. 3, June 2002, pp. 451 – 496.

90 Jeffrey Henderson, Peter Dicken, Martin Hess, Neil Coe, and Henry Wai-Chung Yeung, "Global Production Networks and the Analysis of Economic Development", *Review of International Political Economy*, Vol. 9, No. 3, August 2002, pp. 436 – 464.

may create opportunities for the few players that can actually innovate, but for the vast majority who cannot—whether for reasons of inadequate resources, knowledge, or supporting institutions—the terms of competition have become brutal. "[91] The result as far as China is concerned has generally been that the industrialization process has remained rather shallow, technology transfer has been limited, and the tendency toward dualism has persisted because "the highly internationalized and competitive sector has not significantly helped the modernization of the rest of the economy"[92].

The failure of industrial upgrading and technology transfer is invariably attributed to either a general lack of state capacity[93], or more specifically to the impact of decentralization and the consequent "lack of production networks and organic linkages among domestic firms or between foreign and local enterprises"[94]. And yet, while there are obvious difficulties facing China's policy makers in actually achieving the degree of control or direction over industrial development that they might wish, the state in China remains developmental in orientation and ambition. One of the hallmarks of Japan's "mercantile realism", or its integrated developmental, strategic, and foreign policies, was a lively awareness of the importance of technological mastery in underpinning national economic and military security.[95] In China, too, there is a similar determination, if not capacity, to adopt a "comprehensive" approach to technological upgrading, security, and development.[96]

Whatever the merits of this approach to industrial development, the

---

91 Edward S. Steinfeld, "China's Shallow Integration: Networked Production and the New Challenges for Late Industrialization", *World Development*, Vol. 32, No. 11, November 2004, p. 1974.

92 Francoise Lemoine and Deniz Unal-Kesenci, "Assembly Trade and Technology Transfer: The Case of China", *World Development*, Vol. 32, No. 5, May 2004, p. 831.

93 Tsai and Cook, "Developmental Dilemmas in China".

94 Wang, "China's Dualist Model", p. 387.

95 Eric Heginbotham and Richard J. Samuels, "Mercantile Realism and Japanese Foreign Policy", *International Security*, Vol. 22, No. 4, Spring 1998, pp. 171 – 203.

96 Adam Segal, "Chinese Technonationalism: Autonomy and Security in the World Economy", in Saadia M. Pekkanen and Kellee S. Tsai (eds.), *Japan and China in the World Political Economy*, London: Routledge, 2005, pp. 205 – 222. Definitions of security are famously more "comprehensive" than they are elsewhere, something which explains the frequent desire to link conventional strategic goals with a wider array of economic policies and political goals. See Muthiah Alagappa, "Asian Practice of Security: Key Features and Explanations", in Alagappa (ed.), *Asian Security Practice: Material and Ideational Influences*, Stanford, Calif. : Stanford University Press, 1998, pp. 611-676.

significant point to emphasize here is that it persists despite the best efforts of organizations like the WTO and a more inclement ideational climate internationally. Indeed, even in the area of finance—the sector of economic activity that is widely considered to have become most "global" and resistant to national proclivities—China's domestic structures and practices remain surprisingly distinct and impervious to reform. Despite widespread criticism and alarm about the health of China's banking system, especially the extent of non-performing loans, Chinese banks continue to lend primarily to SOEs.[97] The reasons are not hard to discern and are a powerful reminder of both the importance of domestic politics and the resultant stickiness of institutions. As Victor Shih puts it:

> continuing gross inefficiency in the financial sector can best be understood by examining the political and careerist incentives of those who decided the policies... Their concern for political survival produced a bundle of policies that maximized their financial control, bolstered their administrative accomplishments, and minimized policy risks.[98]

In other words, the nature of policy, the role of the state, and the durability of institutionalized relationships that have apparently passed their use-by dates can be largely explained by the continuing influence of contingent political forces. While this may not tell us anything about the type of state this will produce or the policies it will pursue, it does suggests that differences persist even in the most fungible sectors of formerly discrete national economies.

Can Difference Persist?

Even if it is accepted that in the absence of major crises or shocks, institutional inertia or stickiness is likely to impart a degree of path dependency to policy frameworks and the underlying constellations of power that inform them. Yet we might still expect that a more generalized process of policy convergence might occur as particular ideas become more

---

97 Edward S. Steinfeld, "Market Visions: The Interplay of Ideas and Institutions in Chinese Financial Restructuring", *Political Studies*, Vol. 52, No. 4, December 2004, p. 646.

98 Victor Shih, "Reform Equilibrium, Chinese Style: Political Incentives and Reform Stagnation in Chinese Financial Policies", *Comparative Political Studies*, Vol. 40, No. 10, 2007, p. 1257.

influential.[99] There is, after all, an extensive public policy literature that points to the possibilities of policy learning and transfer[100], as well as more critical studies that emphasize the hegemonic role of transnational class forces in encouraging, if not compelling, change along neoliberal lines.[101] And yet, the reality is that, as the varieties of capitalism literature reminds us, national diversity persists at an underlying structural level, and the policy initiatives associated with neoliberalism have been actively resisted in East Asia.[102] There are a number of reasons to believe that resistance to Anglo-American forms of capitalism may actually intensify.

China's rise is widely predicted to have a major impact on the distribution of power and influence in the international system.[103] Again, views differ about the possible impacts of China's economic development, but to state them briefly they may be divided between those that expect China's rise to lead to inevitable hegemonic competition and conflict[104], and those that believe that China's political and economic elites are being socialized into cooperative behavior as a consequence of their increasingly active and sophisticated participation in international institutions.[105] Either way, there is widespread agreement that China's rise matters enormously,

---

99　Beth A. Simmons and Zachary Elkins, "The Globalization of Liberalization: Policy Diffusion in the International Political Economy", *American Political Science Review*, Vol. 98, No. 1, 2004, pp. 171 – 189.

100　Mark Evans and Jonathan Davies, "Understanding Policy Transfer: A Multi-Level, Multi-Disciplinary Perspective", *Public Administration*, Vol. 77, No. 2, Summer 1999, pp. 361 – 385; David P. Dolowitz and David Marsh, "Learning from Abroad: The Role of Policy Transfer in Contemporary Policy-Making", *Governance: An International Journal of Policy and Administration*, Vol. 13, No. 1, January 2000, pp. 5 – 24.

101　Paul Cammack, "The Governance of Global Capitalism: A New Materialist Perspective", *Historical Materialism*, Vol. 11, No. 2, 2003, pp. 37 – 59; David Harvey, "Neoliberalism as Creative Destruction", *ANNALS of the American Academy of Political and Social Science*, Vol. 610, 2007, pp. 22 – 44; William I. Robinson, *A Theory of Global Capitalism: Production, Class, and State in a Transnational World*, Baltimore, Md. : John Hopkins University Press, 2004.

102　Beeson and Islam, "Neo-Liberalism and East Asia".

103　See Mark Beeson, "Hegemonic Transition in East Asia? The Dynamics of Chinese and American Power", *Review of International Studies*, Vol. 35, No. 1, 2009, pp. 95 – 112.

104　John J. Mearsheimer, *The Tragedy of Great Power Politics*, New York: W. W. Norton, 2001; Steve Chan, *China, the U. S. , and the Power-Transition Theory*, London: Routledge, 2008.

105　Alastair I. Johnston, "Is China a Status Quo Power?", *International Security*, Vol. 27, No. 4, Spring 2003, pp. 5 – 56; David C. Kang, *China Rising: Peace, Power, and Order in East Asia*, New York: Columbia University Press, 2007.

and that it has the potential to influence the system of which it is a part. The difference between the most recent ascents of China and Japan is, therefore, striking and merits emphasis.

Japan's initial attempt at carving regional hegemony ended disastrously and culminated in its defeat and occupation by the United States. [106] The most striking feature of Japan's subsequent foreign policy has been its "reactive", passive, and ineffectual nature: Strategic subordination to the United States has meant that Japan has been unable to play the sort of international political role that we might have expected from a country of its material capabilities. [107] Although China, by contrast, displays no such inhibitions, as Goldstein observes, there is "scant evidence that China is likely to abandon its current, relatively conservative approach and instead adopt a grand strategy that would seek to overturn, rather than adjust to or attempt to reform, the international order it faces"[108]. But while Chinese policy makers may be relatively content with the broad geopolitical parameters within which they operate, this does not mean they will not attempt to shape them to their advantage.

In the dialectical interplay of material and ideational factors that constitutes the international system and approximates "global governance", two developments are especially noteworthy and likely to encourage the persistence of difference in East Asia. First, China's increasingly sophisticated diplomacy is reinforcing its growing material presence and helping to establish a "Beijing Consensus" as an alternative to the more familiar, frequently unloved Washington variety. [109] China's own stellar developmental record might be expected to lend the Beijing Consensus intrinsic appeal, but its "pragmatic" approach to public policy and tolerance of authoritarianism make it even more attractive to countries where

106　For a more detailed discussion of this period and of the different historical roles played by Japan and China in East Asia, see Mark Beeson, "Geopolitics and the Making of Regions: The Fall and Rise of East Asia", *Political Studies* (forthcoming).

107　Richard J. Samuels, *Securing Japan: Tokyo's Grand Strategy and the Future of East Asia*, Ithaca, N. Y.: Cornell University Press, 2007.

108　Avery Goldstein, *Rising to the Challenge: China's Grand Strategy and International Security*, Stanford, Calif.: Stanford University Press, 2005, p. 211.

109　Joshua C. Ramo, *The Beijing Consensus*, London: The Foreign Policy Centre, 2004; Joshua Kurlantzick, *Charm Offensive: How China's Soft Power Is Transforming the World*, New Haven, Conn.: Yale University Press, 2007.

development is stalled or failing. The second factor that may give China a surprising degree of ideational influence is the array of problems affecting its principal rival: The rapid decline in the status and strength of the U. S. economy is not simply undermining the material foundations of American power, it is also changing the way the United States is perceived. [110]

For decades America's undoubted military primacy was underpinned by economic strength. Indeed, the conventional wisdom in East Asia, and a major constraint on the foreign policy of Japan in particular, was the assumption that East Asian development was dependent on continuing access to North American markets. While there is still something in this, the recent turmoil in the American economy has seen a rapid change in its ideational status and an even more tangible shift in its material position. The fact that America's largest bank had to go cap in hand to China's new sovereign wealth funds for emergency funding highlights the rapid shift that has occurred in the international balance of economic power. [111] For some American commentators the emergence of Chinese-style "state capitalism" means "the reality may be that the era of free markets unleashed by Margaret Thatcher and reinforced by Ronald Reagan in the 1980s is fading away. In place of deregulation and privatization are government efforts to reassert control over their economies and to use this to enhance their global influence. It is an ill wind that blows"[112].

Whether one agrees with the view that the resurgence of East Asian forms of state-dominated capitalism is any worse than a neoliberal model that is wracked by crisis and distinguished by grotesque, unsustainable-looking levels of inequality is a moot point. [113] What matters here is that the

---

110 William Pesek, "U. S. Financial Clout Loses Sway", *International Herald Tribune*, April 4, 2007, online at www. iht. com/articles/2007/04/04/business/Sxpesek. php; Julian Borger, "Sun Sets on U. S. Power: Report Predicts End of Dominance", *The Guardian*, November 20, 2008.

111 Thorold Barker, "On Wall Street: Sovereign Wealth Funds to Drive Hard Bargain", *Financial Times*, November 16, 2007, online at www. ft. com/cms/s/0/2535fffe-947a-11dc-9aaf-0000779fd2ac. html; Larry Summers, "Sovereign Funds Shake the Logic of Capitalism", *Financial Times*, July 30, 2007, online at www. ft. com/cms/s/0/8c9dea94-3e30- 11dc-8f6a-0000779fd2ac. html.

112 Jeffrey Garten, "The Unsettling Zeitgeist of State Capitalism", *Financial Times*, January 14, 2008, online at www. ft. com/cms/s/0/f0f2a32ec2d6-11dc-b617-0000779fd2ac. html.

113 Will Hutton, "This Reckless Greed of the Few Harms the Future of the Many", *The Observer*, January 27, 2008, p. 35.

declining reputation and performance of neoliberal, Anglo-American capitalism means that it is unlikely to win new admirers in an East Asian region that has profited from rather different developmental models. On the contrary, even prominent champions of neoliberalism are now concerned that the balance of ideational influence may be shifting. [114] In such circumstances, it is not simply possible that East Asia's distinct political economies with their tradition of state interventionism and suspicion of neoliberalism may actually persist. It is entirely possible that they will actually look increasingly attractive compared to their damaged and somewhat discredited Western rivals.

▪ Conclusion

At the broadest level, it might seem redundant even to ask whether states in East Asia remain developmentally oriented or whether the state continues to influence economic activity: All states are involved in providing the regulatory and social context in which economic activity of any sort can occur—an especially important consideration in capitalist economies. [115] Despite an association with corruption and more recently inefficiency, aspects of the developmental state pioneered by Japan and emulated to varying degrees elsewhere remain—for better or worse—institutionally embedded in the East Asian region. Consequently, if we understand East Asian developmentalism as being about an overall orientation to public policy and the role of the state, rather than about a specific set of policy prescriptions or bureaucratic agencies, it is clear that East Asia's distinctive forms of political and economic organization persist despite significant structural and agential reformist pressures.

It is also evident that, for all China's profound developmental challenges and unpromising socialist heritage, interventionist public policies have played an important role in underpinning its remarkable recent economic development—despite inferior state capacity and a less permissive external environment. While there is much in common with Japan's high growth

---

114 Martin Wolf, "Why the Credit Squeeze is a Turning Point for the World", *Financial Times*, December 11, 2007, online at www. ft. com/cms /s/0/90126fca-a810-11dc-9485-0000779fd2ac. html.

115 Bob Jessop, *The Future of the Capitalist State*, Cambridge: Polity, 2003.

phase in terms of overall policy orientation and developmental intention, "socialist" China must negotiate ideological constraints that Japan did not. As Dani Rodrik points out, while state intervention has clearly contributed to the speed and direction of industrialization in China, the "appropriate criterion of success for industrial policy is not that 'only winners should be picked' (an impossible task) but that 'losers should be let go'"[116]. Given the SOE's powerful political connections and their continuing importance in the labor market, this will be no easy task.

The danger for China is that it may succumb to the same kinds of problems that overtook Japan—in short, institutional inertia and an inability to overcome powerful vested interests that are resistant to change. Like Japan, China may end up with the worst of both worlds: an old model that is no longer as effective, legitimate, or relevant as it once was, and a new model that is insufficiently developed or embedded to sustain future development. An additional problem for China is that some of the adverse impacts of a more Western-style, market-based model are becoming painfully clear in China's increased levels of inequality and unemployment[117], at precisely the same moment that the Anglo-American model itself appears to be less stable and sustainable.

However, the intention here has not been to provide an assessment of the relative merits of East Asian developmentalism compared to alternatives elsewhere, although there does seem to be very persuasive evidentiary base which suggests that the East Asian model has been central to the region's overall rise and may yet provide something of a template for other would-be industrializing nations. Rather, the preceding discussion has sought to demonstrate why the developmental state was such a powerful force in East Asia, how it became so deeply institutionalized, and why it continues to exert an influence as a consequence—even if that influence is taken to be malign, self-serving, inappropriate, anachronistic, or inefficient.

But while we may no longer wish to praise the developmental state quite

---

116 Dani Rodrik, "What's So Special about China's Exports?", *China & World Economy*, Vol. 14, No. 5, September-October 2006, p. 17.

117 Dali L. Yang, " Economic Transformation and Its Political Discontents in China: Authoritarianism, Unequal Growth, and the Dilemmas of Political Development", *Annual Review of Political Science*, Vol. 9, June 2006, pp. 143 - 164.

as unreservedly as we once did, it is too soon to bury it either. Even if enduring elements of Japan's developmental state may have blocked what some take to be necessary reforms, and even if China's developmental state risks becoming predatory and less sympathetic to democratic reform[118], we cannot wish it away. Indeed, it is less and less obvious why we would necessarily want to do so given the recent underwhelming performance of the Anglo-American alternative. In the continuing saga of competing capitalisms, there may yet be life in East Asian developmentalism.

■ References

Mark Beeson, *Regionalism, Globalization and East Asia: Politics, Security and Economic Development*, Basingstoke: Palgrave, 2007.

Richard F. Doner, Bryan K. Ritchie, and Dan Slater, "Systemic Vulnerability and the Origins of Developmental States: Northeast and Southeast Asia in Comparative Perspective", *International Organization*, Vol. 59, No. 2, Spring 2005, pp. 327 – 361.

Peter Evans, *Embedded Autonomy: States and Industrial Transformation*, Princeton, N. J. : Princeton University Press, 1995.

Eric Heginbotham and Richard J. Samuels, "Mercantile Realismand Japanese Foreign Policy", *International Security*, Vol. 22, No. 4, Spring 1998, pp. 171 – 203.

Chalmers Johnson, *MITI and the Japanese Miracle: The Growth of Industry Policy, 1925—1975*, Stanford, Calif. : Stanford University Press, 1982.

Joel S. Migdal, *Strong States and Weak Societies: State-Society Relations and State Capabilities in the Third World*, Princeton, N. J. : Princeton University Press, 1988.

Saadia M. Pekkanen and Kellee S. Tsai (eds.), *Japan and China in the World Political Economy*, London: Routledge, 2005.

T. J. Pempel, *Regime Shift: Comparative Dynamics of the Japanese Political Economy*, Ithaca, N. Y. : Cornell University Press, 1999.

Susan L. Shirk, *China: Fragile Superpower,* Oxford: Oxford University Press, 2007.

Edward S. Steinfeld, "China's Shallow Integration: Networked Production and the New

---

118 Minxin Pei, *China's Trapped Transition: The Limits of Developmental Autocracy,* Cambridge, Mass. : Harvard University Press, 2006.

Challenges for Late Industrialization", *World Development*, Vol. 32, No. 11, November 2004, pp. 1971—1987.

Richard. Stubbs, *Rethinking Asia's Economic Miracle*, Basingstoke: Palgrave, 2005.

Kellee S. Tsai, *Capitalism Without Democracy: The Private Sector in Contemporary China*, Ithaca, N. Y. : Cornell University Press, 2007.

Steven K. Vogel, *Japan Remodeled: How Government and Industry are Reforming Japanese Capitalism*, Ithaca, N. Y. : Cornell University Press, 2006.

Shahid Yusuf, Kaoru Nabeshima, and Dwight H. Perkins, *Under New Ownership: Privatizing China's State-Owned Enterprises*, Washington, D. C. : World Bank, 2006.

图书在版编目（CIP）数据

当代中国政治发展 = The Political Development
in Contemporary China：英文/吕增奎，王新颖编.
—北京：中央编译出版社，2011.4
（寻求变革）
ISBN 978 - 7 - 5117 - 0816 - 8

Ⅰ.①当…
Ⅱ.①吴… ②王…
Ⅲ.①政治制度-研究-中国-现代-英文
Ⅳ.①D621

中国版本图书馆 CIP 数据核字（2011）第 045735 号

Seeking Changes: The Political Development in Contemporary China

出 版 人	和　龑
策划编辑	贾宇琰
责任编辑	侯天保　杜永明
责任印制	尹　珺
出版发行	中央编译出版社
地　　址	北京西单西斜街36号（100032）
电　　话	（010）66509360（总编室）　　（010）66509367（编辑室）
	（010）66161011（团购部）　　（010）66130345（网络销售）
	（010）66509364（发行部）　　（010）66509618（读者服务部）
网　　址	www.cctpbook.com
经　　销	全国新华书店
印　　制	北京中印联印务有限公司
开　　本	787×1092　1/16
印　　张	22.5
版　　次	2011 年 5 月第 1 版第 1 次印刷
定　　价	66.00 元

本社常年法律顾问：北京大成律师事务所首席顾问律师　鲁哈达